SEA

I. Grande | Punta de Manzanillo
Portobelo | Nombre de Dios
La Guaira
María Chiquita | P.N. Portobelo
Colón | Cuango | Tubualá
Sabanitas | Parque Nacional Chagres
Río Alajuela | Las Salinas
El Valle
El Porvenir (Gaigirgordub) | Cayos Limones | Cayos Holandeses (Maoki)
Archipiélago de San Blas
Golfo de San Blas | Gardi | Cayos Coco-Bandero (Ordupuquip)
Sugdub | Garti | Tupile
Guna Yala (Guna Yala) | Playón Grande (Uggubseni)

COMARCA GUNA YALA

Akuna Guna | Serranía de San Blas | Punta Mosquito
L. Bayano | I. Pino (Dubbag)
Comarca de Madugandí | Morti | I. Ucuptuma
Chepo | Río Chepo | Navagandí | Punta Escocés
Pacora | Cuevas de Majé | Comarca de Wargandí
Tocumen | Panamá | 1439 | Torti | Comarca de Mulatupo
Panamá | Chinina | Serranía de Majé | R. Chucunaque
La Chorrera | Armila
Panamá | Capurganá

THE CANAL AND CENTRAL CARIBBEAN COAST

PANAMA CITY

Panamá

Punta Chame | I. Taboga | Santa Fé
I. Otoque | Puerto | **DARIÉN AND THE EAST**
Bejuco | I. Bona | Río Congo
Playas Gorgona and Coronado | I. Saboga | I. Chapera | La Palma | Comarca Emberá-Wounaan
Playa Santa Clara | I. la Mina | Punta Alegre | Chepigana
I. Viveros | Reserva Punta Patiño | Mogué | La Marea | Yaviza
I. P. Gonzáles | Golfo de San Miguel | Taimatí
I. del Rey | La Chunga | Pejivasal | Darién
Archipiélago de las Perlas | I. San Telmo | Garachiné | Puerto Indio (Sambú) | Boca de Cupé
I. San José | Playa Muerto | R. Sambú | R. Balsas | Parque Nacional Darién

Golfo de Panamá | R. Sambú | Comarca Emberá-Wounaan
Serranía del Sapo | Riosucio

Ocrí | Jaqué | **COLOMBIA**
I. Iguana | Refugio de Vida Silvestre Isla Iguana
Pedasí | Punta Mala
Playa Los Destiladeros | Jurado | R. Atrato

OCEAN | Bellavista

INSIGHT ◉ GUIDES

PANAMA

PLAN & BOOK
YOUR TAILOR-MADE TRIP

BRAZIL   CHILE   ECUADOR

TAILOR-MADE TRIPS & UNIQUE EXPERIENCES CREATED BY LOCAL TRAVEL EXPERTS AT INSIGHTGUIDES.COM/HOLIDAYS

Insight Guides has been inspiring travellers with high-quality travel content for over 45 years. As well as our popular guidebooks, we now offer the opportunity to book tailor-made private trips completely personalised to your needs and interests. By connecting with one of our local experts, you will directly benefit from their expertise and local know-how, helping you create memories that will last a lifetime.

HOW INSIGHTGUIDES.COM/HOLIDAYS WORKS

STEP 1

Pick your dream destination and submit an enquiry, or modify an existing itinerary if you prefer.

STEP 2

Fill in a short form, sharing details of your travel plans and preferences with a local expert.

STEP 3

Your local expert will create your personalised itinerary, which you can amend until you are completely satisfied.

STEP 4

Book securely online. Pack your bags and enjoy your holiday! Your local expert will be available to answer questions during your trip.

BENEFITS OF PLANNING & BOOKING AT INSIGHTGUIDES.COM/HOLIDAYS

PLANNED BY LOCAL EXPERTS

The Insight Guides local experts are hand-picked, based on their experience in the travel industry and their impeccable standards of customer service.

SAVE TIME & MONEY

When a local expert plans your trip, you save time and money when you book, even during high season. You won't be charged for using a credit card either.

TAILOR-MADE TRIPS

Book with Insight Guides, and you will be in complete control of the planning process, from the initial selections to amending your final itinerary.

BOOK & TRAVEL STRESS-FREE

Enjoy stress-free travel when you use the Insight Guides secure online booking platform. All bookings come with a money-back guarantee.

WHAT OTHER TRAVELLERS THINK ABOUT TRIPS BOOKED AT INSIGHTGUIDES.COM/HOLIDAYS

Trip to Portugal

Every step of the planning process and the trip itself was effortless and exceptional. Our special interests, preferences and requests were accommodated resulting in a trip that exceeded our expectations.

Corinne, USA ★★★★★

Trip to Vietnam

The organization was superb, the drivers professional, and accommodation quite comfortable. I was well taken care of! My thanks to your colleagues who helped make my trip to Vietnam such a great experience. My only regret is that I couldn't spend more time in the country.

Heather ★★★★★

DON'T MISS OUT
BOOK NOW AT
INSIGHTGUIDES.COM/HOLIDAYS

CONTENTS

Introduction

The best of Panama 6
Hats off, Panama! 17
A bridge between lands 19
    ○ Conservation issues 22

History & features

Decisive dates 26
Early history 29
Spanish conquest 33
Striving for independence 39
    ◎ Life in the Canal Zone 44
Modern history 47
    ○ Operation 'Car Wash' and
        other scandals 55
People 59
Music and dance 67
    ○ Rubén Blades – Panama's
        musical megastar 71
Traditional crafts 73
Wildlife 79
    ◎ Frogs 84
Outdoor activities 87
Food and drink 93
The Canal 99

Places

Introduction 111
    ■ PANAMA CITY 117
    ○ Islas de las Perlas 138
    ■ THE CANAL AND CENTRAL
        CARIBBEAN COAST 141
    ○ Transiting the Canal 146
    ◎ Festivals 162
    ■ CENTRAL PANAMA AND THE
        PACIFIC BEACHES 165
    ■ THE AZUERO PENINSULA AND
        VERAGUAS 181
    ■ CHIRIQUÍ AND WESTERN PANAMA 203
    ○ Coffee 219
    ◎ Birdwatching 220
    ■ BOCAS DEL TORO 223

- Bocas and the banana boom 241
- COMARCA GUNA YALA 243
- Traditional dress 260
- DARIÉN AND THE EAST 263
  - Scotland's doomed Darién
    adventure 277

Travel tips

TRANSPORTATION
Getting there 280
Getting around 281

A – Z
Accommodations 283
Addresses 283
Admission charges 284
Budgeting for your trip 284
Children...284
Climate...284
Crime and safety..............................285
Customs regulations 285
Disabled travelers............................285
Eating out..286
Electricity 286
Embassies and consulates 286
Etiquette 286
Festivals and events........................286
Health and medical care.................287
Internet 287
Left luggage 288
LGBTQ travelers...............................288
Maps...288
Media..288
Money...288
National parks and protected areas..........289
Opening hours...................................289
Photography......................................289
Postal services..................................289
Public holidays 290
Religious services............................290
Restrooms...290
Shopping 290
Tax 290
Telephones..290
Time zone 291
Tourist information 291
Tour operators and travel agents 291
Visas and passports 291
Websites and apps...........................291
Weights and measures 291

LANGUAGE
Pronunciation tips.............................292
Greetings..292
At the hotel..292
Shopping 292
Traveling...293
Sightseeing 293
Eating out...293
Menu decoder 293
Health..294
On the road...294
Emergencies......................................294
Useful words/phrases 294
Days of the week 294
Months of the year/seasons 294
Numbers 295

FURTHER READING
The Canal 296
Pirates and politics 296
Guna culture 296
Fiction 297
Biography...297
Birdlife...297

Maps
Panama..112
Central Panama City.........................114
Panama City and around..................120
Casco Viejo 122
The Canal and central Caribbean coast 142
Central Panama and the Pacific beaches ..166
The Azuero Peninsula........................182
Veraguas 187
Chiriquí and Western Panama.................205
Bocas del Toro 224
Bocas del Toro archipelago 226
Guna Yala 244
Darién and the East 264

Inside front cover Panama
Inside back cover Central Panama City

LEGEND
- Insight on
- Photo story

THE BEST OF PANAMA: TOP ATTRACTIONS

△ **Casco Viejo.** Hip rooftop bars and chic restaurants dot leafy plazas, ancient churches, and stately colonial buildings in Panama City's historic center. See page 119.

▽ **The Panama Canal.** The 20th century's greatest feat of engineering is astonishing to behold, whether you're observing giant container vessels squeezing through the locks, or experiencing the magical tropical scenery on a boat or in a kayak on the Canal's rainforest-protected reservoir, Lago Gatún. See page 141.

△ **Colonial forts.** The ruined colonial forts of San Lorenzo and Portobelo are impressive reminders of the defenses the conquistadors needed to protect their plundered treasure from marauding pirates. See pages 155 and 158.

△ **Partying in the Azuero.** From the seriously hedonistic Carnavales to the religious celebrations of Corpus Christi or small-town *patronales*, it's hard to beat the revelry of the Azuero Peninsula. Expect flamboyant costumes and exuberant music and dancing washed down with lashings of seco, the country's potent spirit. See page 183.

△ **Parque Nacional Soberanía.** Only a short hop from Panama City, this wildlife paradise has almost guaranteed sightings of toucans, parrots, sloths, and monkeys. See page 147.

◁ **Bocas del Toro.** A popular Caribbean destination, Bocas offers a chilled party scene, with great drinking, dining, and dancing, as well as rainforested islands, and watersports and beaches galore. See page 223.

▷ **Parque Nacional Darién.** It's no easy matter to get here, but the rugged mountains, towering rainforest canopy, and immense biodiversity in the country's largest wilderness area – and Unesco World Heritage Site – is worth the effort. See page 268.

△ **Guna Yala.** The Comarca Guna Yala stretches along the Caribbean coast, home to a host of palm-topped islands and the indigenous Guna, who have fiercely defended their mores and lifestyle against outsiders for centuries. See page 243.

▽ **Santa Catalina and Coiba.** This isolated fishing village is Panama's best surfing destination and also the gateway to Coiba, the country's top marine reserve and most unexplored island. See page 199.

△ **Chiriquí Highlands.** Whether ziplining, birdwatching, hiking through cloudforest, or watching the sun rise from the summit of Volcán Barú – Panama's highest peak – most visitors find time to sample some of the world's finest gourmet coffee. See page 203.

THE BEST OF PANAMA: EDITOR'S CHOICE

Guna Yala beach.

BEST BEACHES

Western Guna Yala. Dozens of tiny islets boast idyllic white-sand beaches, sheltered by coconut palms and lapped by the warm waves of the Caribbean. See page 243.

Isla Saboga. One of the Pearl Islands' best kept secrets, Isla Saboga hides two glorious soft-sand beaches along its western flank: the delightfully secluded Playa Encanto, complete with upscale beach bar, and the empty salt-and-pepper stretch of Playa Larga. See page 139.

Playa El Estero, Santa Catalina. A lovely flat belt of sand, it is bookended by a shallow stream to the west and a rocky headland to the east, and is the ideal spot for beginners to learn to surf. See page 199.

Punta Chame. Along a lengthy spit, offering splendid views across the bay to the cordillera rising up from the mainland, this flat belt of sand is Panama's premier kitesurfing location. See page 168.

Playa Bluff. This five kilometers of sand pounded by surf seems to stretch endlessly up the eastern coast of Isla Colón, in Bocas del Toro. See page 229.

Isla Gámez. Laying claim to two glorious beaches a stone's throw apart and either side of this tiny Robinson-Crusoe islet, Isla Gámez is a favored day-trip destination in the Golfo de Chiriquí. See page 218.

BEST WILDLIFE-WATCHING

Chiriquí Highlands. The cloudforests of the contiguous national parks of Barú and Amistad are the most reliable places to spot the dazzling resplendent quetzal, as well as a host of other highland birds. See page 203.

Humedales de San San Pond Sak. An early morning boat ride through these little-known wetlands, brimming with birdlife, is your best chance of seeing the shy and extraordinary manatee. See page 238.

Isla de Cañas. At certain times of the year, the 14km (9-mile) belt of flat beach at Isla de Cañas witnesses the extraordinary mass nesting of the olive ridley turtle, as well as the more conventional egg-laying of green turtles, leatherbacks, and hawksbills. See page 194.

Parque Nacional Soberanía. The unique observation deck of the Canopy Tower peeks above the treetops, offering top-notch birdwatching and a good chance of seeing monkeys and kinkajous. See page 147.

Isla Coiba. The waters off Central America's largest island are teeming with spectacular marine life, including whale sharks, manta rays, and humpback whales. See page 200.

Volcano hummingbird.

BEST HIDEAWAY LODGES

El Otro Lado.

driftwood-hewn bungalows that gaze out across the Caribbean, where you can slip into the sea straight off your private deck. www.alnaturalresort.com.

Isla Palenque. Eight exquisitely designed thatched bungalows set back from the beach make this private tropical island resort a special place; gourmet food, rainforest trails, and snorkeling trips complete the picture. www.islapalenque.com.

Mount Totumas. Set in spectacular cloud-forested mountains, this is Panama's best mountain lodge. Offering outstanding hospitality, comfort, and character – and even a treehouse – it's a nature-lover's dream, with trails galore and great guiding. See page 211.

El Otro Lado. Beautifully decorated with Afro-Panamanian art, this high-quality retreat looks across the bay to colonial Portobelo. With its own waterfall, lake, and slice of tropical forest, it also supports a laudable social program. www.elotrolado.com.pa/en.

Al Natural. At the eastern tip of Isla Bastimentos, this isolated, idyllic oasis offers open-fronted

BEST ADVENTURES

Ziplining. Though there are several canopy trails in Panama, the adrenaline-fueled Boquete Tree Trek stands head and shoulders above the rest, soaring above the valleys of the Chiriquí Highlands. See page 206.

Rafting and kayaking. Whether rafting the rapids of the Chiriquí Viejo, or paddling down the mighty Chagres to Fuerte San Lorenzo, a memorable day out is guaranteed. See page 88.

Travel in the Darién. A trip to the Darién is the ultimate adventure: sleeping in an Emberá village, sweeping round the meanders of the Río Sambú, and hiking through the rainforest. See page 268.

Surfing. With a world-class point break in Santa Catalina, and some fine spots in Bocas, plus a laid-back après-surf scene to match, Panama is a great place to ride the waves. See page 90.

Surfing in Bocas del Toro.

BEST FESTIVALS

Festival de Congos y Diablos. Fearsome devils brandishing whips, dancing to drum beats and satirical costumes are the hallmarks of this hugely enjoyable Afro-Panamanian festival. See page 158.

Corpus Christi. Tiny Villa de los Santos in the Azuero is the place to head for the country's best celebrations, featuring a carpet of flowers, an array of bizarre costumes, and more devils than you shake a trident at. See page 189.

Los Carnavales. The country's major bacchanal, with the most extravagant celebrations occurring in Las Tablas. Panama City comes a close second, though the aquatic parade in Penonomé wins marks for originality. See page 162.

La Mejorana. The festival where you're least likely to get a dose of reggaeton, La Festival de la Mejorana, named after Panama's five-stringed guitar, is a marvelous tapestry of folk dancing, costumes, rural traditions, and parades. See page 191.

Festival de las Mil Polleras. Unashamedly touristy, this annual January parade in Las Tablas aims to showcase Panama's elaborate national dress, the *pollera*, in all its glory as women sashay though the streets. See page 191.

Panama Jazz Festival. Now attracting more than 30,000 visitors over its duration, this January music fest features local and international artists and culminates in a free open-air concert in the Ciudad de Saber. See page 67.

Donning traditional polleras.

Casco Viejo facade, Panama City.

Guna woman showing off her mola and bracelets (winis).

Centennial Bridge over the
Panama Canal.

HATS OFF, PANAMA!

Boasting cloud-forested highlands, idyllic palm-topped islands, vibrant indigenous cultures, riotous festivals, and Central America's most ebullient capital city, Panama offers surprising variety for such a small country.

Young capuchin monkey.

For so long in the shadow of Costa Rica, Panama is only now emerging as a wildlife destination in its own right, and one without the tourist buses. Boasting over a thousand bird species, from shimmering resplendent quetzals to fearsome harpy eagles, plus parrots, toucans, and hummingbirds galore, Panama is primed for some of the world's best bird-watching. And if its mammals you're after, the isthmus harbors all seven of Central America's monkeys, which are easily spotted, along with sloths and agoutis, some even in the center of Panama City. Less visible, stealing through the undergrowth of Darién and Amistad – the vast wilderness national parks that bookend Panama – are the country's elusive 'Big Five' cats, as well as tapirs, anteaters and peccaries.

Cast your eye around from the summit of Volcán Barú, Panama's highest peak, and the country's natural beauty is immediately apparent. Its mountainous spine, cloaked in tropical forests, extends into the distance with two glittering oceans stretching out either side, dotted with dreamy islands, soft-sand beaches, and mangrove-strewn coastlines. These stunning landscapes provide the perfect settings for a wealth of adventure activities, from zip lining and white-water rafting in Boquete to surfing the waves in Bocas or Santa Catalina, scuba-diving with sharks, or backpacking through jungle along the Camino Real – following in the footsteps of the Spanish conquistadors.

Baby brown-throated sloth.

Despite the devastation wreaked by the Spanish Conquest, eight of Panama's indigenous populations survive, and continue to fight to preserve their cultural identities in a rapidly modernizing society. Unique opportunities exist in a number of Guna, Ngäbe, and Emberá communities to experience village life – be it in a raised Emberá *rancho* in the rainforest or a cane hut on a coconut isle in Guna Yala, lapped by the turquoise Caribbean Sea.

And then there's the Canal. More than just an iconic waterway, it was the impetus to the founding of the Panamanian republic and a magnet that attracted people from all over the world. Panama's fusion of Amerindian, African and European heritage – facilitated by the Canal – is precisely what makes Panama such a vibrant and enchanting country to visit today.

Volcán Barú, shrouded in mist.

A BRIDGE BETWEEN LANDS

Sandwiched between two vast oceans and forming a narrow bridge between two huge land masses, Panama's landscapes are indelibly shaped by its unique location.

Though experts may not agree on the timing, they all consider the formation of the volcanic isthmus of Panama to be one of the planet's most important geological, oceanographic, and biogeographic events. The gradual closure of what was known as the Central American Seaway, caused by the collision of two geological plates, gradually pushed up the landmass that is Panama today. This in turn resulted in changes to ocean currents and wind patterns – including the formation of the Gulf Stream – with wide-reaching effects. Marine populations' migratory routes were blocked, meaning the eventual development of new species either side of this new land bridge. At the same time, the nascent terrestrial link kick-started what paleontologists call the Great American Interchange of land and freshwater wildlife between North and South America. Only through the construction of the Canal – some three million or more years later – were sea links symbolically reopened.

Isla Diablos in Guna Yala.

GEOGRAPHY

Squeezed between seven and nine degrees north of the equator, between Costa Rica, to the northwest, and Colombia, to the southeast, Panama's narrow eel-shaped territory is located firmly within the tropics. And it has the climate to match: relentlessly hot and humid in the lowlands (which cover around two thirds of the country), with more variation in the highlands, where temperatures change significantly with altitude and can be chilly at night. The forested mountainous spine that runs along much of the country's 800 plus kilometers (500 miles) – often vaguely referred to as the Cordillera Central – clearly separates Panama into Pacific and Caribbean climates and cultures.

Most of the country's population is spread along the Pacific coastal belt, which enjoys two distinct seasons. 'Verano' (summer), roughly mid-December to the end of April, is characterized by azure skies and high temperatures of around 85°F (30°C). These can rise even higher in some parts of the interior, particularly round the Arco Seco (Dry Arch), the arid belt that curves into the Azuero Peninsula. In 'invierno' (winter), which lasts between May and early December, there are intense and frequent downpours, though along the coastal plains these sometimes only last a few hours, leaving plenty of sunny, dry periods to enjoy.

In contrast, some areas of the Caribbean coast can receive up to three times as much rain as the Pacific. What's more, there's virtually no recognizable dry season, although the islands of Bocas del Toro enjoy two slightly drier spells around March and October. The Caribbean communities also bear the full brunt of the trade winds; when they are at their strongest (Dec–Feb), rough seas make the outer islands of Bocas del Toro and Guna Yala – the two archipelagos at either end of the country – almost inaccessible.

Lapped by two warm oceans, Panama's combined coastlines extend over 2,500km (1,500 miles), including more than 1,500 islands, providing a seemingly endless mosaic of beaches, mangroves, cliffs, and coral reefs to explore. Panama's largest island, Coiba, is also the largest in Central America and

Açaí palm berries.

forms the centerpiece of a national park. Its years of isolation – in part as an island-prison – have left much of its forests relatively untouched, allowing some species that have now vanished from the mainland to flourish, and other local endemics to develop.

Given the narrow shape of the Panamanian isthmus, you are rarely too far from the sea – as the crow flies, at least. From the summit of Volcán Barú (3474 meters/11,398ft) in the Western Highlands, the country's highest peak, you can survey both the glistening Caribbean and Pacific oceans, dotted with dreamy islands.

VEGETATION

An estimated 10,000 plus vascular plant species grow on the isthmus, predominantly in the country's luxuriant tropical rainforests – which by definition receive an annual rainfall of more than 2 meters (6ft 6in) – that cover an estimated 45 percent of the land. Most are found along the Caribbean slopes and cloak the Darién, the country's greatest wilderness and most biodiverse area at the far eastern end of the country. In these complex ecosystems, most animal and plant activity is found in the forest canopy and the sub-canopy, where dangling vines and lianas provide vital transportation links. Poking out of this forest 'roof,' which filters out more than 90 percent of the sunlight, are a sprinkling of robust emergent trees, generally around 60–70 meters (197–230ft) tall, able to withstand being buffeted by storms and scorched by sunlight.

Most easily recognized, and visible from a great distance, is the ringed silvery grey trunk of the cuipo (*cavanillesia platanifolia*), which exhibits a bare umbrella-like crown during the dry season. Particularly abundant in the Darién, it is a favorite nesting site of the harpy eagle. Equally distinctive from above is the lofty guayacán (*tabebuia guayacan*), whose brilliant golden flowers stand out against the dense green canopy carpet, blooming a month in advance of the first rains. Not atypically, both species drop their leaves in the dry season to reduce water loss through evaporation. From the forest floor, the vast buttress roots of the ceiba (silk-cotton or kapok tree; *ceiba petandra*), or thinner versions on the Panama tree (*sterculia apetela*), are more striking. So too are the vicious protective thorns on the spiny cedar (*pachira quinata*), or the swollen midsection of the aptly named barrigón (*pseudobombax septenatum*) – 'barriga' meaning 'pot belly' in English – which can double its waist size to store water and whose pretty pompom flowers open for evening pollination.

Dominated by vines, ferns, saplings, and shrubs typically 10–25 meters (30–80ft) tall, the forest understory and forest floor below are relatively sparsely populated in the cathedral-like primary forest, in contrast to the dense and tangled vegetation of secondary forest. It's in these lower layers that you'll come across the pinkish hues of heliconias, such as the vividly named lobster's claw (*heliconia rostrata*), edged with yellow, and the more solid beefsteak (*heliconia mariae*), a 'medium-rare' dark pink, or the pouting scarlet bracts of the Warholian hotlips (*psychotria poeppigiana*), which lure butterflies and hummingbirds to the almost invisible central flowers.

Topping the higher mountainous ridges, especially prevalent in the Cordillera de Talamanca of western Panama, and almost permanently enveloped in mist, are dense patches of eerie fern-filled cloudforest, characterized by shorter, stockier trees covered in lichen and dripping with mosses. Boughs here are more heavily laden with epiphytes, including many of Panama's 1,000-plus species of delicate orchid and vibrant bromeliads, whose leaves trap moisture, providing water for numerous tree-dwelling organisms.

Back down on the coast, some 1,500 sq km (580 sq miles) of mostly red, white and black mangroves constitute a vital buffer zone for both terrestrial and marine ecologies. The largest swathe lines the Golfo de Panamá east of Panama City. West of the capital, the mangroves – as well as the hinterland – have been cleared for development or agriculture, such as shrimp farming. Yet, as the coast curves into the Azuero Peninsula, amidst the pastureland, pockets of rare dry tropical forest maintain a precarious foothold, aided by recent reforestation efforts.

A Panamanian orchid, pretty in pink.

Ø ORCHIDS

With 1,200–1,500 orchid species, Panama is an orchid-lover's paradise, though many of its species are considered endangered through habitat loss and orchid trafficking. That is the case with Panama's national flower, the Flor del Espiritú Santo (Holy Ghost or Dove Orchid; *peristeria elata*), which also grows in Ecuador and Colombia. It only blooms once a year (July–Oct), but the 4–12 marble white flowers speckled with violet are extremely attractive and the dove-shaped center – hence the name – extremely distinctive. It's epiphytic and grows at the moist edges of mature forest, close to the ground at around 1,100 meters (3,600ft). This is lower than most orchids in Panama, which prefer higher altitudes of between 1,500–2,800 meters (5,000–9,000ft). Since these striking flowers are such a big deal in Panama it's no surprise that there are several annual festivals, notably in Santa Fé de Veraguas in August, and a larger one in Boquete every March/April. If you're keen to seek out orchids at other times, APROVACA (www.aprovaca.com) in El Valle, which aims to protect and reintroduce species back into the wild, has a nursery that can be visited, as well as a hostel located inside the orchid conservatory. The staff are extremely knowledgeable and are on hand to answer your questions.

CONSERVATION ISSUES

The main conservation issues facing Panama apply to many tropical countries, especially those with high rural and indigenous populations.

Environmental Impact Assessments before forging ahead.

DEFORESTATION

Although the large-scale extraction of tropical hardwoods has come under greater control in recent years, the lumber industry continues to be a major

Deforestation in Panama.

In Panama, the familiar interlinked tales of deforestation, environmental degradation and pollution, loss of biodiversity, and threatened livelihoods are played out against a backdrop of climate change, economic hardships, and increasing urbanization. In 2018 alone the Ministerio del Ambiente dished out $2.2 million in fines to developments that had failed to carry out proper

contributor to deforestation, particularly in the Darién region, as illegal logging, and more insidiously, selective thinning continues.

But by far the main driver of deforestation is colonization, clearing the land for cattle ranching and subsistence agriculture, and, more recently, lucrative palm oil cultivation. Encroaching urbanization, particularly the continued expansion of Panama

City, is another contributor. Having already denuded the entire Azuero Peninsula and most of the Pacific slopes of central and western Panama, *colonos*, or 'colonists,' have been moving into eastern Panama for several decades along the Darién highway and Caribbean coast. This has included impinging on protected areas, in addition to indigenous lands, often with the collusion of government officials. Panama's coastal mangrove forests – considered to be the most extensive, diverse, and healthiest in all Central America – are critically threatened.

Small-scale initiatives across the country aim to improve environmental awareness, ranging from assistance for micro-enterprises, such as plant nurseries and agroforestry projects, to tree-planting and recycling, often backed by NGOs and international environmental organizations.

MINING AND HYDROELECTRIC PROJECTS

Another area of environmental concern is the mining industry, which has been poorly managed in terms of enforcing environmental standards. In 2008, Panamanian environmental watchdog CIAM (Centro de Incidencia Ambiental) revealed that the amount of land involved in mining concessions that had either already been granted or were awaiting consideration totaled three times the country's surface area. Though many projects have not yet been realized, or have stalled since then, significant degradation has already been caused. Indigenous populations are frequently threatened by mining and hydroelectric projects that encroach upon their lands. As trees are felled to make way for access roads and dam construction, valleys have been flooded and river ecosystems gravely affected by changing water patterns.

Thankfully, Panama is now also looking toward alternative, more renewable energy sources, establishing its first large-scale photovoltaic power station on the Azuero Peninsula in 2014, and, a year later, a wind farm outside Penonomé – the largest in Central America.

TOURISM

Two areas at serious risk from unregulated tourism are the fragile marine environments of Bocas del Toro and western Guna Yala. Improved roads to Guna Yala have meant faster, cheaper access. Day-trippers from Panama City and beach-loving backpackers put untold pressure on the natural resources of these postage-stamp-size islands, especially in summer, while coral-mining has degraded many reefs and undermined the environment's ability to withstand coastal erosion. The beautiful islands of Bocas del Toro, the most visited region outside the capital and Canal area, suffer from similar problems. Though the islands are larger, many of the hotels guzzle energy as they accommodate ever more tourists. As the Panamanian government continues to promote tourism, serious challenges lie ahead to develop the sector in a sustainable way.

Mining in the forest.

Cutting a path across the Isthmus of Panama during Spanish rule.

DECISIVE DATES

EARLY HISTORY

c.11,000 BC
The likely first settlement is established on the isthmus, a fishing village on the Azuero Peninsula.

2500–1200 BC
Pottery is made on the Azuero Peninsula; archeological finds in the area provide the earliest traces of pottery-making in the Americas.

500–600 AD
An eruption of Volcán Barú likely brings an end to the Barriles culture – one of the most important pre-Columbian societies.

SPANISH CONQUEST

1501–02
Spanish explorers Rodrigo de Bastidas and Christopher Columbus visit modern-day Panama.

1505
The Spanish conquest intensifies; indigenous populations are massacred or enslaved, though some resist.

1513
Vasco Nuñez de Balboa crosses Panama, becoming the first European to see the Pacific Ocean.

1519
Panama City is founded on August 15 by conquistador Pedro Arias de Ávila (known as Pedrarias).

1533
The Camino Real flourishes as the main transit route for plundered riches from South America bound for Spain.

1596–1739
The Spanish are constantly threatened by European pirates and privateers; Henry Morgan sacks Panamá Viejo in 1671, forcing the Spanish to relocate and rebuild Panama City in its present location in 1673.

1746
Spain reroutes the treasure fleet around Cape Horn, resulting in economic decline.

STRIVING FOR INDEPENDENCE

1821
Panama declares independence from Spain, and joins the confederacy of Gran Colombia (Bolivia, Peru, Ecuador, Venezuela, Colombia, and Panama).

1830
Panama becomes a province of Colombia after the dissolution of Gran Colombia.

1850–55
The California gold rush prompts construction of the Panama Railroad across the isthmus.

1881
French architect Ferdinand de Lesseps begins excavations for the Panama Canal. Some 20,000 workers die before the venture is abandoned in 1889.

1902
End of three-year civil war between the Conservative and Liberal parties – La Guerra de

Panama Canal locks, 1918.

los Mil Días (War of a Thousand Days) – which claims 100,000 lives.

1903
Backed by the US, Panama declares separation from Colombia but in return essentially hands the US control of the future Canal Zone 'in perpetuity.'

THE CANAL UNDER US CONTROL

1914
The Canal is completed. Around 56,000 people from 97 countries have had a hand in its construction. The official death toll is 5,609, though the real figure is probably much higher.

1925
The successful Dule Revolution results in the Guna people being promised a measure of cultural autonomy.

1936
Despite a treaty limiting US rights, tensions continue to build between Panama and the US territory of the Canal Zone.

A group of men start a street fire during anti-government demonstrations in 1988.

1940
Fascist president Arnulfo Arias Madrid sets about disenfranchising Afro- and Chinese Panamanians while pursuing racist immigration policies.

1953
The first comarca is legally established in Panama under the authority of the Guna General Congress.

1964
'Martyrs' Day' flag riots protest the US occupation of the Canal Zone: 21 Panamanians are killed and over 500 injured.

1968
Omar Torrijos, chief of the National Guard, overthrows President Arnulfo Arias and imposes a military dictatorship.

1977
Torrijos secures a new canal treaty with US president Jimmy Carter, who agrees to transfer the Canal to Panamanian control in 1999.

1983
Colonel Manuel Noriega becomes de facto military ruler. He is initially supported by the US, but also cultivates drug-cartel connections.

1988
The US charges Noriega with rigging elections, drug smuggling, and murder; Noriega declares a state of emergency, dodging a coup and ruthlessly repressing opposition.

1989
US troops invade Panama and oust Noriega, but also kill and leave homeless thousands of civilians.

1992
US court finds Noriega guilty of drug charges, sentencing him to 40 years in prison.

1999
Mireya Moscoso, widow of Arnulfo Arias, becomes the country's first female president, and presides over the handover of the Canal to Panama in December.

MODERN HISTORY

2004
Martín Torrijos, son of former dictator Omar Torrijos, is elected president; in a national referendum plans for a Panama Canal expansion plan are passed.

2009
Right-wing supermarket magnate Ricardo Martinelli becomes president after a landslide victory, and sets about building a metro for Panama City.

2011
Silvia Carrera is elected the first female cacique of the Ngäbe, Panama's most numerous indigenous people. Noriega is extradited back to Panama, after prison terms in the US and France, to serve another 20 years.

2012
Countrywide protests by the Ngäbe over mining and hydroelectric concessions on their land end in police violence, leaving thousands wounded and three dead.

2016
The Panama Canal expansion is inaugurated, two years overdue and $1.6bn over budget.

2018
Panama qualifies for the soccer World Cup for the first time and celebrates with a public holiday. Former president Martinelli is extradited from the US to face charges of espionage and corruption.

2019
Panama City celebrates 500 years since its foundation and receives its first papal visit.

Carte de l'Isthme

EARLY HISTORY

Although humans have lived on the isthmus of Panama for thousands of years, very little is known about these early settlers.

In geological terms, the Panamanian isthmus is still fairly young, since it probably came into being a mere three million years ago – though some experts date its emergence to several million years prior to that. What is not in doubt, however, is that its location as a slender bridge between two vast continents has been as crucial to its development as its eventual link between two expanses of ocean, the Panama Canal.

Panama's scant archeological remains give little clue to the societies that once inhabited the region, in part because many of the first excavations in the early 1900s were poorly executed and finds were damaged or looted. Fast-forward to the 21st century, and matters have scarcely improved. Archeology in Panama continues to be characterized by state apathy, underfunding, and negligence: the country's national anthropological museum in Panama City has been closed to the public since 2013 and several of the regional museums are dilapidated.

What's more, lacking the huge stone structures and sophisticated carvings that epitomize the Maya, Aztec, and Toltec civilizations of Mesoamerica, the trading societies of Central America have always taken a historical backseat. Yet central Panama boasts the earliest traces of pottery-making in the Americas, with ceramics from Monagrillo, in the northern Azuero Peninsula, carbon-dated to 2500–1200 BC. A nearby fishing village in Sarigua is considered to be the oldest settlement of the isthmus, dating from around 11,000 BC. These early dwellers are thought to have descended from hunter-gathers from Eurasia, experiencing little contact with other cultures until the conquest. Much of what has been learned, or can be deduced, about early societies has come from the diaries

Coclé ceramic plate.

and reports of conquistador soldiers or officials, since the indigenous peoples did not develop systems of writing and therefore left no first-hand accounts.

Archeologists generally discuss the pre-Columbian isthmus in terms of three broad regions: Gran Darién, from present-day Panama province and eastward; Gran Coclé for the central region, including the Azuero; and Gran Chiriquí to the west, extending to Bocas del Toro. Radio carbon-dating and analysis of the stylistic development of ceramics has been used to draw inferences about the nature of the societies that once flourished here.

The most sophisticated societies inhabited central Panama, in the area of Gran Coclé.

This is reflected in their ceramics, dating from about 200BC, which display great skill in their use of multiple luminous, rich colors, zoomorphic and anthropomorphic figures – especially reptiles, birds, and marine life – and symbolic representations. This was confirmed by the country's richest finds unearthed in the 1930s in the necropolis of Sitio Conté, outside Penonomé, and, more recently, from around 2006, in the nearby necropolis of El Caño, outside Natá. In Sitio Conté these early excavations by American academics opened up around 100 tombs

standing stones that might have offered some clues. New excavations undertaken since 2006 by Panamanian archeologist Julia Maya and her team are producing fascinating finds: analysis of the gold artifacts, for example, has proved that these were made locally, thus confirming an excellent local understanding of metallurgy. Despite the lack of monumental structures, early society around central Panama was clearly sophisticated and hierarchical, capable of working intricate gold pieces and ceramics even though it is presumed that their living quarters

Ancient artifacts on display in Sitio Barriles.

to reveal thousands of intricate gold pieces of jewelry alongside polychrome ceramics displaying exquisite artistry and other artifacts dating back to the first century. At the time, the discovery constituted the greatest haul of gold artifacts in the western hemisphere, most of which were shipped off to the United States. Yet the area, which lies on private agricultural land, has not been touched by archeologists since 1940.

At El Caño, near Natá, an elaborate burial site dates from around 700–1000 AD. It has a number of similarities to the Sitio Conté site, though its original function and significance is unknown, not helped by the fact that a US adventurer decapitated more than 100 basalt

were simple structures of wood, wattle, and thatch that have rotted away over time. Unlike Sitio Conté, El Caño is open to the public (see page 176).

In the Western Highlands, outside Volcán, another important site indicates the existence of what has been termed the Barriles culture, which gained its name from the barrel-shaped stones they carved. It was at its apogee around 500–600 AD, after which, it has been suggested, the population might have disappeared on account of a massive eruption from Volcán Barú. One of the more curious discoveries, however, are stone statues of a figure wearing a conical hat, carrying another on its shoulders, which lie in Panama City's anthropological museum. The bearer's seemingly African features have been used as evidence that Africans were living on the isthmus before the arrival of the Spanish. A large ceremonial grinding stone, or *metate*, adorned with human heads – also in the museum – has also led to speculation about human sacrifice. Earlier investigations considered Barriles to be a ceremonial center, but a more recent excavation (this century) uncovered evidence of village living. Sprinkled round Sitio Barriles and elsewhere in western and central Panama, on moss-covered boulders, are numerous petroglyphs, which have also baffled archeologists; they may be ritual or narrative depictions, markers of territory or maps, or symbols related to water or fertility. In some Ngäbe groups, petroglyphs have been assimilated into their oral histories, made by the fingers and toes of the mythical Evia. The largest petroglyph uncovered so far is La Piedra Pintada outside El Valle, but the collection in El Nancito – just north of the Interamericana between Las Lajas and Tolé – is of greater interest.

⊘ TREASURE TROVE IN EL CAÑO

In 2008, in a dusty field in the neglected site of El Caño, a tomb was discovered that caused a wave of excitement across the archeological world. In it lay an elite warrior with gold breastplates and beaded belt and arm cuffs. News of the find soon spread, attracting more funding and further excavations. In 2011, the archeologists were rewarded by even greater treasures. A multi-level burial pit was unearthed revealing a skeleton also dressed in gold, but surrounded by a careful arrangement of 25 bodies covered in pieces of ceramic. These were possibly slaves or human sacrifices, and a bowl of fishbones belonging to a poisonous species may signal how they met their end. Amidst the skeletons were tiny gold adornments meant for a child of status. A more recent excavation uncovered the tomb of a high-ranking 10-year-old, accompanied by 47 dead bodies, indicating a system of inherited wealth. So far, a stash of gold, copper, ceramic, and emeralds has been found, along with axe heads, animal teeth, and bones. However, it's not known where the pieces are being kept, or where or when they will eventually be displayed. By the end of 2017, archeologists were onto their seventh tomb. In the meantime, a special edition of stamps depicting some of the gold pieces was released in Panama in 2018. Until the country has a fully functioning archeological museum, the stamps are likely to be the nearest anyone gets to seeing one of the Americas' most important archeological finds in decades.

Vasco Nuñez de Balboa crushing indigenous resistance.

SPANISH CONQUEST

Bloody, brutal, and bruising – the Spanish Conquest of Panama had a devastating and lasting impact on the isthmus.

ARRIVAL OF THE SPANISH

The first European credited with setting foot on the isthmus of Panama was the Spanish aristocratic notary Rodrigo Galván de Bastidas, who made a low-key appearance in 1501, trading his way peacefully up the Caribbean coast as far as present-day Colón. In contrast, the arrival of Christopher Columbus (Cristóbal Colón), who embarked a year later on his fourth and final voyage to the 'New World,' was anything but low-key. Heading for the western and central Caribbean coast, keen to lay his hands on its legendary gold, Columbus came ashore on the eponymous Isla Colón, in the Bocas del Toro archipelago. Attempting to establish the first European settlement on the isthmus, he was soon engaged in violent conflicts with indigenous populations on the mainland. Though relations between Columbus and the local chief or cacique, Quibián, known as 'El Señor de la Tierra,' were initially friendly, the mood changed once it became clear the Spanish intended to stay. When Columbus left his garrison at Santa María de Belén (in present-day Veraguas) to seek reinforcements, Quibián rallied local leaders to destroy the settlement, but was captured by Columbus's brother Bartolomé, who had been left in charge. While being transported as a prisoner downriver to Belén, the chief dived out of the dugout and was presumed drowned. He survived, however, and went on to lead an assault against the invaders, forcing them to flee.

The respite was short-lived. In 1505 the king of Spain, Ferdinand II, intent on expanding his empire, dispatched two men to take charge of what had been named 'Tierre Firme' (extending from present-day Venezuela to Panama). The first, Alonso de Ojeda, was to govern the land

Balboa ordering indigenous peoples to be torn to pieces by dogs.

between Cabo de la Vela in present-day Colombia through to the Golfo de Urabá, known as Nueva Andalucía. Diego de Nicuesa was to oversee the west from the gulf to Gracias a Dios on what is now the border between Honduras and Nicaragua (and was known as Castilla de Oro, after its supposed riches). Both campaigns ended in disaster.

Though estimates of the indigenous population at the time of the Spanish conquest vary from 200,000 to 2 million, the speed at which the local communities were decimated was indisputably swift, as much by disease brought by the conquistadors as through massacre and enslavement. The remainder retreated to inhospitable remote mountain areas, where they either lay low or continued their resistance against the invaders. The Spanish Crown instituted a feudal-style system of *encomiendas*, theoretically entrusting 'free' indigenous peoples to the stewardship of colonizers for their well-being and instruction in the Catholic faith in return for labor and other tributes; in practice, workers were more often treated like slaves. The aim was to concentrate the subjugated population in one place, making it easier to convert them to Catholicism and to manage their financial and laboral exploitation. Though

the *encomienda* system was abolished in 1720, it did not spell the end of intense hardships for much of the rural population.

The annihilation or resistance of much of the indigenous population left the conquistadors with a labor shortage, which was exacerbated after they 'discovered' Perú and sent many to work in the mines. The Spanish addressed the shortage by importing slaves from various parts of Africa, initially to work in the ports and on the ships, and later to undertake the grueling crossings of the isthmus, accompanying the mule train.

Balboa 'discovering' the Pacific.

⊘ CACIQUE URRACÁ

With a park named after him in central Panama City, and his head on the one cent coin, the mighty indigenous chief Urracá is the most famous of three Guaymí (forefathers of the Ngäbe) leaders in western Panama – the others being Natá and Parita, after whom the Spanish named settlements. Over a nine-year period, Urracá provided the colonizers' fiercest resistance as they attempted to make inroads into Panama. Managing to unite community chiefs who were traditional enemies against a common foe, he conducted guerrilla-type raids from his mountain stronghold above Santa Fé de Veraguas. After repeatedly failing to defeat Urracá, and following numerous

bloody clashes, the Spanish resorted to deception, luring him down to Natá under the pretense of negotiating a peace settlement – the same tactics they used later against Bayano in Darién. When he showed up, with two of his men, Urracá was immediately seized and taken in chains to Nombre de Dios, from where he was to be deported to Spain. Managing to escape, he returned to his people, vowing to fight the invaders to the death. By this stage, however, the Spanish were so afraid of him and his warriors that they avoided conflict with them whenever possible, while the chief continued his resistance until he died in 1531.

BALBOA AND THE MAR DEL SUR

Though an instrumental figure in the development of the isthmus, there's little in Vasco Nuñez de Balboa's early life to suggest he would rise to prominence. After arriving in the region as a member of Bastidas' expedition, he settled on Hispaniola, where, failing as a pig-farmer, he fled his creditors by stowing away on a boat bound for the mainland. Upon discovery, he was saved from being thrown off the ship thanks to his knowledge of the isthmus. As the incipient Spanish settlements struggled to survive, including the new forests of the Darién. On September 25, 1513, so the story goes, he was standing on top of a mountain when he became the first European to look out onto the Pacific Ocean. Several days later, in true imperialist fashion, Balboa waded into the water in full body armor, sword in one hand, statue of the Virgin Mary in the other, and claimed possession of the 'Mar del Sur' in the name of the king of Spain. Yet he received scant reward for his 'discovery' – in 1519 his jealous superior Pedro Arias de Ávila, known as Pedrarias the Cruel or Furor Domini (Wrath of God),

regional center San Sebastián de Urabá, Balboa recommended relocating across the gulf. Santa María de la Antigua del Darién (on the other side of the current Panama–Colombia border) was thus established on a site that had been seized from followers of Cacique Cémaco, a pivotal leader of indigenous resistance. It was the first successful Spanish settlement on the isthmus, eventually becoming the capital of Castilla de Oro until the seat transferred to Panama City in 1524.

Meanwhile Balboa continued his acquisition of power by subjugating, negotiating, and making peace with local peoples. Hearing about another sea to the south and land dripping in gold and pearls – possibly the Inca civilization – Balboa set off on an expedition with just under 200 men, determined to find a route through the

⊘ PIRATES AND BOOTY

During the 16th and 17th centuries, Nombre de Dios and later Portobelo became two of the most enticing targets for cut-throat pirates and privateers – pirates with a Royal license to plunder. The towns were particularly vulnerable at the ports' annual trade fairs. These were held when the Spanish fleet, having returned from escorting the booty-filled galleons to Spain, returned to unload their silks and luxury goods to trade, before stocking up once again with silver. Two of the most persistent headaches for the Spanish were Englishman Francis Drake and Welshman Henry Morgan.

the first governor of Castilla de Oro, put him on trial on trumped up charges of rebellion and high treason, before having him, and four of his companions, beheaded.

PANAMA CITY AND THE CAMINO REAL

In the face of appalling losses from disease, Pedrarias eventually moved his base from the Caribbean side to the slightly more salubrious Pacific coast, where he founded Panama City (Panamá La Vieja) in 1519. The new settlement became the jumping-off point for further Span-

At the height of silver production at the end of the 16th century, over 200 tons of silver were being transported across the isthmus annually by mule train.

and privateers, the first of whom, the Englishman Francis Drake, successfully raided Nombre de Dios. He received support from the *cimarrones*, communities of escaped African slaves

Welsh buccaneer Sir Henry Morgan.

ish inroads north and south along the coast, and, after the conquest of Peru in 1533, it began to flourish as the transit point for the fabulous riches of the Incas on their way to fill the coffers of the Spanish Crown. From Panama City, cargo was transported across the isthmus on mules along the paved Camino Real to the port of Nombre de Dios, and later Portobelo, on the Caribbean coast. A second route, the Camino de Cruces, was used to transport heavier cargo to the highest navigable point on the Río Chagres, where it was transferred to dugout canoes to be carried downriver to the coast.

The flow of wealth attracted the attention of Spain's enemies, and the Caribbean coast was under constant threat from European pirates

who lived in the jungle and often collaborated with pirates in ambushing mule trains and attacking their former masters. In the most daring assault, in 1671, Welshman Henry Morgan and his men sailed up the Río Chagres, having destroyed the fortress at San Lorenzo at the rivermouth en route, and crossed the isthmus to ransack Panama City. Though the area around present-day Panamá La Vieja was destroyed, the city was rebuilt in 1673 on today's Casco Viejo, behind defenses so formidable that it was never taken again. However, the raiding of the Caribbean coast continued until Spain finally rerouted the treasure fleet around Cape Horn in 1746. With the route across the isthmus all but abandoned, Panama slipped into decline.

Pedro Arias de Ávila attacking the indigenous population.

The Californian gold rush in the mid 1800s sparked a flurry of traffic across the Panamanian isthmus.

STRIVING FOR INDEPENDENCE

After shrugging off Spain, and then Colombia, Panama offered itself to the US with the promise of a canal.

INDEPENDENCE FROM SPAIN

By the turn of the 19th century, independence movements in South America, headed by Simón Bolívar and José de San Martín, were gathering pace. Though the isthmus initially remained fairly detached from the process, it was not devoid of nationalist sentiment. On 10 November 1821, the tiny town of La Villa de Los Santos unilaterally declared that it would no longer be governed by Spain, in what was known as the *Primer Grito de la Independencia* (First Cry for Independence); the rest of the country followed suit, declaring independence on November 30. It retained the name of Panama, as a department of what historians have subsequently termed 'Gran Colombia'; with the secession of Ecuador and Venezuela it quickly became Nueva Granada. Almost immediately conflicts emerged between the merchants of Panama City, eager to trade freely with the world, and the distant, protectionist governments in Bogotá, leading to numerous, if half-hearted, attempts at separation. As the century wore on, US influence asserted itself, most notably in the 1846 Mallarino-Bidlack Treaty, which granted the US government rights to build a railroad across the isthmus and, significantly, accorded them power to intervene militarily to suppress any secessionist uprisings against the New Granadan government – a theoretically mutually beneficial accord that was to seriously backfire on Bogotá.

The discovery of gold in California in 1849 sparked an explosion in Gold Rush traffic across the isthmus. Travel from the US east coast to California via Panama – by boat, overland on foot, and then by boat again – was far less arduous than the trek across North America, and thousands of 'Forty-niners' passed through on their way to the goldfields. In 1850 a US

Construction of the Panama Canal.

company began the construction of a railroad across Panama. Carving a route through the inhospitable swamps and rainforests proved immensely difficult – thousands of the mostly Chinese and West Indian migrant workers died in the process – but when the railroad was completed in 1855, the Panama Railroad Company

The Panama Railroad cost 6,000–10,000 lives and $8 million to construct, making it the most expensive track per kilometer in the world. However, the hefty $25 transit fee in gold helped it earn $7 million in profit over the first six years alone.

proved an instant financial success. However, it also marked the beginning of a new era in foreign control: within a year, the first US military intervention in Panama had taken place.

THE FRENCH CANAL VENTURE

In 1869, the opening of the first transcontinental railroad in the US reduced traffic through Panama, but the completion of the Suez Canal that same year made the long-standing dream of a canal across the isthmus a realistic possibility. Well aware of the strategic advantages such a waterway would offer, the French secured a concession to build a canal, as well as purchasing the Panama Railroad, from the New Granadan government. In 1881, led by ex-diplomat Ferdinand de Lesseps, the driving force responsible for the Suez Canal, the Compagnie Universelle du Canal Interocéanique began excavations.

Despite de Lesseps' vision and determination, the 'venture of the century' proved to be a disaster, not least because of his technical ignorance and arrogance. In the face of impassable terrain – forests, swamps, and the shifting shales of the

Ferdinand de Lesseps visiting Panama.

The War of the Thousand Days.

⊘ THE WATERMELON WAR

The completion of the Panama Railroad left many Panamanian laborers, including the new immigrant workforce, unemployed and resentful of their well-paid US counterparts, some of whom showed scant respect for their hosts or local customs. On April 15, 1856, tensions spilled over. An intoxicated white American named Jack Oliver, who had been killing time in the bars waiting for the boat, grabbed a slice of watermelon from a local black vendor and refused to pay. When the trader drew a knife, Oliver drew a gun. An attempt to disarm the American resulted in a bystander getting shot, prompting a full-scale anti-US riot. Many Americans holed up in the railroad depot and gunfire was exchanged with the crowd, which was attempting to batter down the door. Rather than control the situation, the police joined in the affray, which continued until a trainload of the vigilante Isthmus Guard arrived to disperse the mob. While the number of casualties in the so-called 'Watermelon War' – 17 dead and 29 wounded, predominantly American – was not disputed, blame for the violence was. Amid claims and counterclaims of racism, the US government dispatched two warships to Panama and occupied the train station (albeit for only three days) but their demand for total control of the railroad was refused.

continental divide – the proposed sea-level canal proved unfeasible, while yellow fever, malaria, and a host of other unpleasant diseases ravaged the workforce. In 1889 the Compagnie collapsed; $287 million had evaporated as a result of financial mismanagement and corruption, implicating the highest levels of French society. Hundreds of thousands of ordinary French investors lost everything.

THE WAR OF THE THOUSAND DAYS

At the end of the 19th century the simmering feud between the Conservative and Liberal parties erupted into a bloody three-year civil war called the War of the Thousand Days (*Guerra de los Mil Días*). Though there were ideological differences, there were also many factions and much infighting. Essentially, the ruling elite Conservatives supported strong central government, limited voting rights, and close bonds between Church and State, whereas the merchant class and educated Liberals wanted more decentralized, federal government, universal voting rights, and a greater division between Church and State. The violence was triggered by alleged election fraud

The US agrees to build the Panama Canal.

⊙ PEDRO PRESTÁN AND THE FIRE OF COLÓN

One of the uglier episodes in the factional feuding of the War of the Thousand Days occurred in 1885, with the public hanging of Pedro Prestán. Prestán, a Liberal revolutionary, had taken advantage of the absence of Colombian troops in Colón – they had headed over to Panama City to quell an attempted coup – by seizing control of the city. After looting businesses to raise money, he and his band of rebels purchased arms from the US, which had arrived on a steamship anchored in the bay. When the ship agent refused to unload the arms, Prestán took the agent, US consul, and several other Americans hostage, threatening to kill them if the US naval vessel stationed nearby landed troops and

the arms were not handed over. Though the weapons were promised and the hostages released, the Americans reneged on the deal. Fleeing to Monkey Hill outside the city, Prestán and his poorly armed combatants got caught up with the Colombian troops now back from Panama City. The rebels were routed and the city caught fire; built of wood, it was totally destroyed, killing 18 and leaving thousands homeless. Prestán, who had fled by boat to his native Cartagena, became the scapegoat. Many of his men were rounded up and executed while Prestán himself was later captured, tried and convicted by a partisan jury, and hanged above the railroad tracks in Colón.

by the landed Conservatives in their bid to remain in power, but by the time the bloody conflict had ended in 1902, claiming 100,000 lives, it was hard to pinpoint what much of the fighting had actually been about. It's also unclear whether key Liberal protagonists were motivated more by the desire for separation than for social justice; regardless, most Liberals were subsequently elevated to the status of nationalist heroes.

The initial Liberal revolt was led by Belisario Porras, the popular exiled lawyer, who later won three periods of office as president of Panama.

With the support of the presidents of Nicaragua and Ecuador, Porras entered western Panama on March 31, 1900, with an invasion force commanded by Colombian Emiliano Herrera, at the insistence of President Zelaya of Nicaragua. Their antagonism was a major factor in the ultimate Liberal failure. Moving toward Panama City, they gathered numerous supporters, but slow progress allowed reinforcements to arrive from Colombia. On arrival outside the capital, Herrera rejected Porras's attack plan and led a botched single-pronged assault on the city in which 1,000

USS Wisconsin passes through Gatún Locks.

⊙ VICTORIANO LORENZO

These days Victoriano Lorenzo is regarded as a nationalist hero in Panama; three plaques commemorate him on Plaza de Francia, where he was executed by firing squad. Whatever his motivations for joining the Liberal struggle, he was, above all, a champion of social justice for the rural poor. Born in the 1870s and of predominantly indigenous heritage, Lorenzo was well educated and worked in the municipality of Penonomé in the central province of Coclé. When Porras and his troops swept through the country in 1900, Lorenzo and his supporters threw their lot behind the Liberal cause, conducting a number of guerrilla raids on Conservative forces down on the plains. From the moment the peace deal was signed between

the Liberal and Conservative elites, however, and Lorenzo refused to lay down arms, he was doomed. Some maintain that his arrest, in contravention of the amnesty, was a sordid – and racist – collusion between both Conservative and Liberal social elites, scared at the power he wielded among the rural populations, and their potential to destabilize US support for an independent Panama. Alternatively, he was simply a convenient scapegoat. Others contend that Porras supported the populist leader, but that his words went unheeded. Whatever the truth, Lorenzo's fears about the peace accord were well founded, as the new Panama showed frequent disregard for social inequalities and the needs of the poor.

died. Though the Conservatives reasserted their authority, small bands of Liberal sympathizers ran riot in the interior, especially in the central rural areas under the leadership of Victoriano Lorenzo, a local official of predominantly indigenous ancestry from Coclé and a champion of the indigenous population. In 1901, a second Nicaraguan-backed Liberal force managed to take Colón and effectively immobilize the railroad, forcing the Colombian government to ask the US to broker an armistice. Meeting on the US battleship *Wisconsin* on November 21, 1902, the Liber-

becoming a major sea power. At first the favored route was through Nicaragua, but the persuasive lobbying of Philippe Bunau-Varilla, former acting director and major shareholder in the French company, swung the Senate vote in Panama's favor. His masterstroke was to buy 90 Nicaraguan stamps that showed an erupting volcano – a major argument against the Nicaragua route – and send one to each senator just three days before the vote. In 1903 a treaty allowing the US to build the canal was negotiated with the Colombian government, whose senate refused to ratify it, under-

als, fearing intervention by the US government, agreed to the peace conditions, but Lorenzo refused to accept the terms. Surprisingly, it was Herrera, the Liberal general, who disregarded the amnesty detailed in the accord and ordered Lorenzo's arrest. He was summarily tried, found guilty, and executed by firing squad that same night on May 15, 1903, in the Plaza de Armas (today's Plaza de Francia) of Panama City. Six months later Panama separated from Colombia.

SEPARATION FROM COLOMBIA

Despite the French canal debacle, the dream of an interoceanic waterway remained as strong as ever. US President Theodore Roosevelt, in particular, felt that the construction of a canal across Central America was an essential step to

standably wary that the US would not respect their sovereignty. Outraged that 'the Bogotá lot of jackrabbits should be allowed to bar one of the future highways of civilization,' Roosevelt gave unofficial backing to Panamanian secessionists.

In the event, the separation was a swift almost bloodless affair with only one casualty. The small Colombian garrison in Panama City was bribed to switch sides and a second force that had landed at Colón agreed to return to Colombia without a fight after its officers had been tricked into captivity by the rebels. On November 3, 1903, the Republic of Panama was declared and immediately recognized by the US, whose gunship standing offshore prevented Colombian reinforcements from landing to crush the rebellion.

📷 LIFE IN THE CANAL ZONE

A US state within a state, the Panama Canal Zone even had its own postal service, with 17 post offices and its own stamps.

In 1903, when work first started on the US canal venture, the Canal Zone was established. It was effectively a slice of US territory, 8km (5 miles) either side of the canal, managed by the Isthmian Canal Commission (ICC). It remained under US jurisdiction until 1979, before transitioning to joint US-Panamanian control, until its handover in 1999. From the outset, work was carried out under an apartheid labor system – an extension of the racial inequalities of the railroad and French canal construction eras. Employees were either 'gold roll' or 'silver roll;' the former, almost exclusively white US citizens, were paid in gold (almost twice the value of silver) and the rest – the vast majority of whom were black West Indian workers from present-day Barbados and Jamaica – in silver. This categorization permeated every aspect of life. The Americans enjoyed more spacious housing, better food, health care, and schooling. White workers were encouraged to bring their wives and were offered rent-free housing – not so the black workers. For these minority white 'gold roll' employees, the Zone was in many ways a tropical paradise, especially once the canal was completed, with plenty of clubs, societies, sports amenities, theaters, and movie theaters for entertainment, and trips to the beach on weekends. At the center of zonal social life stood the grand Tivoli Hotel; as well as accommodating VIP visitors – from presidents and royalty to movie stars, who all flocked to Panama to gawp at the 'Big Ditch' – it also hosted weekly dances, school proms, weddings, and balls. By 1908, there were over 1,000 US families and the ICC was spending $2.5 million annually on games and entertainment for the gold roll employees. There was no entertainment budget for the black workforce.

The Miraflores Locks at the Pacific side of the Canal consist of two sets of lock chambers.

A fence separates the Canal Zone from the rest of Panama City. Running right through the heart of Panama, the Canal Zone divided the country in two, making it difficult for Panamanians to travel freely around their own country. To cross Panama, they were forced to pass through land under US jurisdiction.

Infrastructure built for the construction of the Panama Canal.

The Tivoli Hotel at Ancón in the Canal Zone.

The 'silver roll' heritage

Life was very different for the 'silver roll' laborer. Assigned barrack-type singles living quarters, some married workers rented squalid lodgings in Panama City or Colón, or used salvaged materials to build a shack in the jungle. For the black worker it was a constant tale of rain, mud, exhaustion, and daily danger from accidents, landslides, and disease. Though health conditions gradually improved, malaria, pneumonia, typhoid, and tuberculosis persisted, compounded by the inferior medical care that black employees received. Unsurprisingly, their mortality rate, even in the US canal period, was four times higher than among whites. A visit to the Museo Afroantillano in Panama City (see page 133) is a poignant reminder of the huge sacrifice and contribution of the West Indian workforce.

US President Theodore Roosevelt refusing to pay Colombia 'millions' for canal rights in 1903.

Vintage stamp from the Canal Zone.

Workers digging the Panama Canal. During the US construction period, Panamanians made up a surprisingly small percentage of the work force: the Americans were wary of growing resentment at US control and were reluctant to highlight the disparity between life in the Canal Zone and how the rest of the population lived.

Patient in a yellow-fever cage in Ancón Hospital.

MODERN HISTORY

Post-independence Panama has survived two dictatorships, an invasion by the US, and gained sovereignty over the Canal, but a string of corruption-plagued presidencies and financial scandals is widening the gap between the 'haves' and the 'have-nots.'

THE CANAL

As the War of the Thousand Days neared its conclusion, liberal elites became preoccupied with promises of wealth from building a canal, and, as a result, abandoned the concerns for social justice that had initially attracted indigenous peoples to their cause. Panamanian independence, declared in 1903, was backed by the US, whose politicians and businessmen were keen to control the Canal venture.

In a speech to Congress, President Roosevelt made clear his view on the Canal: 'No single great material work which remains to be undertaken on this continent is of such consequence to the American people.'

Philippe Bunau-Varilla.

A new canal treaty was quickly negotiated and signed on Panama's behalf by slippery French businessman Philippe Bunau-Varilla, who had managed to get himself appointed a special envoy, theoretically only with negotiating powers. The Hay-Bunau-Varilla Treaty of 1903 gave the US 'all the rights, power and authority... which [it] would possess and exercise as if it were the sovereign,' in perpetuity over an area of territory – the Canal Zone – extending 8km (5 miles) either side of the canal. In return, the new Panamanian government received a one-off payment of $10 million and a further $250,000 a year. (Of particular interest to Bunau-Varilla was the $40 million the French canal company received for all its equipment and infrastructure, in which he was a major shareholder.) Even American secretary of state John Hay admitted

the treaty conditions were 'vastly advantageous to the US and we must confess... not so advantageous to Panama.' Panama's newly formed national assembly found the terms outrageous, but when told by Bunau-Varilla that US support would be withdrawn were they to reject it – a claim he invented on the spot – they ratified the treaty, and work on the Panama Canal began.

The completion of the Canal was an unprecedented triumph of organization, perseverance, engineering, and, just as crucially, sanitation, during which time chief medical officer Colonel William Gorgas established a program that eliminated yellow fever from the isthmus and brought malaria under control. As a result, the death toll – though still numbering some

5,600 workers, predominantly of West Indian descent – was substantially lower than it would otherwise have been. Meanwhile the two men in charge, John Stevens, a brilliant railroad engineer, and his successor George Goethals, a former army engineer, managed to solve the problems that had stymied the French. The idea of a sea-level canal was quickly abandoned in favor of constructing a series of locks to raise ships up to a huge artificial lake formed by damming the mighty Río Chagres. Stevens was responsible for maximizing the potential of the

ran through the continental divide, required a mind-boggling 27,000 tonnes of dynamite. The end result, overseen by Goethals, was the largest concrete structure, earth dam, and artificial lake that the world had ever seen, accomplished with pioneering technology that set new standards for engineering. On August 15, 1914, the SS *Ancón* became the first ship to officially transit the Canal, which was completed six months ahead of schedule.

An enormous migrant workforce, at times outnumbering the combined populations of

Construction of the giant lock chambers.

railroad, devising an ingenious pulley system that enabled them to excavate over 170 million cubic meters (222 million cu yds) of earth and rock, three times the amount removed at Suez. The 13km (8-mile) Gaillard Cut, which

The eventual mosquito control program in the US canal era significantly reduced the death and hospitalization rates among workers. In 1906, the death rate was 12 percent; by 1909 it had been reduced to 1 percent. Hospitalization was reduced from 10 percent in 1905 to 2 percent by 1909.

Panama City and Colón, was imported to work on the Canal's construction, and many of these laborers – Indians, Europeans, Chinese, and above all West Indians – stayed on after its completion, indelibly transforming the racial and cultural make-up of the country. Work was carried out under an apartheid labor system where white Americans were paid in gold and everyone else (mainly black workers) were paid in silver. Not only did gold-roll employees and their families enjoy higher wages, they also benefitted from superior accommodations, better nutrition, health care, and schooling; even toilets and drinking fountains were set aside for the exclusive use of one group or the other.

THE NEW REPUBLIC

Though their economy boomed during the Canal's construction, it was soon apparent to Panamanians that they had exchanged control by Bogotá for dominance by the US. The government, largely controlled by a ruling oligarchy known as the 'twenty families,' was independent in name only; the US controlled everything – trade, communications, water, and security. Moreover, the de-facto sovereignty and legal jurisdiction that the US enjoyed within the Canal Zone made it a strip of US territory in which

Following an armed revolt led by *Sailas* (chiefs) Nele Kantule and Olokindibipilele (Simral Colman), which resulted in around 20 fatalities on each side, the Guna declared independence. Forestalling government retaliation, the US stepped in and mediated a peace agreement that granted the Guna the semiautonomous status they still retain.

The Republic of Panama's first president, the respected Conservative Manuel Amador Guerrero (in power 1904–8), was actually from Colombia. But the first Panamanian president of real impact was Belisario Porras, elected to

Painting of the SS Ancon, the first ship to pass through the Panama Canal on opening day, August 15, 1914.

Panamanians were denied the commercial and employment opportunities enjoyed by the US 'Zonians,' a situation that lasted well beyond the completion of the Canal. The US agreement to guarantee Panamanian independence came at the price of intervention whenever the US considered it necessary to 'maintain order,' a right they exercised on several occasions.

One such action followed the Dule or Guna Revolution in 1925, a result of the Panamanian government refusing to recognize the relative autonomy granted by the Colombian authorities in 1870 through the Comarca Tulenega. Pressure mounted when outside groups were given concessions to plunder Guna resources and persistent attempts were made to suppress Guna culture.

office in 1912 for the first of three terms (1912–16, 1918–20, and 1920–24). A trained lawyer and prominent Liberal leader from the War of the Thousand Days, he is largely credited with establishing the basic infrastructure necessary

When Belisario Porras had the huge Hospital Santo Tomás built in Panama City in 1924, it was considered a white elephant for being far too big for the population. Ironically, by the time Porras fell terminally ill 20 years later, there was no bed free, so he ended his days in a private hospital.

for a newly independent state – roads, bridges, hospitals, schools, libraries, a legal system, communication networks, and even the cherished national lottery.

While all Panamanians were initially delighted at having shrugged off the yolk of Colombian rule, it did not take long for the isthmian elite to take over and the usual social hierarchies to be re-established. The state did not deliver on the rights that many rural people – and indigenous populations above all – had craved and fought for. Instead, its politicians encour-

while going on to become one of the country's most popular leaders. A Harvard graduate of middle-class farming stock, he founded Acción Communal, the political precursor to the Partido Nacional Revolucionario and present-day Partido Panameñista (PP), which espoused his nationalistic and initially racist doctrine of Panameñismo. After assisting his older brother Harmodio Arias Madrid to the presidency in 1932, he won office himself in 1940, for the first of three periods (1940–41, 1949–51, and 1968). During his first term he set about disenfran-

Anti-American riots in Panama.

aged settlement of migrants, and made laws to facilitate their acquisition of land. The 'civilizing' program of nation-building took hold, including the establishment of state education, with its narrow curriculum that excluded the histories, cultures, and perspectives of the indigenous, Afro-Panamanian, and minority populations.

THE RISE OF NATIONALISM

Despite a new treaty limiting the US right of intervention in 1936, resentment of American control became the dominant theme of Panamanian politics and the basis of an emerging sense of national identity. Arnulfo Arias Madrid, a fascist and Nazi sympathizer – earning him the nickname 'Führer Criollo' – exploited this

chising Afro-Antillean and Chinese- Panamanians and pursuing overtly racist immigration policies. On the positive side, he instigated the social security system, improved many workers' rights (a policy strand abandoned in his later term), modernized banking, and gave the vote to women. Crucially, he was adamant about pushing for a better deal with a US government intent on expanding its military defenses outside the Canal Zone. But the US-backed Panamanian Policía Nacional (National Police) and its successor, the Guardia Nacional (National Guard), made sure that no president who challenged the status quo lasted long in office and Arias was ousted by military coup each time, the last after only two weeks.

Nevertheless, anti-US riots erupted periodically over the next 30 years. The 10,000-strong protest in 1947 against the US attempt to extend the lease on World War II-era bases outside the Canal Zone helped persuade the deputies not to ratify the proposal. By 1948, the US military had withdrawn from outside the Zone. The most infamous disturbances, however, were the so-called flag riots of 1964. The flying of flags was a trivial but symbolic battleground for Panamanian-US antagonism. When the US flag was flown on its own for two days in succession in Balboa High School – not along with the Panamanian flag, as had been agreed – 200 Panamanian students arrived at the school to rectify the situation. A skirmish broke out and the Panamanian flag was torn, prompting full-scale mob violence. The 21 Panamanians who died were later elevated to the status of national martyrs, commemorated annually on January 9, *Día de los Mártires* (Martyrs' Day).

THE NEW CANAL TREATY

After a brief power struggle following the coup to oust Arnulfo Arias Madrid in 1968, Lieutenant Colonel Omar Torrijos of the National Guard established himself as leader of the new military government. Fracturing the political dominance of the white merchant oligarchy (known disparagingly as the *rabiblancos*, or 'white tails') in his pursuit of a pragmatic middle way between socialism and capitalism, he was a charismatic, populist leader. Over 12 years he introduced a wide range of reforms – a new constitution and labor code, nationalization of the electricity and communications sectors, and expanded public health and education services, especially for the poor. This he managed while simultaneously maintaining good relations with the business sector, establishing Colón's Zona Libra (Free Trade Zone), and initiating the banking secrecy laws necessary for Panama's emergence as an international financial center.

Often seen wearing his trademark bush hat, Omar Torrijos never took the title 'president,' but rather 'Líder Máximo de la Revolución Panameña' and 'Comandante de la Guardia Nacional.'

Rather more darkly, he was extremely intolerant of political opposition and his critics were often imprisoned or simply 'disappeared.' Several mass graves from the period were unearthed during a Truth Commission instigated by President Moscoso, though there was no evidence of Torrijos' direct involvement in the atrocities, and blame was generally apportioned to his head of military intelligence, Manuel Noriega.

Central to Torrijos' popular appeal was his insistence on gaining Panamanian control over the Canal. After lethargic negotiations with the

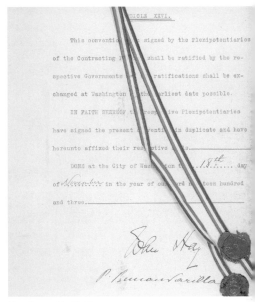

Hay-Bunau-Varilla Treaty.

Nixon and Ford administrations, Torrijos signed a new canal treaty with US president Jimmy Carter on September 7, 1977. Under its terms, the US agreed to a gradual withdrawal, passing complete control of the Canal to Panama on December 31, 1999; in the meantime it was to be administered by the Panama Canal Commission, composed of five US and four Panamanian citizens. Even so, the US retained the right to intervene militarily if the Canal's neutrality was threatened. Under pressure from Washington to democratize, Torrijos formed a political party, the Partido Revolucionario Democrático (PRD), and began moving Panama toward free democratic elections. In 1981, however, he died in a plane crash, near the national park that bears his name. It was rumoured that his accident was plotted by the CIA or Colonel Manuel Noriega, Torrijos' former military intelligence chief.

US INVASION

After a period of political uncertainty, Noriega took over as head of the National Guard, which he restructured as a personal power base and renamed the Fuerzas de Defensa de Panamá (Panama Defense Forces or PDF), becoming the de-facto military ruler in 1983. Although the 1984 elections gave Panama its first directly

US Armed Forces occupy the Canal Zone.

elected leader in nearly two decades, Nicolás Ardito Barletta, the real power lay in the hands of Noriega, backed by the US government.

A career soldier, Panama's new military strongman had been on the US Army's payroll as early as the 1950s and the CIA's from the late 1960s, before becoming chief of intelligence for the National Guard in 1970. In the early 1980s, Noriega assisted the US by supporting its interests elsewhere in Central America, especially Nicaragua. Whereas Torrijos had supported the leftist Sandinistas in Nicaragua's civil war, Noriega allegedly provided covert US military support for the Contras, helping to funnel money and weapons to the guerrilla force – a charge he denies. At the same time, Noriega was busy

> *Ironic tunes requested from radio listeners to the station aimed at flushing out Noriega included Bon Jovi's 'Wanted Dead or Alive,' The Animals' 'We Gotta Get Out of This Place,' and Led Zeppelin's 'Your Time is Gonna Come.'*

building relations with the Colombian cocaine cartels in Medellín. Although this extracurricular activity was ignored by the US for years, in 1986 the Iran-Contra Affair – in which the US government sold weapons illicitly to Iran and used the proceeds to fund the Contras – brought an unwelcome glare of publicity on the cozy arrangement between Noriega and the CIA. Deciding it was politically expedient to drive Noriega from power, the US government began economic sanctions in 1987, followed by Noriega's indictment on drug charges in the US in February 1988.

On 20 December 1989, US president George H.W. Bush launched the ironically named 'Operation Just Cause,' and 27,000 US troops invaded Panama. They quickly overcame the minimal organized resistance offered by the PDF. Bombers, helicopter gunships, and even untested stealth aircraft were used against an enemy with no air defenses, and hundreds of explosions were recorded in the first 12 hours. The poor Panama City barrio of El Chorrillo was heavily bombed and burned to the ground, leaving some 15,000 people homeless; a Human Rights Watch report noted that civilian deaths were more than four times higher than military casualties among the PDF. Noriega himself evaded capture and took refuge in the papal Nunciature. He was eventually forced to surrender on January 5 after the US bombarded him using 'music torture' – a round-the-clock diet of ear-splitting heavy metal and rock music was blasted from a local radio station in the parking lot.

Noriega was extradited to the US, convicted of drug trafficking, and sentenced to 40 years in a Miami jail. Estimates of the number of Panamanians killed during the invasion vary from several hundred to as many as 10,000. That the invasion was illegal, however, was clear: it was condemned as a violation of international law by the United Nations and the Organization of American States, both of which demanded the immediate withdrawal of US forces. Despite most Panamanians being relieved to see the back of Noriega, they were outraged at the excessive use of force and America's blatant disregard for Panamanian sovereignty. After serving his prison term in the US, Noriega was returned to Panama in 2011, where he was imprisoned until his death in 2017.

THE NEW CENTURY

In an interesting twist, the presidential elections of 1999 were contested between Martín

Moscoso's term in office got off to a rocky start when, before the first budget vote, she gave Cartier watches and jewelry as 'Christmas presents' to the 72 members of the legislative assembly. It set the tenor for the presidency, which was scarred with accusations of corruption and incompetence. Her term ended in similarly controversial fashion as she tried to push through construction of a tarred road linking Boquete and Cerro Punta through the national park of Volcán Barú. Opposition to the outrageous plan successfully united numerous national and international

Omar Torrijos addresses the nation on live TV following his return to Panama.

Torrijos, illegitimate son of the former military ruler, and the widow of Arnulfo Arias (the man Torrijos ousted in 1968). The latter, Mireya Moscoso, became Panama's first female leader and on December 31 presided over the seamless handover of the Canal, which is now efficiently managed by the independent Autoridad del Canal de Panamá. The US withdrawal was a mixed blessing for Panama's economy: many jobs disappeared with the closure of the bases, but the valuable real estate and infrastructure Panama inherited created investment opportunities in what are now referred to as the Áreas Revertidas (see page 144). That said, a number of former US buildings lie abandoned, and relations with the US remain complex.

environmental groups and became a major election issue allowing Martín Torrijos, heading the PRD, to become president.

Though Torrijos junior was elected on a platform of 'zero corruption,' it did not take long before scandals started to emerge. Nor was his administration's record on the environment particularly laudable, approving countless hydroelectric projects in Chiriquí and Bocas del Toro provinces with scant environmental assessment studies and little negotiation with the indigenous populations most affected. He did, however, help to tighten measures against drug trafficking and money laundering. And in his biggest gamble, he green-lighted the Canal expansion project (see page 102).

RECENT TRENDS

The elections in May 2009 broke the political stranglehold that the PRD and PP had enjoyed for the previous 70 years as conservative multi-millionaire supermarket magnate Ricardo Martinelli swept to power. Head of the new Cambio Democrático (Democratic Change) party, he immediately launched several popular initiatives: increasing the minimum wage; establishing pensions; ensuring free books and uniforms for schoolchildren, and laptops for students; and launching a free public Internet service across

Panama City skyscrapers.

many parts of the country. Panama enjoyed sustained economic growth – though the gap between the 'haves' and 'have-nots' continued to increase – and the government spent a staggering $20 billion on roads, schools, and bridges across the country. In the capital countless skyscrapers sprang up, the new Metrobus and Metro systems were established, and the Cinta Costera – an ambitious land reclamation project – was extended, including a highly controversial orbital road round Casco Viejo.

However, as with Martinelli's predecessors, corruption scandals mounted and his increasingly autocratic ruling style, curtailment of the press, and overuse of police force – especially against indigenous communities – provoked

much criticism at home and internationally. In the 2014 elections, Martinelli's estranged vice-president, Juan Carlos Varela, who had fallen out with his former ally after being dismissed as foreign minister, won a surprising victory for the Partido Panameñista.

The vastly overbudget Canal expansion was inaugurated in 2016 and early indications are that the huge investment is paying off. In a likely related move, Panama cut ties with Taiwan and began diplomatic relations with China (a major user of the Canal), signing 19 cooperation agreements. As economic growth slowed down, unemployment rose and the Lava Jato cash-for-contracts scandal broke, Varela's popularity plummeted. In particular, his vehement denial and subsequent admission that he had accepted campaign money from the Odebrecht construction company at the heart of the scandal did little to endear him to the population. Varela's continued detention of his predecessor, Martinelli, on charges of illegal wire-tapping, compounded his ratings, being viewed as nothing more than a personal vendetta.

> In 2018 Panama's soccer team qualified for the World Cup for the first time, a feat marked with a national holiday.

This long-term, endemic lining of pockets by top government and business officials has diverted funds and attention away from addressing the Panamanian people's more pressing concerns: inadequate health, transportation, and education services; continued erosion of indigenous populations' rights; widening social inequalities; worsening environmental degradation; and rising levels of unemployment and crime. In the wake of various corruption revelations, 2017 witnessed widespread anticorruption and anti-government street protests, but several distracting celebrations – Panama making it to the World Cup, the 2019 papal visit, and the 500-year commemorations of Panama City, as well as national elections – have disrupted the rhythm of the groundswell of dissent.

OPERATION 'CAR WASH' AND OTHER SCANDALS

Operation 'Car Wash', a run-of-the-mill money-laundering sting in Brazil, has spiraled into an international corruption scandal engulfing 12 Latin American countries.

At the center of the storm is Brazilian construction behemoth Odebrecht, responsible for many of the continent's mega-projects. In Panama, the company has been involved in contracts from the Cinta Costera, the highway between Panama City and Colón, to the Tocumen airport expansion program and the Metro.

By way of plea-bargaining, Odebrecht's former CEO, Marcel Odebrecht, who was arrested in 2015, confessed to shelling out millions of dollars in bribes, paying off senior politicians, and funding presidential campaigns, in return for overpriced contracts. He even admitted to the company having a special department for kickbacks.

In Panama's case, two former presidents, Martín Torrijos and Ricardo Martinelli, are currently under investigation for accepting campaign funds and/or cash-for-contracts, while the most recent presidential incumbent, Juan Carlos Varela, has admitted accepting a campaign 'donation' but has so far escaped official scrutiny. One hundred million dollars is said to have been paid in bribes. In March 2018 Transparency International pointed the finger at four of the countries involved, including Panama, for being too slow to take action over the matter. A few months later a group of Panamanian journalists launched their own independent investigation into the scandal, entitled Lava Jato – Conexión PTY. The explanation for state lethargy in addressing the charges is aptly summarized in a slogan that has appeared frequently on protest banners across the Americas since the story broke: *'El sistema no puede combatir la corrupción porque la corrupción es el sistema'* (The system can't combat corruption because the system is corrupt).

At the end of 2018, the Public Prosecutor's Office announced that investigations would probably be complete in 2019, and congratulated themselves on their five convictions, 76 ongoing investigations, and their recovery of $255 million in money and goods. This last claim is not as impressive as it sounds, given that most of that sum covers the fine that Odebrecht has agreed to pay back as part of their goodwill gesture and cooperation with the government enquiry. When, despite all that has happened, Odebrecht was awarded the new contract to build the Metro link to the airport in 2018, the Panamanian public questioned whether it was another case of business as usual.

PANAMA PAPERS AND BLUE APPLE

Lava Jato is not the only corruption scandal festering in Panama. The 'Panama Papers' have provided some unsavory revelations, too. Although many felt that the country's reputation was being unfairly tarnished by the sobriquet – only 20 percent of the companies exposed in the leaked documents actually operated out of Panama – it hasn't helped that the two founders of the now defunct firm at the center of the leak, Mossack Fonsecca, have been arrested on charges of money laundering, with possible links to Lava Jato. And then there's the Blue Apple affair, another huge web of deceit, featuring fraud, bribery, and money laundering that has been simmering since 2017. Under the legal microscope so far are seven companies and 33 people, including former ministers and the sons of ex-president Martinelli, who are also facing similar charges related to Lava Jato. As time passes, the threads of corruption become increasingly longer and more difficult to untangle.

January 2018 rally against corruption, Panama City.

Guna women in traditional dress.

PEOPLE

A veritable ethnic melting pot, Panama's population has been shaped by the Spanish conquest, a string of construction enterprises, and centuries of migration for trade and commerce.

It may be a cliché to talk about Panama as a land of contrasts, but in the case of its people, this statement is emphatically true. Indeed, the country's diverse population, which has resulted from several key events in its history, is one of its attractions to visitors. Of the indigenous groups that survived the Spanish conquest, eight are officially recognized today, comprising 12 percent of Panama's estimated 4 million-strong population. Many of these live in semi-autonomous regions known as *comarcas*, struggling to preserve their lands, traditions, and cultural identities, while adapting to modern living on their terms. Some have relocated to the city and been assimilated into urban modernity; others lead a more fluid existence, moving seasonally in and out of the *comarca* in search of employment.

The arrival of the Spanish in the 16th century precipitated a huge shift in demographics, as the first major influx of Africans hit the isthmus, brought over as slaves. The building of the railroad in the mid-19th century attracted further migrants of African heritage, mainly from Jamaica, as well as Malaysians, Chinese, and people from various corners of Europe. More Jamaicans arrived for the French canal construction period, along with the French. There was a greater migration for the US canal – again West Indian workers formed the core – mainly from Barbados this time, alongside many Spanish and North Americans, although some laborers came from as far as Australia and Armenia. At the same time, the banana boom was kicking off in the Caribbean in Bocas del Toro, attracting yet another migrant workforce, with

Emberá boatman on the Río Chagres.

Jamaicans featuring strongly once again. Although many thousands died on these enterprises, and some of those who survived returned home, a fair number stayed on the isthmus after the project had ended – the ancestors of today's Panameños.

Two thirds of these Panameños are *mestizo*, a mix of diverse heritages – generally European, Amerindian, and African – often lost over the generations, but with varying identities and aspirations, marked by levels of education, wealth, and rural or urban location. Well over two-thirds of modern Panamanians are urbanites, with close to half living in ever-expanding, cosmopolitan Panama City. Beyond the capital lies a completely different country, predominantly rural and agricultural, dotted with a few small provincial towns, and characterized by a marked ethnic geography. Though most of the country's GDP is produced in Panama City by the service sector, from businesses primarily related to the canal, agriculture is still important. And as you speed along the Panamerican Highway across the Pacific lowlands, you'll pass plenty of farmland: maize, sugar cane, and cattle farming, for example, while on the coast you'll see fishing boats bringing in their catch and shrimp farming.

fairly fluid, with many of the men in particular migrating to Panama City for casual labor when necessary.

More numerous by far are the Ngäbe, totaling around 260,000. They share a vast *comarca* in mountainous western Panama, spanning Bocas del Toro, Chiriquí, and Veraguas provinces, with around 27,000 Buglé. The groups are culturally similar but speak mutually unintelligible languages. Suffering the country's highest levels of poverty, many Ngäbe and Buglé from the *comarca* migrate for seasonal jobs on banana,

Panamanian youth at a bicycle-rental shop.

INDIGENOUS PEOPLES

According to the last census in 2010, more than 400,000 people claimed to belong to one of Panama's eight indigenous groups. The country's most high-profile people, the Guna, number around 80,000. Their Comarca Guna Yala – a semi-autonomous state – was the first such territory to be established in 1953, after they had risen up in revolt against the Panamanian government in 1925. Stretching along eastern Panama's Caribbean coastal strip to the Colombian border, it incorporates more than 400 tiny islands, where most communities live, as well as a swathe of forested mainland. The smaller inland *comarcas* of Wargandi and Madugandi were added later. The population is

coffee, and sugar plantations to earn cash to sustain them the rest of the year.

In Eastern Panama, the Emberá (31,000) and Wounaan (7,000) share a *comarca* in the forests of the Darién, having probably migrated there from present-day Colombia in the 1700s. Some relocated to the Chagres river basin nearer Panama City in the 1960s, for economic reasons. Around a third live in two *comarcas*; others are scattered among 40 riverine communities across the province.

At the other end of the isthmus, in Bocas del Toro province, the Naso, also known as the Teribe, number under 4,000 and live around the banana town of Changuinola and along the scenic Río Teribe heading up into the mountains and

Parque Nacional Amistad. They are on the cusp of being granted a *comarca*, for which they have been lobbying for years; it was passed by the National Assembly in 2018, and reaffirmed again in 2019, following a presidential veto. A few kilometers north, on the banks of the Río Sixaola, straddling the Costa Rican border, live around 2,000 Bri-Bri. A similar number of the oft-forgotten Bokota, who are frequently mistaken for Buglé since they speak Buglere, inhabit the area around the Bocas–Veraguas provincial boundary in the Comarca Ngäbe-Buglé.

of slavery, remaining where they were set free, such as in the towns of the Azuero. Having been longer on the isthmus, the Afrocolonials are all Spanish-speaking.

In contrast, the West Indian Afro-Antillanos came later, as laborers for the railroad and both the French and US canal construction periods. Most came from English-speaking islands, such as Barbados and Jamaica, and with a Protestant colonial experience. Descendants of these pioneers constitute the population of Colón, and areas of Panama City, with communities in areas

Wounaan boy in a hammock in the Darién.

AFRO-PANAMANIANS

Although some archeological evidence points to African presence on the isthmus before the arrival of the Spanish, most ancestors of Panama's Afro-Panamanian population come from two distinct heritages. Collectively they make up around 15 percent of the population. Communities along the Costa Arriba, Darién and the Pearl islands are mainly descendants of black slaves, brought to Panama from various parts of Africa during the era of the Spanish conquest. Otherwise referred to as Afrocoloniales, their ancestors either escaped from the colonizers to hide in the jungle and form centers of resistance (*palenques*), or they were freed later, following the abolition

such as Río Abajo. At the same time as the canal labor influx, other Caribbeans, mainly Jamaicans, migrated to Bocas del Toro to work on the banana plantations. Their descendants are very much in evidence today, particularly on Isla Bastimentos, where they still speak a Panamanian English Creole, similar to the one in Jamaica. While some of Panama's black population maintain these distinct ethnic identities, others prefer to claim a more general Afro-Panamanian identity.

OTHER SOCIAL GROUPS

The first wave of Chinese settlers also came to build the railroad, with subsequent migrations from both Taiwan and China during the canal construction periods. The substantial Chinese-Panamanian population is increasingly visible in commerce; they operate most of the convenience stores, mid-size supermarkets, and various trading warehouses, from Bocas to Darién. Inevitably, given the history of the canal, there are a lot of North Americans on the isthmus – around 25,000 in various pockets of the country. When the Canal Zone was dissolved in 1999, many Zonians returned to the US, but others – some with dual citizenship – stayed, moving to other parts of the country. In more recent decades they have been joined by US retirees, drawn by incentives offered by the Panamanian government.

The construction of the railroad and Canal both brought opportunities for trade, which encouraged further immigration. Other sizeable populations include Panama's 15,000-strong Hindu population – of Indian heritage but often via Caribbean countries such as Guyana. Many came for the canal construction but have remained, working in

Ngäbe family resting by the Río Caldera in Boquete.

⊘ THE FIRST FEMALE NGÄBE CACIQUE

In September 2011, Silvia Carrera was voted in as the first female *cacique* of the Comarca Ngäbe-Buglé. A woman of extraordinary strength and resilience, Carrera was working the fields at 12 and a mother by 13.

The excitement was short-lived, however, as conflict over the Barro Blanco hydroelectric project on the Río Tabasará dogged her tenure. Approved by the government back in 2007, the dam had been consistently rejected by the *comarca* on account of its negative social, environmental, and cultural impact, which over the years resulted in construction being periodically suspended. Carrera had always vehemently opposed the project, and caused outrage when she green-lighted the dam in 2016. She was promptly ousted from office in a coup – for signing an accord without due consultation with congress – a move she and her supporters dismissed as unconstitutional.

Carrera maintains that she's always opposed the dam, but since it was practically complete by this stage – construction had continued despite ongoing negotiations – she felt a government accord would at least guarantee jobs for the *comarca* and a share in the profits. The government also agreed not to flood the area without further consultation. Her critics accused her of selling out, pointing to the appointment of her son as ambassador to Bolivia. When, despite assurances, the dam's floodgates were opened in 2018, her detractors felt vindicated.

shipping and commerce. They own the majority of stores lining Avenida Central in Panama City, and were involved in setting up Colón's Zona Libre. Panama also boasts large Lebanese and Syrian Jewish communities, whose economic success has attracted Jewish migrants from other countries.

SOCIAL INEQUALITIES

There's no getting away from the fact that Panama is a highly stratified society, with marked social and racial hierarchies, which the rural peasant class. Though some Afro- and indigenous Panamanians – notably the Guna – have achieved social and economic success, on the whole, the black and indigenous populations face much discrimination. Symptomatic of such prejudice was the reaction to the 2018 election of Ngäbe Rose Iveth Montezuma as Miss Panama, the first indigenous woman to represent the country at Miss Universe. Though a source of great pride among the Ngäbe, she faced a barrage of racial abuse on social media from other

Ngäbe children in Chiriquí.

translates economically and geographically. Those who identify as white (around 13 percent in the last census) and can trace their ancestry back to a European, usually Spanish, heritage consider themselves to be of higher social status. These include Panama's oligarchy that remains top of the pile. Known colloquially as the *rabiblancos* (white-tails), they are the elite families that have ruled the country since independence. Occupying the senior positions in government and big business, they look out for each other, intermarry, and can be found sipping cocktails at the exclusive Club Unión. Otherwise, socio-economic status tends to determine the pecking order, and urbanites tend to look down on

sections of society, who cast doubt about her nationality and made racial slurs while denigrating her traditional dress (*nagua*).

Such prejudice translates into both social and economic inequalities. While Panama's national economy enjoys one of the highest growth rates in Latin America, the distribution of wealth remains highly skewed, with the poorest 20 percent living below the poverty line and receiving less than 1.5 percent of the earnings. This includes most of Panama's indigenous citizens – especially those living in the *comarcas* – as well as the people of the provinces of Darién and Bocas del Toro, which also have high indigenous and Afro-Panamanian populations. Employment rates are quite high in Panama, but many people remain in poorly paid jobs, struggling to cope with the rising cost of living. There is also a significant urban-rural divide, where rural populations have less access to basic services such as water, sanitation, electricity, health care, and education – again, especially among the indigenous populations living in the *comarcas*. Deficiencies in these services are associated with lower life expectancy and higher child mortality rates.

Gender inequality is also pronounced in

Felipe Baloy.

certain areas. Although women play an active role in both the political arena and in the formal employment sector, only 42 percent of women are employed (compared to two thirds of men), though of course this doesn't include the growing informal sector – such as selling in the street – something the government has been trying to 'clean up' in recent years in Panama City. Only 30 percent of businesses have female board members and yet women have more years of schooling on average. In the indigenous communities of the Guna, Emberá, and Wounaan, in particular, some women earn a good income from their fine-quality craft work. This has not only made them less economically dependent but has

also helped improve their status within their respective communities.

INDIGENOUS RIGHTS

Panama has been more progressive than some states – at least on paper – in recognizing the rights of its indigenous citizens. A number of communities have been allocated land in the form of *comarcas* and allowed a measure of autonomy. In practice, however, successive governments have followed a development trajectory that puts big business and making big bucks first.

The greatest success in defending their rights against the state has been enjoyed by the Guna, who are the most organized politically. As well as their own congress, the Guna possess several representatives at national government level. The other main indigenous groups have tended to follow the Guna model, electing a General Congress consisting of a *cacique* (chief) and community representatives. There is also a national body, with representatives from all indigenous groups, which aims to tackle attempts to marginalize them or incorporate them into models of development they do not espouse.

Although the *comarcas* cover a fifth of Panama's land, these territories, as well as those of indigenous communities residing outside their boundaries, are under constant threat. Some lands lie within national parks and reserves, which has enabled government, generally through its environmental wing, to apply restrictions on traditional lifestyles in the name of conservation, while simultaneously allowing mining or hydroelectric projects to go ahead often with minimal or no consultation with indigenous authorities and no compensation to those forced to relocate. Government and big business are not the only threats: poor cattle farmers, *colonos*, desperate for fresh grazing land, have been encroaching on indigenous lands for years, particularly in eastern Panama.

Better health, education, transportation, and access are consistent demands being made of government since many in the *comarcas* live without access to clean water, health care, electricity, decent schooling, or paid employment. The statistical comparisons are stark:

life expectancy for an indigenous woman in the *comarca* is 11 years less than the average for the whole population; similarly, the maternal mortality rate is a staggering five times higher than the national average.

LOOKING TO THE FUTURE

As in many post-colonial states, great effort is put into forging a unified Panamanian identity. For many years the narrative centered on Panama–US relations and reclaiming the Canal. Now, a strong 'unity in diversity' theme

government coffers, and revelations from the Odebrecht and other corruption scandals spiraling out of control, ordinary Panamanians are fed up with officials lining their pockets and want to see some benefit from this wealth. As Panama celebrates 500 years since its capital was founded in 1519, and a new government takes office, it would be a good moment for the country's leaders to reflect on what needs to be done to ensure all Panamanians get to enjoy the benefits of the country's biggest asset – after its people: the Canal.

Congos festival in Portobelo.

is played out in the country's countless festivals. The government supports and promotes Panama's diverse ethnic groups in celebrations of their cultural identity, be it the Congos festival in Portobelo (see page 158), the Mil Polleras in Las Tablas (see page 191), where even women from groups who don't wear a *pollera* are invited to participate, or the Día de la Etnía Negra. Yet for all the annual celebrations of traditions and culture, which provide fantastic entertainment for locals and visitors alike, critics point out that such festivities are merely window-dressing and do little to address the underlying issues of persistent social inequality and discrimination. With the expanded canal now bringing in around $2 billion annually to

⊙ CLUB UNIÓN

Panama's most exclusive club was established in 1909, and is now, as it was then, the place for the country's most powerful people – usually men – to meet, socialize and plot their continued social dominance. Formerly in Casco Viejo, the club transferred to a prime piece of real estate with stunning sea views in exclusive Punta Paitilla in the late 1960s. It now boasts top-notch sport and leisure amenities, including a library with over 3,500 books, and a collection of comfortable bars, lounges, and restaurants. Cash is not used, but the club card with a limit of $2,000 manages to cover most needs.

Dancing shoes.

MUSIC AND DANCE

Panamanians are party people, which means plenty of music and dancing, be it at a hip club in Panama City, at a colorful festival in the Azuero, or in a small community in the Darién.

Spend any amount of time traveling by bus in Panama and you soon realize how much Panamanians love their music: from bachata to salsa, rock to reggaeton, pop to *pindín*. Inevitably, given the melting pot of cultures that Panama is, styles are wide-ranging, drawing on instruments and rhythms from elsewhere in the Americas, Africa – often via the Caribbean – and Spain, combined with indigenous traditions.

SALSA AND JAZZ

Salsa is one of the rhythms most readily associated with Latin America, though it actually developed in the late 1960s and 70s in New York, drawing on Afro-Cuban son montuno and Puerto Rican bomba and plena, subsequently soaking up a variety of other musical sounds. Panamanian Rubén Blades, a salsa pioneer, is still one of its greatest stars. Since 1990 he has been backed by fellow Panamanian bassist and singer Roberto Delgado and his *orquesta*. Other big-name salsa bands in Panama include La Kshamba, which features one of the genre's few female singers – Anita Barroso – and Orquesta Yaré. Omar Alfanno is another Latin Grammy-winning *salsero* of note from Panama.

Many visitors intending to spend some time in Panama are keen to take salsa lessons, yet finding a class, or even a venue to listen to a band, is not as easy as you might think, especially outside Panama City, since reggaeton has rather taken over the scene. In the capital though, some of the big hotels and casinos, such as the Majestic Casino, Radisson, and Marriot offer weekly classes, so you can practice your moves before joining the experts when the live band shows up and the serious dancing follows later in the evening. The Paradise Dance Hall, too, has been offering lessons for years. Spanish schools in Panama City, Bocas, and Boquete

Emberá music and dance.

usually have dance classes as part of their extra-curricular program, though these days they also tend to include other popular tropical rhythms such as merengue, bachata – a slower rhythm from the Dominican Republic – and the ubiquitous reggaeton.

Latin jazz is also often infused with salsa and other Latin rhythms. Panama's biggest jazz name is award-winning pianist and composer Danilo Pérez, who organizes and frequently performs at the Panama Jazz Festival (Wpanamajazzfestival. com). This annual musical extravaganza takes place in the Ciudad de Saber, close to the Miraflores Locks, in mid-January. Packed with local and international talent providing concerts and workshops, it always ends with a hugely enjoyable free open-air concert. For jazz in a more refined intimate atmosphere, *Danilo's Jazz Club*, adjoining the *American Trade Hotel* in Panama City, puts on high-quality performances. At the other end of the country, the annual Boquete Jazz & Blues Festival (www.boquetejazzandbluesfestival.com) is a relaxed four-day open-air musical jamboree.

ROCK, POP, AND DISCO

There's a diverse array of pop and rock to be heard across Panama, usually of Latin American or Spanish origin, or by Latino musicians from the US. Over the drier summer months, when the bulk of Panama's festivals are held, concerts pop up all over the Pacific coast – even at more traditional festivals – and at agricultural shows. While no big-time international stars hail from Panama, the country's most enduring rock band, which tours across Latin America and the US, is the ska rock fusion outfit Las Rabanes, from Chitré, which has over a dozen albums to its name. Señor Loop, playing a blend of reggae and Latin dance rhythms that been dubbed 'alternative Latin rock,' is another household name. In terms of solo artists, singer-songwriter Cienfue has developed a uniquely isthmian style fusing local folk music with rock. He also runs a bar in Casco Viejo aimed at nurturing young rock talent. Women, as usual, are underrepresented, though Lolas is a locally successful hard rock trio (formerly a quartet).

In many *discotecas* – the word 'nightclub' in Panama denotes a strip joint – and on radio playlists, *música varieda* is the order of the day, so that you'll get a few songs of one genre before the DJ moves onto the next. While electronica or trance music was all the rage in clubs in the early naughties, reggaeton and bachata tend to rule the roost now.

MÚSICA TÍPICA

What is considered by many to be traditional Panamanian folk music – *música típica*, *pindín* or just *típica* – has its heart in the central provinces of Coclé, Veraguas, Herrera, and Los Santos. Essentially a *mestizo* confection, *típica*, nevertheless, is a potpourri of Andalusian, African, and indigenous influences. Played with abandon on the provincial Coaster buses, or at festivals on the Azuero, these

Danilo Pérez.

ⓘ DANILO PÉREZ

A jazz pianist and composer of international renown, Danilo Pérez is also a keen social activist and philanthropist. Born into a musical family, he was studying classical piano by the age of 10 and went on to win a Fullbright Scholarship and studied jazz composition at the prestigious Berklee College of Music. However, it was his experience playing with Dizzie Gillespie's United Nations Orchestra in 1989 that taught him the power of music as a tool to bring cultures together. This message was reinforced later that same year when he'd no sooner landed back in Panama to perform a concert than the US invaded. Naturally, the event was cancelled, but Pérez and his fellow musicians went ahead anyway with an improvised show – despite the bombs and bullets flying around. Though the audience included people both for and against the military action, he recognized that for those two hours music had acted as a life-affirming, unifying force. This philosophy has endured in Pérez' philanthropic activities, including acting as a goodwill ambassador to UNICEF and a Unesco artist for peace. Pérez has won several Grammy nominations and a host of other awards for albums such as *Central Avenue* (1989), *Motherland* (2000), and *Across the Crystal Sea* (2008). Often characterized as a Pan-American jazz pianist, his music incorporates other sounds from Latin America and beyond, drawing on folk and classical traditions.

chirpy tunes epitomize celebrations in central Panama. Arguably the most popular exponents of this music are the brother-and-sister duo Samy and Sandra Sandoval.

An array of instruments are used to perform the various *típica* songs and dances, starting with the all-important rhythm, beaten out on one or more drums – all of African origin. The *pujador* and *repicador* are both cylindrical wooden drums with animal skin stretched over the top; the former provides the bass, whereas the latter produces high-pitched sounds. In contrast, the *caja* or *tambora* is the military-style circular drum played with drumsticks. String instruments include the European violin, or the local more rustic version – a simple three-stringed *rabel*. Panama's most emblematic chordophone, however, is the five-stringed *mejorana*, a small guitar-like instrument with a shorter neck, after which the country's premier folk festival is named (see page 191). A four-stringed *socavón* or *bocona* is an alternative. Distinctive smaller pre-Columbian percussion instruments, usually made from hollow gourds, include maracas and the *churuca* – also called *guaracha* or *güira*. This last instrument is an elongated hollow gourd with horizontal markings across its center that produces sounds when scraped up and down with a metal comb. The accordion and harmonica probably came to the Americas via merchant boats in the late 19th century, and the former, in particular, is now integral to many folk groups.

Panama's national song and dance is the *tamborito*, accompanied by a full percussion section and a female singer who leads an all-female chorus in a call-and-response routine, very typical of Africa. The courtship dance between couples involves the woman swishing her *pollera* provocatively, one minute seemingly inviting the man, the next rejecting him. The man in turn advances and retires, taking small steps, as they both circle round each other. In *El Punto*, a more sedate dance also performed in couples, the action starts off with the man on bended knee doffing his sombrero to the woman, and often features the violin more strongly. Other popular dances include Panamanian cumbia – also with African origins, and *mejorana*.

AFRO-PANAMANIAN

Afro-Panamanian culture is arguably more 'traditional' than the *típica* of the Azuero, since much of the inspiration, rhythm, and instrumentation for

what the *mestizo* majority consider to be national culture, comes from Africa. Yet Afro-Panamanian musical traditions per se have not been celebrated to the same extent as those more readily associated with the central provinces, although in 2018 the Congos were recognized by Unesco as part of the country's living heritage. Dances to look out for include the *bunde* in the Darién, which was incorporated into Christian traditions and is associated above all with Christmas, when the main singer and chorus of clapping women celebrate the arrival of Jesus as couples come to

Musician playing traditional music.

pay they respects to the baby Jesus (represented by a doll) by dancing in front of a makeshift altar. The *bullerengue*, in contrast, is a joyous celebratory dance associated with fertility and love – a more upbeat, relaxed, and sensuous version of the tamborito – with more *pollera* swishing, provocative hip movement, and advances and brush-offs between couples.

INDIGENOUS MUSIC AND DANCE

Even less is written about indigenous music and dance, which tends to be rooted in the natural world, depicting specific animals and relating to harmony with nature and agricultural cycles. The Ngäbe, for example, crouch down like apes in the monkey dance, or coil round in single file as a snail. The Emberá women 'fly' in a circle with their arms outstretched, dipping them high and low to resemble a swallow in flight. The musical accompaniments generally involve instruments such as wooden or bamboo pipes, maracas made from gourds and seeds, and horns. In the most practised Guna dance, Noga Gobbe, women shake the maracas (nasis) to beat the time as they dance while the men play the pan pipes (ganu). It is said that when Ibeorgun – the Guna cultural leader – came to Earth he brought with him 12 different kind of flutes.

Traditional Congo dance performance.

CLASSICAL MUSIC

Despite boasting a wealth of fine musicians, Panama's classical music scene is a niche interest and has struggled for years with a lack of funding and support. That said, the Orquesta Sinfónica Nacional de Panamá (www.facebook.com/osnpanama) manages regular, if infrequent, concerts in their home venue, the splendid Canal-era Teatro Balboa, but performs in other arenas too. Though the national ballet company has only been in existence since 1972, it usually puts on around 40 performances annually across the country, often in non-traditional venues such as shopping malls and metro stations in order to try and widen its appeal. An even greater newcomer to the country's cultural scene, the Fundación Operá Panamá (www.facebook.com/fundacionoperapanama.com) celebrated 10 years in 2018, and is helping to nurture young operatic talent. Full productions are usually performed in the Teatro Nacional, though recitals are also given. Serious aficionados should keep their eye out for live streaming from the Metropolitan Opera House in New York, screened at the Miraflores Locks. Central America's oldest classical music fest, the Festival Internacional de Música de Alfredo de Sant Malo (www.asmfestival-panama.com) occurs in late May. Named in honor of Panama's fine 20th-century violinist, who played with many of the world's top orchestras, it brings local and international artists together in a range of workshops, concerts and competitions for young musicians. It also gives exposure to the Sinfonía Concertante de Panamá, a youth orchestra aimed at underprivileged children.

⊘ REGGAETON

Love it or loathe it, reggaeton's heavy beat is immensely popular with the Panamanian youth, and you can't fail to miss it blasting out of cantinas, discotecas, and bus music systems. Though debates rage on about whether Panama or Puerto Rico invented the genre, few would dispute that it was Panama's development of reggae en español in the 1970s that paved the way for its development. Originating among the Jamaican and other Afro-Antillean communities on the isthmus, with the pioneering trio of The General, Nando Boom, and Renato, it wasn't until the 1990s in Puerto Rico that the term reggaeton was more generally recognized as the stew of Jamaican dancehall, hip-hop, rap, and Latin rhythms that it is today. The music's focus on gang violence, drugs, and a propensity for explicit sexual lyrics and 'dirty dancing' videos, have caused more than their fair share of upset and controversy. However, reggaeton's popularity has continued to spread across Latin America and among the Latino youth in the US, and even to Europe. Among Panama's current favorite exponents are Eddy Lover, Joey Montana, and Flex. Reggaetoneras are few and far between in a music form that has often been accused of being misogynistic, but Dempha and Anyuri are two popular female artists based in Panama. In 2017 Luis Fonsi's Latin-pop-reggaeton hit 'Despacito' became a global hit. Featuring the 'King of Reggaeton,' Daddy Yankee, the song broke the YouTube record for being the most streamed video ever, suggesting that the genre is here to stay.

RUBÉN BLADES – PANAMA'S MUSICAL MEGASTAR

Rubén Blades has done it all – he's a multi-Grammy-award-winning salsa icon, acclaimed movie and TV actor, social activist, politician, and Harvard-trained lawyer.

Despite turning 70 in 2018, Rubén Blades shows no sign of slowing down. He is still making music, touring, and acting, and was recently appointed as the inaugural scholar-in-residence at the Steinhardt School of Culture, New York University, with a brief to work with staff and students to bring about social change and promote diversity.

Born in Panama City to Cuban-Colombian parentage with a musical pedigree, Rubén Blades arguably had a head start in music; he played from a young age, and continued even while he was completing his law degree in 1972 to please his parents. But the family's stay in Panama didn't last long as his father, a former detective for the secret police, fell foul of Manuel Noriega, then head of military intelligence, and was forced into exile in the US. Blades followed suit, eventually ending up in New York 'with $100, a bag, and a guitar.' Over the next 10 years he shot to stardom, initially with New York Puerto Rican salsa star Willie Colón; their 1978 album *Siembra* ('Sowing' in English) became one of the best-selling salsa albums of all time. It features two of Blades' best-known songs, *Plástico* and *Pedro Navaja*, which characterize his oft-dubbed 'thinking man's salsa,' as he writes engaging narratives about working-class characters and provocative political lyrics, championing Latin Americanism while refuting anti-imperialism. Going on to form his own band, *Seis del Solar* (Six from the Tenement), he scored similar success with *Buscando América* in 1984 before taking a break to bag a Master's degree in law at Harvard. Since then he's gone on to pen and perform over 40 albums, constantly innovating – mixing salsa with jazz, Irish folk, and even tango – and clocking up 17 Grammy wins along the way.

Then there's his life as a successful screen actor. He has worked alongside the likes of Denzel Washington, Harrison Ford, Jack Nicholson, and Bruce Willis, and won three Emmy nominations for his performances in *The Josephine Baker Story* (1991), *Crazy from the Heart* (1992), and *The Maldonado Miracle* (2003).

His forays into politics, however, have been less successful. He returned to Panama in 1993 and formed his own political party, Movimiento Papa Egoró (loosely translating as 'Mother Earth Movement'), running for president the following year. He came a distant third, garnering 17 percent of the vote, from those who were tired of the mainstream political elite. Others, however, felt he was

Rubén Blades in concert.

out of touch with Panama, having spent so many years in the US, escaping the realities of living under a dictatorship. Though the party gained six seats first time round, Blades' frequent absence from the country was generally believed to account for the party's poor showing in the polls four years later, when it didn't win sufficient votes to continue. Not one to give up easily, Blades then served time as Minister for Tourism in the government of Martin Torrijos (2004–9), during which political cartoonists constantly used his own lyrics to satirize his absences. If you want to know more about what makes Panama's international superstar tick, seek out the recently released biopic – award-winning, naturally – *Yo No Me Llamo Rubén Blades* (My Name is Not Rubén Blades).

TRADITIONAL CRAFTS

From appliqué textiles to coiled basketry, wood-carving to mask-making, palm fibers to papier-mâché, the range of materials and products in Panama reflects its multi-ethnic make-up.

Although some exquisite items can be picked up in the boutique shops of Casco Viejo, it's more rewarding for everyone if you buy them from the remote villages or home-based workshops where they are crafted, learning more about the intricate production processes and cultural significance of your purchase at the same time.

MOLAS

You can't walk far in Casco Viejo without tripping over *molas* – literally, as they're spread out on pavement and draped over park benches. Panama's most abundant and distinctive textile is made by and for Guna women and *omeggid* – 'third gender' males. Traditionally worn as decorative panels on the front and back of their blouses, they are now an important part of the Guna economy. These reverse appliqué textiles comprise various layers of brightly colored cloth, with shapes cut out and overturned edges painstakingly stitched. The quality of the *mola* (and therefore the price) is determined by such factors as the number of layers, the evenness, width, and skill of the cut-outs, the fineness of the stitching and other embroidery and embellishments, as well as the overall design. Though the older geometric designs that evolved from body painting are still popular, you are just as likely to come across a helicopter or Spiderman. What's more, the art has nowadays been applied to a whole range of goods, from cushion covers and slippers to oven gloves and cell phone cases.

Striking devil mask.

MASKS

Devil masks are central to the extravagant celebrations of Corpus Christi and the pre-Lenten Congo festivals along the Caribbean coast. They are made predominantly from papier-mâché coated on a greased clay or earthen mold; their horns, wooden teeth, and eyes – usually ping-pong balls or marbles – are added later. The most famous mask makers hail from around Chitré and La Villa de los Santos, in the northern Azuero, their workshops stuffed full of salivating dragon or gargoyle-like monsters in kaleidoscopic colors.

An entirely different tradition of mask-making is passed down through generations of women in the Wounaan and Emberá communities, employing the same palm fibers used for basketry, but with more colorful dyes (which have generally spent longer in the pot). Rainforest animals important in folklore, such as tapirs, jaguars, macaws, toucans, and monkeys inspire fanciful elaborate masks and head-pieces, with some of the largest and finest taking months to make. They were originally used in Emberá shamanic cleansing rituals; although shamanism is dying among communities, due

Most striking is the broad necklace, or *ngu-ñunkua* (*chaquira* in Spanish); once worn by Guaymí warriors, the modern-day equivalent is donned by both female and male Ngäbe as a marker of cultural identity. You can find them dangling from roadside stands on the Interamericana, close to Tolé, as well as in craft shops of Bocas del Toro and Panama City. *Wini* – the colorful bands sewn round Guna women's forearms and calves – are also made from colored beads these days. Smaller versions to wear as a bracelet or

Bracelets and chokers for sale.

in part to the spread of Evangelism, mask-making continues to thrive and evolve as a vital source of income. These days, as a result of tourist demand, you may also find the occasional lion, zebra, or flamingo making an appearance among the rainforest fauna.

JEWELRY

The jewelry and adornments worn by indigenous women and men were once fashioned out of natural products such as dyed shells, seeds, pebbles, and bone. Nowadays, most are made from synthetic beads bought in bulk in Panama City, but are attractive, colorful, and skillfully made, for all that.

anklet make popular souvenirs, and the vendor will happily stitch it round your wrist or ankle with cotton. The *wini* usually lasts several months before it falls apart, but the cotton is easily cut if you fancy a change earlier.

Beads have also made their way into *tembleques*, the elaborate hairpieces worn as accessories to the flowing *pollera de gala* in parades over much of central Panama. On closer inspection, you see that most resemble flowers, modern replacements for actual flowers such as hibiscus, which used to be worn in the past, when they were more readily available. Butterflies, dragonflies, peacocks, and other creatures are also sometimes incorporated into the

How you wear your sombrero also has meaning. Having both the front and back turned up – known as 'a la pedrá' – suggests the wearer feels successful, or ready for a fight. Just the back part turned up implies they are knowledgeable, whereas turning up the front suggests they're on the lookout for a woman.

BASKETRY AND BAGS

The Wounaan women, and, to a slightly lesser extent, the Emberá of eastern Panama are renowned worldwide for their exquisite coiled basketry. The finest examples are so tightly woven that they can even hold water. Originally plain *canastas* for everyday use designed to carry and store goods, they have evolved into highly sophisticated works of art, sold to tourists and collectors, with the really large *hösig di* (meaning 'fine baskets' in Wouneu) fetching several thousand US

design. Crucially they are fashioned using soft, pliable wire so that the *tembleque* –

Street stall with hand-made souvenirs.

which means 'shaking' in Spanish – does just that in time to the dancing rhythm of the wearer. As designs have diversified, so have materials – a prestigious festival queen these days might wear an ornate *tembleque* consisting of Swarovski crystals or pearls, as well as being decked out in fine gold earrings, chains, pendants, and hair combs elaborated by skilled goldsmiths and handed down through the generations, totaling several thousand dollars. The average parade participant, however, is more likely to have hair accoutrements made of ribbons, imitation gold, or pearl, of the sort that are more often sold to tourists at craft stands.

⊘ NATURAL DYES

The process of dying natural fibers for indigenous baskets, masks, and bags is complex, time-consuming and handed down the generations. The bark, leaves, roots, seeds, and fruit of specific plants are ground, mixed and boiled in water with the fibers, and sometimes subjected to other processes. Generally, the longer the dyes are 'cooked,' the darker the colors. In the Darién rainforests, black can be produced by boiling cocobolo shavings and burying them in mud. Yellow and gold come from the root of *yuquilla* (turmeric) or *achiote*; pucham produces a pinkish-red but combines well to make various colors. More commonly seen as body art, *jagua* can also be used to dye fibers blue-black.

dollars. Traditional designs and motifs are sold alongside more modern depictions of flora and fauna.

It's a lengthy process, as first the relevant palm leaves have to be collected from the rainforest. Collecting the 'chunga' palm (*astrocaryum standleyanum*) is no easy task given the vicious spikes on its trunk. It is then split into strands of varying thickness, and left to dry and bleach in the sun before being dyed and dried again. Only then can the actual weaving begin. Nahuala or weaving begins, fibers have to be dyed, separated, and hand-spun into yarn, a technique involving the spinner stretching the fibers over the big toe of her outstretched leg to produce tension, and rolling them in her hands. Coming in all shapes and sizes, used by both men and women, the bags serve a variety of purposes: a small one hanging across the shoulder may be a purse, yet a large one slung across the back can be used to carry a large bunch of plantains or even a baby. Designs still generally adhere to geo-

Making a Panama hat.

'Panama hat' palm (*carludovica palmata*) is commonly used for the coils, with the dyed chunga palm filaments used to sew the coils together and produce the pattern. The two main weaving techniques are rib stitch, which accentuates the individual coils, and silk stitch, which, as it sounds, produces a smooth, silky sheen.

In contrast, the Ngäbe *kri* (*chácara* in Spanish) is a relatively simple, but very versatile, string bag, which can also involve intricate weaving. It's made from fibers of pita, cabuya, or cortezo plants; each has different properties and extraction methods, with the softest, most lustrous finish provided by the pita (*aechmea magdalenae*). Before the metric designs, evoking folklore, historical events, and natural surroundings. Given the time needed to make a traditional *kri*, it's no wonder that many Ngäbe women these days use recycled plastic or nylon thread to make their own bags.

HAT-MAKING

Though Panama's hat-making industry shows due deference to the 'true' Panamas that originate in Ecuador, it produces a fine array of its own *sombreros*, made from sisal, *junco*, or *bellota*, the oft-dubbed 'Panama hat palm' (*carludovica palmata*). These are fabricated for working in the fields as much as for special occasions.

Recently recognized by Unesco as an important part of Panama's cultural heritage is the best-known *sombrero pintado* (or *pintao*) – the 'painted hat' from Coclé, whose name derives from the decorative black rings in the weave. Quality is primarily determined by the number of rings (*vueltas*), but also takes into consideration the consistency and fineness of the weave. While the basic seven-ring weave can be finished in a week, the most sophisticated examples, known as *finos* on account of the finer, denser weaving, take

Pintada, in Penonomé, is a good place to go if you're interested in acquiring one.

WOODCARVING

Wounaan and Embera men are as renowned at woodcarving as their womenfolk are at basketry. Initially embellishing household utensils and shamanic spirit sticks, which are also often found in tourist shops, these craftsmen now also fashion free-standing animals from cocobolo, an attractive reddish-brown tropical hardwood, which produces its

Plate decorated with traditional Panamanian wood carvings.

several weeks or months to make as they can only be made in the morning or in the evening, to avoid quality being compromised by the sweat that builds up on the weaver's hands. As a result, they cost hundreds of dollars. Other popular styles include the *sombrero mosquito*, which includes rings of small black v-shapes, resembling the wings of said insect, and the simple off-white *sombrero Ocueño*, made and worn by men and women of Ocu, in the Azuero Peninsula.

Ngäbe and Buglé artisans produce some of the finest quality straw hats, though most *sombreros* found in craft markets and shops come from the *mestizo* cottage industries in the provinces of Herrera and Coclé. La

own polished sheen when rubbed with sandpaper. They also craft intricate animals from tagua nuts, or 'vegetable ivory', harvested from a variety of palms in the *phytelaphas* genus. Poison-dart frogs are a favorite subject matter. Since the nuts are never much larger than a couple of inches in diameter, the animals too are necessarily tiny, though sometimes the artist fuses several nuts together. They are painted using natural dyes, or bought paints from Panama City.

Less refined woodcarving skills are needed to produce the equally colorful painted, glazed Ngäbe trays (*bateas* in Spanish), which are ornamental versions of the plain ones used to toss rice and grain.

In Panama, the last refuge of the scarlet macaw is on Isla Coiba.

WILDLIFE

Bridging two continents, Panama hosts deer and coyotes common to temperate North America as well as jaguars and capybaras from the tropical South, plus a cornucopia of astounding marine life.

Panama's emergence as a bridge between the continental masses of North and South America some three million years ago and its location within the tropics have resulted in a staggering biodiversity for such as tiny country. Although just smaller than South Carolina and slightly larger than Ireland, the isthmus has recorded around 1,000 bird species – more than the US and Canada combined, and greater than any other central American state – as well as accommodating just under 300 mammals, around 250 reptiles, and over 200 amphibians.

BIRDS

It is Panama's birdlife that tends to grab the international headlines: the 17km (10.5-mile) Camino del Oleoducto (Pipeline Road) in the former Canal Zone alone boasts a species list of more than 400. Even the sprawling metropolis of Panama City harbors an amazing variety, from egrets to elaenias, parakeets to pelicans; avian-rich locations within the greater city boundaries include the Metropolitan and other parks, Panamá Viejo, the Amador Causeway and round Cerro Ancón and Balboa.

Acting as a continental funnel, Panama sees many migrants, with numbers peaking in September and October and returning in more dispersed fashion from March through May. During this period, more than one million shore birds carpet the Pacific coastal mud flats, though it is the raptor migration that captures the imagination. Hundreds of thousands of vultures and hawks ride the thermals, wheeling their way along the isthmus (late Oct–Nov), a spectacular sight best

Volcano hummingbird.

appreciated from the summit of Cerro Ancón or one of Gamboa's several canopy lookouts.

Panama has more than its fair share of dazzling birds. The cloudforests of Chiriquí afford an unparalleled opportunity to spot the iridescent emerald-and-crimson resplendent quetzal – especially visible and striking during spring courtship displays – while the Darién jungle maintains a similar reputation for the harpy eagle, Panama's gigantic national bird with its distinctive tousled crest and ferocious giant talons (see page 274). Other glamour birds include the country's multicolored, raucous parrots (*loros*), including five species of endangered macaw (*guacamaya*), with the scarlet macaw making its last stand on the island of Coiba. Panama's seven varieties of toucan (*tucán*), including toucanets and aracaris, are a more common psychedelic feature of the landscape; their oversized rainbow-colored bills help pluck hard-to-reach berries and regulate their body temperature. Abundant in the Canal area and round Cerro Ancón, they are most easily spotted croaking in the canopy in early morning or late afternoon. Other avian pin-ups include shimmering hummingbirds (*colibrí*; see page 149), lustrous tanagers, smart trogans, and

Baird's tapir.

the distinctive racquet-tailed motmots.

Birds more notable for their behavior include lily-trotting jacanas, whose vast, spindly feet enable them to stride across floating vegetation; minute fluffy manakins conduct manic acrobatic courtship displays in their communal mating arenas known as *leks*; and the prehistoric-looking nocturnal potoo camouflages itself on the end of a tree stump during the day, invisible to would-be predators. Spend enough time in the Western Highlands, especially in the breeding season (Mar–Aug), and you're likely to hear the distinctive 'boing' of the strange-looking three-wattled bellbird, complete with what look like strands of liquorice hanging from its beak; audible from

almost a kilometer (half a mile) away, it is considered one of the loudest bird songs on earth. More varied are the constant gurgles, chimes, and melodies of the ubiquitous oropendola (gold pendulum). These large, generally russet-toned birds, with outsize pointed beaks and golden tails, are renowned for their colonies of skillfully woven hanging nests, which dangle from tall trees like Christmas decorations.

MAMMALS

Spotting many of Panama's mammal species – half of which are small bats – requires luck and persistence and is nigh on impossible when it comes to the 'big five' wild cats, which in descending size order are the jaguar, puma (mountain lion), jaguarundi, ocelot, and margay. Nocturnal and shy at the best of times from years of human predation, they are most numerous in the country's two remaining wilderness areas at either end of the isthmus: the Darién and Amistad.

Spotting tracks in the morning mud is the closest you're likely to get to a jaguar in the wild. Referred to as a '*tigre*' (tiger) by indigenous populations and revered as a symbol of power and strength, the jaguar is the world's third largest feline, after the lion and tiger, weighing in at around 60–90kg (130–200lbs), and with leopard-like markings. You're more likely to encounter its dinner, however, be it deer (*venado*), the raccoon-like coati (*gato solo*) or large rodents such as the agouti (*ñeque*) or the nocturnal paca (*conejo pintado* – literally 'painted rabbit' on account of its white spots). Panama also harbors the world's largest rodent, the capybara, which can tip the scales at 65kg (143lbs); resembling a giant guinea pig, it wallows in the shallows round Gamboa

Uniquely, around 2,000 humpback whales from both Alaska and Antarctica converge in Panamanian waters to mate and calve (July–mid-Oct). They can be seen in the Pearl Islands, off the Azuero Peninsula and Coiba, and among the islands of the Golfo de Chiriquí.

and grazes at Punta Patiño, in the Darién. A more ambitious feature of the jaguar's diet is the peccary, a kind of wild boar: the more frequently seen collared peccary (*saíno*) lives in small herds, whereas the elusive, aggressive white-lipped peccary (*puerco de monte*) can travel in battalions of several hundred, and is dangerous when threatened.

One of the largest, most extraordinary-looking mammals in the Neotropics is Baird's tapir (*macho de monte*), which resembles an overgrown pig with a stubby prehensile nose and

herbivore, with a paddle-like rudder and flabby fleshy snout, found in the Caribbean Humedales de San San Pond Sak. Over in the Pacific, humpback whales mate and calve in the calm, warm waters though the young can easily become prey to predatory orcas (killer whales).

REPTILES AND AMPHIBIANS

More than 400 species of reptiles and amphibians inhabit Panamanian forests, with the country's tiny colorful frogs generating the

Poison-dart frog.

upper lip used to grip branches and eat the leaves and fruit. More commonly espied are sloths (*perezosos*) and anteaters (*hormigueros*). Panama's two-toed and three-toed sloths spend much of their time literally hanging around treetops, either curled round a branch camouflaged as an ants' nest, or gripping with their long curved claws, doing everything in slow motion to conserve energy. Inexplicably, they make a near-suicidal descent to ground level once a week to defecate.

Marine mammals that capture the attention of tourists include bottle-nosed dolphins, often glimpsed swimming round the archipelago of Las Perlas and in Bocas del Toro; and the manatee, or sea cow, an amiable elephantine

most interest (see page 84). As regards reptiles, snakes are the most numerous, though relatively few are venomous and snakebites are rare since they tend to be wary of humans. The most feared, accounting for almost all fatal snakebites in Panama, is the lowland fer-de-lance pit viper. Commonly dubbed *'equis'* ('X') for the markings on its well-camouflaged brown, cream, and black skin, it often exceeds 2 meters (6ft) in length. The female gives birth to 50–80 live young, which are venomous from birth. Initially arboreal, feeding on frogs and lizards, they become terrestrial with age. The world's largest pit viper, the dangerous bushmaster, can reach 3 meters (10ft), but fortunately is only encountered in remote forests and, like most pit vipers, is nocturnal. Panama's various species of coral snake, both venomous and benign, all possess striking black, red, and yellow-banded markings. Since it's difficult to differentiate among them, it's best to assume danger. Positively mellow in comparison – though packing a powerful bite if provoked – the giant boa constrictor is Panama's only endangered snake, hunted for its prized skin.

Similarly under threat are the five species of marine turtles found around the coast (see page 195). So too is the green iguana, which actually ranges from lime-green to dusty brown in color and is pursued for its eggs and tasty meat, earning it the nickname 'gallina de palo' (tree chicken). Despite its dragon-like appearance, it is a docile forest-living herbivore that likes to be near water; the large dewflaps under its chin are used to regulate body temperature and for courtship and territorial displays. The tetchier, charcoal-grey spiny-tailed or black iguana is most commonly found on the Azuero Peninsula. The world's fastest

Geoffroy's tamarin.

⊘ MONKEYS

Charismatic, playful, acrobatic, mischievous, or just plain loud, monkeys of some sort are an almost guaranteed sighting in Panama, which hosts all seven Central American species. A distinctive feature of the tropical landscape, the large, shaggy mantled howler monkey (*aullador negro*) is more likely to be heard before being seen. The ape's stentorian cries travel for kilometers, with large troops announcing dawn and dusk and even the onset of heavy rain. The other two more widespread species are the cherub-like Geoffroy's tamarin (*mono tití*), found in central and eastern Panama, and the larger, highly intelligent

white-throated capuchin (*mono cariblanco*). Named for their physical resemblance to brown-robed Capuchin friars, the monkey's pink anthropomorphic face has led to it becoming a popular pet. Catching sight of a troop of black-headed spider monkeys (*mono araña negro*) – which are critically endangered – elegantly gliding through the canopy is a magical experience. Owl or night monkeys (*mono de noche*), with their saucer-like eyes, are restricted to the Caribbean lowlands of Bocas, while over on the Pacific side, the delicate squirrel monkey (*mono ardilla*) is occasionally sighted in the Burica Peninsula in southwestern Chiriquí.

lizard, it escapes predators by hitting speeds of up to 35km/h (22mph). The miniature version, a 30cm (12in) basilisk, takes flight across water on its hind legs and partially webbed feet, earning it the nickname 'Jesus Christ' lizard.

Lurking in Panama's mangrove-filled estuaries and mud-lined waterways, including around Lago Gatún and Lago Bayano, are the endangered, aggressive American crocodile and the smaller more docile spectacled caiman.

INSECTS

Insects don't generally set the pulse racing, but butterflies are the exception. With 16,000 species, Panama hosts approximately 10 percent of the world's Lepidoptera, from the enormous owl butterfly, so-called after the large 'eyes' on its mottled brown wings, to the tiny delicate glasswing, whose translucent wings resemble a stained-glass window. Most magnificent of all, is the iridescent blue morpho.

Ants can be found in abundance; tiny Isla Barro Colorado alone has over 200 species. Most distinctive are the packed highways of industrious leafcutter ants bearing enormous segments of leaf to their vast underground complex, where they are pulped to cultivate a 'fungus garden,' which in turn feeds the ants. Also easy to spot, and one to avoid, is the enormous black bullet ant. The size of a large grape and prevalent in low-lying forests, it holds the dubious distinction of causing the world's most painful insect sting.

FISH

With coastlines on two oceans, Panama's marine biodiversity is also impressive, especially where warm ocean currents and upswellings of cool nutrient-rich waters converge along the Pacific's Golfo de Chiriquí. In the first half of the year (Feb–July), you may be lucky enough to catch sight of the gargantuan but placid whale shark, the world's largest fish, as it moves submarine-like through the waters round Coiba. Hammerhead and tiger sharks are occasionally spotted though white-tipped reef sharks are more common. From October through December schools of diamond-shaped golden rays glide like

floating autumn leaves, occasionally leaping 2 meters (6ft) into the air, as do more solitary manta rays. Boasting a colossal 6-meter (20ft) wingspan, one weighs as much as a small car.

In general, the Pacific coast boasts a greater number of large pelagic fish – blue and black marlin, amberjack, wahoo, dorado, and tuna, to name a few. Off both coasts, however, lie extensive coral reefs, which in turn nourish and shelter countless fish. On the Pacific side, the main reefs lie round the Pearl Islands and in the marine parks of Coiba and the Golfo de

Monarch butterfly.

Chiriquí. On the Caribbean side, they are most prominent around the archipelagos of Bocas del Toro and western Guna Yala. Crucial to the health of these reefs are the distinctive colorful parrot fish, whose serrated parrot-like 'beaks' gnaw harmful algae and coral polyps off the reef.

Colorful parrot fish eat and digest dead coral, which is excreted as sand – up to an estimated 90kg (200lbs) per fish annually, contributing to the formation of Panama's glorious white-sand beaches.

 **FROGS**

Thumb-sized, and with markings as varied as wallpaper, brilliantly colored poison-dart frogs are the miniature poster boys of the tropical forest floor.

Panama's frogs make up some of the country's most compelling creatures, especially the dazzling poison-dart frogs (*dendrobatidae*), whose coloration ranges from gold, through copper to cobalt blue, scarlet or bottle green, and black, sporting a range of designs, including the 'blue jeans' look. Their threatening name derives from the lethal toxin secreted by some, which was traditionally used by the Chocó (ancestors of the present-day Emberá) to coat darts and arrows for hunting. Since dart frogs are diurnal, they can often be spotted hopping around leaf litter under trees, especially in Bocas del Toro.

Their lustrous pigmentation aims to alert would-be predators to the poison beneath their skin (a strategy known as aposematic coloration), but the devoted parenting in some species is equally striking. After eggs have been laid and fertilized, one parent – usually the male – periodically returns to keep them moist. The tadpoles, once hatched, are then transported by piggy-back, and deposited in safe pools of water, sometimes fed on unfertilized eggs dropped into the water later by the conscientious parent.

Other equally extraordinary amphibians inhabit Panama's forests, though being arboreal and primarily nocturnal, they are less visible: tiny lime-green glass frogs, whose inexplicably transparent belly affords you the dubious pleasure of observing their viscera and digestive processes; red-eyed tree frogs (*agalychnis callidryas*) that hide their characteristic bulging scarlet eyes and bright side stripes during the day, leaving their lime-green body perfectly camouflaged against a leaf; and common milk frogs (*trachycephalus venulosus*) – so named after the toxic mucous they secrete when threatened.

Vanishing robber frog.

The variable harlequin frog (also known as the clown frog) often remains in the same area for a long time. It is critically endangered, and can only be found in western Panama and Costa Rica.

Strawberry poison-dart frogs actually come in a range of different colored 'morphs' and patterns.

Red-eyed treefrog.

The Amphibian ark

The lethal chytrid fungus, which has been decimating the planet's amphibians, hit western Panama in the early 1990s, moving gradually eastward over the following two decades. The waterborne disease, which attacks the skin and suffocates the animal, was thought to have wiped out the wild population of Panama's emblematic and endemic *rana dorada*, or golden frog (*atelopus zeteki*). Herpetologists and conservationists worldwide started up the Amphibian Ark project, airlifting healthy specimens to safety to breed in captivity. Panama's own rescue mission (www.amphibianrescue.org), headed by the Smithsonian and working with several US zoos, also established two amphibian centers. The one in El Nispero zoo in El Valle (see page 170), home of the *rana dorada*, is open to the public. Here, you can see the much-revered frog alongside other captive species. A third display opened in 2017 in Punta Culebra in Panama City. The good news is that recent research suggests that some species thought to be extinct are making a comeback, possibly developing resistance to the fungus. What's more, golden frogs have bred successfully in captivity, so they, and other relatives, may eventually be able to return to the wild.

cente's poison frog is endemic to Veraguas and Coclé ovinces in central Panama.

eminis' dart frog has a limited range in the Río Belén asin in Colón province.

Panama's golden frog is actually a species of toad. The species is sadly critically endangered.

Rainforest walk.

OUTDOOR ACTIVITIES

With two oceans, a coastline dotted with tropical islands, and plenty of rainforest and mountains in between, Panama has plenty to offer the outdoors adventurer.

Panama is home to a whole host of outdoor activities, from swinging through the rainforest canopy on a zip line to tracking tapir prints in the mud of the Darién, kayaking round deserted islands or lolling on a deserted beach. Some of these pursuits can be experienced as efficient pre-booked packages from Panama City; others will need to be arranged more informally on the spot and a few require no organization whatsoever. Already renowned as a world-class bird-watching and sport fishing destination, Panama also affords outstanding diving, surfing, snorkeling, white-water rafting, and wilderness hiking.

Several excellent tour operators, providing knowledgeable bilingual or multilingual guides, work out of Panama City and offer activities around the country. Outside the capital, the three main outdoor-activity centers are Boquete, in the Chiriquí Highlands, Santa Catalina, on the Pacific coast, and Bocas Town, on Isla Colón in the Bocas del Toro archipelago. For these locations, it makes more sense to organize your fun with a local operator there.

El Valle view.

HIKING

Although there are no hiking maps, and relatively few developed trails in Panama, the country's mountainous and forested landscapes offer a myriad of hiking opportunities, provided you go with an experienced guide. What's more, the fact that organized hiking is in its infancy means that in many places you can often have the forest all to yourself. The most scenic hiking terrain lies in western Panama, in the cloudforested peaks of the Chiriquí Highlands, laced with spectacular waterfalls. The area round the charming mountain village of Santa Fé, in Veraguas, is also delightful. Note that although the whole country lies in the tropics, you'll need warm clothes for chilly nights up in the mountains.

National parks which have a couple of established trails each are Soberanía, Coiba, Altos de Campana, and Volcán Barú, where the Sendero de los Quetzales, which meanders through fabulous cloudforest between Boquete and Volcán, is probably the country's best loved hike.

The vast wilderness areas such as La Amistad and the Darién are ideal for adventurous multiday treks across the isthmus, often involving bivouacking, staying in indigenous villages, fording rivers, and wading through meters of mud, though it is essential to go with someone who knows the terrain. Aside from the Panama City operators, mountain guides can be engaged locally in places

There are virtually no organized campsites in Panama, though a few lodgings allow tents if asked, or provide tents to rent in summer. Camping is permitted in national parks – in limited places – though facilities may be lacking.

such as Santa Fé, Boquete, and Cerro Punta, at far less cost, though they may only speak Spanish. In and around all the *comarcas*, including in

the Darién, independent travelers can easily contract the services of an indigenous local guide to explore the forests. Otherwise, a few specialist operators offer strenuous jungle treks in the Darién, or the opportunity to cross the isthmus in the footsteps of the conquistadors by traipsing through rainforest along the Camino Real.

RAFTING AND KAYAKING

The fast-flowing rivers that tumble down from the highlands of western and central Panama, carving their way through dramatic scenery, have put

Rafting on the Río Chiriquí Viejo.

⊘ PANAMA'S NATIONAL PARKS

Almost a quarter of Panama's land lies within the boundaries of its 14 national parks – add in reserves, refuges, and other protected areas, and the figure is more than a third. Under siege on all sides from urban development, pollution, and deforestation, they nevertheless constitute one of Panama's major attractions, where you can trek through pristine rainforest, explore Spanish colonial forts, haul yourself up volcanic peaks, or swim with sharks and manta rays. Some of these protected areas, such as the legendary Darién, Central America's largest wilderness, and Cerro Hoya, at the tip of the Azuero Peninsula, are particularly inaccessible and involve a lot of planning, perseverance, and often money to reach; others, such as Soberanía, and

Altos de Campana, lie a stone's throw from Panama City, making an easy day-trip and providing a great opportunity to see some of Panama's dazzling birdlife.

Since the country is so slender, many of the parks offer a hugely varied topography; several straddle the continental divide and range from lofty moss-covered cloudforest pierced by rugged peaks to humid lowland rainforest; others protect dense swathes of mangrove, harboring caimans, crocodiles, and crustaceans while protecting vital mud flats for thousands of migratory birds. Panama's three main marine parks offer coral reefs, turquoise waters, and islands encircled with sugar-sand beaches and coated in tropical forest.

According to some, Panama means 'abundance of fish' in the indigenous Cueva language, and nowhere is that more apparent than when diving in the stunning Pacific waters off Isla Coiba.

Panama on the map for whitewater rafting and kayaking. The top destination is the Río Chiriquí Viejo, which runs parallel with the Costa Rican border. Though the descent is shorter and less wild since its damming for a hydroelectric project, it's still an impressive run, with Category II to III rapids. The rivers are at their wildest during the heavy rains (roughly May to mid-Dec), but you'll manage to find enough water flowing somewhere to raft and kayak year-round. Boquete operators are best placed to organize Chiriquí highland destinations, while companies in the capital head for rivers in the Chagres basin or in neighboring Coclé province. Kayaking on Lago Gatún is particularly special, as you get to witness the Panama Canal in action, up close, as giant container vessels glide past. A day's kayaking down the Río Chagres to the ruined colonial fort of San Lorenzo is another special experience.

Sea-kayaking is also growing in popularity, offering a great way to explore rocky coastlines and mangroves, and to access remote beaches on Panama's many islands. Multi-day guided kayaking and camping adventures in high-quality kayaks are available round the island of Coiba from Santa Catalina (www.fliudadventures.com), and in Guna Yala (www.xtrop.net). Fun day-trips around Santa Catalina and the Golfo de Chiriquí usually include some beach time and snorkeling. Various island accommodations in the latter, as well as in the Pearl Islands and parts of the Bocas del Toro archipelago, provide basic sit-on-top kayaks for guest use to explore the local surroundings.

DIVING AND SNORKELING

Diving in Panama can be truly spectacular, particularly in the Golfo de Chiriquí and the Archipiélago de las Perlas. Pick the right time of year and you're likely to spot manta rays, moray eels, sharks, schools of dolphins, and migrating humpback and sperm whales – some scuba operators offer whale-watching tours. Large pelagic fish such as marlin, sailfish, amberjack, dorado, and

tuna also abound, which reel in sport fishing enthusiasts too. The jewel in this marine crown is Isla Coiba; located on the edge of the second-largest reef on the Pacific side of the Americas, it offers world-class diving.

Among the coral reefs of Bocas and Portobelo on the Caribbean side, diving can also be enjoyable, if not as spectacular as at some other Caribbean destinations. Visibility can vary enormously, especially after heavy rain. However, the rainbow-colored soft corals of Cayo Crawl off Isla Bastimentos make for breathtaking snorkeling, with the

Zip lining in El Valle.

⊘ HIKING GEAR

Since hiking is not a mainstream recreational activity in Panama, it follows that good quality hiking (and camping) equipment is not readily available in the country. That said, basic gear can often be bought at any of the Novey or Do It Best stores in the main cities, though a better selection (albeit still fairly limited and expensive) is found at the branches of Outdoor Adventure in Albrook Mall (tel: 303 6120) and several other malls in the capital, as well as in Chitré and Santiago. Do It Center in Albrook Mall sometimes stocks water filters and water-purification tablets, but you are better off bringing them with you.

Golfo de Chiriquí, and Coiba in particular, a close second and the Islas de las Perlas not far behind.

Reputable local dive shops operate out of Bocas, Portobelo, Santa Catalina, Isla Contadora, and Pedasí on the Azuero Peninsula, while Scuba Panama (www.scubapanama.com), the country's oldest outfit, organizes expeditions from Panama City. It offers divers unique bragging rights with a dive-trip to both the Pacific and Atlantic (Caribbean) oceans the same day.

SURFING

With two long coastlines, Panama offers hundreds of waves of all kinds to suit novices and expert surfers. Away from the renowned hot spots you can have the beach almost to yourself, though the surfing infrastructure (hostels, bars, restaurants, and regular public transportation) may also be lacking. The three main surfing centers – Bocas, Santa Catalina, and Playa Venao – all offer board rental and surf lessons.

Local surfers confined to Panama City tend to dash to the nearby Pacific beaches of Coclé for a weekend escape, such as El Palmar and Playa Malibu. For top-drawer surfing on the Pacific coast (generally best Apr–Nov), head for the internationally renowned breaks round Santa Catalina. In April waves here can reach 4 meters/yds or more, with the high season continuing until August (though a good ride on 2-meter/yd breakers is guaranteed year-round). Playa Venao on the south coast of the Azuero Peninsula arguably offers the country's best-known beach break, a party scene, and also attracts international competitions; the more remote Cambutal, which has beach and point breaks, and can catch big waves, lies farther west. On the eastern side of the peninsula, the small town of Pedasí is within reach of several surfing spots; remote Playa Morillo, down the western coast is for hard-core adventurers, prepared to brave the no-frills accommodations and the sand flies.

On the Caribbean coast (best Dec–Mar), Bocas del Toro is the standout surf center, offering varied breaks for beginners and experts – including the monster reef bottom wave of Silverbacks off Isla Bastimentos – plus welcoming bars and a decent après-surf scene. Less well-known spots to ride the waves lie east of Portobelo, such as Isla Grande or Nombre de Dios and Palenque. The Panamanian surfing association's website

(www.surfeapanama.com) and Facebook page are good places to start for information (in Spanish); check also Magic Seaweed (www.magicseaweed.com) for the swell history and forecasts for the best-known spots.

SAILING

With so many islands, atolls, and cays to explore, Panama is made for sailing. For most tourists, though, sailing equals lazing around on a catamaran and being sailed from one delightful island to another, dropping anchor to swim or snorkel, or

Surf's up at Playa Venao.

⊘ SAFETY IN THE SEA

El Sistema Nacional de Protección Civil (SINAPROC) is in its infancy when it comes to providing protection on Panama's beaches. Lifeguards are a recent institution, and are only deployed to the country's most popular beaches for peak summer vacation periods (Dec–Apr). Similarly, the flag warning system – red (keep out of the water), yellow (enter with caution) – is not consistently applied, nor necessarily enforced or heeded. Rip tides are a common feature along both coastlines, though warning boards are few and far between; rogue waves, jellyfish, and rays are also an occasional hazard. It therefore pays to seek advice before plunging into the sea, however inviting it looks.

In the delightful mountain village of Santa Fé, in Veraguas, tubing down the Río Santa María is pure joy: at times bubbling over rapids, at others gliding past kingfishers and herons.

make the occasional foray onto dry land. The most idyllic place for this is in the Comarca de Guna Yala (www.sanblassailing.com), where you can charter a boat and crew for a week or more. Alternatively, popular catamaran day-trips head out from Bocas Town around the archipelago, and from Contadora, in the Pearl Islands. Here, you can also take the tiller yourself and have sailing lessons (www.sailing-clubpanama.com). Windsurfing and stand-up paddle-boarding (SUP) are also on the menu.

HORSEBACK RIDING

Tourist-oriented horseback riding in Panama is more about getting out in the countryside and admiring the scenery for a few hours, rather than galloping over the fields. Most places also cater to people who have never been on a horse, though you won't always get a safety helmet or a saddle that fails to remind you for the next week what you've been doing. Scenic places to saddle up include El Valle, Santa Fé de Veraguas, and across the rolling hills of Caldera, south of Boquete. Over in Bocas de Toro, a couple of stables offer excursions that guarantee splendid sea views too, while a ride along the Costa Arriba near Portabelo takes you through fabulous rainforest. On the Azuero Peninsula, from Pedasí or Playa Venao, you're likely to explore dry tropical forest and maybe a beach or two.

FISHING

The Bahía de Piñas on the Pacific coast of the Darién, location of the exclusive Tropic Star Lodge (www.tropicstarlodge.com), is widely considered to be the world's top saltwater sport fishing destination. Foreign-owned fishing lodges are mushrooming along other parts of the Pacific coast, most of which offer multiday package deals that cover accommodations, meals, and fishing excursions costing up to several thousand dollars. Recommended outfitters include Panama Big Game Fishing (www.panama-sportfishing.com), Coiba Adventure Sportfishing, (www.

coibaadventure.com), and Pesca Panama (www.pescapanama.com).

A wholly different experience is to try your hand at a spot of artisanal fishing from a dugout canoe, using a simple piece of nylon and a hook tied to a stick. This can often be arranged when staying in an indigenous community in the Chagres basin, Darién, Guna Yala, or Bocas del Toro.

OTHER ACTIVITIES

Although there are several zip lines in Panama, the Boquete Tree Trek (www.boquetetreetrek.com)

Horse riding on the beach.

is undoubtedly the canopy adventure to top them all, boasting a dozen cables that whizz you across spectacular mountain scenery. More modest versions exist in El Valle, along the Río Piedra near Portobelo, and at Cañas, at the bottom of the Azuero Peninsula. Mountain-bikers in search of company might consider contacting Boa Panama (www.facebook.com/groups/boapanama) for English- and Spanish-speaking contacts and a What's App group; this association of recreational off-road cycling enthusiasts organizes weekend outings. On the other hand, if kitesurfing is your sport – or you'd like to learn how to do it, head for Punta Chame, a 12km (7.5-mile) sandy spit on the Pacific coast west of Panama City. Several places offer instruction during the season (Dec–May).

A traditional tamal.

FOOD AND DRINK

From Spanish colonial times through to the railroad, Canal, and banana boom eras, Panama's diverse immigrant population brought with them a wealth of culinary traditions.

The isthmus' history as a major global trading crossroads has led to a wonderfully varied cuisine infused with countless influences, notably indigenous, Spanish, French, Indian, Chinese, American, and Afro-Antillean. Cosmopolitan Panama City inevitably offers the greatest diversity in terms of gastronomy and price, from an inexpensive plate of noodles and chicken in the public market to ornate fusion cuisine served on damask tablecloths. In the capital, traditional Panamanian dishes (*comida típica*) rarely feature on the menus of the mid- to high-end restaurants, the exception being unashamedly tourist-oriented venues, such as El Trapiche (www.eltrapicherestaurante.com), Las Tinajas (tel: 263 7890) or Diablicos (www.diablicopanama.com). At the other end of the price range, on the other hand, in markets, hole-in-the-wall *fondas* (basic, informal restaurants), or *cafeterías* (self-service establishments), it's much easier to find local specialties, as it is in restaurants away from Panama City and the tourist hotspots of Boquete and Bocas.

Street food.

Mid-range and high-end restaurants charge a seven percent sales tax (ITBMS), which is not usually included in the advertised menu prices. Some places even add a 10 percent service charge to the bill, although it is no longer legal.

COMIDA TÍPICA

Traditional home cooking varies depending on where you are in Panama, but it's often heavy on starch, and frequently fried. Panama's filling *desayuno típico* (traditional breakfast) is aimed at sustaining workers for a hard day in the fields. Deep-fried favorites include *tortillas* (thick cornmeal cakes), *carimañolas* (mashed boiled yuca – cassava or manioc – stuffed with ground beef), and *hojaldres* (discs of sweetened leavened dough), which at best are delightfully crispy and tasty but at worst are chewy and dripping in grease. They may accompany beef steak, *salchichas guisadas* (chopped frankfurters stewed in a spicy tomato sauce), chicken, or eggs. Costa Rica's national dish, *gallo pinto* (literally 'speckled rooster'), is also popular, though it's also a lunchtime favorite. A moist rice, beans, and onion mix, it is often accompanied with a dollop of *natilla* – a local sour cream that is also lavished on strawberries in the Chiriquí Highlands – and fried or scrambled eggs.

For something lighter, head for a *panadería* (bakery) for a pastry and a shot of coffee, or pick up fresh fruit at the local market. In the more expensive hotels in Panama City and in foreign-owned establishments outside the capital, you can also expect combinations of cereals, fruit, yogurt, and toast.

While in urban and tourist areas it's possible to grab a light lunch – a flaky *empanada* (pasty)

Outside the main tourist centers, vegetarians may struggle since, as elsewhere in Central America, even the veggie staple of beans or lentils and rice can be cooked in pork fat. The safest bets are Chinese restaurants and pizzerias; alternatively, head for the nearest fruit and veg market.

ejecutivo – a fancier and pricier set menu, but still good value – to their business clientele.

Baked empanadas.

with a beef-, pork-, chicken-, or cheese-based filling or an *emparedado* (sandwich) – for most Panamanians lunch is the main meal of the day. Evening meals, in contrast, are more low-key, and in local restaurants in remote rural areas, dinner may merely be the leftovers from lunch.

In the *fondas* and cheaper restaurants ordering an *almuerzo* or *menú del día* (lunch of the day) will get you a filling plate of chicken with rice, plus beans or lentils – or maybe fish and plantain down on the coast – for a few dollars. Some places throw in a soup starter and dessert to give you a three-course set meal at very little extra cost. More upscale restaurants in the city will sometimes offer a *menú*

Panama's national dish, *sancocho de gallina*, is a firm midday favorite. It's a tasty slow-cooked soup, containing chicken with root vegetables such as yam or cassava, flavored with onion, garlic, oregano, chili peppers, and lots of cilantro. Modern variations often include sweetcorn too. Corn also features in another of Panama's much loved foods: *tamales*, which entail corn dough stuffed with beef, chicken, or pork, and other goodies, wrapped in a bijao leaf and then boiled. Common throughout Latin America, in Panama they're often served at Christmas, at weddings, and on other special occasions.

In the province of Los Santos, in the Azuero Peninsula, pork sausages (*chorizo*) – seen dangling from roadside stands – make a change from beef and chicken, while in the Chiriquí Highlands, locally farmed trout is a common alternative source of protein.

Panama's indigenous populations also have their own classic foods. For example, the Guna are renowned for their succulent lobster, and *moe* – a cream of pumpkin soup thickened with otoe, yam, and cassava, mixed with smoked fish, chili peppers and green bananas; more modern versions add coconut milk and lime juice. Smoked fish is also

meal. Examples include *cabanga*, a sticky confection consisting of green papaya, grated coconut, and honey, and *suspiros*, light cinnamon-flavored cookies that are a specialty of the province of Coclé.

CARIBBEAN CUISINE

With so much ocean and coastline, the Panamanian palate is inevitably treated to plenty of fish – red snapper, grouper, sea bass, tuna – and an array of other seafood, such as lobster, langoustines, prawns, conch, octopus, mus-

Caribbean-style jumbo shrimps in Bocas del Toro.

favored by the rainforest-dwelling Emberá and Wounaan, who traditionally eat it with *bodochi*, a ball of unsalted rice wrapped in a *bijao* leaf and boiled.

> *Over 250,000 cases – each case containing nine 750ml bottles – of Panama's own firewater, Seco Herrerano, are consumed annually.*

Traditional desserts are thin on the ground and quite simple, as are the few (very) sweet treats and cakes that are more often than not eaten as a snack rather than after a main

sels, clams, and calamari. Popular accompaniments the country over are *patacones* (flattened fried slices of green plantain), while a tangy *ceviche* (fish, shrimp, or other seafood marinated in lime, with onion, cilantro, garlic, and a touch of chili pepper) is a common tasty starter. However, it's along the coast and islands of the Caribbean that some of the most delicious seafood is served, by the Afro-Panamanian community. With roots in Caribbean island cuisine, their culinary traditions in turn draw on a mix of African, Indian, Amerindian, and European influences. Dishes include *rondón*, a spicy soup of fish marinated in lime and cilantro, cooked in creamy coconut milk, with assorted root vegetables and the kick of Scotch Bonnet pepper. *Pescado escaveche* also stars on many menus: flour-coated strips of fish marinated in lime, fried and further cooked in a sauce of vinegar, curry spices, onion, garlic, and hot pepper. Along the coast in Colón province, conch (*cambombia*) is especially favored. The above dishes are usually served with *patacones* or *arroz con coco* (coconut rice), often cooked with pigeon peas (*guandú*).

Whether on the coast or inland, the absence of green vegetables and salads – beyond the ubiquitous garnish of a lettuce leaf with a slice of tomato – is striking, though tourist-oriented restaurants usually fare better, especially in the Western Highlands, where most of the country's greens are grown.

STREET FOOD AND SNACKS

The mainstay of the country's many festivals, and sold occasionally on buses, Panama's street food can range from chunks of fresh pineapple or watermelon to *empanadas* (pasties usually stuffed with ground beef or

Arroz con pollo (chicken rice).

☉ LA NUEVA COCINA PANAMEÑA

Panama is finally developing a fine-dining identity of its own: *la nueva cocina Panameña*, which gives traditional dishes a sophisticated twist, and emphasizes local ingredients and isthmian culinary traditions. For decades, Charlie Collins has been at the forefront of such innovation. His mantra *'de la huerta a la mesa'* ('straight from the garden to the table') emphasises freshness. Other pioneering chefs include Cuquita Árias de Calvo and Mario Castrellón. The latter's restaurant, Maito in Panama City, is the first Panamanian establishment to make it into San Pellegrino's Top 30 restaurants of Latin America – a feat achieved three years in a row (2016–2018).

chicken) and plantain crisps (*platanitos*) deep-fried on the spot. Small roadside grills often serve *carne en palito* (meat on a little stick) – fairly tiny kebabs comprising slivers of (occasionally spicy) marinated beef, which take the edge off your appetite.

During the day, you'll also see men pushing carts laden with fluorescent liquids and blocks of ice around the main squares, peddling *raspados* – paper cones filled with shavings of ice, drizzled over with a sickly flavored liquid, made still sweeter by a slurp of condensed milk and much loved by kids. Other sweet treats include *churros*, long finger-like ridged waffles, sprinkled with icing sugar, and oozing a gooey filling such as *manjar blanco*, a reduced and thickened confection of sweetened milk, sugar, and vanilla, occasionally pepped up with cinnamon.

QUENCHING YOUR THIRST

Water quality is excellent in many areas of Panama, so much so that iced tap water is generally served on arrival in restaurants. Exceptions include Bocas, the Darién, and Guna Yala, where water may be purified or you will have to purchase the bottled variety.

In addition, you've a wide choice of alcoholic or non-alcoholic beverages. Delicious fruit-based drinks feature prominently; in most parts of the country you can enjoy them with ice, safe in the knowledge that the water is drinkable. Mango, pineapple, soursop, passion fruit, tamarind, and a host of other fruits can be savored in a range of forms: as a *jugo natural* (pure fruit juice), a *licuado* (a fresh fruit, water, and sugar shake – unless you specify 'sin azúcar'), a *batido* (a milk shake, also usually with additional sugar) or a *chicha* (a sweet maize-based fruit concoction, not to be confused with its alcoholic cousin *chicha fuerte*). The similar-sounding *chicheme*, a tasty Panamanian specialty of ground maize, milk, vanilla, and cinnamon, should also be sampled, and is a particular typical of La Chorrera. Along the Caribbean coast, *agua de pipa* or *agua de coco* – fresh coconut water sipped through a straw straight from the shell – is another must.

Outside the country, Panama's reputation as the world leader in producing gourmet coffee is a secret known only to connoisseurs; you can sample the most prized beans in Boquete and Panama City, though elsewhere you're more likely to be sipping the more mundane but perfectly satisfying Café Durán, which will be strong and is sometimes offered with condensed milk. While black tea is widely available in cities and tourist areas – though it may be served with hot milk, unless specified otherwise – tea lovers are better off contenting themselves with herbal varieties: chamomile (*manzanilla*) or cinnamon (*canela*) are the most common.

Beer is the most popular alcoholic drink. Panama's four main labels (Soberana, Panamá, Balboa, and Atlas) are all fairly inoffensive lagers, with Balboa, slightly more full-bodied; they now all sell low-alcohol versions too. Though none will set the pulses of beer aficionados racing, when ice-cold they do hit the spot. Imported beers such as Heineken and Budweiser, and even Guinness, are available in Panama City and tourist towns, but are more expensive. Over the last couple of years, craft beers are growing in popularity in Panama City and the major tourist and expat residential areas.

The national tipple, the transparent, throat-singeing *seco* (a rough sugar-cane spirit),

Ngäbe picker harvesting coffee in Boquete.

is significantly more potent (35 percent) and more commonly consumed by men in the interior, and at fiestas – as is rum. *Chicha fuerte* (also *chicha brava*) a potent fermented maize firewater, is made in bulk for special celebrations, particularly among indigenous and *campesino* communities. Another lethal home-brew favored by *campesinos* is *vino de palma*, made from fermented palm sap, whereas *guarapo* is sugar-cane juice distilled to knockout strength. Although Panama doesn't possess any vineyards, wine – usually Chilean, Argentinian, or Californian – is widely available in restaurants in Panama City and in tourist areas such as Bocas, Boquete, and Santa Catalina.

The Panama Canal under construction.

THE CANAL

Despite the superlatives and the hype, and the rights and wrongs of its construction, it's hard not to be impressed by the Panama Canal.

Whether peering down at the port of Balboa from the Puente de los Américas, watching giant ships squeeze through the locks at Miraflores, or glimpsing Lago Gatún through the tropical undergrowth from the train, the Canal is truly mesmerizing. Part of its allure is the juxtaposition of a commercial behemoth and triumph of engineering with the immense beauty of the surrounding rainforest. Add to that the backstory of its construction – a gripping tale of power politics, human folly, exploitation, endeavor, and sacrifice – and you have some clue as to its enduring, magical appeal.

Gatún Locks.

British historian, politician, and former ambassador to the US, James Bryce famously described the Canal as 'the greatest liberty Man has taken with nature.'

CONSTRUCTION OF THE CANAL

In a nutshell, there were two phases to the Canal's construction (see page 47). First, came the French period (1880–1889) led by Ferdinand de Lesseps, a major force behind the building of the Suez Canal. A combination of technical ignorance, arrogance, and a tropical environment rife with ill-understood diseases resulted in immense loss of life, financial ruin, and failure. The US took up the mantle in 1903. Directed by engineer John Stevens, and then George Goethals, the Americans determined to build a locks-based canal, which would raise the ships up to a vast artificial lake – created by damming the

Río Chagres – and down the other side. With advances in medicine, sanitation, and technology, the 'Big Ditch' claimed fewer lives the second time round; even so, thousands of members of the predominantly West Indian workforce died. In 1914, just as World War I broke out, the world's greatest – and most scenic – shortcut finally opened.

THE MECHANICS

The Canal runs roughly 80km (50 miles) northwest from Panama City, on the Pacific coast, to Colón, on the Caribbean, or Atlantic coast – in canal-speak. It's a tribute to the quality of its design and construction that much of the original structure and components are as they were when it opened more than 100 years ago. From the Pacific side, ships first pass through the two-chamber Miraflores Locks, which raise them approximately 16.5 meters (54ft) – depending on the tide – to the level of tiny Lago Miraflores, an artificial body of water that leads into the single-lock chambers of Pedro Miguel. Here the boat is raised a further 9 meters (30ft) before heading into 13km (8 miles) of the sinuous Culebra (Gaillard) Cut, the Canal's narrowest channel, which in turn opens out into Lago Gatún. This in the reservoir. This is because the Culebra Cut was originally too narrow to accommodate two vessels passing. Although the channel has now been widened, some of the traffic is still too broad to pass safely, so, by and large, traditional transit patterns still prevail. The new sets of locks at Cocolí, just west of Miraflores, and Agua Clara, east of Gatún, each have three chambers along a single lane.

The original lock chambers measure 304.8 meters (1,000ft) by 33.53 meters (110ft), affording huge Panamax vessels – so-called

Miraflores Locks.

vast picturesque reservoir, fed by the Río Chagres, actually constitutes around 40 percent of the Canal's length, as the route weaves 33km (20 miles) round forested islands before arriving at the largest of the old locks at Gatún, where three lock chambers lower boats down to the Atlantic.

Each set of these original locks operates two 'lanes', which were designed to allow ships to pass through in both directions simultaneously. But in practice ships tend to head in the same direction, northward from the Pacific, through Miraflores and Pedro Miguel in the morning, at the same time as southbound vessels enter Gatún Locks from the Atlantic, with transit schedules ensuring that ships cross as they are the largest size that can fit through the locks – a mere 0.6 meters (2ft) of leeway either side. They are kept aligned by cables attached to pairs of electric locomotives known as mules (*mulas*). The new locks, which are more than half as big again, demand an even trickier, and more dangerous, operation,

The Panama Canal is the only place in the world where a ship's captain relinquishes control of their vessel – to a canal authority pilot, who takes charge for the duration of the transit.

One of the more curious canal happenings is the annual Ocean to Ocean cayuco race (www.cayucorace.org) that usually takes place over three days in April, with teams of enthusiasts paddling traditional wooden dugout canoes – or fiberglass replicas – from the Atlantic to the Pacific side.

since the mules have been abandoned in favor of tugboats, which are attached to the bow and

stern of these colossal Neopanamax ships, and squeezed into the same lock chamber as the towering metal monsters they're guiding.

FERRIES AND BRIDGES

Ferries and service bridges across the locks (when shut) were the order of the day in the early years of the Canal. It wasn't until 1962 that the magnificent Bridge of the Americas, which spans the Pacific entrance, was inaugurated, effectively joining the two halves of the country. Then in 2004, spanning the Culebra

Bridge of the Americas, spanning the mouth of the Panama Canal.

⊙ THE ORIGINAL CANAL IN NUMBERS

Years taken to build
9 years (French era) & 10 years (US era)

Workers involved
56,000 (US era) of 97 nationalities

Lives lost
Est. 22,000 (French era); 5,600 (US era)

Money spent
$375 million (US era)

Dirt dug
205 million cubic meters

Dynamite used
30,000 tons

Concrete used

2.5 million cubic meters (60 Empire State buildings)

Water used per transit
52 million gallons (78 Olympic swimming pools)

Kilometers saved
15,000km round Cape Horn

Cheapest transit
Swimmer Richard Halliburton (36 cents)

Most expensive cruise transit
NCL Pearl $450,000

Average container vessel transit
$150,000; over $450,000 for Neopanamax

Contribution to Panama's GDP
$2 billion annually

Cut, the Puente Centenario was built to help alleviate the increasing road traffic. Long overdue, a bridge across the Atlantic entrance to the Canal (Puente del Atlántico) is finally being constructed, and is scheduled to open in 2019, making the one remaining car ferry obsolete.

SEEING THE CANAL IN ACTION

There are several ways to appreciate what the Canal is about, all of them within easy striking distance of the capital, though none are cheap. Most people take a trip to the Atlantic side's Miraflores Locks – a short bus ride out of Panama City from the Albrook bus terminal – which has a well-situated visitor center containing a museum and an observation platform, offering a fine view of ships as they pass through: northbound up until 9.30am, then southbound after 3pm. The exhibition on the Canal is spread over three floors but only one deals with the remarkable history of the Canal, which is covered in much greater depth in the Museo del Canal in Casco Viejo.

The new Agua Clara Locks, near Colón.

⊙ THE $5-BILLION CANAL EXPANSION

Two years overdue and several billion dollars over budget, the Panama Canal expansion was finally inaugurated on June 26, 2016, amid much fanfare, fireworks, and flag waving. The bold investment aimed to accommodate Post-Panamax vessels (ships that are too large for the original Canal locks) through an entirely new lane of traffic and two larger sets of locks, thereby tripling the size of the ships the Canal can accommodate, and doubling its capacity. It took roughly 40,000 workers nearly 10 years to complete, while enough earth was dredged to fill the Great Pyramid at Giza 25 times over.

Initially budgeted at $5.3 billion with a completion date of 2014, the project was not without its setbacks, including strikes and cost overruns – the construction consortium is demanding billions in compensation from the Panamanian government, which is likely to keep the courts busy for years to come. Another concern is the huge amount of fresh water necessary to operate the increase in traffic. Although the new Cocolí and Agua Clara locks include water-recycling devices, overall the canal now needs twice the amount of water as it did previously, which, given current climatic variability, may prove difficult in the future. For this reason, plans for further expansion have been shelved until at least 2025 and an alternative water source has been found. The uncertainty in world shipping has been another worry. Initial signs are, however, that the gamble has paid off as 2017 and 2018 each saw record tonnage shipped through the world's most famous shortcut.

A further 10 minutes up the road from Miraflores toward Gamboa, you can peer at the Pedro Miguel Locks through some fencing by the roadside. The waterway's other official observation site, however, lies an hour's drive across the isthmus, on the Atlantic side, at the new Agua Clara Visitor Center, just south of Colón. Sited on a hilltop, the viewing platform overlooks the new Agua Clara Locks. You get a fine view and live commentary about its operations, including the workings of the new sliding lock gates, and the storage basins for

on weekdays, crossing the isthmus to Colón, and returning to Panama City at the end of the working day. Popular with tourists, the train journey offers comfortable period carriages and old-world elegance – with air-conditioning – though the more modern observation car and open viewing deck provide better views, assuming it's not raining. The journey runs parallel to the Canal for much of the crossing, offering tantalizing glimpses of Lago Gatún, transiting ships, and plenty of rainforest, but is over all too quickly. Most visitors buy a one-

Container ship leaving the Miraflores Locks for the Pacific Ocean.

recycling the water. The vantage point also affords a panoramic vista across the shimmering expanse of Lago Gatún beyond, where ships often have to wait in line for their turn to pass through the old Gatún Locks (now closed to the public), which lie to the west.

A different perspective again is offered by train along the renovated old Panama Railroad. A morning commuter service leaves Corozal train station (just before Miraflores)

way ticket for the morning train, and catch the infinitely cheaper bus back to the capital.

More leisurely explorations of Lago Gatún are offered by fishing, boating, or kayaking trips, which are a great way to appreciate the natural beauty of one of the world's most scenic reservoirs. With a good guide, exploring the backwaters, inlets, and islets, you may see monkeys, sloths, green iguanas, and a host of birds, as well as vast ghostly tankers gliding past.

The most obvious, and arguably the best way to get your head around the technical brilliance, natural beauty, and sheer magnitude of the world's eighth wonder is to travel along it ('transit') by boat.

Every ship that passes through the Canal must pay a toll based on the vessel's cargo space.

Soberania National Park.

San Pedro on Isla Taboga.

El Valle de Antón.

INTRODUCTION

For such a slender country, Panama has a dazzling array of attractions: lush rainforest, an ebullient capital, evocative colonial ruins, fascinating indigenous cultures, and idyllic deserted islands – not to mention the world's grandest canal.

Resplendent quetzal.

The vast majority of visitors fly in to cosmopolitan Panama City, where brash skyscrapers stare across the bay at the rocky peninsula of colonial Casco Viejo, the city's historic center. Here, the elegantly restored mansions, ancient churches, and leafy plazas demand a day's leisurely exploration. Though the capital offers little else in the way of sights, it makes a comfortable base from which to make forays across the isthmus – kayaking down the Río Chagres, birdwatching in Soberanía, or exploring the Spanish colonial forts of San Lorenzo and Portobelo. For those who need a quick fix of beach, a day-trip to the dreamy Pearl Islands fits the bill perfectly. What's more, all these varied pursuits are possible without forgoing the epicurean pleasures of the capital's sophisticated bars and restaurants in the evening.

And then there's the monumental canal – after you've prepped on your history in the downtown museum, you're ready to take on the eighth wonder of the world, either marveling at its technical brilliance from land, at Miraflores or Agua Clara, or experiencing it up close, from the deck of a boat as you transit through the locks yourself.

Many travelers on a short visit then fly over to David and head straight for the Highlands and scenic Boquete, home of specialty coffee, resplendent quetzals, and emerald cloudforest, streaked with waterfalls, hiking trails, and zip lines. Alternatively, a flight to Bocas is just as easy, where you can sample the Caribbean vibe and the soft-sand beaches of Bastimentos.

Boquete town.

A flight back to Panama City could easily round off a 'highlights' tour, but so much more would be missed: riotous costumed festivals in the Azuero; world-class scuba diving and snorkeling in the mangrove-rich marine parks of Coiba and Chiriquí; or the unique culture of Guna Yala, home to Panama's most politically independent and culturally distinct indigenous people.

Few visitors venture east of Panama City to the Darién jungle, which has gained almost mythical status. Requiring patience, money, and more than a smattering of Spanish, the rewards are ample: sinuous river journeys by dugout, great canopies of cathedral-like rainforests sheltering some of Panama's most spectacular fauna, and remote Emberá and Wounaan communities, keen to share their skills and culture with visitors.

Panama

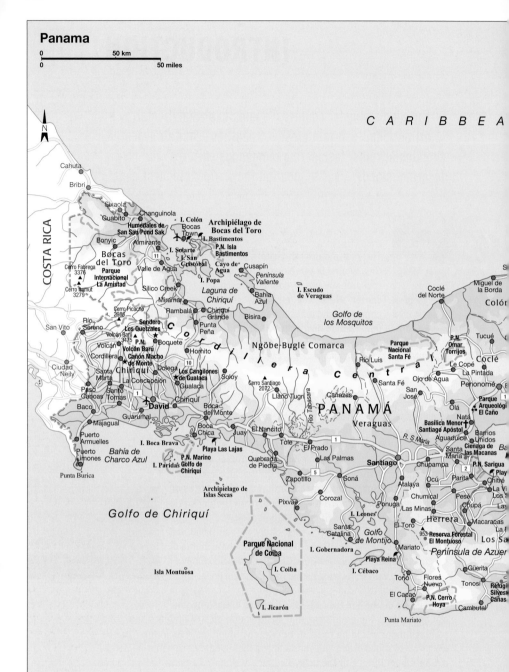

0   50 km

0   50 miles

C A R I B B E A

Cahuta

Bribri

Sixaola

Guabito   Changuinola

Humedales de   I. Colón   **Archipiélago de**
San San Pond Sak   Bocas   **Bocas del Toro**

Bonyic   Almirante   Town   I. Bastimentos

P.N. Isla

Bocas   I. Solarte   Bastimentos

del Toro   I. San

Cerro Fabrega   Valle de Agua   Cristóbal   Cayo de   Cusapín

3376   **Parque**   Agua

Internacional   I. Popa   Península

La Amistad   Valiente

Cerro Itamut   Sílico Creek   Bahía   I. Escudo

3279   Miramar   **Laguna de**   Azul   de Veraguas

Cerro Picacho   Rambalá   **Chiriquí**

2986   Chiriquí   **Golfo de**

Río   **Sendero**   Grande   Bisira   **los Mosquitos**

San Vito   Sereno   **Los Quetzales**   Punta

Volcán Barú   Peña

3475   **P.N.**

Volcán   **Volcán Barú**   Boquete   **Ngöbe-Buglé Comarca**   **Parque**

Cordillera   **Cañón Macho**   Hornito   **Nacional**

Ciudad   **de Monte**   Río Luis   **Santa Fé**

Neily   Santa   Dolega   **Los Cangilones**

Marta   La Concepción   **de Gualaca**   Soloy   Ojo de Agua

Paso   Santo   Gualaca   Cerro Santiago   Santa Fé   San

Canoas   Tomás   2072   Llano Tugrí   José

Baco   **David**   Chiriquí   Boca   Cañazas   **P A N A M Á**   Olá

Guarumal   del Monte   **Veraguas**   Nata

Majagual   Boca   Juay   El Nancito   Aguadulce

Puerto   Chica   **I. Boca Brava**   Tole   El Prado   Santa

Armuelles   **Playa Las Lajas**   María

Puerto   **Bahía de**   **P.N. Marino**   Quebrada   Las Palmas   **Santiago**   Chupampa

Limones   **Charco Azul**   **I. Paridas Golfo de**   de Piedra   Ocú

Punta Burica   **Chiriquí**   Zapotillo   Soná   Atalaya

Archipiélago de   Pixvae   Corozal   Chumical   Pesé

Islas Secas   Ponuga   Las Minas   Chupá

Golfo de Chiriquí   **I. Leones**   **Herrera**

Santa   El Toro   Reserva Forestal   Macaracas

Catalina   **Golfo**   **El Montuoso**

Parque Nacional   **de Montijo**   Mariato   **Península de Azuero**

de Coiba   **I. Gobernadora**

Playa Reina

Isla Montuosa   **I. Coiba**   **I. Cébaco**   Toño   Güerita

Flores   Tonosí

El Cacao   Nuevo

I. Jicarón   **P.N. Cerro**   Cambutal

Hoya

Punta Mariato

Cerro Fabrega

Bocas
del Toro

11

Chiriquí

10

David

1

5

2

P A C I F I

A

Punta de
I. Grande Manzanillo
Nombre de El Porvenir Cayos **Archipiélago de San Blas**
Portobelo La Guaira Dios (Gaigirgordub) Limones **Cayos Holandeses**
aría Chiquita **P.N. Portobelo** Cuango Golfo de San Blas (Maoki)
Tubualá Gardi **Cayos Coco-Bandero**
Sugdub (Ordupuquip)
Parque Nacional Cartí Tupile
Chagres **Guna Yala**
n Sabanitas L. Alajuela Las (Kuna Yala) Playón Grande
Cristoba Sainas El Valle **Serranía de San Blas** (Uggubba)
P.N. 9 Playón Achutupu
Soberanía Espavé Chepo L. Bayano Chico (Assudub)
Barro Gámboa **San** San Ignacio Mamitupu
olorado **Miguelito** Pacora Rio Chepo de Tupile (Mammidub)
arterita Cuevas **Comarca de** Usdub Punta Mosquito
Arraiján **Tocumen** de Majé **Madugandí** Navagandí I. Pino
Panamá Chinina **Panamá** Morti (Dubbag)
rrera **(Panama City)** 1439 Torti Comarca de I. Ucuptuma
á I. Flamenco **Serranía de Majé** Wargandí Mulatupo
e I. Taboguilla Bahía de Punta Escocés
mpaña Punta I. Taboga Panamá
N. Altos Chame Santa Fé Armila
Campana I. Otoque Puerto Píto
Bejuco I. Bona I. Saboga I. Chapera Lara Metetí Capurganá
Playas Gorgona I. la Mina Rio **Comarca**
and Coronado I. Víveros Congo **Emberá-**
ara I. P. Gonzáles La Palma **Wounaan**
nta Clara **Archipiélago** I. del Rey Punta Alegre Chepigana
de las Perlas **Reserva**
I. San Telmo **Punta Patiño** Mogué La Marea Yaviza 1875
I. San José Golfo de Taimatí
Golfo de Panamá Garachiné San Miguel La Chunga Pelivasal Boca
Puerto Indio de Cupé
Playa Muerto (Sambú) **Darién**
Comarca
ana **Emberá-** **Parque Nacional**
gio de Vida **Wounaan** **Darién**
stre Isla Iguana Serranía del Sapo
Mala Riosucio
os
deros Jaqué **COLOMBIA**

Jurado

R. Atrato

Bellavista

C E A N

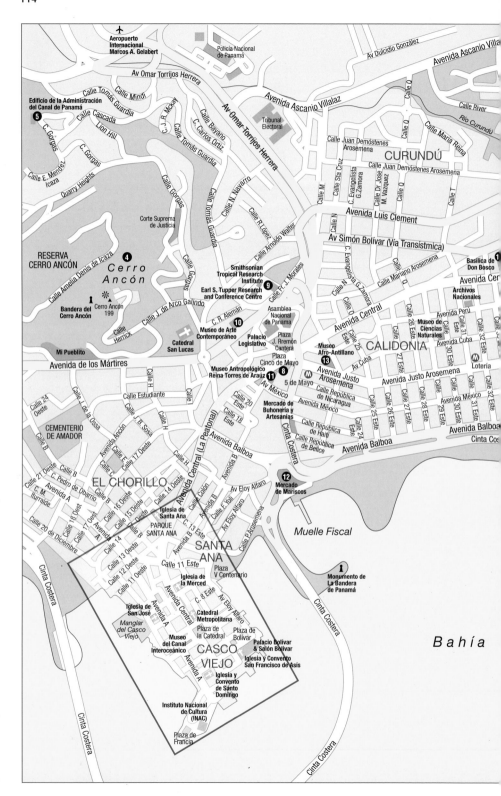

✈ Aeropuerto Internacional Marcos A. Gelabert

Policía Nacional de Panamá

Av Dulcidio González

Avenida Ascanio Villa

Av Omar Torrijos Herrera

Calle Tomás Guardia

Calle Mindi

Edificio de la Administración del Canal de Panamá
5

Calle Cascada

Lion Hill

C. Gorgas

C. Gorgas

C. J. R. McKay

Calle Bayano

C. Carlos Ortíz

Calle Tomás Guardia

Av Omar Torrijos Herrera

Tribunal Electoral

Avenida Ascanio Villalaz

Calle River

Río Curundú

Calle María Reina

Calle Juan Demóstenes Arosemena

CURUNDÚ

Calle Q

Calle Q

Calle Sta Cruz

C. Evangelista G.Zamora

Calle Dr. José M. Vazquez

Calle Q

Calle T

Calle Juan Demóstenes Arosemena

Calle E. Méndez Icaza

C. Gorgas

Quarry Heights

Corte Suprema de Justicia

Calle N. Navarro

Calle R.López

Calle Arnoldo Walter

Calle M

Avenida Luis Clement

Av Simón Bolívar (Vía Transístmica)

Basílica de Don Bosco **1**

RESERVA CERRO ANCÓN

Calle Amelia Denis de Icaza

4

Cerro Ancón

Calle Gorgas

Smithsonian Tropical Research Institute

Earl S. Tupper Research and Conference Centre **9**

Calle Fr. J. Morales

C. Evangelista G.Zamora

Calle N

Calle Mariano Arosemena

Avenida Cer

Archivos Nacionales

☀ Bandera del Cerro Ancón

Cerro Ancón 199 ▲

Calle J. de Arco Galindo

C. R. Alemán

Asamblea Nacional de Panamá

Calle N

Calle Q

Avenida Central

Calle 26 Este

Avenida Perú

Museo de Ciencias Naturales **1**

Avenida Cuba

Calle Herrick

Mi Pueblito

Catedral San Lucas ✝

10 Museo de Arte Contemporáneo

Palacio Legislativo

Plaza J. Rremón Cantera

Museo Afro-Antillano **13**

CALIDONIA

Calle 27 Este

Calle 30 Este

Calle 32 Este

Avenida de los Mártires

Calle H

Museo Antropológico Reina Torres de Aráuz **11**

Plaza Cinco de Mayo

8

Av Cuba

Avenida Justo Arosemena

Calle 25 Este

Loteria Ⓜ

Calle 20 Este

5 de Mayo Ⓜ

Avenida Justo Arosemena

Avenida Justo Arosemena

Calle 26 Este

Calle 27 Este

Calle 28 Este

Calle 29 Este

Avenida México

Calle 30 Este

Calle 31 Este

Calle 32 Este

Calle Estudiante

Calle 24 Oeste

Calle L.de la Ossa

Calle H

Calle H

Calle 18 Este

Av México

Calle República de Nicaragua

Avenida México

Calle República de Haití

Calle República de Belice

Avenida Balboa

Calle 24 Este

Avenida Balboa

Cinta Cos

CEMENTERIO DE AMADOR

Calle B

Avenida Ancón

Calle F

Calle 17 Oeste

Avenida Central (La Peatonal)

Avenida Balboa

Calle B

Cinta Costera

Calle 21 Oeste

Calle B

Avenida A

C. Pedro de Obarrio

C. M. Iturralde

Calle B

Calle 16 Oeste

Calle 15 Oeste

Calle 14 Oeste

EL CHORILLO

Av Eloy Alfaro

Mercado de Maríscos **12**

Calle 18 Oest

Calle 20 de Diciembre

Calle 17 Oest

Avenida A

Calle 14

Iglesia de Santa Ana

PARQUE SANTA ANA

Avenida B

Calle Colón

Av Eloy Yoll

Av Eloy Alfaro

Av Eloy Alfaro

Muelle Fiscal

Calle 13 Oeste

Calle 12 Oeste

Calle 11 Oeste

Calle 13 Este

C. 13 Este

SANTA ANA

Calle 11 Este

Plaza V Centenario

Monumento de La Bandera de Panamá ⓘ

Iglesia de la Merced

C. 8 Este

Av Eloy Alfaro

Iglesia de San José

Avenida Central

Cinta Costera

Manglar del Casco Viejo

Museo del Canal Interoceánico

Catedral Metropolitana

Plaza de la Catedral

Plaza de Bolívar

Palacio Bolívar & Salón Bolívar

Bahía

CASCO VIEJO

Avenida A

Iglesia y Convento San Francisco de Asis

Iglesia y Convento de Santo Domingo

Instituto Nacional de Cultura (INAC)

Cinta Costera

Plaza de Francia

Cinta Costera

Central Panama City

0   500 m
0   500 yds

Corredor Norte

Calle Rubén Darío

Calle Heliodoro

River

Calle Martín Sosa

Estadio Óscar
Suman Carrillo

Instituto Geográfico
Nacional
'Tommy Guardía'

Av Arturo del Valle

Av Arturo del Valle

Av Simón Bolívar (Vía Transístmica)

JARDÍN
UNIVERSITARIO
DE LA TRANSÍSTMICA

EL CANGREJO

Av Octavio Méndez Pereira

Octavio
Méndez
Pereira

Universidad de Panamá
JARDÍNES
DE LA COLINA

Vía Argentina

Einstein's
Head Monument

Complejo
Hospitalario
Dr. Arnulfo
Arias Madrid

Calle Martín Sosa

Calle José de Fábrega

Av 1a Perejil Norte

Calle 2a Perejil

Calle 1a

Perejil

Av J.A. Guizado

Av Cabo Verde

ement

on Bolívar (Vía Transístmica)

LA CRESTA

Avenida 2 Norte

Avenida 1 Norte

Calle 53 Oeste

Calle Eric del Valle

Calle 53 Oeste

Av Manuel Espinosa Batista

Calle Enrique Geenzier

Calle Augusto Samuel Boyd

Calle Eusebio A. Morales

Iglesia
del Carmen
17

Hotel
El Panama

Vía Veneto

Calle Hercilia Lamela

OBARRIO

Avenida Central

Avenida Perú

Vía España

Vía España

Supermercado
Rey

Calle 52 Este

Calle 45 Este

Calle 44 Este

Calle 43 Este

Calle 42 Este

Avenida Justo Arosemena

Iglesia del
Carmen

Calle Elvira Méndez

Calle R. Arias

Calle A. Arango

Av Samuel Lewis

Santuario
Nacional

Calle 53 Este

Av R. Arango

Calle 54 Este

Avenida Cuba

Santo Tomás

EXPOSICIÓN

BELLA
VISTA

Calle 45 Este

Calle 44 Este

Calle 47 Este

Calle 50

Calle 52 Este

Calle 51 Este

Calle 50

Calle San Lucas

Calle 37 Este

Calle 38 Este

Calle 36

Calle 36 Este

Calle 37 Este

Calle 38 Este

Calle 39 Este

Calle 40 Este

Calle 41 Este

Calle 42 Este

Calle 43

Museo Ricardo
J. Alfaro

Avenida Frederico Boyd

Calle 48 Este

Calle Colombia

PARQUE
URRACÁ
20

Calle 45 Este

Calle
49 Este

Calle República de Uruguay

Calle Aquilino de la Guardia

Calle 50

Soho Mall

MARBELLA

Hospital
nto Tomás

Calle República de Chile

Calle 37 Este

Avenida Balboa

Calle 47
Este

Calle 48 Este

Av 5a B. Sur

Calle Las Acacias

Calle Margarita A. de Vallarino

Calle 53 Este

World Trade
Center

Plaza
New York

El Tornillo
16

19
mento a
co Núñez
e Balboa

Cinta Costera

Club de
Yates y Pesca

Cinta Costera
18

Av 5a B. Sur

Avenida Balboa

Calle 54 Este

Calle 55 Este

Calle 50 Este

Centro Médico
Paitilla

Vía Israel

Matasnillo R.

Boulevard El Hayek

Hard Rock
Hotel

Multicentro

Calle Ramón H. Jurado

anamá

Anfiteatro

Plaza de la
Democracia

Plaza
Paitilla

Cinta Costera

Avenida Balboa

Calle Juan XXIII

Avenida Italia

Avenida Italia

C. República de China

Calle Gil Colunge

PUNTA PAITILLA
21

Calle W. Churchill

PARQUE
PUNTA
PAITILLA

Playa de
la Rampa

Arco Chato, Convento de Santo Domingo.

PANAMA CITY

Love it or loathe it, few cities in Latin America can match the diversity and cosmopolitanism of Panama City: polyglot and postmodern before its time, its soaring skyline seems to spread endlessly along the coast.

Being hemmed in between rainforest-clad mountains, the protected canal basin, and the Pacific Ocean has confined the capital's haphazard expansion to a thin coastal strip. From the old colonial city center that protrudes into the southwest end of the bay, the modern city's tentacles extend 30km (19 miles) northeast through the eastern suburbs toward the Darién jungle. In the other direction, the impressive Puente de los Americas spans the Panama Canal, feeding into the Panamerican Highway that sweeps through a never-ending string of satellite towns to the inviting countryside beyond.

Visitors naturally head first for colonial Casco Viejo – established in 1673 by the Spanish, two years after the sacking of the original settlement, Panamá Viejo, by Welsh buccaneer Henry Morgan. Home to most of the capital's historical sights, the area offers classy boutique accommodations, casual cafés, and fine-dining, sprinkled among ancient churches and restored mansions, as well as a growing trendy nightlife scene. The ruins of Panamá Viejo, the first European city to be founded on the Pacific coast of the Americas, some 8km (5 miles) northeast of the center, constitute the only other significant remains from the conquest era.

El Cangrejo skyline.

A few kilometers northeast of Casco Viejo rise the shimmering skyscrapers of El Cangrejo, Marbella, and Obarrio, the modern banking and commercial district that hosts the main chain hotels and is bursting with bars, restaurants, glitzy shopping malls, and nightclubs. These in turn are fronted by the oceanfront penthouse apartments of Punta Paitilla and Punta Pacífica. The old and new cities are connected by the sweeping four-lane Cinta Costera, aimed at easing traffic congestion. Built on reclaimed land, it also

Main attractions

Casco Viejo
Museo del Canal
  Interoceánico
Calzada de Amador
BioMuseo
Cerro Ancón
Parque Natural
  Metropolitano
Cinta Costera
Panamá Viejo
Isla Taboga
Archipiélago de las Perlas

Maps on pages
114, 120 and 122

provides a welcome recreational space, where city residents stretch their legs, catch the ocean breeze, and soak up the views. Canal history buffs will also want to explore the buildings and monuments in the former US Canal Zone district of Balboa, with its distinctive clipped lawns and restrained utilitarian architecture. From the canal's original breakwater, nearby Calzada de Amador, you can watch the vast container ships glide past 24 hours a day. Behind, the attractive forested hilltop of Cerro Ancón affords stunning panoramic views across both the canal and the city. It also harbors a surprising array of wildlife, as does the larger Parque Metropolitano.

TRADE, TRAVEL, AND TOURISM

From its inception, Panama City has been located on one of the world's great crossroads, and it has thrived on trade, attracting migrants from all over the world to a melting pot bubbling with energy and ambition. Since the late 17th century, its fortunes have

waxed and waned in rhythm with the relative international importance of the isthmian trade route: from the glory years of the Spanish Camino Real, through decades in the doldrums until the 19th-century boom periods of the Californian Gold Rush, construction of the railroad, and the French and US Canal ventures. Once the mighty waterway finally opened in 1914, Panama City's position as a global trading center was secured; a wealth of new cultural influences had transformed the city and its inhabitants, who by 1920 totaled almost 60,000. Now the capital is home to 1.7 million – well over a third of the country's population – and although it is the undisputed political, economic, and social center of Panama, the city has very little in common with the rest of the country, which is often vaguely referred to as 'el interior.'

For the vast majority of visitors to the country, Panama City provides their first point of contact, via Tocumen International Airport, 24km (15 miles) northeast of the city center.

Panama Metro.

Some can't wait to escape the oppressive heat, traffic mayhem, and construction noise in search of the 'real Panama.' However, many spend their entire stay here, since it makes a good base from which to explore many of the country's attractions while enjoying the material comforts of sophisticated city living. The Canal, a handful of national parks, and the Caribbean coast as far as Portobelo can all be visited on day-trips. You can also reach the quaint flower-filled island of **Taboga** (see page 126) by ferry, or the desert-island beaches of the **Archipiélago de la Perlas** (see page 138), and still be back in time for a cocktail at sunset.

CASCO VIEJO

Exploration of Panama City is best started on foot in the old colonial heart of **San Felipe**, more commonly referred to as **Casco Viejo** (sometimes Casco Antiguo). Indeed, many visitors never move beyond this sector as most of the city's historical monuments and tourist attractions are packed into its narrow streets and there are plenty of accommodations and places to eat.

For centuries San Felipe was the hub of Panama City's social and political life but by the 1970s it had fallen into neglect. Since 1997, when it was declared a Unesco World Heritage Site, much of it has been restored to its former glory, a mix of Spanish and French-colonial architecture plus more modern neoclassical buildings. Boutique hotels, chic stores, and galleries now jostle for space with upscale restaurants, rooftop bars, and cafés. Though the area's gentrification has not been without its critics, as many of the poorer residents have been forced out, Casco Viejo is an exceedingly pleasant place for a leisurely stroll or intimate dinner.

Entering the historic center via Avenida Central in the morning you pass rows of lottery ticket sellers on the left-hand side. Numbering more than 10,000 across the country, they do a brisk trade along the sidewalk in front of the striking blue-and-white-striped Art Deco building, one of two homes for

⊙ Eat

A fabulous indulgence after tramping the streets of Casco Viejo, Grandclément (Mon–Thu 11.30am–8pm, Fri & Sat 11.30am–9.30pm, Sun noon–8pm), a French-style artisanal ice-cream parlor, offers chocolate every which way and an array of mouthwatering sorbets, though at a price.

Colorful buildings in Casco Viejo.

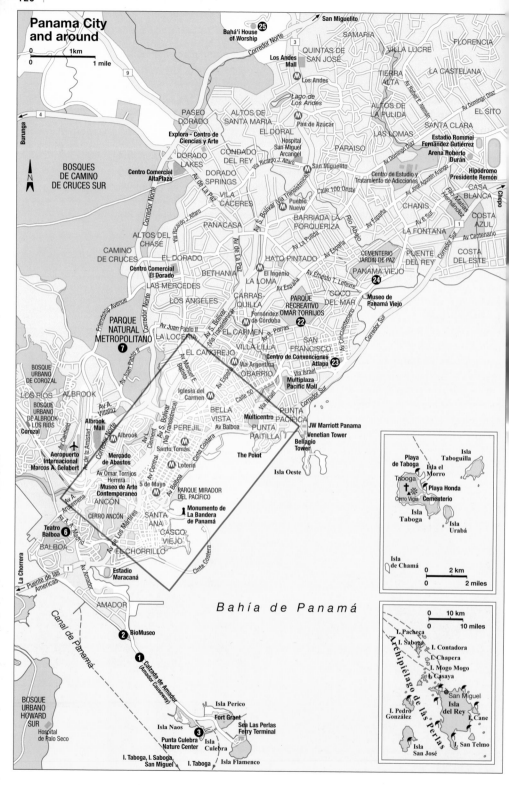

Panama City and around

0 — 1km
0 — 1 mile

Bahá'i House of Worship 25

San Miguelito

Corredor Norte

SAMARIA

VILLA LUCRE

FLORENCIA

QUINTAS DE SAN JOSÉ

3

TIERRA ALTA

LA CASTELANA

Los Andes Mall

Los Andes

Lago de Los Andes

ALTOS DE LA PULIDA

EL SITO

Av Rafael E. Alemán

Av Domingo Díaz

Burunga

4

9

PASEO DORADO

ALTOS DE SANTA MARIA

Pan de Azúcar

ALTOS DE LA PULIDA

SANTA CLARA

Explora - Centro de Ciencias y Arte

EL DORAL

Hospital San Miguel Arcangel

PARAISO

LAS LOMAS

Estadio Rommel Fernández Gutiérrez

Arena Roberto Durán

BOSQUES DE CAMINO DE CRUCES SUR

Centro Comercial AltaPlaza

DORADO LAKES

CONDADO DEL REY

San Miguelito

Centro de Estudio y Tratamiento de Adicciones

Hipódromo Presidente Remón

Av Domingo Díaz

Av José Agustín Arango

CASA BLANCA

N

DORADO SPRINGS

VILA CÁCERES

Pueblo Nuevo

Calle 100 Oeste

CHANIS

Rio Matias Hernández

Av 6 Sur

Corredor Norte

Av Ricardo J. Alfaro

Av de La Paz

Av S. Bolívar Vía Transístmica

Río Abajo

COSTA AZUL

Chepo

PANACASA

BARRIADA LA PORQUERIZA

Av España

LA FONTANA

1

Av Centenario

ALTOS DEL CHASÉ

Corredor Norte

EL DORADO

Av de La Paz

HATO PINTADO

CEMENTERIO JARDIN DE PAZ

PUENTE DEL REY

Corredor Sur

COSTA DEL ESTE

CAMINO DE CRUCES

Centro Comercial El Dorado

BETHANIA

El Ingenio

LA LOMA

Av España

Av Ernesto T. Lefevre

PANAMA VIEJO

24

LAS MERCEDES

CARRAS-QUILLA

COCO DEL MAR

Museo de Panamá Viejo

Friendship Avenue

LOS ÁNGELES

Fernández de Córdoba

PARQUE RECREATIVO OMAR TORRIJOS

22

PARQUE NATURAL METROPOLITANO 7

Av Juan Pablo II

Av S. Bolívar Vía Transístmica

EL CARMEN

Av B. Porras

Av Cincuentenario

Corredor Sur

Corredor Norte

LA LOCERIA

VILLA LILLA

SAN FRANCISCO

BOSQUE URBANO DE COROZAL

Av Juan Pablo II

EL CANGREJO

Centro de Convenciones Atlapa 23

Av Manuel E. Balboa

OBARRIO

Vía Argentina

Vía Israel

LOS RÍOS

ALBROOK

Iglesia del Carmen

Calle 50

Multiplaza Pacific Mall

BOSQUE URBANO DE ALBROOK LOS RÍOS

Av A. Villalaz

Albrook Mall

BELLA VISTA

Multicentro

PUNTA PACIFICA

Corredor Sur

Corozal

Albrook

Av S. Bolívar Vía Transístmica

Av L. Clement

PEREJIL

Av Balboa

Cinta Costera

PUNTA PAITILLA

JW Marriott Panama

Venetian Tower

Aeropuerto Internacional Marcos A. Gelabert

Av Cañfield

Mercado de Abastos

Santo Tomás

The Point

Bellagio Tower

Isla Oeste

Av Omar Torrijos Herrera

Loteria

Museo de Arte Contemporaneo

5 de Mayo

Av Central

Av Balboa

PARQUE MIRADOR DEL PACÍFICO

ANCÓN

CERRO ANCÓN

Av A. Arosemena

SANTA ANA

Monumento de La Bandera de Panamá

Cinta Costera

Teatro Balboa 6

Av de Los Mártires

CASCO VIEJO

BALBOA

Av A. Madrid

Estadio Maracaná

EL CHORRILLO

La Chorrera

Puente de las Américas

Av Amador

AMADOR

Bahía de Panamá

BioMuseo 2

BOSQUE URBANO HOWARD SUR

Calzada de Amador (Amador Causeway)

1

Hospital de Palo Seco

Canal de Panamá

Isla Perico

Fort Grant

Sea Las Perlas Fetry Terminal

Isla Naos

Punta Culebra Nature Center 3

Isla Culebra

I. Taboga, I. Saboga, San Miguel

I. Taboga

Isla Flamenco

Playa de Taboga

Isla Taboguilla

Isla el Morro

Taboga

Playa Honda

Cerro Vigía

Cementerio

Isla Taboga

Isla Urabá

Isla de Chamá

0 — 2 km
0 — 2 miles

---

0 — 10 km
0 — 10 miles

I. Pacheca

I. Saboga

I. Contadora

I. Chapera

I. Mogo Mogo

I. Casaya

San Miguel

I. Pedro González

Isla del Rey

I. Cane

Archipiélago de las Perlas

Isla San José

I. San Telmo

the national lottery (the other lies on Avenida Perú). A little farther along on the left stands the gleaming neoclassical **Casa de la Municipalidad**, seat of the city government.

Next door, across the intersection with Calle 10, the city's oldest church, **Iglesia de la Merced Ⓐ** (daily 6am–7pm; free) is notable mainly because it was reconstructed on its present site in 1680 using the original stones from Panamá Viejo. The Baroque facade is the best-preserved section of the church, which is also the only church in Casco Viejo to retain its original wooden roof and interior columns; the impressive organ has over 1,000 pipes.

PLAZA DE LA CATEDRAL

Midway down Avenida Central the street opens out into the old quarter's main square, **Plaza de la Catedral Ⓑ** – also known as Plaza Mayor and Plaza de la Independencia since the proclamations of independence from Spain and separation from Colombia were both made here. The newly restored **Central Hotel** (www.centralhotelpanama.com), on the east side of the plaza, played a starring role in both events. It was here that crowds gathered in 1903 to celebrate full Panamanian independence by emptying a dozen bottles of champagne over the head of General Huertas, the defecting Colombian garrison commander.

Numerous busts of the nation's founding fathers are scattered beneath the shady trees surrounding the striking central gazebo, with the Republic's first president, Manuel Amador Guerrero, taking pride of place. In the 17th and 18th centuries the square was used for bullfights and theatrical presentations. Even today it hosts the occasional entertainment, and a craft fair every other Sunday.

Dominating the plaza on the west side is the **Catedral Metropolitana** (daily 7am–7pm; free). An unusual design, it displays a mix of neoclassical and Baroque in the olive-and-cream sandstone facade, flanked by gleaming white towers topped with sparkling mother-of-pearl. Like the Iglesia de la Merced, it was built using stone brought from the ruins of Panamá Viejo. Three of its bells were also recovered from its derelict predecessor. Following a complete overhaul ready for the Pope's visit in 2019, the cathedral is now dazzling, with the marble floor gleaming and the imposing large altarpiece carved from seven types of Italian marble covered with plenty of glittering gold leaf. To its right lies a trapdoor marking the entrance to tunnels – not open to visitors – designed as escape routes, connecting the cathedral to the churches of La Merced and San José. During the restoration, an ancient mural was discovered behind the altar, dating from the mid-18th century, making it the oldest work of art in the cathedral.

Southeast of the cathedral, the **Museo de Historia de Panamá** (tel: 228 6231; Mon–Fri 8am–4pm) takes up the ground floor of the splendid

⊙ Fact

The cathedral bells reputedly owe their distinctive tone to a gold ring thrown by Queen Isabella I of Spain into the molten metal from which they were cast.

Catedral Metropolitana.

neoclassical **Palacio Municipal**, built in 1910 on the site of the former city hall. The small rather uninspiring museum offers a cursory introduction to Panamanian history. The reclining languorous nude that greets visitors in the entrance hall is said to represent Panama bathing in the waters of the two oceans.

Tucked away in the corner of the plaza, a restrained French colonial building with mansard roof and shutters houses the **Museo del Canal Interoceánico** (tel: 211 1649; www. museodelcanal.com; Tue–Sun 9am–5pm). Easily the most interesting of the square's attractions, its highly polished marble entrance hall harks back to the museum's former life as the city's grandest hotel before it became the French canal company's headquarters. Rightly on the itinerary of most tour groups, the museum offers a comprehensive history of the 'Big Ditch,' from the founding of the isthmus through the first Spanish attempt to find a passage to Asia to the recent expansion project. The

museum relies heavily on text predominantly in Spanish, so it's worth renting an audio-guide, or taking a guided tour (by prior arrangement). That said, the exhibition is brought to life by an array of photographs, video montages, and maps, enhanced by a few interactive exhibits. Together they highlight the very different working conditions of the French and US canal eras, as well as the apartheid living conditions of gold (white) and silver (black) roll employees in the latter. By the end of the visit, you are left in no doubt about the levels of human endurance, suffering, and technical ingenuity that made the Panama Canal's construction such a phenomenal achievement.

Cross the square and head down a passage (by René Café), which brings you to Avenida Eloy Alfaro and the splendid, if diminutive, Spanish Mudéjar-style **Palacio Presidencial ⓒ**. The palace's original 17th-century building had served variously as a private mansion, customs house, teacher training college, and even a prison. In 1922,

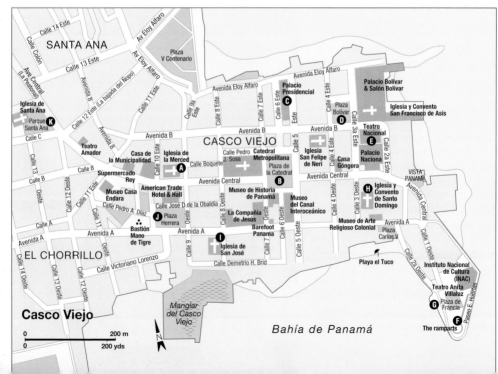

under the orders of President Belisario Porras, it was rebuilt as the presidential residence in grandiose neo-Mudéjar style, oozing marble and mother of pearl. It is commonly known as the 'Palacio de las Garzas' after the white egrets – 'garza' meaning egret – given to Porras by his poet friend Ricardo Miró; egrets have lived freely around the patio ever since. The only way to see the palace interior is on a guided tour, which only covers a few rooms, though it is at least free. It includes the long Salón Amarillo (Yellow Hall) complete with presidential throne, gilt mirrors, and heavy drapes. Striking murals by Roberto Lewis – Panama's pre-eminent artist of the time – here and in the state dining room offer a selective pictorial run through Panama's history.

PLAZA BOLÍVAR

Walk east a block along Eloy Alfaro, then another block back from the waterfront along Calle 4 Este and you reach Casco Viejo's most elegant square, **Plaza Bolívar D**, overlooked by a couple of notable churches and a palace. A central monument to independence leader Símon Bolívar or 'El Libertador' (The Liberator), topped by a giant condor, presides over topiary trees and leisurely pavement café-restaurants. At lunchtime, the peace is interrupted by the cries of young schoolchildren spilling out of class seeking out *raspados* (snow-cones) from the waiting vendors. Extending along the eastern edge of the square, the smart **Palacio Bolívar** (Mon–Fri 8am–4pm; free) is worth a quick peek inside. Having served as part of a convent, military barracks, and a school, the beautifully restored building now houses the Ministry of Foreign Affairs. To the right as you enter is **Salón Bolívar**; formerly the chapter house of a Franciscan monastery, it is now home to a small museum commemorating the

Congreso Anfictiónico of 1826. Organized by Bolívar, the congress was the first Panamerican gathering aimed at unifying the newly independent Latin American countries. Although the great man's plans of unity ultimately foundered, the congress was judged a success. Today's exhibits include a replica of the Liberator's gold ceremonial sword, encrusted with more than 1,000 diamonds, and the congress' original documents.

On the southeastern corner of Plaza Bolívar, the renovated **Iglesia y Convento de San Francisco de Asís** (daily 7am–7pm; free) reopened in 2016 after years of neglect and stop-start restoration. Established by the Franciscans in the 17th century, it was later taken over by the Jesuits, who were responsible for its present design, adding the imposing bell tower in 1918. The top of the bell tower offers the best view of Casco Viejo in town, but is currently under restoration. Note the restrained interior, which features delightful modern stained-glass windows laden with Franciscan symbolism, and a

◉ Tip

To arrange a free guided tour of the Palacio Presidencial (Mon–Fri 8.30am–4pm, hourly) in Spanish or English, e-mail Eguiasdepalacio@presidencia. gob.pa, or deliver a hand-written letter to the Oficina de Guías – at the back of the yellow building on the waterfront by Calle 4 – two weeks in advance, suggesting your preferred possible dates. You also need to provide a scan of your passport, and address your request to: Office of the First Lady of the Republic, Protocol Direction, Office of Palace Guides.

Monument to Simon Bolívar in Plaza Bolívar.

beautifully restored mural composed of Venetian mosaics. As you enter the church, to your right you'll also notice a huge shiny silver *anda*; bought in time for the papal visit in early 2019, it is used to parade the Virgen Dolorosa round the streets on Good Friday. Far less imposing, on the opposite corner of the plaza, is the **Iglesia San Felipe de Neri** (daily 7am–7pm; free), one of Casco Viejo's earliest churches, built in 1688. It served as a shrine to the cathedral and later as a children's home and orphanage.

Follow Avenida 'B' out of the plaza for 100 meters/yds to arrive at the handsome **Teatro Nacional** Ⓔ (tel: 262 3525). One of the first grand, national buildings to be commissioned by the newly independent Panamanian state, this magnificent Italianate neoclassical edifice is well worth a closer look. Designed by Genaro Ruggieri, the theater has had mixed fortunes ever since. Though it opened its doors to the public in 1908 to initial success, it failed to survive the global depression of the 1930s,

becoming a movie theater for a while before falling into decline. After substantial restoration work, the theater reopened in the 1970s with a performance by British ballerina and long-term Panama resident Margot Fonteyn. Her bronze bust adorns the lobby, alongside that of Roberto Lewis, whose allegorical frescoes depicting the birth of the nation adorn the vaulted ceiling of the splendid Baroque interior. The theater was forced to close again in 2015 for a multi-million-dollar makeover but is due to reopen in 2019, when occasional theatrical productions will resume.

Turn right out of the theater, then right again to reach the steps that lead to the Paseo Esteban Huertas, a delightful, breezy, bougainvillea-covered promenade that runs some 400 meters/yds along the top of **the ramparts** Ⓕ. The walkway along the defensive seawall is a favorite haunt of smooching couples, hence its nickname Paseo de los Inamorados (Lovers' Walk). Guna traders also display

Teatro Nacional.

their handicrafts to passing tourists; many can also help arrange a trip to their home islands in Guna Yala.

PLAZA DE FRANCIA AND AVENIDA 'A'

Squeezed onto the southeastern tip of Casco Viejo, down the steps from the ramparts, the focus of the **Plaza de Francia**  is the French Canal venture. A large monument pays homage to the thousands of workers who died in the fiasco. Topped by a proud Gallic cockerel, the central obelisk is ringed by busts of the key characters, including Ferdinand de Lesseps, the French diplomat who first conceived of the canal yet whose ignorance and vanity were central to the project's ultimate failure (see page 99). Note the small plaque (also on the seawall) commemorating nationalist hero Victoriano Lorenzo, who was executed in the plaza in 1903 (see page 42).

Formerly the Plaza de Armas, the colonial city's main square is an irregularly shaped space bounded by a fortified seawall and the renovated arches of Las Bóvedas (vaults), Spanish dungeons that also functioned as storehouses, prison cells, and barracks for the fort that occupied the plaza until the early 20th century. The Bóvedas now contain a chic restaurant of the same name and a couple of smart stores. The large gleaming-white building nearby is home to the **Instituto Nacional de Cultura** (INAC), the body responsible for maintaining the country's few museums. It was spruced up for the James Bond film *Quantum of Solace*, in which it featured as a Bolivian hotel.

Turning right up either Calle 1 or 2 brings you into Avenida A, where you'll pass a further string of religious buildings. First is the 17th-century **Iglesia y Convento de Santo Domingo** . It is most famous for the Arco Chato (flat arch) over the main entrance. Just 10.6 meters (35ft) high, but spanning some

15 meters (50ft) with no keystone or external support, it was reputedly cited as evidence of Panama's seismic stability when the US Senate was debating where to build an interoceanic canal. Ironically, the arch inexplicably collapsed just after the centenary celebrations for Panama's independence in 2003, but has subsequently been restored.

Next door, the **Museo de Arte Religioso Colonial** (Mon–Fri 8am–4pm), which gives access to the Arco Chato, has a small collection of religious paintings, silverwork, and sculpture dating back to the colonial era, though the detailed information panels are only in Spanish. Four blocks farther down Avenida 'A,' after crossing Calle 7 Oeste, stands the careworn facade of La Compañia de Jesús.

Diagonally opposite, slightly set back from the road, the **Iglesia de San José**  (daily 7am–7pm; free) is worth a peek, if only to see the legendary Baroque Altar de Oro (Golden Altar), which illuminates the otherwise gloomy interior. A carved

◷ Tip

The northern end of the ramparts gives you the best view across the bay to the skyscrapers of Punta Paitilla and Punta Pacífica. At the other end, at the head of the steps onto Plaza de Francia, you get a fine view across to the Biomuseo and the Puente de los Americas.

Bust of Símon Bolívar.

mahogany extravaganza gilded with 22-carat gold leaf, it was one of the few treasures to survive Henry Morgan's ransacking of Panamá Viejo in 1671, thanks, apparently, to having been painted or covered in mud to disguise its true value. Legend has it that when Morgan demanded to see the gold, the priest explained its absence by pleading poverty, even persuading the buccaneer to make a donation to the church.

Continue walking and in 100 meters/yds Avenida A opens out into **Plaza Herrera 🅹**, marking the western limit of Casco Viejo. An elegant square, it was named in honor of General Tomás Herrera, the military leader of Panama's first short-lived independence attempt in 1840 (see page 42), whose equestrian monument stands proudly in the center. The northern side is dominated by the gleaming white facade of the renovated American Trade Hotel, which dates back to 1917. The hotel is also home to Danilo's Jazz Club, owned by Grammy award-winning Panamanian jazz superstar Danilo Pérez (see page 68). Just to the west of the square lies a crumbling and indistinct pile of masonry that is **Bastión Mano de Tigre** (Tiger Hand Bastion), the last remaining section of the city's original defensive walls on the landward side. Beyond, the road soon dissolves into the poor *barrio* and no-go area of El Chorrillo, which was devastated during the US invasion, leaving hundreds dead and thousands homeless. The neighborhood has since been rebuilt, but the colored concrete tenements that replaced the old wooden slum housing are already run-down. Despite a substantial increase in police presence, and investment in leisure facilities, it's still a dangerous place, day or night.

Doubling back onto Avenida Central takes you back out of Casco Viejo the way you came in, via **Parque Santa Ana 🅚**. The social hub of the impoverished neighborhood of the same name, the park marks the transition between the old colonial center of Casco Viejo and the more commercial modern city. As

Ⓞ ISLA TABOGA

Around 20km (12 miles) off the coast, the lush hills of Isla Taboga have provided a popular weekend escape for Panama City residents for centuries. Dubbed the Isla de las Flores for its fragrant and colorful blooms, the place is packed on summer weekends, though quiet at other times. But Taboga's present-day tranquility belies a turbulent past. The Spanish wasted no time in enslaving the native Cueva inhabitants and constructed a fort on adjoining Isla El Morro; its cannons are still sprinkled round the island. The excellent natural harbor later provided a launchpad for Francisco Pizarro's conquest of Peru, and a hiding place for numerous pirates and privateers.

Most visitors to the island are day-trippers – though you can overnight here – lounging on the beach, lingering over a seafood lunch, and strolling the traffic-free streets of San Pedro fishing village, where most of the thousand or so inhabitants live. The main plaza, and Taboga's social hub, is filled on summer afternoons as villagers of all ages gather to watch or play sport, or just to hang out. At one end stands the gleaming white Iglesia San Pedro, built in 1550; a short distance away from the opposite end is a shrine to the Virgen del Carmen, the island's patron saint.

Every July 16, she is honored with an aquatic procession followed by general merrymaking and fireworks. Opposite the shrine is the house where Pizarro apparently lived, while a nearby plaque commemorates the sojourn of French painter Paul Gauguin, who worked on the Canal briefly before heading off for the South Seas.

Since the main beach and surrounding waters are not especially clean, it's worth summoning the energy for one of the island's two hikes. The first is an easy 20-minute stroll to the large cross on the eastern headland – take Calle Abajo out of the village along the main 'road,' and turn left down a dirt track after the cemetery. Alternatively, stay on the road as it winds up to the 300-meter (984ft) summit of Cerro Vigía, Taboga's highest point. The *mirador* on top of an old US military bunker affords truly spectacular panoramic views. Other popular activities include guided walking tours, boat trips that take a closer look at the island's pelican population, and snorkeling. Two boat services leave for Taboga from Panama City's causeway: the leisurely Calypso (www.thebeachhousepanama.com/barcoscalypso/) from Mi Playita; or the faster Taboga Express from Isla Flamenco on the causeway (www.tabogaexpress.com).

the center of activity outside the city walls in the early 19th century, it hosted colorful markets and bullfights; now it offers some respite from the swirling traffic. On the corner stands **Café Coca Cola** (daily 7am–11pm), which claims to be the oldest café in Panama. The unprepossessing exterior hides a city institution, where older locals like to drink coffee, read the paper, and discuss the news. The rather tatty, traffic-free section of Avenida Central, on the park's northeastern side, leads down to Plaza Cinco de Mayo and the modern city.

THE BREEZY CAUSEWAY

Away from the heat and traffic of downtown Panama City, the breezy **Calzada de Amador ❶** (Amador Causeway) – the Canal's Pacific breakwater – is a popular weekend recreational area for middle-class Panamanians. Built in 1913 from dirt and rock that was excavated during the Culebra Cut, it links four islets – Naos, Culebra, Perico, and Flamenco – to the mainland. El Causeway, as

it's more commonly known, was part of the US Canal Zone until the handover in 1999, when the government opened it to the public. In recent times, its popularity has risen and fallen according to the stop-start construction of new developments. Currently, it is on the up. A new dual carriageway, regular bus service – including the hop-on-hop-off tourist bus (www.hop-on-hop-off-bus.com) – a cycleway, park benches, and viewpoints are helping to fill the bars and restaurants once more; you can wine and dine while enjoying close-ups of transiting ships or more distant views of the modern city's skyline. On Friday nights you'll find plenty of activity: families riding four-seater bicycles, booze cruises round the bay, and *chivas parranderas* – old buses done up as party buses with flashing lights, pumping music, and plenty of rum.

On your right, shortly after reaching the causeway, you pass the **Plaza de Etnías y Culturas**, featuring an odd-looking rocket-shaped monument designed to represent Panama's status

The most colorful way to get around Panama City, by these diablos rojos.

⊘ ALTOS DE ANCÓN

A stroll up Cerro Ancón takes you past the entrance to the exclusive, leafy, residential area of Altos de Ancón. Formerly known as Quarry Heights, its elevated position and proximity to the canal administration made it the ideal base for the US military command center within the Canal Zone. The name derived from the adjacent quarry, which had provided the construction rock for both the Pedro Miguel and Miraflores locks. Following the canal handover, the desirable residences came under private ownership. It's worth a quick detour to admire the classic Zonian architecture: two-story wooden structures with large windows, wide wraparound verandas, and overhanging eaves to keep out the heavy tropical rain.

as the bridge across two oceans and the country's ethnic diversity. Beyond, on the oceanfront, the Balboa Yacht Club has a pleasant waterside bar open to all. Next up is the Zona de la Rumba, an enclosed nightclub area and the enormous Vegas-style Centro de Convenciones Figali, which is under renovation.

Just before entering the causeway proper, crumpled multicolored roof plates announce the star attraction, the $100 million Frank Gehry-designed **BioMuseo** ❷ (www.biomuseopanama.org; Tue–Fri 10am–4pm, Sat–Sun 10am–5pm). Taking over a decade to build, it highlights Panama's rich biodiversity, informed by the country's unique position as a land bridge between the two Americas. It also devotes space to Panama's human history. Although the permanent exhibition comprises just eight rooms, plus a couple of outdoor exhibits, its state-of-the-art interactive screens and large-scale audio-visual presentations are undeniably impressive, though it's arguable whether it's worth the hefty entry fee. An aquarium

The impressive Frank Gehry-designed BioMuseo.

and more exhibition rooms are still under construction. Outside, a biodiversity park is still in its infancy, showcasing endemic and other native plants.

Farther down the causeway, the Smithsonian's Tropical Research Institute runs the child-friendly **Punta Culebra Nature Center** ❸ (www.stri.si.edu; Jan–Feb Tue–Sun 10am–6pm, Mar–Dec Tue–Fri 1–5pm), where visitors can explore the marine and coastal environment on trails through the tropical dry forest and various exhibitions of native flora and fauna. Its most recent attraction is an exhibit showcasing some of Panama's endangered frogs, threatened by the spread of a deadly fungus (see page 85). Next door, the sheltered harbor of Mi Playita is the departure point for the Calypso ferry to Isla Taboga (see page 126).

Islas Perico and Flamenco host an array of strip malls full of bars and restaurants, as well as a couple of flashy marinas. During US control, the strategic location of Isla Flamenco's rocky knoll resulted in the construction of a military base; these days, the island hosts the command center for the ACP (see page 129), which controls all canal traffic. Canal transit cruises, the Sea Las Perlas ferry (www.ferrypearlislands.com) to Islas de las Perlas, and the Taboga Express to Isla Taboga all depart from the marina at Isla Flamenco (see page 126).

CANAL MONUMENTS AND GREEN CITY SPACES

Visible from most of the surrounding area, the huge Panamanian flag fluttering in the breeze on the summit of **Cerro Ancón** ❹ is one of the city's most distinctive landmarks. The hilltop itself affords the best vistas of both the city and the Canal. What's more, it is covered with a protected area of secondary forest that harbors a wealth of wildlife, from agoutis to

white-faced capuchin monkeys, and is well worth the 30-minute stiff walk. Alternatively, a taxi can take you halfway up, though the final section is now off-limits to motor vehicles on account of subsidence. By the *mirador* overlooking the city, and below the flagpole, sits the serene bronze figure of poet Amelia Denis de Icaza, who is remembered for the nationalist poem *Al Cerro Ancón*. At the hill's base, the neighborhood of Balboa still retains a number of Canal-era buildings since it, as well as Cerro Ancón, were formerly part of the US Canal Zone.

Sprawling over the western slope of Cerro Ancón, Balboa's main attraction is the impressive if austere **Edificio de la Administración del Canal ❺** (Canal Administration Building). As well as being the ACP's seat of authority, it houses four arresting murals that celebrate in graphic detail the Herculean achievement of building the Canal. Decorating an elegant domed marble rotunda, just inside the main entrance, they were painted by New York artist William Van Ingen, known for his work in the Library of Congress in Washington DC. A series of evocative lithographs adorn the outer walls of the rotunda. To peek inside at any hour, present your passport to the security guard at the car park and explain that you want to see the murals (*los murales*). Round the back of the building, a steep set of steps descends to the **Monumento a Goethals**, which commemorates the achievement of the canal's chief engineer George Goethals (see page 48). The cream monolith represents the canal, with water cascading over three stepped marble platforms – symbolizing the three original sets of locks – into a pool below. Diagonally opposite stands the former Balboa High School, site of the dramatic 'flag riots' of 1964 (see page 51); the 21 Panamanians who died in the skirmish are honored in a memorial near the back of the building, where their deaths are remembered every January 9 on Día de los Mártires (Martyrs' Day). Today, the old school houses the **Centro de Capacitación Ascanio**

Calzada de Amador.

Panama City skyline.

Arosemena (Mon–Fri 7.15am–4.15pm; free). In addition to providing technical training to Canal employees, it contains a small but evocative historical exhibition which shows items including porcelain from the Tivoli Hotel – the grandest hotel of the Canal Zone era – and Goethals' hat rack, along with an excellent collection of photographs of the waterway's construction.

Goethals' monument stands at the head of **El Prado**, a palm-lined grassy rectangular boulevard, measured to match the length and width of an original lock chamber. At the far end, **Circulo Stevens** (Steven's Circle) represents a low-key celebration of the canal's first engineer. Across busy Avenida Arnulfo Arias Madrid, the faded Art Deco **Teatro Balboa** ➏ (tel: 501 4109) is worth a quick look inside for its splendid mosaic floors. Home to the Orquesta Sinfónica Nacional de Panamá, it hosts occasional classical concerts.

A short taxi-ride from the city center along Avenida Juan Pablo II, the **Parque Natural Metropolitano** ➐ (tel: 232 5552; www.parquemetropolitano.org; daily 6.30am–4.30pm) offers an accessible slice of semi-deciduous tropical forest. The birdwatching is excellent and five short but well-marked trails with several viewpoints give tantalizing glimpses of the city. Arriving early in the morning enhances your chances of seeing sloths entwined around branches, agoutis or koatis snuffling in the undergrowth, and some splendid colorful birds. Guided tours of the park can be organized in Spanish or English with a day's notice, and periodically Panama's Audubon Society (www.facebook.com/audubonpanama) leads guided birdwatching walks, open to all. In 2018, a butterfly house (www.mariposariometropolitano.com; Tue–Sun 9.30am–4.30pm) opened next to the visitors' center, which will provide you with a map for your entry fee.

CENTRAL PANAMA CITY

In contrast to the relative calm of the city's historical center and ancient remains, the modern streets of central Panama City reverberate with

traffic noise. Sidewalks are packed with people squeezing in and out of a patchwork of stores, banks, hotels, and restaurants or threading their way through street vendors, hawkers, and other pedestrians. Stretching around the Bahía de Panamá, from Plaza Cinco de Mayo – home to a cluster of government buildings – to the original skyscraper city of Punta Paitilla, the area ranges from the older residential and commercial districts of Calidonia and La Exposición, via the more affluent area of Bella Vista, to the Área Bancaria (Central Business District) *barrios* of El Cangrejo and Marbella linked by the reclaimed Cinta Costera. Heading farther east, the former exclusively residential neighborhoods of Obarrio and San Francisco are being gradually gobbled up by yet more skyscrapers and brash businesses, a number of which are merely fronts for money laundering.

The traffic-free stretch of Avenida Central, lined with tired and tatty stores, leads down from Casco Viejo and spills out into the turbulent traffic

of **Plaza Cinco de Mayo** ❽. Though not particularly attractive, this irregularly shaped plaza is the city's main square and home to the seat of government, the **Asamblea Nacional de Panamá**. Unremarkable government buildings stand on the western side of the square in the raised Parque José Antonio Remón Cantera, named after a former president who was mysteriously gunned down at the hippodrome in 1955. Peer behind the towering black monolith at its center and you are greeted by an enormous head of the murdered president, protruding from the granite.

Behind the government buildings, a set of steps and a footbridge across Avenida de los Mártires take you to two places of interest. Turning right after the bridge, onto Avenida Roosevelt, leads to the **Smithsonian Tropical Research Institute's Earl S. Tupper Research and Conference Center** ❾ (www.stri.si.edu; Mon–Fri 9am–5pm; free). Set in leafy grounds, it hosts a research library and an impressive bookstore, where you can arrange

Fruit and veg for sale off Avenida Central.

Fresh fish on display at Mercado de Mariscos.

visits to Isla Barro Colorado (see page 152). Turning left, you reach the privately owned **Museo de Arte Contemporáneo** ⑩ (tel: 262 8012; www.macpanama.org; Tue–Sat 10am–5pm, Sun 10am–4pm). The city's main art gallery, it houses a modest permanent collection of works by Panamanian artists in a range of media, and periodically hosts interesting temporary exhibitions. Behind the art gallery, a leafy back road leads up and around Cerro Ancón, skirting the old Gorgas Hospital (see page 47) and the Corte Suprema de Justicia (Supreme Court).

On the south side of Plaza Cinco de Mayo, the neoclassical building that was originally the proud Panama Railroad Pacific terminal is in the process of being restored to house the **Museo Antropológico Reina Torres de Araúz** ⑪. There have been many announcements heralding its imminent reopening since it closed to the public in 2013. The latest date is late 2019. Part of the reason for the delay is to habilitate a space with the requisite security to house the more recently discovered

treasures from El Caño (see page 176). The exhibition space will be given a facelift to display the valuable pre-Columbian ceramics, gold *huacas*, weapons, and tools currently held in the vault.

Heading downhill from Cinco de Mayo toward the ocean, along Calle 23 Este, you will pass the **Mercado de Buhonería y Artesanías** (Mon–Sat 9am–5pm). Due to move to a new location in 2019, it currently inhabits a series of pink shipping containers and is an inexpensive place to shop for souvenirs – though since the place is hemmed in by heavy traffic on both sides and the overpass above, the location is hardly conducive to a leisurely browse. A block farther on, you reach the southern end of the Cinta Costera. Head across the road to the distinctive blue-roof of the **Mercado de Mariscos** ⑫ (Mon–Sat 6am–6pm; closed first Mon of the month for fumigation). A fabulous place to wander around, you'll see all shapes and sizes of seafood on sale, some waving their antennae from tanks. The market's comings and

⊙ REINA TORRES DE ARAÚZ

Appropriately, Panama's finest anthropological collection is named after its pre-eminent anthropologist, ethnographer, and university professor, Reina Torres De Araúz. Born in 1932, she was the driving force behind the country's national and regional museums, and tirelessly pursued the illegal removal of archeological artifacts, writing to US museums personally to demand their return. Totally fearless, she took part in the four-month Trans-Darién expedition of 1959–1960, alongside her husband, Amado Araúz. The couple have three children together.

The author of the first main published work on Panama's indigenous peoples, she also excelled on the international stage, speaking a total of five languages, including Ancient Greek and Latin, and serving as vice-president of Unesco's World Heritage Committee, among other offices. An extraordinarily driven woman, she became the youngest recipient of the Orden de Vasco Nuñez de Balboa, Panama's highest honor, and the first of several she received. All of this she achieved before the age of 49, when she died after a long battle with cancer.

goings are easily observed from a table upstairs at the seafood restaurant.

Heading out of Cinco de Mayo in a northerly direction along Avenida Justo Arosemena (also known as Avenida 3 Sur) takes you almost immediately to the diminutive **Museo Afro-Antillano** ⑬ (tel: 501 4130; www.samaap.org; Tue–Sun 9.30am–3.45pm). Housed in an unmarked, wooden, former church and dwarfed by giant tower blocks, this small but worthwhile museum is dedicated to the important history and culture of Panama's large West Indian population. The Church of the Christian Mission, as it used to be, constituted the social center of the *barrio* of El Marañon, once a thriving Afro-Antillean community dating back to the construction of the railroad (see page 39). Today's exhibits highlight the pivotal role that Afro-Antilleans played in building both the railroad and the Canal, as well as illustrating the harsh working and living conditions of black 'silver roll' Canal workers, which contrasted acutely with the privileges of white American 'gold roll' employees,

in the days of the Canal Zone (see page 48). The museum also helps organize the annual Afro-Antillean Fair that takes place during Carnaval at the Centro de Convenciones ATLAPA.

Beyond Plaza Cinco de Mayo, Avenida Central continues north, through Calidonia, and La Exposición. Consisting of a dense grid of streets, these twin *barrios* are crammed with budget hotels, and sprinkled with small parks and a couple of museums to provide welcome relief. This older section of the modern city dates back to the boom construction eras of the Panama Railroad and Canal in the mid- and late 19th century. The area's population expanded yet further when non-US-Canal laborers and their families were gradually forced out of the newly created Canal Zone in the early 20th century. As new high-rise developments continue apace, the working-class residents and their small businesses are gradually being squeezed out. Along Avenida Perú, between calles 33 and 34, by La Lotería metro station, **Plaza Belisario Porras** ⑭ honors

Bella Vista, Campo Alegre and Obarrio in the early evening sun.

the country's three-time president and founding father. Amid the neatly trimmed flowerbeds and shady trees rises a vast monument in which Porras cuts a dashing figure, overlooked by splendidly restored government buildings and the balustraded Spanish Embassy. With your back to the monument, looking up Calle Ecuador to Avenida Central, you can spy the rose window of the neo-Romanesque **Basílica de Don Bosco** ⓯ (daily 6am–6pm; free), built in the 1950s. As well as being pleasantly airy with some lovely stained glass, the place is a glittering blue mass of modern mosaics, crafted in Italy and brought to Panama for the city's centennial celebrations.

SOARING SKYSCRAPERS

Continuing broadly northeast, the major arteries of Vía España and Calle 50 transect the neighboring areas of Bella Vista, Marbella, El Cangrejo, and Obarrio. These form the financial and commercial core of Panama City – what is often nebulously referred to as the Área Bancaria – which is replete with skyscrapers. The most distinctive of these is the spiraling green tower known as **El Tornillo** ⓰ (The Screw), which houses a bank. Bella Vista, on either side of Calle 50, once a leafy *barrio* brimming with 1930s colonial mansions, has all but been taken over by modern tower blocks. The legendary Calle Uruguay was for many years a fulcrum of nightlife, a contiguous strip of bars and clubs. Though still with some vibe, the smart young set now party more in Casco Viejo, while the street, recently restricted to pedestrians only, has yet to redefine itself. To the north on Vía España stands the incongruous 20th-century neo-Gothic wedding cake, the **Iglesia del Carmen** ⓱ (daily 7am–7pm; free). Particularly impressive when illuminated at night, the stained-glass windows along the aisles depict tropical flowers, while those higher up in the nave relate tales from the Old and New Testaments. Equally striking is the neo-Byzantine mosaic altarpiece. The church marks the beginning of El Cangrejo, home to many of the city's high-end, high-rise

⊘ LA CINTA COSTERA

It's hard to miss the Cinta Costera – the broad belt of land that sweeps round the Bahía de Panamá, skirting the Mercado de Mariscos and including the raised highway loop over the water around Casco Viejo. The aim of this multimillion-dollar land reclamation project was to ease traffic congestion while providing an oceanfront promenade, complete with trees, benches, and leisure amenities. Controversy dogged its ten-year construction, from the choice of contractor, Odebrecht – currently embroiled in the world's biggest bribery scandal (see page 55) – to opposition to the Casco Viejo beltway. A tunnel was initially planned beneath the historical center but, at the last minute, was replaced with a loop road. Loud objections were raised, not least from Unesco, which threatened to revoke Casco Viejo's World Heritage status, while local residents and businesses protested vociferously – though to no avail. Although the project has delivered far more concrete than the green spaces that were originally promised, the Cinta Costera has marginally improved the traffic flow, and its jogging path and cycleway are well used by residents and visitors.

Whether strolling, jogging, skateboarding, cycling, or merely lazing on a bench admiring the sunset, the Cinta Costera is a hive of activity on summer evenings and weekends. Sunday mornings in particular offer a spread of recreational pursuits, most of them free. During Ciclovía Panamá (6am–noon) the regular cycleway is extended northeast all the way to the museum at Panamá Viejo, from where you can pedal southwest as far as the Estadio Maracaná, the other side of Casco Viejo – 15km (9 miles) one way. Around 300 free bikes are available for this weekly event, on a first-come-first-served basis; you'll find them opposite the Hilton Hotel at Calle Alquilino de la Guardia, in the middle of the Cinta Costera (show your passport), though several places also rent bikes. Free exercise classes are also on offer at 7 and 8am: choose from yoga, boxercise, and Zumba. Turn up suitably attired at the Fuente Anayansi, and treat yourself to a raspado when you've finished. For a few dollars, you can also attend classes on weekdays, in the early morning or evening.

hotel chains and restaurants, as well as upmarket stores and shopping malls, which extend into adjacent Bella Vista, Marbella, and Obarrio.

The sweeping arc of Avenida Balboa, which connects the city's historical heartland, Casco Viejo, to its symbols of industrial progress, Punta Paitilla and El Cangrejo, now forms part of the **Cinta Costera** ⓲, a four-lane highway built on reclaimed land, with some landscaped recreational areas. It is also the focus of Panama City's Carnavales, which, outside the Azuero, are the country's most extravagant. The main sight of note is the vainglorious **Monumento a Vasco Núñez de Balboa** ⓳, positioned midway round the bay (Bahía de Panamá). Erected in 1913, it celebrates the 16th-century conquistador's 'discovery' of the Southern Ocean. Opposite, but set back across Avenida Balboa, is the grand neoclassical facade of **Hospital Santo Tomás**, the largest public medical facility in the country. A further 800 meters/yds along the embankment from the Balboa monument, past the swanky yacht club, the pleasant **Parque Urracá** ⓴ is named after the indigenous chief who famously defeated the Spaniards and later escaped from captivity (see page 34). Hemmed in by highrises, this welcome green space comes alive in the late afternoons on weekends as locals congregate to play soccer and socialize. At the time of writing, the park was undergoing renovations.

Jutting out into the sea at the northeastern end of the bay, the artificial peninsula of **Punta Paitilla** ㉑, packed with more than 50 shimmering skyscrapers, constitutes one of Panama City's most emblematic views. Built around 1970, it marked the beginning of Panama City's skyscraper craze. The 40-story high-rises and their luxury apartments, many of which lie empty due to absent or fictitious owners, immediately became one of the city's most exclusive residential areas. It's also a major Jewish neighborhood, with a synagogue and kosher food stores and restaurants in the vicinity. Around the headland, the newer, taller skyscrapers of **Punta Pacífica** house

La Cinta Costera.

⊘ Fact

One of the city's many curiosities sits in a tiny park just off Vía Argentina. A common reference point for El Cangrejo, 'La Cabeza de Einstein' (Einstein's Head) is just that – a huge sculpture of Albert's head protruding from a lawn amid the traffic. Commissioned by the local Jewish community organization, it was crafted in 1968 by celebrated Panamanian sculptor Carlos Arboleda, and bears a marvelous likeness to the great scientist.

Panamá Viejo ruins set against modern skyscrapers.

yet more opulent ocean-view residences, with the sail-shaped 70-story JW Marriot Panama (formerly the Trump Tower) easily the most distinctive. Both exclusive enclaves form part of the broader district of San Francisco, which is also gradually falling prey to the country's skyscraper addiction and houses some of the city's finest dining options.

The area has two main landmarks of interest of visitors, both along Avenida Belisario Porras. First is **Parque Recreativo Omar Torrijos** ㉒ (www.parqueomar.org; daily 4am–10pm), generally shortened to Parque Omar. After the Parque Metropolitano, this is the city's second largest green space, though it also hosts the national library. Hundreds of residents take their morning exercise here or laze about on the grass. There's a jogging track, plus basketball and tennis courts, and a lovely outdoor swimming pool, which is packed with families on weekends. A kilometer farther along Avenida Belisario Porras takes you to the **Centro de Convenciones Atlapa** ㉓ (www.

atlapa.gob.pa). Boasting two auditoriums and exhibition space, the city's main convention center hosts a wealth of cultural and business events.

PANAMÁ VIEJO

Eight kilometers northeast of Casco Viejo, along Avenida Cincuentenario, lie the ruins of the original Panama City, **Panamá Viejo** ㉔ (www.patronatopanamaviejo.org), founded by notorious conquistador Pedrarías Dávila in 1519. Despite the surprisingly swampy location, the city prospered as the Pacific terminal of the Spanish Crown's treasure trail, sending silks and spices from the East alongside plundered silver and gold from Peru to Europe via the isthmus. By the early 17th century, it boasted an impressive cathedral, seven convents, numerous churches, a hospital, 200 warehouses, and around 5,000 houses. The city's location on the booty-laden trade route led to the construction of a huge customs house, a treasury, and a mint; these were built in the most heavily fortified area of the Casas Reales (Royal Houses), the symbol of

⊘ BIRDS IN THE BAHÍA DE PANAMÁ

The mudflats and mangroves by Panamá Viejo mark the western boundary of the Bahía de Panamá's RAMSAR site – indicating a wetland of international importance – which is one of five in the country. It's worth taking some binoculars when visiting the ruins since a well-located viewing platform enables you to watch a carpet of waders moving in unison while probing the exposed sand at low tide. Extending some 300km (186 miles) eastward, the wetlands play host to between 1 and 2 million migratory shorebirds annually, including significant populations of Western sandpipers, semi-palmated plovers, and whimbrels, as well as more than 30 other species. September and October are the best months to catch the migrants, which return in more dispersed fashion from March to May. In recent years, the site has been under threat from pollution and deforestation due to agricultural and urban development. The situation got so bad that the area's protected status was suspended for a while in 2012, but following some serious lobbying from environmental pressure groups, it was eventually reinstated in 2013. Even so, its future remains precarious.

the Spanish Crown's might, originally separated from the rest of the city by a moat and wooden palisade.

When the place was sacked by Welsh pirate Henry Morgan in 1671 (see page 36), it was razed to the ground. Though Morgan is generally blamed for the deed, the likely culprit was the Spanish commander, who wanted to make sure that nothing fell into enemy hands. At the time, as many as 10,000 people lived here, though thousands died in the attack. When the settlement was moved to present-day Casco Viejo, which could be better defended, much of the stone went with it.

A Unesco World Heritage Site, the few ruins that remain are largely surrounded by modern suburbs. To make the most of your visit, stop by the visitors' center first, which has a model of the city before it was destroyed, as well as a few exquisitely preserved Pre-Columbian artifacts. Then follow the path along the shoreline and across the road to the Iglesia del Convento de la Concepción, the city's only convent

for women, built in 1597, and the best-preserved building in this sector. Crossing the main road again brings you to the restored Plaza Mayor, overlooked by an imposing bell tower from what was Panama's original cathedral. The view from the top gives you some sense of the city's former grandeur. There is also an onsite craft market to browse.

The white egg-shaped dome visible on the hillside from Panamá Viejo's belltower is the **Baha'í House of Worship** ㉕ (tel: 231 1191; daily 9am–6pm; free). It's the focus of attention for an estimated 60,000 Baha'í followers in Panama and following the opening of nearby San Isidro metro station in 2015, from where there's a shuttle service, it's attracting increasing numbers of tourists. Interested visitors can attend the 10am Sunday service or simply wander through the delightful flower-filled gardens and soak up the splendid vistas across to the Pacific. Note that you will need to be suitably attired to visit; no shorts, flip-flops, or T-shirts.

⊘ Fact

Some of the uninhabited, rainforested Islas de las Perlas (see page 138) have been a favorite location for the *Survivor* reality TV shows over the years. More recently they have been hosting Bear Grylls' survival series, *The Island*.

Bahá'í House of Worship.

⊘ DAY TRIPS FROM PANAMA CITY

Panama's diminutive size and elfin shape means that much of the country is accessible on a day trip. From the comfort of the capital, you can head out in the morning to tramp though jungle, marvel at the Canal, or soak in the sea, but be back in time to dine off damask by candlelight or hit the dance floor in downtown Panama City. Local tour operators offer an array of destinations and activities, from birdwatching and hiking in Parque Nacional Soberanía to visiting indigenous Emberá villages up the Río Chagres. If lolling on the beach seems like the ideal antidote to frenzied city life, then the azure waters of Archipiélago de las Perlas are within easy reach, though some prefer to head west to the Pacific playas round Santa Clara and Coronado. More active pursuits that can be arranged include kayaking, horseback riding, surfing, scuba-diving, or even kite-surfing, in season. The evocative Spanish colonial forts of Portobelo and San Lorenzo on the Caribbean coast also make for intriguing excursions. For Canal enthusiasts, keen to explore every inch of the mighty waterway, it's often worth engaging the services of a taxi driver for the day, which is easily arranged through your accommodations.

ISLAS DE LAS PERLAS

Comprising over 200 tropical islands and cays set in coral-rich crystalline waters only a short hop from Panama City, visiting the Archipiélago de las Perlas (Pearl Islands) is an alluring prospect.

Spread over around 1,700 sq km (656 sq miles), only a handful of the Islas de las Perlas are inhabited; even fewer are set up for tourism, and many remain under-explored. Currently, the attractive Isla Contadora is the only island with a developed tourist infrastructure, though the golden beaches of nearby Isla Saboga and cream-colored sands of Isla Bolaños and Isla Viveros – close to the archipelago's largest land mass, Isla del Rey – are beginning to draw visitors, particularly on good-value day-trips from Panama City (www.sealasperlas.com). If you're not on a budget, consider flying in to the wonderful coral and sand of private Isla San José, only accessible via the exclusive Hacienda del Mar (www. haciendadelmar.net).

Pristine archipelago waters.

BRIEF HISTORY

Little is known about the original indigenous population, who were soon wiped out once news of the islands' prolific black-lipped pearl oysters had reached the ears of the greedy conquistadors. Needing labor to harvest the gems, the Spanish then brought over slaves from Africa – the ancestors of most of the archipelago's current population. Over the next few centuries, the maze of islands provided hideouts for pirates plundering Spanish galleons en route from Peru, often with the help of local bands of *cimarrones* (escaped slaves). Yet the end of Spanish rule did not spell the end of the pearl trade, which thrived until the oyster beds became diseased in the 1930s. Though they have recovered to an extent – pearl fishers still operate from Isla Casaya – there's little chance of anyone bringing up a new gem to rival the archipelago's most famous find, the pear-shaped Peregrina ('pilgrim'). Plucked in the 16th century, it belonged to Spanish and English royalty before ending up with Hollywood legend Elizabeth Taylor – a Valentine's Day gift from husband Richard Burton. Taylor then had the pearl set in a Cartier diamond-encrusted necklace. After her death in 2011, it fetched a record $11 million at auction.

Tourism in the archipelago took off in the 1970s when businessman and diplomat Gabriel Lewis Galindo bought Isla Contadora for a bargain $30,000. By constructing roads and selling off plots to other wealthy Panamanians, he established Panama's first resort island, which soon became a favorite destination for the rich and famous. John Wayne, Elizabeth Taylor, Sofia Loren, and the Kennedys all vacationed here, while the island's most unlikely resident was the deposed Shah of Iran, who took refuge on Contadora for a while after fleeing the 1979 Islamic Revolution. The pulse of this luxury playground was the glorious but now defunct Contadora Hotel & Resort, whose ruins are gradually being reclaimed by the forest at the back of Playa Larga; the hotel's rusting old ferry still lies like a beached whale on the sand. While the wealthy mansion-owners are glad to have the island to themselves again – day-trippers aside – the population of nearby Isla Saboga laments the loss of jobs. These days, a sprinkling of small hotels, B&Bs, and restaurants dot the island, which still hosts the archipelago's only public airstrip, but prices are high as everything has to be imported from the mainland.

ISLA CONTADORA

Contadora has 11 beaches, all very different in character, and the island is small enough that you can explore them all on foot in a day, though golf buggies are on hand for rental. Playa Larga, on the eastern side, provides the longest strand and most sheltered swimming in shallow, warm water. Heading south round the promontory, Playa de las Suecas ('Swedish Women's Beach'), Panama's only public nudist beach, is suitably secluded. It also offers Contadora's best snorkeling, by the headland, where sharks, stingrays, and turtles can often be seen. Continuing west, and skirting the end of the airstrip, brings you to the island's loveliest swathe of soft, sugary sand: Playa Cacique. Backed by lush vegetation, it looks across turquoise waters to Isla Chapera. On the northern side of the island, the charming sheltered cove of Playa Ejecutiva stands out, fringed by manicured grass dotted with shady trees. Farther east, at the northern end of the airstrip, the Point Hotel surveys Playa Galeón, where the ferries arrive and depart, and fishermen can take you to Isla Saboga or farther afield. Away from the shoreline, Contadora's wooded areas provide shelter and food for a surprising array of wildlife, including deer, agoutis, and iguanas. The center of the island is occupied by a small whitewashed church overlooking a soccer field, which comes alive in late afternoon. Only a handful of families are permanently resident on the island, while workers from nearby Isla Saboga commute daily to service the 180 luxury villas, which remain empty for much of the year.

In addition to its fine selection of lovely soft-sand beaches, Contadora provides a sound base for water-based activities (www.coral-dreams.com) elsewhere in the archipelago: snorkeling and diving trips to the corals and crystalline waters of neighboring islands, visits to seabird colonies, and sailing trips – including a glorious multi-day cruise camping out on deserted beaches and cooking over a campfire (www.sailingclubpanama.com). Between July and October, whale-watching tours (www.whalewatchingpanama.com) are a major attraction; over 2,000 humpbacks visit the coastal waters of Panama to breed, so the chances of catching sight of these majestic ocean-faring mammals is high.

ISLA SABOGA

After the slightly surreal atmosphere of Contadora, neighboring Isla Saboga – where there are some accommodations and beach camping – offers a dose of reality. The island's 400 inhabitants populate the main village, Puerto Nuevo, perched on the hilltop above a pink-shell beach. Many villagers commute to Contadora to work; others fish and ferry tourists in their boats or carry out subsistence agriculture. The island's 18th-century hilltop church is a rare trace of Spanish occupation left in the archipelago. Most visitors head across the island to delightful Playa Encanto, where some relatively discreet high-end developments are taking hold at the back of the beach. At low tide, it's an exciting two-hour scramble south over rocks and across coves to the soft salt-and-pepper expanse of the island's premier stretch of sand, Playa Larga. From there, it takes under 30 minutes to hike back down a track to the village.

As elsewhere in Panama, high season in the archipelago coincides with the dry season, but since the islands receive far less rainfall than the mainland it's worth considering a visit at other times, when prices are lower and beaches less crowded. Daily flights are available from Air Panama (www.airpanama.com), while daily ferry crossings by Sea Las Perlas (www.sealasperlas.com) leave from the Causeway.

Isla Contadora.

Río Chagres, Gamboa.

THE CANAL AND CENTRAL CARIBBEAN COAST

The majestic Panama Canal scythes through wildlife-rich tropical forests before spilling into the Caribbean, a magnet for historians, nature-lovers, and adventure enthusiasts.

Running 77km (48 miles) across the isthmus between the Pacific and Atlantic oceans, straddling the provinces of Panama and Colón, the Panama Canal is a gargantuan engineering feat and a triumph of human endeavor and sacrifice – a truly awe-inspiring sight and justifiably the country's top tourist attraction. What's more, it can easily be explored on an excursion from Panama City. Uniquely, it carves its way through pristine rainforest, and across a vast artificial lake. The four national parks of Soberanía, Camino de Cruces, Chagres, and Portobelo, formed in order to protect the Canal's watershed, all offer the opportunity to walk along the partially cobbled remnants of the historic Camino de Cruces and the Camino Real. Of the four, Parque Nacional Soberanía is the most accessible, containing some excellent hikes and opportunities for birdwatching in tropical rainforest, while Isla Barro Colorado – plum in the middle of Canal – is home to the world-renowned Smithsonian Institute. Both support an exceptional degree of biodiversity and are easy day-trips from the capital. Scattered round the fringes of Lago Gatún and along the banks of the Río Chagres are various Emberá communities which welcome visitors.

The Canal reaches the Atlantic at Colón, historically Panama's second city, synonymous with poverty and crime in the minds of many Panamanians, yet compelling and rich in history, with a strong Afro-Antillean and Afro-Colonial heritage. To the west, along what is known as the Costa Abajo, the formidable remains of the Fuerte San Lorenzo are the country's most impressive colonial ruins, still guarding the mouth of the Río Chagres amid untouched tropical rainforest. To the northeast lies the Costa Arriba, an isolated region of rich coral reefs and laidback fishing villages, much of

Main attractions

The Panama Canal
Esclusas de Miraflores
Parque Nacional
   Soberanía
Lago Gatún
Esclusas de Agua Clara
Fuerte San Lorenzo
Portobelo

Map on page 142

Purple gallinule.

which is nominally protected by Parque Nacional Portobelo, set around the ruins and beautiful natural harbor of the old Spanish port of Portobelo.

Marking the narrowest point across the isthmus, the history of this section of Panama is inevitably linked to its function as a link between two oceans. Though a network of trails made by the indigenous population predated the arrival of the conquistadors, the first jungle 'highway' to be written about is the Camino Real (see page 36), the colonial mule train from Panamá Viejo to the Caribbean coast, constructed around 1519. Nombre de Dios was the initial shipment point, where galleons laden with loot headed off to Spain; the main port was then relocated west to

the better defended Portobelo in 1597, whose fortifications are still visible today. The transisthmian routes taken some 250 years later by the Panamanian Railroad, and then, more recently, by the Canal, run roughly parallel and west of the Camino Real. This time the Caribbean port and rail terminal was Colón, whose development has been sorely neglected by successive governments over many decades since those times of prosperity and commerce.

THE PACIFIC CANAL ENTRANCE

Completed in 1962, the impressive **Puente de los Américas ❶**, suspended high above the sea, marks the Pacific entrance to the Canal. Down

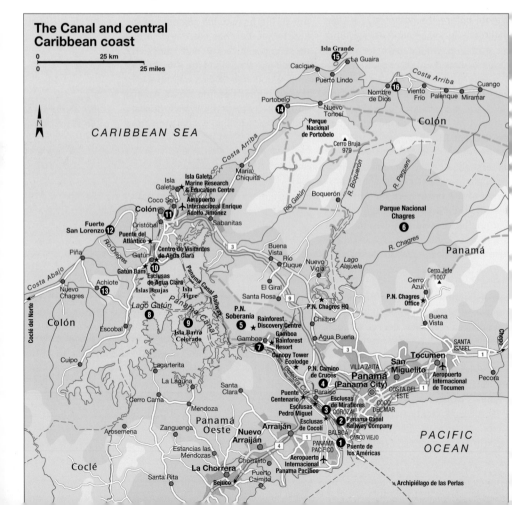

The Canal and central Caribbean coast

below, stacks of shipping containers and serried ranks of cranes indicate the port of **Balboa**. Alongside, Avenida Omar Torrijos runs northwest out of Panama City, broadly parallel to the great waterway, ending some 30km (19 miles) later in somnolent Gamboa, a small Canal-era town on the shores of Lago Gatún. On the way lie some of the Canal's key sights and access roads to the rainforested national parks that aim to protect its watershed.

Shortly after the port, on the left-hand side is the **Corozal terminal** of the **Panama Canal Railway Company** ❷ (tel: 317 6070; www.panarail. com; Mon–Fri 7.15am departure). The original Panama Railroad, built in the 1850s during the California Gold Rush, transported more than $700 million in gold before the completion of the Union Pacific Railroad across the US in 1869 made it obsolete, forcing it into bankruptcy. Following a short revival during the Canal's construction, the railroad fell into disrepair until 1998 when the government agreed to privatize it. Though the railroad company predominantly ferries freight to and from the Atlantic and Pacific container ports, it offers a weekday commuter passenger service to Colón that is also very popular with tourists. A supremely comfortable way to enjoy the Canal, the one-hour traverse of the isthmus serves up old-world elegance in wood-paneled, carpeted railcars with large windows.

Just over 1km (0.6 mile) farther along the road, on the right, is the entrance to the **Ciudad de Saber** (City of Knowledge; www.ciudaddelsaber. org). Founded in 1995 on the site of Fort Clayton and one of around 15 US military establishments in the former Canal Zone, the enclave is a center of academic, scientific, technological, and business innovation. It currently hosts several North American University outreach programs as well as UN bodies and innovative enterprises. It also has various places of interest to visitors, namely the newly restored 1935 Zonian movie theater, which has been transformed into a smart Spanish Colonial Revival-style theater, the Ateneo, and a

Panama Canal Railway carriage.

⊙ BUILDING THE PANAMA RAILROAD

Overshadowed by the building of the Canal, the Panama Railroad was the world's first transcontinental railroad and a phenomenal engineering feat in its own right. Anticipating the gold rush, wealthy US businessman William Aspinwall constructed a 76km (47-mile) track linking the Atlantic and Pacific oceans to facilitate trade between the East Coast and rapidly developing California. At a total cost of almost $8 million, it became the most expensive track per kilometer in the world, though the first-class transit fee, $25 in gold, made it one of the most profitable.

The human costs were brutal. During the five years of construction an estimated 6,000–10,000 workers died, though, appallingly, records were only kept of the minority white employees. The high death toll enabled the railroad company to sustain a grisly side-business in pickling bodies in barrels to sell to hospitals worldwide. Most of the laborers were Caribbean, but others migrated from as far as Ireland, India, China, and Malaysia. Despite the constant influx of workers, construction occasionally stalled since at any one time only a third of the men – who spent long days up to their waists in swamp, attacked by mosquitoes and disease – were fit enough to wield a shovel.

Few recalled the dreadful human cost when the inaugural transit was made in 1855 amid much pomp and champagne. Today, the journey remains one of the most scenic and enjoyable in Panama.

⊙ Eat

Location, location, location – Atlantic & Pacific Co (Miraflores Locks; tel: 232 3120; atlanticpacificrestaurant.com) offer a unique opportunity to dine within touching distance of vast Panamax vessels as they transit through the locks. The lunchtime buffet can be crowded, but bag a table on the terrace at night for some à-la-carte organic neo-Panamanian fare when the ships are illuminated like Christmas decorations.

pleasant sport and recreation area, run by the Kiwanis and open to all (www.ciudaddeportivakiwanis.org). Of historical interest is the **Centro Interpretativo**, full of Canal Zone history, displayed in the restored house that was formerly occupied by the US military commander in chief, though they have yet to provide any information in English. If you're visiting Panama in January, it's worth noting that the Ciudad de Saber is also the venue for the annual jazz festival (www.panamajazzfestival.com).

MIRAFLORES LOCKS AND BEYOND

Roughly opposite the Ciudad de Saber, and a mere 15 minutes from downtown Panama City, a short access road leads to one of the must-see sights on any Canal tour: the **Esclusas de Miraflores** ❸ (Miraflores Locks). The four-story Centro de Visitantes de Miraflores (tel: 276 8617; www.pancanal.com; daily 8am–5pm) has a couple of observation decks overlooking the famous locks, as they raise or lower vessels 16.5 meters (54ft) between sea level and the artificial Lago Miraflores in two stages. These provide the best vantage points for observing the Canal action close up. Optimum viewing times for vessels transiting are before 9.30am, when ships are usually entering the Canal from the Pacific, and after 3pm, when they are exiting. It's advisable to get there early in high season as the viewing platforms can get very crowded.

The building also contains an informative introductory museum on the Canal's history and workings, which serves to promote the Autoridad del Canal de Panamá (ACP) – particularly through the 3D film (shown in Spanish and English at different times) – as much as to inform you about the Canal. Both the French and US construction efforts are squeezed into the first-floor exhibition – more in-depth coverage is provided in the Canal museum in Casco Viejo (see page 122). Against a vast montage of historical photos and a soundtrack of blasting dynamite, the bare bones of the enterprise are covered through impressive scale models and bilingual texts. Sound effects continue on the second floor as the focus shifts to the biodiversity of the Canal's catchment area, while on the floor above, the spotlight turns to engineering. Highlights include a virtual high-speed transit of the Canal, complete with illuminated 3D topographic map, and the chance to experience life inside a lock culvert (thankfully without the water). Buses to Miraflores Locks leave Albrook Bus Terminal at regular intervals and taxis are relatively inexpensive.

Southwest of Miraflores, action in the new, larger, three-chambered **Esclusas de Cocolí** – inaugurated in 2016 as part of the Canal expansion program – is only visible from the road that skirts the western flank of the new channel, though only four to eight ocean-faring giants currently pass through per day. Just over 3km (2 miles) beyond Miraflores lie the

⊙ THE ÁREAS REVERTIDAS

The transfer of the Canal to the Panamanian government was accompanied by the gradual handover of the adjacent Canal Zone land and properties – known as the Áreas Revertidas. These included everything from bowling alleys to gas stations, air bases to hospitals, schools to residential townships. In 1993, a government authority was established to oversee the management of the newly acquired assets for the 'maximum benefit of the whole country.' The reality has inevitably been very different: many un- or under-used buildings fell into dereliction; informal settlements have spread; and illegal land use has flourished. Land lots and properties are periodically auctioned off, raising millions of dollars for the government, used more often to pay off their debts rather than finance the social development projects that were originally promised. Corruption and controversy over sales are never far from the surface, resulting in periodic protests, most notably in Colón in 2012 and 2013, as the government of the day threatened to sell off land in the Zona Libre (Free Trade Zone), then later in a residential neighborhood, where many descendants of the Canal's black workforce live today.

smaller **Esclusas de Pedro Miguel**. These are closed to the public, but it's possible to park in the small pull-off and peer through the chainlink fence to watch the ships maneuvering, saving yourself the Miraflores entry fee in the process.

Beyond the Miraflores Locks the Canal narrows into the infamous **Corte de Culebra** (formerly the Gaillard Cut), where more than two-thirds of all the original Canal excavation occurred. A graveyard for many workers, its 13km (8-mile) stretch posed the most persistent technical headache for engineers, and severe landslides continued long after the eventual opening of the Canal.

A little beyond the community of Paraíso, the Canal's former dredging headquarters, rows of small white crosses mark the **French Cemetery**, which sits on the continental divide, a poignant reminder of the doomed French attempt to build a canal in the 1880s (see page 99). The road then climbs, passing a turn-off to the elegant, cable-stayed **Puente Centenario**, opened in 2004 to celebrate Panama's hundred years of independence. After 3km (2 miles) of dense rainforest the road forks: to the right it cuts through Parque Nacional Soberanía to the Transístmica and the new expressway, both of which link Panama City with Colón, while to the left it crests the continental divide, where there is a municipal park-cum-zoo, with some sad-looking cages, before the road winds its way to Gamboa.

A TRIO OF NATIONAL PARKS

Two national parks border the eastern edge of the Canal; a third, the Parque Nacional Chagres, is set farther inland.

CAMINO DE CRUCES

A couple of bends after the Pedro Miguel Locks, the Carretera Chivo Chivo leads 2km (1.2 miles) to the office of the **Parque Nacional Camino de Cruces** ❹ (tel: 500 0839). Despite bearing the name of the conquistadors' famous trade route across the isthmus (itself named after Cruces, a settlement now submerged under Lago Gatún), this small park is often

Superbly sited Fuerte San Lorenzo.

TRANSITING THE CANAL

To fully appreciate both the engineering brilliance and majestic beauty of the Panama Canal, you need to experience it on a boat.

You may feel you've 'done' the Canal after a morning gazing at ships maneuvering through the locks from the observation deck at the Miraflores Visitor Center. But it's hard to beat the excitement of gliding under the Puente de los Américas, and approaching the mighty miter lock gates head-on, as they open and empty before you. Unless you're on a cruise ship, or have wangled a job as a line-handler on a yacht, the only way to go through the Canal is on a full or partial transit (crossing), organized from Panama City.

Most transits are northbound, starting from the tip of the Amador Causeway in Panama City and ending in Gamboa (partial transit) or Colón (full transit). Progressing up the side of the causeway, you get a close-up of the multicolored roof of the Frank Gehry BioMuseo, before cutting under the bridge with a tingle of anticipation as you enter the Canal proper. Skirting looming giant cranes and stacked containers of the port of Balboa, with frigate birds swirling overhead, the boat arrives at Miraflores. Once inside the first lock chamber, with the gates shut behind, you can appreciate the technical genius and simplicity of work that is over 100 years old as the upper valves open to allow the chamber to flood, using gravity alone. The whole process – filling enough water to fill 44 Olympic swimming pools – is over in a mere eight minutes. Once the water has risen to the level of the second lock

En route to Pedro Miguel Locks.

chamber, the giant gates ahead are opened, and the boat slides into the new chamber, where the same happens again. In total, the vessel is raised around 16.5 meters (54ft) (depending on the Pacific tide) to the level of Lago Miraflores, a small artificial body of water that leads to the single set of locks at Pedro Miguel. Here the boat ascends another 9 meters (30ft) before entering the notorious Corte de Culebra (also Gaillard Cut); so named after its serpentine shape, it was more aptly dubbed 'Hell's Gorge' by the laborers. Many lost their lives here. After sweeping under the glorious Puente Centenario, the narrow channel opens out into Lago Gatún, where the boat pulls into Gamboa.

The full transit from Panama City to Colón (from where you are bussed back to the capital) takes in the most breathtaking tropical scenery, crossing Lago Gatún and weaving among tiny forested islands. You'll glide past a silent stream of giant ships before passing through the enormous three-chambered Gatún Locks. Here, the process is repeated in reverse, as the boat is lowered back to sea level and released into the Atlantic.

BOOKING YOUR TOUR

Though countless tour operators sell Canal transits, only two companies actually operate them: Canal & Bay Tours (www.canalandbaytours.com) and Panama Marine Tours (www. pmatours.net), with the latter the preferred option for foreign tourists. Both can be booked online. The cost includes transfer between the port and the boat (and maybe a hotel pick-up), bilingual guided commentary, soft drinks, and a buffet meal. In the tourist season (Dec–Apr) there are almost daily excursions and boats can be very crowded – especially on the open viewing deck; out of season there are fewer options, with a full crossing often only once a month. Departure times are only confirmed the day before since the tourist boats have to fit round the timetables of the mega-fee-paying cargo vessels. Generally, though, northbound trips leave early morning, whereas the transfer bus for the southbound ones departs a couple of hours later. Although completing a full transit might hold a certain cachet, the advertised 8–9 hours can often be a lot longer if you get caught up in one of the frequent log-jams at Gatún Locks. A partial transit, lasting 4–5 hours, provides enough excitement and interest for most people.

overlooked, with neighboring Soberanía attracting far more visitors. And while it is hard to escape the dull sound of traffic along the Autopista Panamá–Colón highway that cuts cross the corner of the reserve, and as recently as 2018 a large chunk of forest was cut down without due process, it is a prime location for spotting sloths and a recently revamped 3km (2-mile) circuit leads to a mirador with good views across the Canal.

SOBERANÍA

Next door, a mere 30-minute drive away from the skyscrapers of Panama City, **Parque Nacional Soberanía** ⑤ (tel: 232 4192; daily 8.30am–4.30pm) is one of the country's most visited national parks and well worth exploring. Stretching north and west from the park office, it hugs the Canal and encircles Gamboa, covering more than 190 sq km (73 sq miles). It encompasses a stretch of the majestic Río Chagres, the Canal's lifeblood, which you can explore by boat or kayak; there are also several well-maintained trails either side of Gamboa, including a stretch of the historic Camino de Cruces and a world-renowned birding hot spot, the Camino del Oleoducto. The trails are not particularly close to each other or the park office, however, making the logistics difficult unless you have your own transportation, or you go as part of a tour. Several Panama City agencies offer hikes to the Camino de Cruces and the Sendero del Oleoducto, but you can hire a ranger from the park office as a guide if one is available – a much cheaper option, and one which helps supplement their low income. However, they are unlikely to speak any English.

Although most of Soberanía's trails are easy and safe enough to walk on your own, you're strongly advised to hike the Camino de Cruces on a tour or with a guide as the path is overgrown and difficult to follow in places. The route begins 6km (4 miles) up the road that forks right at the park office, ending up at the shores of the Río Chagres, site of the barely distinguishable remains of the Ruinas de Venta de

⊘ Tip

To avoid returning the same route on the Camino de Cruces in Parque Nacional Soberanía, you can hike half of it in a northwesterly direction, then turn off down the Sendero de la Plantación to join the Gamboa road, where you can catch a bus back to Panama City.

Enjoying the view from Rainforest Discovery Center's canopy tower.

⊘ CANOPY TOWER ECOLODGE

The unique Canopy Tower birdwatching lodge occupies a former US military radar tower on a hilltop surrounded by lush rainforest. It offers multi-day packages, including guided walks accompanied by a top-notch bilingual specialist guide, and excursions for non-birders too. Half-day visits, which have to be organized in advance, also include a guided walk, on which you're likely to spot manakins, antbirds, tinamous, sloths, coatis, and agoutis. You get a meal, and, best of all, time on the truly special canopy-level observation deck, which affords surreal panoramic views: watching monkeys feeding in the branches, with the city's skyscrapers in the distance, or giant container vessels peering above the trees. The deck is equipped with a telescope and sun loungers, which allow you to indulge in top armchair birdwatching.

Cruces, which served as a resting post for weary, booty-laden mules and conquistadors. Independent travelers can pick up a map and pay the park fees at the office or at the entry barrier to the Camino del Oleoducto (Pipeline Road), if there is someone there when you arrive.

You don't have to venture that far to get a flavor of the history – after a 10-minute hike, your guide should be able to point out a restored section of the original 16th-century paving stones. A much easier prospect is the 5km (3-mile) **Sendero de la Plantación** (Plantation Trail) along the gravelly remnants of a paved thoroughfare that once led to the largest private agricultural venture in the old Canal Zone, harvesting rubber, coffee, and cocoa, which you can still occasionally spot growing wild amid the rainforest. The entrance to the trail, where there is a small parking lot, is about 20km (12 miles) from Panama City and 6km (4 miles) before Gamboa. Adjacent is the entrance to Semaphore Hill, which snakes steeply up to the unusual

Exploring Lago Gatún by boat.

Canopy Tower Ecolodge (tel: 264 5720; www.canopytower.com), a former US military installation that became a world-famous birding lodge.

By far the most tramped trail in Soberanía is the unpromising-sounding **Camino del Oleoducto** (Pipeline Road), so named because it was originally built to service an oil pipeline constructed across the isthmus by the US in World War II. The pipeline was never used but the 17.5km (11-mile) dirt-road service track, which lies 1km (0.6 mile) beyond Gamboa, draws birding enthusiasts from around the world. Though it's visually unremarkable – this is no wilderness trail – the likely wildlife sightings more than compensate. Even casual nature lovers cannot fail to be impressed by the array of brightly colored birds; you'll see a great deal more if you go with a good birding guide. Two kilometers (1.2 miles) along the trail is the **Rainforest Discovery Center** (tel: 6450 6630; www.pipelineroad.org; daily 6am–4pm), which boasts an impressive canopy observation tower that has multilevel

viewing platforms. There is also a series of short trails and an interpretive center, whose main draw is the observation deck, where bird feeders attract scores of dazzling humming-birds. The entrance fee is substantial, however, especially if you arrive during prime birding time (6–10am), though it's worth the outlay if you are a keen bird-watcher. Profits go toward environmental education, research, and conservation projects.

PARQUE NACIONAL CHAGRES

The third park that protects the Panama Canal Basin, and encompasses large tracts of Colón and Panama provinces, is **Parque Nacional Chagres ⑥**. It stretches from the northern rain-soaked mountains overlooking the Caribbean to the park's highest peak, Cerro Jefe, in the south. The tropical vegetation harbors large but elusive populations of tapirs, endemic salamanders, and an abundance of bird-life, including harpy eagles and the rare Tacarcuna bush tanager, and is laced with waterfalls and rivers rich in fish as well as otters, caimans, and crocodiles. Hikers are also drawn to the area, particularly by the prospect of following in the steps of the conquistadors along the historic Camino Real, which slices across the western edge of the reserve, skirting the eastern shores of Lago Alajuela. A couple of tour companies offer multi-day hikes along the whole trail.

At the heart of the park, the powerful Río Chagres and its tributaries – home to several Emberá and Wounaan villages that accept visitors – carve their way through rugged terrain. They spill into the elongated Lago Alajuela reservoir at the park's southwest corner, built to help regulate the water level in Lago Gatún farther downriver.

Providing most of Panama's water, as well as electricity through hydro-electric power, the Río Chagres is of vital importance to the country, and is the park's main artery. In order to protect the river and its catchment area, the national park was formed in 1985, its 1,296 sq km (500 sq miles) making it one of the country's largest reserves.

Most tourist activities take place along the Río Chagres, be it whitewater rafting the cascading torrents of the upper river, or more leisurely kayaking along the slower, lower stretches, both of which are generally organized as day-trips from Panama City. An equally enjoyable way to experience the park is by visiting one of the numerous Emberá communities sprinkled along the banks of the Chagres and its tributaries (see page 151). The Emberá, together with the closely related Wounaan, have been relocating from the Darién since the late 1960s. Given their traditional means of livelihood – semi-nomadic subsistence agriculture and hunting – are now largely denied to them thanks to the restrictions of living within a national park, they are being encouraged to make a living from eco-tourism. However, there are important caveats. Publicity brochures glibly talk

(see page 151)

> **⊙ Fact**
>
> The Río Chagres supplies 40 percent of the water necessary for the Canal to function and 80 percent of the country's domestic water supply.

Rainforest flanks the Río Chagres.

⊙ Fact

Following the damming of the Río Chagres in 1910, the waters took three years to rise to form Lago Gatún. At the time it was the largest artificial lake in the world, covering 425 sq km (164 sq miles) – roughly the size of Barbados.

Emberá craft work.

about the Emberá 'living much as their ancestors did centuries ago' although you don't need to look farther than the use of outboard motors, cell phones, and Spanish – not to mention the jeans and T-shirts often donned once the tourists have evaporated – to see that the Emberá are undergoing radical change. Staying overnight, or preferably for several nights, affords a better opportunity to interact with villagers and learn more about the challenges of their changing lifestyles, though some communities do not accommodate overnight stays. A longer visit also allows travelers to venture deeper into the forest. It is certainly worth timing your visit to avoid a cruise ship tour, as the village is inevitably overrun with too many tourists, which makes for an uncomfortable and unsatisfying visit.

That said, if you are lucky, day-tours can still offer a fascinating partial snapshot of traditional Emberá life and culture, and there are obvious benefits to communities: income that will afford them greater self-determination, renewed cultural pride, and a revival

of ancestral skills and traditions. For a less touristy scene, a visit to an Emberá community in the Darién (with far fewer and smaller tour groups) generally allows visitors to learn about village life without disrupting it.

GAMBOA AND LAGO GATÚN

Sleepy, isolated **Gamboa** ❼ – its only road access via an old single-track bridge shared with the Panama Railroad – was built in 1911 as a settlement for around 700 'silver roll' employees and their families (see page 48). Its population did not increase significantly until the Canal's dredging division relocated here from Paraíso in 1936. By 1942, Gamboa's residents exceeded 3,800, much more than the current population, and the community boasted a movie theater and golf course. But once the Panama Canal Authority started to transfer operations to Panama City following the 1977 treaties, services began to close and the town dwindled, although the golf course has recently been upgraded (www.summitgolfpanama.com).

Surrounded by the luxuriant vegetation of Parque Nacional Soberanía and bordered by the impressive Río Chagres and Lago Gatún, into which the river spills, Gamboa is the portal to many attractions on and off the water, most of which are organized as day-trips from Panama City. For nature lovers and birding enthusiasts in particular, Gamboa provides access to the legendary Camino del Oleoducto and the adjacent Rainforest Discovery Center, as well as serving as the arrival point for partial Canal transits. The town is easily accessed by frequent buses from the main bus terminal in Panama City, and though some activities need organizing in advance, others can be arranged on the spot. There's little to do in Gamboa itself but soak up the tranquil yesteryear feel: taking in the attractive (and often empty) Canal-era architecture; indulging in a little birdwatching around the wooded fringes; and strolling along the Chagres, looking out for iguanas and turtles sunning themselves along the riverbanks. The main center of activity is the sprawling Gamboa Rainforest Resort (www.gamboaresort.com), which occupies an enviable location on a bluff overlooking the river, and is really the only place to grab a drink and a bite to eat.

Gamboa also marks the point where the Canal opens out into **Lago Gatún** ❽. This vast reservoir comprises more than 40 percent of the waterway's total length – with the ships following the original course of the Río Chagres, where the lake is at its deepest. The undulating topography ensured that after the river was dammed and this impressive reservoir developed into a place of great beauty, with dozens of peninsulas and tree-topped islands, and a myriad of inlets easing their tentacles into the lush rainforest, all of which are best explored by boat. A popular route is round islas Tigre and Brujas. You can't land on the 17 or so islands, but with a good pair of binoculars you can usually observe the islands' monkeys cavorting in the trees while marveling at the constant procession of container ships. Panama

⊘ VISITING AN EMBERÁ COMMUNITY

Although villages vary in setting and character, excursions to Emberá communities are similar. Prices and tour-group sizes vary; even traveling in a small party is no guarantee you won't be cheek by jowl with other tourists once you're in the village, especially during the cruise ship season (Oct–Apr). Morning pickups from Panama City (8am–8.30am) are followed by an hour's bus journey to Lago Alajuela, where life-jacketed tourists fan out toward different villages in motorized dugouts. The boat trip (30–60min, depending on the village location and river water levels) is itself a highlight, gliding through vine-laden forest with raptors wheeling overhead and metallic kingfishers flashing past. At the villages, traditional wood-and-thatch buildings sit on stilts, and you'll be greeted by enthusiastic kids and women who form a dazzling collage of fluorescent sarong-like skirts (uhua) and multicolored bead-and-silver-coin necklaces, their hair often adorned with hibiscus flowers.

Activities generally include a village tour, a talk about the traditional Emberá way of life, and a demonstration of basketry or woodcarving as well as a short walk into the rainforest

to a waterfall, or with a village elder to learn about medicinal plants. A simple lunch precedes traditional dances accompanied by drums, bamboo flutes, and maracas, after which tourists can get their bodies painted with jagua dye, frolic with the kids in the river, and peruse the finely made crafts on display. Unlike the Guna, the Emberá are fairly comfortable being photographed and general shots of the village (though not inside homes) and dances are allowed, though permission should always be sought from individuals. Most tours pile back into the dugouts at 2.30–3pm for the return trip.

It is cheaper and far better to organize a visit directly with the community – several of the communities have their own Facebook page with contact details but you'll still need to call a couple of days in advance to ensure a boat ride. Getting from Panama City to Puerto de Corotú, the departure point for most villages on Lago Alajuela, takes around 90 minutes. Take the Metro Line 1 to the end at San Isidro, then take the bus bound for La Cabima, where a second bus can take you to Puerto Corotú, at the lake. Some communities can arrange transportation for you from the capital.

City tour operators offer water-based excursions on Lago Gatún, as does the tour operator in the Gamboa Rainforest Resort. Unfortunately, some operators can't resist the urge to feed the monkeys, so it's worth enquiring about their policy before signing up. Other wildlife to look out for, which can easily be spotted while on a fishing trip, includes crocodiles and caimans slithering in the muddy shallows, as well as sloths and snakes entwined round branches. The lake is famous for its prolific peacock bass, and fishermen hanging out at the public dock, before the bridge that leads into Gamboa, will happily take you out for a few hours angling.

Following the lake shore, 1km (0.6 mile) beyond the park in Gamboa you come to the jetty for the boat to **Isla Barro Colorado** . Probably the earth's most studied patch of rainforest, it hosts the Smithsonian Tropical Research Institute field station (tel: 212 8951; www.stri.org). As well as attracting a constant stream of biologists from all over the world to pore over the 16 sq km (6 sq miles) of flora and fauna, Barro Colorado can also be visited on a day-long tour. The island, whose name derives from the dominant reddish clay (*barro* being Spanish for clay), makes for an informative outing if you want to gain a deeper understanding of the forest than just how to spot monkeys in the trees.

Tours can be booked online. After a short talk, you set out on a guided walk, during which you'll learn about some of the island's 1,300-plus plant species and around 110 species of mammal, more than half of which are bats. A favorite route leads to the 'Big Tree,' an enormous 500-year-old kapok with a 25-meter (82ft) diameter, laden with epiphytes. Although the small island is home to both ocelots and pumas, you're unlikely to see more than their prints in the mud. Much more visible are the vast colonies of leafcutter ants, estimated to chew 15 percent of all leaves produced in the forest to feed the fungus they eat in their subterranean nests. After lunch in the cafeteria, you can watch for wildlife in the immediate vicinity of the research station, where you're likely to see howler monkeys, but you are not allowed back in the forest unaccompanied.

THE ATLANTIC CANAL ENTRANCE

Marking the original Atlantic (Caribbean) entrance to the Canal are the **Esclusas de Gatún**, the largest and most impressive of the original locks. Comprising three sets of double lock chambers, they stretch for 3km (2 miles) – if you include the approach walls – which made them the greatest concrete structure in the world until the Hoover Dam's completion in 1930. Unfortunately, the viewing platform has now been closed, but you can see them in the distance when crossing the Canal using the new **Puente del Atlántico**. A couple of kilometers west of the locks is **Gatún Dam**. Despite

Howler monkey.

being the longest in the world when it was built, at 2.3km (1.5 miles), and a brilliant technical achievement, the earthen Gatún Dam is not as visually impressive as it should be, though the curved concrete spillway at its center can be an awe-inspiring sight when the floodgates are opened following exceptionally heavy rains. To watch ships negotiating locks on the Atlantic side, you have to swing by the new mammoth three-chambered **Esclusas de Agua Clara ⑩**, which lie to the east of the original locks and cater to the Neopanamax ships. The locks are overlooked by the **Centro de Visitantes de Agua Clara** (tel: 443 5727; www.pancanal.com; daily 8am–4pm), on a headland, which offers a totally different perspective on Canal proceedings. Note the more modern sliding lock gates (as opposed to the old swing miter gates) and the use of a tugboat, which has replaced stabilizing mules. Beyond the locks themselves, you can see the vast water recycling tanks, which aim to retain 60 percent of the water that would otherwise be lost to the ocean

each transit. It's worth bringing your binoculars as the elevated observation platform offers the best views you can get of Lago Gatún. There's no museum as in Miraflores, but the steep entry fee includes an introductory video (in English or Spanish) on the canal expansion. There's also a restaurant and some shady picnic spots.

COLÓN

Located at the Atlantic entrance to the Panama Canal, with a population of around 42,000, **Colón ⑪** makes it into few holiday brochures; for most Panamanians its name is a byword for poverty, violence, and urban decay. Most foreign visitors come here solely to shop at the Zona Libre (Duty Free Zone), a walled enclave on the eastern edge of the city that is world's second-largest duty-free zone after Hong Kong. Yet, vestiges of the city's former grandeur do remain, and a few historic buildings have recently been renovated alongside some 'beautification' of a couple of parks. It's worth a quick drive round (by taxi, for safety reasons)

The Panama Railroad.

⊘ PANAMA'S NEGLECTED SECOND CITY

The Panama Railroad brought many immigrants and a degree of prosperity to Colón despite the constant threat of yellow fever, malaria, and cholera. Since then, wealth – via Canal construction, a spell as a fashionable cruise-ship destination in the 1950s, and the success of the Free Zone, founded in 1949 – has come and gone, and Panama's Atlantic port predominantly remains a slum city. In the face of extreme poverty and soaring unemployment levels, it is little surprise that crime rates are high, particularly drug and arms trafficking. Many residents see the apparent lack of concern and failure by successive predominantly white and *mestizo* governments to develop the predominantly Afro-Panamanian city as a continuation of the racial discrimination that ran throughout the Canal Zone era. A major plan to renovate the city center that was launched in 2015 has only recently started to materialize. So far, though, there's been little beyond some superficial landscaping and the demolition of a few blocks, forcing residents to move outside the city center. Fears that the area will eventually be gentrified for the elite – as has happened with Casco Viejo in Panama City – at the expense of the local populace have fueled dissatisfaction, which has been compounded by the continued inaction on the provision of basic services such as water, sanitation, and protection from high levels of crime.

before heading out to several tourist destinations within striking distance.

BRIEF HISTORY

As work began on the construction of the Panama Railroad in 1850, the settlement now known as Colón began to mushroom on a low-lying lump of coral known as Isla Manzanillo. Surrounded by mosquito- and sandfly-infested mangrove swamps and lacking a source of fresh water, the location was so unfavorable that the workers initially lived on a brig anchored in the bay rather than on the island itself. American historian H.H. Bancroft, on his arrival in 1851, summed up the general view: 'The very ground on which one trod was pregnant with disease, and death was distilled in every breath of air.' Nonetheless the Americans in charge of the railroad bewilderingly insisted on establishing the Atlantic terminal here, and in 1852 unilaterally named the place Aspinwall after one of the railroad's owners, a name which the New Grenadan (present-day Colombia and Panama) authorities

refused to accept, insisting that it be called Colón, after Cristóbal Colón (Christopher Columbus).

COLÓN SIGHTS

At the entrance to the center of Colón is the Atlantic terminal of the **Panama Railroad**, where the tourist train from Panama City pulls in. Opposite the train station is the rather dull **Aspinwall monument**, honoring the American founders of the city and railroad owners. A left turn takes you past the bus terminal, behind which lies the port enclave of Cristóbal, then north up dilapidated Avenida del Frente until you reach the **New Washington Hotel** (www.newwashingtonhotel.com), which overlooks the Caribbean. Initially constructed in wood around 1870 to house railroad engineers, the current concrete and cement-block edifice dates from 1913. Like everything else in Colón, it has seen better days, but it's worth stopping to have a peek at the entrance hall, with its chandeliers and ornate double marble staircase – poignant reminders of Colón's former

Kayaking on the Río Chagres.

splendor. To the right of the hotel as you face the sea is the dark-stone **Episcopalian Christ Church by the Sea**, the first Protestant church in Central America, built in the mid-1860s for the railroad workers; it has some delightful stained-glass windows. Four blocks east along the seafront, a statue of **Christ the Redeemer**, arms outstretched, faces down Avenida Central, the city's main street, which is lined with monuments and is showing signs of some rehabilitation work. The **Catedral de la Inmaculada Concepción de María** (daily 6am–6pm; free), built between 1929 and 1934 with high, neo-Gothic arches and some attractive stained-glass windows, can be found three blocks west of Avenida Central on Calle 5. A few blocks east of Avenida Central, at the northeastern end of the peninsula is the only substantial sign of recent redevelopment work: a new park and some sports amenities (though no public washrooms). Along the waterfront of the Bahía de Manzanillo, on the eastern side of the peninsula, Colón 2000, the cruise-ship terminal, holds a collection of stores and restaurants primarily catering to cruise-ship passengers.

FUERTE SAN LORENZO AND THE COSTA ABAJO

After the Canal, the second most popular destinations on the central Caribbean coast are the Spanish colonial forts of San Lorenzo and Portobelo, which together were declared a World Heritage Site in 1980. Twenty-five kilometers (15 miles) west by road from Colón, across the new Puente de los Américas, takes you to **Fuerte San Lorenzo** ⑫ (daily 8am–4pm). Perched high on a rocky promontory, standing guard over the mouth of the Río Chagres, these relatively well-preserved ruins bear witness to its importance during Spanish colonial times. Its spectacular location, commanding views of both the brooding river and the glistening

Caribbean, coupled with its isolation and forest surroundings, make it a far more evocative place than the more accessible and more visited Portobelo, and if you avoid the cruise ship tour groups – especially midweek in the rainy season, you can have the place to yourself.

The fort is set within the 120-sq-km (46 sq mile) **Área Protegida San Lorenzo**, amid a swathe of secondary forest and swampland, which provide excellent birdwatching. Some 435 species have been recorded, some of which can be spotted along the short trails in the forest off the access road to the fort.

Construction of the original sea-level earth-and-wood fort began in 1595 to protect loot-laden Spanish boats sailing down the Chagres to Portobelo from attack by foreign vessels. Though Francis Drake failed to take the place in 1596, it fell to one of Henry Morgan's privateers in 1670, enabling Morgan and his band to pass unhindered up the river and destroy Panama City (see page 36). The fort was

Brown-throated sloth.

rebuilt in coral stone in the 1680s in its present cliff-top location, where it was eventually ruined in 1740 by the British. The attack was apparently in revenge for the Spanish coastguards' wounding of a British merchant captain named Robert Jenkins, in what became known rather farcically as the War of Jenkins' Ear. Although San Lorenzo was rebuilt and further strengthened, the fortifications were never really tested again, though they were used as part of the US military defenses in World War II – note the still visible antiaircraft platform next to the tower.

To explore the fort, cross over the drawbridge (not the original one) and continue through the smart, squat stone-and-brick guardhouse, the main entrance to the fort. You emerge onto the esplanade, which once served to collect rainwater that was channeled off into a water tank over the parapet in front of you; today it offers the best view of the fort. The vast grassy area below is the parade ground, containing the ruined troops' and officers' quarters. Taking the ramp down, follow the

wall along to the ruins of the powder magazine and the tower built into the side of the hill, now scarcely more than a deep hole filled with garbage. Though the adjacent wall parapets and cannons have now gone, the view is as it always was, and it's easy to picture watchmen anxiously gazing out toward the horizon for enemy ships. Before climbing back up toward the guardhouse, peer inside some of the many remarkably preserved vaults underneath the esplanade, used to store equipment and food and, much later, prisoners. Crossing the drawbridge once more you'll find yourself on the exterior platform, with the one surviving sentry box to the left. Here the parapet is still intact, as are the nine cannons pointing out toward the putative enemy.

Though a few old *diablo rojo* buses grind this far along the Costa Abajo from Colón, few tourists make it as far as the hamlet of **Achiote** ⓭. Strung out along the road and backing onto a flower-filled, forested hillside and surrounded by bucolic countryside, it is home to a community ecotourism project based in the no-frills **Centro El Tucán** (tel: 6626 9790 or 6091 3055; www.centroeltucan.org) which provides basic dorm accommodations with use of a kitchen, though there is a *fonda* in the village. The place is primarily frequented by avid birdwatchers, though in the harvesting season (Dec–Jan) a tour of a local coffee farm and a boat trip on Río Lagarto are also offered. The main birdwatching trail is the Sendero El Trogón, which lies 4km (2.5 miles) before Achiote, and was so named on account of the three types of trogon that frequent the area. Although it's a pleasant walk, the birding is often easier (and free) along the more open areas of the main road. If you're willing to dodge the occasional speeding bus or truck, you'll get a chance to see brilliant chestnut-mandibled and keel-billed toucans, blue-headed parrots,

Boats bobbing in Shelter Bay Marina.

and beautiful blue cotingas. Cell phone coverage is intermittent, but if you fail to make contact with the center in advance you can usually find someone to let you in provided you arrive before nightfall.

PORTOBELO

Heading east from Colón takes you along a coastal road – known as the Costa Arriba – that meanders for 100km (62 miles) past popular weekend playas for Colonenses, through increasingly small settlements and skirting windswept deserted beaches until it comes to a halt in the remote outpost of Cuango. Across the river here, a dirt track penetrates the 35km (22 miles) of jungle that lies between Colón province and the Comarca Guna Yala.

Most tourists, however, stop around halfway, at the scenically located town of **Portobelo** ⓮. In Spanish colonial times, this was the most important settlement on the isthmus after Panama City, since all the plunder from South America passed through here en route to Spain. The ruined fortresses, remnants of the conquistadors' attempts to safeguard the treasure from the envious grasp of pirates and privateers, constitute the main tourist attractions in the town, though its two big annual festivals – the lively Afro-Colonial Congos y Diablos and the religious celebration of El Nazareño – reel in the crowds.

It is said that Portobelo got its name from the words of an ailing Christopher Columbus, who, relieved to spot a beautiful sheltered bay, gratefully exclaimed: 'Che porto bello.' While the name stuck, the strategic importance of the natural harbor was not truly appreciated until 1585, when it became clear that Nombre de Dios – then the principal Spanish port on the Panama's Caribbean coast – was too exposed and should be relocated 25km (15.5 miles) westward, to Portobelo. As if to reinforce the point, Sir Francis Drake destroyed Nombre de Dios in 1595 before dying of dysentery – his coffin supposedly lies at the bottom of the ocean at the entrance to the bay at

Portobelo town.

⊘ Fact

The famous Portobello Road in London was named in celebration of Edward Vernon's capture of the port from the Spanish in 1739 in the War of Jenkins' Ear.

Portobelo, near an islet which bears his name.

In 1597 San Felipe de Portobelo was officially founded, prompting further fortification and providing a new target for spoil-hungry pirates and privateers, including notorious buccaneer Henry Morgan in 1668 and 70 years later, British naval commander Sir Edward Vernon, who destroyed the two fortresses. Though new forts were built in the mid-18th century – those still visible today – they were smaller, since Portobelo's commercial importance was already waning as the Spanish had rerouted their ships round Cape Horn. When the Spanish garrison finally abandoned the town in 1821, the town's 150 years of strategic significance came to an end.

On arrival, it comes as rather a shock to find the forts smack in the middle of an economically deprived modern town, with dilapidated houses propped up against the historical ruins and kids playing soccer in what was once a parade ground. The town itself is mostly squeezed along a thin strip

Festival de los Diablos mask.

of land between the main road and the attractive bay, which spills into the Caribbean, and is easy to explore on foot. A half-day provides ample time to wander freely round the colonial relics, leaving you the afternoon to enjoy a nearby beach, a spot of snorkeling, diving, hiking, or kayaking, or – if you feel less energetic – a boat trip around the bay.

PORTOBELO'S FORTS

Fuerte Santiago is the first fort you encounter from the west before entering the town proper, built in the mid-18th century following the destruction of the original fortifications by the British. The main entrance takes you through a vestibule protected by gun ports to the grassy parade grounds, where the ruined walls of the officers' quarters, barracks, kitchen, and artillery emplacement are visible. More impressive are the lower and upper batteries, their cannons pointing out across the bay.

If you've time, it's worth crossing over the road from Fuerte Santiago

⊘ CONGOS AND DIABLOS

On the weekends leading up to Carnaval, Congo societies along the Costa Arriba erupt in colorful explosions of traditional song, dance, and satirical play-acting that originated in the 16th century among outlawed communities of escaped slaves, known as *cimarrones*. Congregating in mock palaces, each with its king and queen togged out in extravagant costumes and ludicrously large crowns, they communicate in their own dialect. The general view is that the characters represent a parody of the Spanish court, though a more recent interpretation suggests they refer back to the Kingdom of Konga in Central Africa. The men sport painted faces, conical hats, and outlandish tattered clothes; the women wear multicolored *polleras*, their hair garlanded with flowers, and dance to beating drums and choral chants. Recently recognized by Unesco, these Afro-Colonial celebrations reach their climax on Ash Wednesday with the Festival de los Diablos. The ferocious scarlet-and-black devils, who have been previously running amok in frightening masks, brandishing whips, are captured by a posse of angels, who drag them off to be baptized. A more formalized biennial Festival de los Diablos y Congos – likely to become annual – in March/April is well worth seeing.

for the steep five-minute climb to the **Mirador El Perú**. The *mirador* is on the site of a watchtower of the former Fortaleza Santiago de la Gloria, whose scarcely visible overgrown ruins are now bisected by the main road below. Across the bay you can make out what little remains of **Fuerte San Fernando** peeking through dense foliage. As with the other forts, many of the original stones were plundered for construction of the Canal. It's worth taking a short boat ride in one of the water-taxis moored at the jetty by Fuerte Santiago. Though smaller than its sibling fort, the scenic spot gives a different perspective on the town.

PORTOBELO TOWN

The small Plaza Central in the town center is dominated by the two-story coral stone and brick **Casa Real de la Aduana** (Royal Customs House), built in 1638 to replace an earlier wooden structure. A third of the world's gold, alongside copious other treasures, passed through this customs house for more than a century; there was only one entrance and one exit to reduce fraud and theft and to ensure the Crown got its full royal cut of the spoils. Destroyed in an earthquake in 1882, and now containing a modest museum, it underwent a $1 million restoration in 1997 and is now under restoration once more.

Just down by the waterside and hemmed in by housing lies **Fuerte San Jerónimo**, the town's largest and most impressive ruin. The former parade ground stretches along the 18 gun emplacements of the lower battery, with nearly all the original rusting cannons intact. It's worth walking along to the high battery, where you can still see the rainwater reservoir, storage rooms for gunpowder, and the latrines, and get a great view of the entrance of the bay.

Beyond the forts, the town's other major landmark, and focus of the annual Festival del Nazareño, is the **Iglesia de San Felipe** (daily 6am–6pm; free), which overlooks a bare square. Although construction started in 1606, the church was only completed

The remains of Fuerte San Jerónimo, Portobelo.

in 1814, making it the conquistadors' last religious building in Panama, with the bell tower added in 1945. Inside you'll find white walls and a large, carved gilt mahogany altarpiece, though the focus inevitably is on the so-called Cristo Negro, a dark-skinned, lifelike statue of Jesus bearing the Cross that peers out from behind a glass casement. Ask for the caretaker of the museum at the back of the church to peruse its wonders: a splendid collection of luxurious velvet robes embroidered with gold and silver thread donated by wealthy devotees for the Nazareño to wear.

ACTIVITIES AROUND PORTOBELO

Portobelo may be famed for its forts and festivals, but there are plenty of outdoor activities to keep you occupied in the rather fragmented and ill-protected tropical environs of the **Parque Nacional Portobelo**, which sweeps down to the coast from the almost 1,000-meter (3,280ft) summit of Cerro Bruja, taking in plenty of rainforest and a large area of the marine environment. The numerous reefs and scuttled ships in the waters round Portobelo makes it one of the country's top diving and snorkeling destinations – though you won't get the diversity and quantity of fish that you can find in the Pacific. Popular dive spots used by local operators include a B-45 plane wreck by Drake's Island, where some still hold out hope of uncovering the privateer's sunken lead coffin amid the encrusted coral; the varied marine flora and fauna of the Three Sister Islands; and the labyrinth of canyons off Isla Grande. The small but reliable Portobelo Adventures offers guided rainforest hikes, kayaking in the mangroves – home to crab-eating raccoons – and birdwatching. Boatmen hanging round the jetty by Fuerte Santiago can be contracted for boat trips round the bay or a drop-off and pick up at Playa Blanca, the area's prettiest beach. Heading back west toward Colón, up the pretty Río Piedra valley, Panama City-based Panama Outdoor Adventures (www.panamaoutdooradventures.com) runs an adventure activity

⊘ EL FESTIVAL DEL NAZAREÑO

In mid-October, Portobelo bursts into a frenzy of religious fervor and wild partying at the Festival del Nazareño – more commonly dubbed the Festival del Cristo Negro (Black Christ Festival) – after Panama's most revered religious icon, a striking, dark-skinned Christ with a penetrating gaze and bearing the Cross, which resides in the Iglesia de San Felipe. The effigy's iconic status was cemented in 1821 when it apparently spared the townsfolk from an epidemic that was sweeping the isthmus.

Though the main procession occurs on October 21, the build-up begins days before as up to 40,000 pilgrims, including general party-goers and a small number of criminals wanting to atone for their crimes, march into town. Thousands walk the 35km (22 miles) from Sabanitas and a handful hoof it from farther afield, many in ankle-length purple robes. Some crawl the last stretch on their hands and knees, urged on by faithful companions wafting incense, rocking miniature shrines in front of their eyes, or even pouring hot wax on their backs. To compound the suffering, the pilgrims are frequently overdosing on carbon monoxide from the festival traffic, which weaves in and out of the bodies struggling along the scorching asphalt. Shelters, food stands, and medical posts are set up along the route while the town itself is jam-packed with makeshift casinos, vendors selling religious paraphernalia, and food outlets dishing out chicken and rice.

At 8pm an ever-changing cohort of robed men begin to parade the icon, bedecked in a claret robe, round the packed town in a rhythmical swaying to the accompaniment of brass and drum and followed by the penitents. Once the candlelit litter has been returned to the church around midnight, the pilgrims discard their robes at the entrance as an explosion of fireworks marks the start of a hedonistic feast of drinking, gambling, and dancing that continues through the night. 'El Naza,' as the statue is affectionately known, gets another celebratory town outing on the Wednesday of Holy Week, this time clothed in purple, though the festivities are not quite as grand.

center offering zip lining, river tubing, and horseback riding.

THE EASTERN COSTA ARRIBA

Only the adventurous with time on their hands – or possibly with their own transportation – venture east of Portobelo. Here the road forks: left takes you down a small peninsula to the small Afro-Antillean island of **Isla Grande** ⑮. Measuring 3 by 1km (2 by 0.6 miles), it's popular as a day or weekend getaway for Panamanian urbanites, which has often led to hyperbolic descriptions of its beaches and overall beauty. In truth, it doesn't measure up to the stunning islands of Guna Yala or Bocas del Toro – especially as its best beach has been all but eroded, but if you're in the area and want a quick shot of Caribbean vibe, a dose of fresh air, and a splash in the sea before tucking into Creole cuisine, then Isla Grande will do very nicely. As there is no ATM on the island you'll need to bring cash, although most of the accommodations take credit cards. Isla Mamey, a tiny islet a short boat ride from nearby Puerto Lindo has some better sand.

Taking the right-hand fork takes you on an undulating road to the most compelling of the coastal settlements, **Nombre de Dios** ⑯. As you arrive, road signs proudly proclaim its fame as the initial Atlantic terminal for the Camino Real, where in colonial times treasure was transferred from exhausted mules to ships bound for Spain. Apocryphally, the village derived its name from the words of its founder, Diego de Nicuesa, who, desperate to land his starving crew, espied the spot and cried out, 'Paremos aquí en el nombre de Dios!' ('Let's stop here in the name of God!'). Sadly no trace remains of the town's historical past, largely thanks to Sir Francis Drake, who razed the place to the ground, thus persuading the Spanish to move their operation to Portobelo. Nevertheless, the village is a scenic place to stroll through, located on the palm-fringed Río Fato, and with a pleasant five-minute meander up to a *mirador* offering a view of the village and the turquoise sea beyond. Playa Damas, a short hop away by boat, is the best local beach.

> **⊙ Tip**
>
> Note that the last ATM and supermarket of any sort along the Costa Arriba is at Sabanitas, the turnoff from the main Panama City–Colón highway.

El Nazareño being paraded through Portobelo at the Festival del Cristo Negro.

📷 FESTIVALS

Panama is awash with festivals –
religious, hedonistic, culturally hybrid,
local, and national. They all involve plenty
of music, singing, and dancing and require
the stamina to party for days on end.

Alongside the numerous commemorations of historical events and public holidays, there are copious Catholic celebrations – including each town's
patron-saint fest, agricultural fairs, and cultural
extravaganzas that reflect the country's cultural
diversity. Whatever the differences in the details,
they all demand the ability to survive several days
and nights of music, dancing, and processions,
fueled on mountains of street food and gallons
of booze. Many also involve the election of a *reina*
(pageant queen), who often has to sit through
hours of competitions. Head and shoulders above
other festivals stands Carnaval – generally referred
to in the plural as Los Carnavales – a five-day
marathon of hedonism at its most outlandish in
the tiny Azuero town of Las Tablas (see page 190),
but a fairly impressive party in Panama City too.
Even the country's religious festivities are fairly
hedonistic, once the religious devotions have been
completed, and are imbued with Amerindian and
African cultural elements. This cultural hybridity is
most obvious during Corpus Christi, which is celebrated countrywide, but most impressively in La
Villa de los Santos. In more recent times, tourism
has driven the establishment of new festivals, such
as the Mil Polleras (see page 191), the Festival de
Congos y Diablos in Portobelo (see page 158),
and the Festival del
Bunde y del Bulleren-
gue in Darién, aimed at
recovering or sustain-
ing aspects of cultural
identity.

Spectacular, colorful float at Carnaval in Las Tablas. The streets are thronged with pageant queens and floats, and music and dance are ubiquitous.

Devil mask detail. These masks are said to represent the evil spirits of the Spanish colonials.

Clothing detail at Mil Polleras.

Congo dancer costume at the Festival de Congos y Diablos.

Dirty devils

You don't need to attend too many festivals to see that Panama is fond of its devils. The stars of Corpus Christi celebrations – once aimed at getting the Catholic message across to the non-literate indigenous population – they also feature in Congos festivities and in Carnaval in Bocas, plus various other events just for the fun of it. Devils come in a variety of outlandish costumes and fearsome masks. The *diablicos sucios* (dirty devils) are the best known – so called because the black and red striped jumpsuits were originally naturally dyed with charcoal and achiote, which inevitably rubbed off with the sweat. The protagonists of one of the nine dances of Corpus Christi, *diablicos sucios* dancers play castanets and bells while brandishing a *vejiga* – an inflated cow's bladder. In strikingly different outfits, the *diablicos limpios* (clean devils), who feature in the enactment of the battle between good (the Catholic Church) and evil, wear a rainbow of silk handkerchiefs tied to their waist, each color of significance: white for peace, green for nature, red for Hell etc. Some of the strangest devils are the Cucúas, from a small mountain community in Coclé, dressed in what look like pajamas fashioned from bark and a mask made to resemble the head of a deer.

'Mojaderas', a thorough soaking during Carnaval.

eligious pilgrims at the Festival del Cristo Negro (Black hrist Festival).

elebrating Carnaval in Panama City involves a spirited ater fight.

Feeling lucky? Lottery tickets for sale at El Valle market.

CENTRAL PANAMA AND THE PACIFIC BEACHES

Often neglected by foreign tourists, Central Panama possesses a number of pleasures: swathes of soft sand, mountainous national parks, and a relaxing spa town in an extinct volcanic crater.

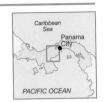

Better known for the farmland that extends over its denuded lowland slopes, and for its peasant farmers, Central Panama is often ignored by foreign tourists as they speed west along the Interamericana. Yet it possesses some fine beaches; strung out along the Pacific coast across the provinces of Panamá Oeste and Coclé, they are within easy access of Panama City. Central Panama also boasts some impressive mountain scenery harboring a wealth of wildlife, particularly the volcanic tors of Parque Nacional Altos de Campana, which afford sweeping vistas of the coastline, while the scenic crater town of El Valle makes a good base for a range of outdoor activities. Farther west, Parque Nacional Omar Torrijos offers mist-shrouded peaks and the potential for wilderness hiking across the continental divide into the lush rainforested slopes of the Caribbean. Back on the coastal plains, two places of historical interest stand out: the pre-Columbian remains of El Caño, an important ancient burial site; and the old colonial church at Natá, which contains wonderful wooden carvings.

Much of Central Panama is taken up with the Provincia de Coclé, which in turn covers a large part of the Pre-Columbian region archeologists term Gran Coclé, which extended across the Península de Azuero and a large part of Veraguas. Here, evidence from the funerary sites of Sitio Conté and El Caño point to a populated area of hierarchical societies organized into chiefdoms, such as Natá. They developed sophisticated and changing styles of ceramics, with the ability to gold and precious stones. When the colonists established their *'reducción de indios'* – administrative settlements to facilitate their proselytizing and financial and social control of the indigenous populations – Penonomé, Coclé's provincial capital, became one of the most

Main attractions

Parque Nacional Altos De Campana
Pacific beaches
El Valle
Cascada Távida & Pozos Azules
La Pintada
Parque Nacional Omar Torrijos
Parque Arqueológico El Caño
Basílica Menor Santiago Apóstol

Map on page 166

El Valle landscape.

important. These days, the population comprises predominantly *mestizo* farmers involved in horticulture and the cultivation of sugar cane, maize, coffee, and beans alongside cattle ranching. The coastal area, meanwhile, thrives on tourism, fishing, and shrimp farming.

PARQUE NACIONAL ALTOS DE CAMPANA

After grinding through the urban sprawl of La Chorerra, 40km (25 miles) southwest of Panama City, the Interamericana crests at Loma Campana. Just before the road swoops down onto the coastal plan, a road to the right climbs up to **Parque Nacional Altos de Campana** 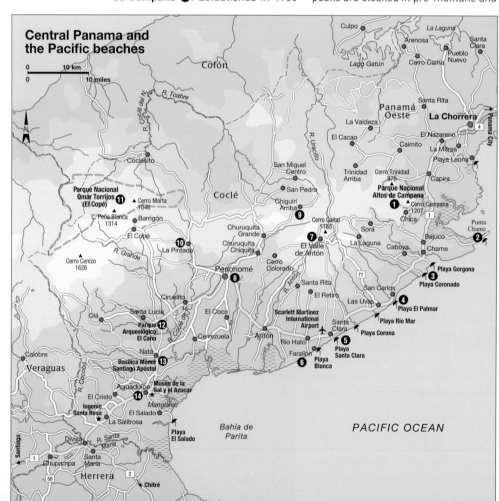. Established in 1966

as part of the protection for the canal basin, Altos De Campana is Panama's oldest national park, and at only 55km (34 miles) from the capital, close to the Intermaricana, one of the most accessible. It's often overlooked by tourists, visited only on weekends by enthusiastic birdwatchers or by fleeing urbanites in search of cool fresh air and exercise. But the stellar views from the park's summits make Altos De Campana a worthwhile hiking day-trip, and its dramatic and singular landscape of craggy tors and lava fields hosts a surprising range of species.

Although the denuded lower western and southern slopes have suffered from deforestation, elsewhere peaks are cloaked in pre-montane and

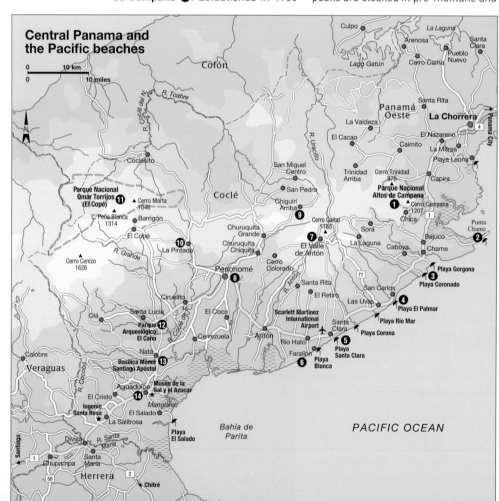

tropical forest. Of the park's 39 mammal species, the black-eared opossum is the most numerous, though it'll be tucked up in its den during the day. More likely sightings include two- and three-toed sloths, coatis, and Geoffroy's tamarin monkeys. Colorful birds also abound, including the striking orange-bellied trogon, rufous motmot, and collared aracari. Above all, though, the 50 sq km (19 sq miles) of park is renowned for its 62 amphibian and 86 reptile species, including the near-extinct golden frog (see page 169) in the area's western fringes.

The park's network of five interconnecting trails is concentrated in the southeastern section. Easily accessible and relatively well demarcated, most are shady strolls, with one a moderately strenuous hike through scenic forest. The main trail, the flattish Sendero Panamá (1.5km/1 mile), leads to the other trails: first to the moderately strenuous Sendero La Cruz, then *senderos* Rana Dorada and Zamora – both are only a few hundred meters/yds long. The slightly longer Sendero Podocarpus is the next turn-off and worth a detour as it takes you through some of Panama's only native conifers of the same name, ending up in the park's campsite at *Refugio Los Pinos*. About 800 meters/yds along the Sendero Panamá, the Sendero La Cruz climbs steeply to the right, through trees dripping with epiphytes, leading eventually to the 1,000-meter (3,280ft) domed peak of **Cerro Campana**, the park's highest point. The large boulder atop nearby Cerro La Cruz affords a slightly better panorama, taking in the meandering Río Chame and the distant Pacific beach resorts, with the rugged ridge of the Cordillera Central disappearing into the distance.

THE PACIFIC BEACHES

Once the Interamericana hits the coastal plain at the western edge of Panama province, roads start to branch off the main artery like blood vessels, feeding the various beaches along the Pacific coast. With locations to suit surfers, swimmers, and sunbathers, and sand ranging from charcoal grey through tan to pale cream, these beaches have become increasingly built up over recent years. The developments – beyond the odd surf spot – primarily cater to weekending capital-dwellers, a few expat communities, and Latin Americans on vacation packages. With little or no regulation there's the odd skyscraper anomaly alongside a colonial-style villa or a rustic thatched bar. Travelers looking for less developed beaches will find offerings in the Azuero, Chiriquí, and Bocas with greater appeal. They are to be avoided at all costs in high season: 4WDs block the beach entrances as there's nowhere to park, and you can scarcely see the sand for screaming partying folk, jet-skis, banana rides, and pumping reggaeton. That said, if you hit the beaches mid-week and out of season, they can be gloriously deserted and really beautiful. Reaching

Bridge at Chorro El Macho.

○ Tip

Any bus bound for Antón or Penonomé can drop you off along the Interamericana at the 'entrada' to any of the beaches, where you can usually get another local bus, a taxi, or walk – the farthest to any beach (barring Chame) is 4km (2.5 miles).

the various playas on public transportation entails taking any west-bound transportation from Panama City to Coclé, such as to Antón or Penonomé.

The least built up of the Pacific beaches is **Punta Chame** ❷, which you access by taking the first beach exit as you travel west along the Interamericana. The road travels the length of a 12km (7.5-mile) sandy spit to a low-key fishing village, where the vast flat beach, strong winds, and choppy waters have transformed this otherwise deserted swathe into Panama's kitesurfing center (season Dec–May) – though beware the stingrays at low tide. Birdwatching is also good here as the tidal pools and mud flats attract a variety of waders. Looking northward across the more sheltered Bay of Chame, you get lovely views of the mainland.

Playas Gorgona and **Coronado** ❸ were once the most fashionable weekend destinations for middle-class residents of Panama City, with beachfront properties overlooking the marbled charcoal sand; Coronado now has a growing expat community. There are two good surfing spots here – Playa Malibu in Gorgona and Punta Teta (predictably dubbed 'Tits' by surfing dudes), 3km (2 miles) down a dirt road not long after the Coronado exit. The only substantial settlement in the area, 12km (7.5 miles) on from the giant El Rey supermarket just off the Interamericana, is **San Carlos**, a pleasant fishing village worth noting mainly as a place to buy provisions and catch a bus. The other surfing hotspots in the area lie down two asphalt roads a few kilometers west of San Carlos at **Playa El Palmar** ❹ and **Playa Río Mar**. Playa El Palmar hosts one of Panama's longest-established surf schools, which specializes in courses for beginners (www.panamasurfschool.com). Non-surfers should continue a further 20km (12 miles) to hit the best beaches on this stretch of coast.

Although large concrete developments are beginning to encroach, and quad bikes and jet skis roar about the place at weekends, **Playa Santa Clara** ❺, 30km (19 miles) east of Penonomé,

Cerro Gaital.

is probably the loveliest beach in the area, and you can have it all to yourself midweek. A seemingly endless belt of pale sand lapped by calm waters, it features a number of pleasantly informal bars and restaurants. A few kilometers farther along the coast from Playa Santa Clara, at the equally impressive beige swathe of **Farallón ⑥** (Playa Blanca), things are even busier, and the local fishing village is becoming increasingly hemmed in among greedy resorts, condominium complexes, and gated retirement communities. Most accommodations can fix up some gentle horseback riding along the beach or a boat trip with one of the local fishermen.

EL VALLE

About 100km (62 miles) southwest of Panama City, just beyond San Carlos, a winding road ascends 600 meters (1,968ft) into the cordillera to **El Valle ⑦**, a small town of around 7,000 inhabitants nestled in the crater of a now-extinct volcano. Undulating hills rise to the south and west, ascending to more dramatic, forested peaks to the north, often shrouded in mist. The picturesque location, cool climate, and relative proximity to the capital (90 mins by car) have made El Valle the vacation-home location of choice for Panama City's elite – a fact that becomes immediately obvious after espying the immaculately kept gardens and luxury residences down the aptly named **Calle de los Millonarios** (Millionaires' Road). Quiet during the week, the place comes alive on weekends and public holidays as a stream of 4WDs arrives from the city and the otherwise still roads resound with the sound of clopping hooves or revving quad bikes. Prices are often higher for lodgings on weekends, and some places insist on a minimum two-night stay (Fri and Sat).

The huge explosion that blew the top off the volcano 3 million years ago left a vast caldera that over time filled with rainwater. When the crater-lake drained, it left behind a flat layer of rich volcanic soil. Perfect for agricultural production, the fertile earth also nourishes the vast expanses of trimmed lawn, abundant fruit and flower-laden trees, and attendant hummingbirds tucked away down El Valle's side streets, which are central to the place's charm. The surroundings are instantly impressive. Spectacular stream-filled cloudforests envelop the elevated mountain reserve of **Monumento Natural Cerro Gaital**, which overlooks the town and provides first-rate birdwatching. If you enjoy fresh mountain air, meanwhile, there are enough decent hiking, horseback riding, and cycling opportunities to keep you in El Valle for several days.

EL VALLE SIGHTS

El Valle's modest attractions peel off the central street as you enter the volcanic town. First up, off to the left, and next to the MiAmbiente office (tel: 983 6411; Mon–Fri 8am–4pm) is the **APROVACA Orchid Nursery** (tel: 983

⊙ Eat

Spanish-Panamanian El Rincón de los Camisones (km 104, La Ermita, Interamericana; tel: 993 3622; daily 11am–10pm) on the north side of the highway has a reputation for dishing up the best seafood in the country (including paella), under a spacious breezy rancho set in a pleasant garden.

⊙ LA RANA DORADA: PANAMA'S GOLDEN FROG

Decorating everything from pre-Columbian talismans to tacky T-shirts and lottery tickets, and star of David Attenborough's *Life in Cold Blood*, Panama's golden frog (*rana dorada; atelopus zeteki*) is one of the country's most enduring cultural icons. It's associated above all with El Valle, since the mountain forests of Coclé provide its only known habitat. In ancient times, the Guaymí (or Ngäbe) revered the frog, carving ceramic and golden likenesses for jewelry and *huacas* – precious objects buried with chiefs and other prominent citizens – of this symbol of fertility and prosperity. Indeed, legend had it that possessing one of these 'true toads' in life would ensure good fortune in the afterlife, as it would transform into a golden *huaca*. Even today it is believed that a glimpse of this dazzling tiny amphibian in the wild will bring good luck, though a sighting is presently highly improbable thanks to the deadly chytrid fungus, which decimated amphibian populations worldwide and wrought devastation in the area in 2006 (see page 85). Recent successful breeding in captivity and isolated sightings in more remote areas give hope that the golden amphibian will once more be seen hopping round the streams of El Valle.

⊙ Tip

The well-established stable, El Hato (tel: 6646 5813), on the street of the same name and close to Hotel Campestre, leads short horseback riding excursions round the backstreets of El Valle, or on longer trails up La India Dormida, or on a four-hour circuit round Cerro Gaital.

6472; www.aprovaca.com; daily 9am–4pm), which nurtures around 500 of Panama's 1,200 orchid species. These include the country's rare endemic national flower, the delicate *flor del Espíritu Santo* – named for the middle of each bloom, which resembles a white dove. The center aims to reintroduce many of the endemic species, which are threatened by poaching, back into the wild.

A few hundred meters farther along Avenida Central, signposted off to the left just before the police station, lies the **Butterfly Haven** (tel: 6062 3131; www.butterflyhavenpanama.com; Jan–Sept & Dec Mon & Wed–Sun 9am–4pm). You get a short guided tour through the butterfly house with around 250 multicolored butterflies flitting around as well as a nursery, where you can learn all about the life cycle of lepidoptera. Directly opposite, a dirt road takes you uphill to **El Nispero** (tel: 983 6142; daily 7am–5pm; EVACC closed Tue), a rather sad zoo that started life as a plant nursery and still functions as such. It crams 55 species of

Sunbathing at El Nispero zoo.

bird, alongside ocelot, margay, capybara, several types of monkey, and even the progeny of Manuel Noriega's tapirs – adopted after the US invasion – into inadequate cages. However, it's worth visiting for the **amphibian rescue center** (EVACC), where El Valle's emblematic golden frog and 16 other threatened native species of frog, toad, and salamander have also been collected for study and breeding in captivity, with a view to releasing them back into the wild once the chytrid fungus is no longer a threat. Shortly afterward, on the main road you come to the hub of activity of El Valle: town life revolves round the daily market, which draws the largest crowds on weekends, especially on Sundays, when farmers and artisans pour in to sell fruit, vegetables, flowers, and handicrafts. Though small, it's Panama's best-known **craft market** outside the capital; as well as straw hats you'll find a decent range of ceramic figurines, painted wooden trays (*bateas*), and soapstone carvings (mostly by Ngäbe or Buglé artists) alongside Guna *molas*, Emberá or

Wounaan basketry, and a host of tacky golden frogs.

The one-room **museum** (Sun 10am–2pm; ask around for access on other days) is hidden behind the tiny white-washed twin towers of **Iglesia San José** along Avenida Central. Amidst a collection of forgettable items are some striking polychromatic pre-Columbian ceramics and interesting carved faces. At the end of the main drag, before it bends round to the right, Calle del Macho leads to what are for many the town's main, albeit low-key, attraction, the *pozos termales* (thermal baths; tel: 6621 3846; daily 8am–5pm). By the banks of Río Antón, they allegedly have medicinal powers. Weekends are hectic, but the shady warm cement pool can be a pleasant experience midweek. A mud face pack is included in the entry price; an extra few dollars gets you a pot of exfoliating, mineral-rich mud (*barro*), which is fun to slather all over your body before rinsing off and taking to the pool. Meanwhile, several boutique hotels offer a more sanitized spa experience.

EXCURSIONS FROM EL VALLE

After crossing the bridge over the Río Guayabo at the west end of Avenida Central, the road forks: a 15-minute walk along the central prong leads to a massive petroglyph known as **La Piedra Pintada**, where there's no shortage of kids offering to guide you to the giant rock face and attempt to explain the mysterious pre-Columbian carved spirals and anthropomorphic and zoomorphic figures. You can continue up the path that follows the stream, past pretty waterfalls, to the mythical ridge of **La India Dormida**. The left fork from the bridge leads to the **Chorro Las Mozas** falls; 15 minutes' stroll from town, it's a popular place for the local youth to splash around, especially on weekends.

The main road that swings round to Cerro Gaital leads past one of El Valle's most popular excursions, **Chorro El Macho** (tel: 983 6547; daily 8am–5pm, last zip line 4pm), a picturesque 35-meter (115ft) waterfall set in a private ecological reserve. A short circular path leads to a viewing platform at the base of the falls, where lizards bask on the rocks and hummingbirds dart through the foliage. It also boasts a five-cable canopy adventure, which ends by taking you across the cascade. If you're heading for Chiriquí you might want to save your cash to do the more impressive Boquete Tree Trek (see page 91). But here the adventure has the potential to combine thrills with a guided (uphill) hike through the rainforest (around 30 mins).

The mountains encircling El Valle offer a wealth of only moderately demanding hiking opportunities. For most hikes you'll need a guide, since trails are not well marked and if the mist descends it's easy to lose your way, though on a clear day you can manage La India Dormida without being accompanied. Although the most direct route up the legendary hill is to

⊘ LA INDIA DORMIDA

The undulating hilltop at the western end of El Valle, known as La India Dormida, is believed to be the slumbering silhouette of Flor del Aire, the beautiful daughter of Urracá (see page 34), the indigenous chief famed for his persistent and fierce resistance to Spanish colonization until his death in 1531. The story goes that while battles were raging, Flor fell in love with one of the adversary Spanish conquistadors, unaware that she was admired by Yaraví, the local Guaymí tribe's most courageous warrior. Failing to get Flor's attention, Yaraví took the drastic measure of hurling himself off a mountain in front of the whole village, including the horrified Flor. Understandably distraught, Flor renounced her love for the Spaniard and wandered off into the forested hills nearby, where she eventually died of grief. Her body, it is said, is immortalized in the shape of a mountain. With a great deal of imagination and a little prompting from a local resident, you can usually make out her recumbent form, denuded of trees except for the distinct forested section to the right-hand side, which more clearly resembles the tresses of her hair. Whether or not you can make out the sleeping maiden, hiking in the surrounding hills is a wonderful and rewarding experience.

follow the path up past the giant petro-glyph, La Piedra Pintada, a better circular route heads out past the baseball stadium, bearing left at the next fork. When the road ends, a path off to the right brings you out on the lower part of what is presumed to be Flor's body (see page 171). Walking north along the deforested ridge, you can enjoy the splendid views across the crater before taking the path down from the 'head' that eventually passes the refreshing waterfalls and natural swimming pools near La Piedra Pintada, where you can cool off.

A more challenging hike scales the area's highest peak, the forbidding forest-clad **Cerro Gaital** (1,185 meters/3,888ft), for which you'll need a permit from MiAmbiente either from the office in town, or the one at the northern entrance to the Monumento Natural Cerro Gaital reserve near La Mesa, which is often unstaffed. The most direct route involves a steep climb from a path behind Hotel Los Mandarinos, for which you'd need a guide. Alternatively, you can labor

7–8km (4.5–5 miles) up the road to La Mesa (or take the bus), bearing right at the fork after the village and arriving, a few hundred meters/yds later, at the entrance to the reserve. The orchid-rich area is a haven for birdwatchers as well as hikers, harboring a rainbow of hummingbirds, honeycreepers, toucanets, tanagers, and trogons, as well as the elusive black guan. A 2.5km (1.5-mile) loop trail, Sendero El Convento, winds through cloudforest, circling the summit, with a turn-off to a *mirador*, which on a clear day affords stellar views down to the coast.

PENONOMÉ AND EASTERN COCLÉ

The capital of the province of Coclé, **Penonomé** ❽ was founded by Spanish colonizers in 1581 and briefly served as capital of the isthmus after the destruction of Panamá Viejo. Standing at the geographical center of Panama (a plaque marks the fact), this bustling market town remains important both as a transit point and for selling goods from the surrounding land, which is

---

Ø FESTIVAL DE TORO GUAPO

The small agricultural town of Antón, just off the Interamericana almost midway between Farallón and Penonomé, really only registers on the tourist radar once a year, during the Festival de Toro Guapo (Fierce Bull Festival; www.facebook.com/fntoroguapoanton) in mid-October, when the pleasant colonial square and whitewashed church are transformed by hordes of visitors. The fun-filled five-day extravaganza takes its name and much of its action from the cattle farming that has defined the area for centuries and is well worth sampling. Alongside the usual array of folkloric dancing, colorful street parades, beauty pageants, and progressively more drunken revelry are *toros* – men who cavort around the streets, charging at all and sundry. They dress in fantastical costumes draped over wooden or bamboo frames, topped with a bull's head adorned with ribbons and mirrors.

Many of the surrounding villages produce such a beast, with the creativity of the costume and acrobatic skills of the wearer a source of local pride, to be displayed during the parade on the final morning. After being blessed in the church, the bulls are led round the town as they playfully harass the *pollera*-swishing dancers, accompanied by bands of drummers. Listen out among the beats for the distinctive chime of the *almirez* – a bell-shaped bronze mortar of Afro-Colonial origin that pharmacists once used to grind their medicinal herbs, and is now a musical instrument unique to Antón.

Other festival highlights include water fights (*mojaderas*), competitions testing traditional rural skills such as carrying firewood, peeling coconuts, and milking a cow, and dancing by extravagantly dressed *diablos limpios*, or 'clean devils' (see page 163). Strangest of all is the *cutarras*, when a poor cow is wrestled to the ground by several farmers, often the worse for wear from *seco*, who then struggle to fix sandals (*cutarras*) over the hooves, recalling an old trick of cattle rustlers attempting to hide the telltale hoof prints.

cultivated for fruit, vegetables, rice, and maize as well as supporting pig, poultry, and cattle farming. The 17,000 inhabitants are predominantly *mestizo*, while some have Arab and Chinese origins. Fittingly for a town that served as a *reducción de Indios* – a place where conquered indigenous groups were forcibly resettled – Penonomé was named after Nomé, a local chieftain cruelly betrayed and executed.

Though a provincial capital and major agricultural center, Penonomé is surprisingly small, with a very rural feel and just a couple of modest sights and a pretty river within walking distance. Its aquatic celebrations for Carnaval are a real crowd-puller, and although the town itself is not especially interesting, it is within reach of several attractions up in the scenic mountains northeast of the town.

The town's main drag, Avenida J.D. Arosemena (also known as Vía Central), runs a few hundred meters/yds from the Interamericana to the pleasant **Plaza Bolívar** (also known as Plaza 8 de Diciembre). Featuring a statue of Simón Bolívar, the square is flanked by government buildings and the **Catedral de San Juan Bautista**, where the early morning or evening light projects dancing rainbows of colors through the new stained-glass windows. East of the cathedral, a small *plazuela* features monuments to Penonomé's glitterati, including a bust of Victoriano Lorenzo, a local nationalist hero who was eventually tricked into capture and executed by firing squad (see page 42). Two blocks south along Calle Damian Carles, then one block west takes you the quiet barrio of San Antonio, the oldest part of town. Here the **Museo de Historia y Tradición Penonomeña** (Calle San Antonio; tel: 997 8490; Tue–Sun 9am–4pm) occupies a tiled blue-and-white *quincha* (wattle and daub) building and contains a modest collection of pre-Columbian ceramics, colonial religious art, and period furniture.

If the heat gets too much, take a five-minute walk northeast out of town to the **Balneario Las Mendozas**, a popular swimming area in the Río Zaratí – this is the location of the aquatic

La India Dormida, El Valle.

parade at Carnaval, when the floats literally bob down the river. Though it's a party place on weekends and during holidays, you can enjoy a quieter dip here at other times, or upstream at **Las Tres Peñas**, a more attractive pool.

From the market area of Penonomé, minibuses head off through the surrounding cultivated fields to villages scattered in the folds of the cool, forested mountains that rise to the north. **Chiguirí Arriba** , 30km (19 miles) to the northeast, makes an easy day-trip, with plenty of good hiking trails – such as to the summit of Cerro La Vieja – and spectacular views across forested limestone hummocks. **Cascada Tavida**, a 30-meter (98ft) waterfall within Villa Tavida's private reserve (www.villatavida. com) is another treat. More adventurous trips can be organized across the mountains to El Valle, or over to the Caribbean rainforests; contact Villa Tavida for the name of a reliable local guide.

If you're in the area in late January, it's worth stopping off at the village of Churuquita Grande, halfway between Penonomé and Chiguirí Arriba, for the citrus-filled **Festival de la Naranja**, to marvel at the elaborate and inventive wood-and-thatch displays overflowing with local produce, all vying for the prize of best stand. Another worthwhile excursion is to the gorgeous **Pozos Azules**, a series of cascades and rocks to clamber over and pristine aquamarine pools to swim in, provided you avoid the weekend crowds. Ask the bus to let you off at the entrance, from where it is a 45-minute hike there (and back!) down a dirt road.

LA PINTADA AND PARQUE NACIONAL OMAR TORRIJOS

When heading up to the hills to the northwest of Penonomé, it's worth making a detour to the village of **La Pintada**, 15km (9 miles) northwest of Penonomé, in the foothills of the cordillera. Aficionados of Panama's hats – as opposed to Panama hats, which are made in Ecuador – will know that the community is famed for its high-quality palm-woven *sombrero pintado* or 'pintao' (see page 77). Although the hats have their origins in indigenous societies, Coclé's version of the *sombrero pintado* ('painted hat'), which takes its name from the black and white design, has become the most popular and emblematic. It is a major and expanding business in the village and surrounding area, involving several thousand individuals. The **Mercado de Artesanías La Pintada** (daily 9am–4pm), which displays the crafts of around 100 local families, sells a wide range of hats in addition to decorated gourds, soapstone carvings, pots, and various knick-knacks, though finding the place open can be tricky, especially in the rainy season. Not so with master hat-maker Señor Quirós, next door, who lives at the back of his shop, **Artesanías Reinaldo Quirós** (tel: 6963 0945; daily 8.30am–4pm), and also has a good collection. Both are on the

Kitesurfing at Punta Chame.

left-hand side of the soccer field and are easy to spot.

Another place of potential interest is the local cigar factory, **Cigarros Joyas de Panamá** (tel: 6660 8935; www.facebook.com/joyasde.panama; Mon–Sat 7am–5pm), garnering an international reputation for its hand-rolled organic Cuban-seed-tobacco cigars. Drop by and witness the dexterity with which workers roll up to 600 cigars a day. Single or boxed cigars can be bought on the spot. The factory lies just off the main road into the village from Penonomé.

Another half an hour up the road takes you to the small community of El Copé, from where it's a further 6km (4 miles) up a steep dirt road to **Parque Nacional Omar Torrijos** ⓫. Although tricky to get to, with only very basic accommodations available, this little-visited, 250-sq-km (96.5-sq-mile) protected carpet of lush forest astride the continental divide is well worth the effort. On the way, you pass the **Cascada Las Yayas** (tel: 6809 6372; daily 8am–6pm). Here, a shady 300-meter/yd trail offers several viewpoints from which to appreciate a series of three falls, the highest of which is 25 meters (82ft). The falls, inevitably, are at their most impressive in the rainy season, though in the dry season there's the pleasure of taking a dip in the pool at the base of the main cascade. The surrounding rainforest is excellent for spotting hummingbirds and amphibians, especially in the late afternoon.

Its full name, Parque Nacional General de División Omar Torrijos Herrera, was given on its formation in 1986 in remembrance of Panama's flamboyant populist leader, whose plane mysteriously crashed into one of the area's highest peaks, Cerro Martha, in 1981. These days it is more usually referred to as 'Parque Omar Torrijos' or 'El Copé' after the nearby village. Averaging 20°C (68°F) in the cloud-forested peaks of the Cordillera Central, the canopy cascades down to the more moist vegetation of the Caribbean side, where temperatures average 25°C (77°F) and the area receives 4 meters (157in)

Petroglyphs at El Valle.

Ⓞ LOS CUCUÁS DE SAN MIGUEL CENTRO

San Miguel Centro, 35km (22 miles) northeast of Penonomé, is home to the Cucuá community, famed for their devil dance conducted in elaborate, cream-colored, pajama-like costumes made from cucuá bark, painted with geometric shapes using natural dyes and topped with a fanciful deer mask complete with real antlers and a peccary's jawbone. As with other devil dances, it was originally associated with Corpus Christi celebrations; at one time in danger of dying out, it is now regularly performed at folk festivals across Panama. The dance is the central attraction of the annual Festival de los Cucuás, which takes place in March in San Miguel Centro. The bark 'material' used for the costumes is beaten against a tree until smooth, then washed in soap and hot water before being laid out to dry. Such has been the demand for the costumes in recent years (they can sell for around $500) that the cucuá tree has become endangered, prompting a recent reforestation program.

Descended from the Guaymí, like the Ngäbe and Buglé, and originally from Veraguas, the Cucuás fled the Spanish colonizers centuries ago to settle in the mountains of Coclé. These days they make a living primarily from coffee cultivation and the sale of *artesanías*; the latter, along with the devil dance, forms a major part of a community-based ecotourism project aimed at preserving and promoting Cucuá culture.

> **Tip**

Near the summit of Cerro Marta, it's still possible to see parts of the wrecked plane that former populist dictator Omar Torrijos crashed in, though it's gradually being reclaimed by the jungle.

of rainfall annually. Some fine wildlife inhabits the mist-shrouded forest: tapirs, peccaries, and all five of Panama's species of large cat roam the undergrowth, while red-fronted parrotlets, orange-bellied trogons, and the extraordinary bare-necked umbrellabird draw bird-lovers. You're more likely to hear than see the three-wattled bellbird, which has one of the loudest birdcalls in the world – a bizarre metallic 'dong' that carries for almost a kilometer (half a mile).

A few hundred meters beyond the park entrance, an informative visitor center, with a rear balcony offering splendid views, marks the start of a couple of fairly short, well-kept circular routes (2km and 4km/1.2 and 2.5 miles) and an interpretive loop, aimed at enhancing visitors' appreciation of the abundant and diverse flora. For longer hikes, you will need to arrange a guide, either via the MIA office in Penonomé, on the Interamericana (tel: 997 7538; Mon–Fri 8am–4pm), or by contacting the Navas family in Barrigón.

A moderately strenuous four-hour trail ascends west from Barrigón aiming for **Cerro Peña Blanca** (1,314 meters/4,311ft), which occasionally emerges from the mist to the west of the park entrance. On a rare clear day you are rewarded at the summit with spectacular views of both oceans. **Cerro Santa Marta** also tops 1,000 meters (3,280ft), but is a much longer climb, and an all-day venture.

The other popular route heads over the continental divide from the park entrance down to the community of **La Rica**, a good four-hour hike away. Set in verdant surroundings laced with waterfalls and natural swimming pools and within reach of giant guayacán, cuipo, and cedar trees, La Rica is the perfect spot to appreciate the park's natural beauty, though getting there can be a very muddy affair for much of the year and a guide is essential.

EL CAÑO AND NATÁ

West along the Interamericana from Penonomé, past the new wind farm – Panama's first and Central America's largest – across the flatlands of Coclé, the terrain becomes duller and drier. Skirting endless fields of sugar cane and cattle, you enter the crescent known as the **Arco Seco** (Dry Arc), which sweeps round the Bahía de Parita west of the Pacific beaches to the eastern section of the Azuero Peninsula. Signposted south off the highway, some 22km (13.5 miles) southwest of Penonomé lies the small village of El Caño; it is the unlikely gateway to one of Panama's most significant pre-Columbian archeological sites, **Parque Arqueológico El Caño** ⑫ (Tue–Sat 8am–3.30pm), which narrowly escaped being bulldozed in the 1970s. An important ceremonial site from 500 to about 1200 AD, El Caño later became a necropolis that remained in use after the Conquest. One of the most fascinating earlier finds was a set of more than 100 basalt statues that formed

Playa Coronado.

what archeologists described as the 'Temple of the Thousand Idols.' These were illegally decapitated by an American Indiana Jones-style adventurer in the early 20th-century, and the best of their zoomorphic and anthropomorphic heads are now scattered in museums in the US, with a few in Panama City's anthropological museum. Only the stone pedestals remain. There are also funeral mounds, six of which have now been excavated (see page 30), displaying many, fairly complete skeletons. One, presumed to be a chief 's burial mound, has thrown up a number of gold and emerald items, which are currently being examined by archeologists, so are not yet on display. Many more burial sites are thought to lie under the nearby sugar cane fields, likely to contain more treasure. The onsite museum, currently closed for renovation, eventually hopes to display some of these finds. Sadly, a combination of plunder, vandalism, and neglect means there is relatively little for the lay visitor to appreciate, while the park's floodplain location makes it a mosquito-infested quagmire in the rainy season. Even so, the well-preserved skeletons in one of the burial pits are quite impressive and definitely worth a look if you're in the area.

It's hard to picture **Natá**, a quiet backwater 10km (6 miles) south of El Caño, as the major Spanish settlement it once was, until you arrive at the plaza to be confronted with the dazzling white Baroque facade of the expansive **Basílica Menor Santiago Apóstol** ⓭ (daily 8am–6pm; free). Possibly the oldest church in the Americas still in use, the church bears testament to the town's historical importance. Founded in 1522 by Gaspar de Espinosa (whose bust surveys the church from the square) and named after the local indigenous chief, the town supposedly gained its subsequent full name, Santiago de Natá de los Caballeros from 100 knights (*caballeros*) – hand-picked by King Charles V of Spain – who were sent to subjugate the local population and spread the Catholic Word. The surrounding fertile plains made Natá a perfect base for confronting the main indigenous

Iglesia de Natá.

⊙ Fact

Archeological evidence indicates that indigenous people have lived in the Aguadulce area since at least AD 800; even then they were extracting salt to barter for other goods.

resistance forces under Cacique Urracá, who relentlessly attacked the site (see page 34), and for providing supplies to the now long-abandoned gold mines on the Caribbean coast.

Aside from the splendid belltower, the basilica's main attractions are the ornately carved wooden altars framed by exquisite columns laden with vines, flowers, and angels, which adorn an otherwise simple wooden interior. Though the least elaborate, the main altar importantly contains images of the patron saint, Santiago el Menor (James the Lesser), and the co-patron, San Juan de Díos, who are removed from their niches and paraded round town on their saint days of July 25 and March 8, respectively.

AGUADULCE AND AROUND

Plum in the middle of the Arco Seco, which transforms into an unpleasant dust bowl in the dry season, stands the important agroindustrial town of **Aguadulce** ⑭, synonymous with sugar, salt and – more recently – shrimp. Coclé's second most important town is

unremarkable, though at the right time of year you can observe its agricultural processes first-hand, while avid bird-watchers head for the saltpans to the southeast. As ever, town life centers on the main square, Plaza 19 de Octubre, where the **Iglesia de San Juan Bautista** exhibits a mishmash of styles, the original altar frescoes having disappeared beneath an expensive pile of red brick – the current altarpiece. Across the plaza the **Museo Regional Stella Sierra** (tel: 997 4280; Tue–Sat 8am–4pm) occupies the mustard-colored, two-story, 19th-century building on the corner, which was formerly the post office. This regional museum, named after a local poet, contains a modest assortment of pre-Columbian relics, photos, and instruments from the early days of the salt and sugar industries; it also houses weaponry and uniforms from the civil war, during which two major battles were fought in the town. Space is also devoted to Aguadulce's two most famous citizens – the aforementioned poet, Stella Sierra, and Rodolfo Chiari, one of Panama's former presidents.

Great egret near Aguadulce.

Of greater interest than Aguadulce's regional museum is a tour around Panama's oldest and most important sugar mill, the **Ingenio Santa Rosa** (tel: 987 8101; www.azunal.com; Jan–Mar Tue–Fri 8am–noon; free). Located 14km (8.5 miles) west of Aguadulce, to the north of the Interamericana, it is reachable via taxi, or a bus can drop you at the bottom of the shadeless 2.5km (1.5-mile) driveway. Here, during the harvesting season, you learn about the fascinating process of production by following the action from the cane fields to the bags of sugar. A small on-site museum, inside the reproduction wooden house of the pioneering Del-Valle family, is stuffed with period furniture and memorabilia. Outside, the grounds are sprinkled with early mill machinery, including old sugar cane presses. At least a day's notice is needed to book a tour (in Spanish). To see the cane-processing, you need to wear long sleeves, long pants, and closed shoes; otherwise you can only visit the museum.

Heading southeast out of Aguadulce, a tarred road navigates 8km (5 mile) between mud and salt flats and shrimp farms to the mangrove-lined coast at **Playa El Salado**. In the dry season, salt is heaped like snow by the evaporation pools while September and October are the best months to catch flocks of migrating waders; among the numerous sandpipers and plovers, look out for striking black-necked stilts probing the mud for crustaceans and lovely roseate spoonbills filtering the tidal pools.

On weekends, many Aguadulceños head this way to escape the heat of the town and to lounge on the pleasant beach or to loll about in **Las Piscinas** – shallow stone baths built on the flats, offering views of the bay. As the tide moves out they become warm pools of salt water, but you need to get out quickly once the tide turns, as they soon become submerged. The biggest attraction for many, though, are the **jumbo shrimp** for which the fishing village is famous, and which you can sample at any one of the restaurants dotted along the road.

Aguadulce mural.

Waterfall on the Azuero
Peninsula.

THE AZUERO PENINSULA AND VERAGUAS

The Peninsula de Azuero delivers on the stereotypes – traditional festivals with pollera-swishing parades and campesinos in sombreros – yet it also offers up great surf spots, island wildlife reserves, and stellar sunsets.

The boxy land mass that protrudes into the Pacific, the Peninsula de Azuero covers a substantial 7,616 sq km (2,940 sq miles). A distinction is often made between the Eastern and Western Azuero since there is no connecting road across the dividing mountainous spine that runs down the western flank. The former comprises the vast bulk of the terrain and the small provinces of Herrera and Los Santos, clustered around their respective provincial capitals of Chitré and Las Tablas, which make good bases for exploring the region. It is here too that the country's most famous and riotous festivals take place. But there's more to the peninsula than partying. For nature lovers, Isla Iguana and Isla de Cañas offer fascinating wildlife experiences: the former is a major nesting site for the chest-puffing frigate birds, boasting coral beaches and rich snorkeling, while the latter affords a rare opportunity to witness the mass breeding of olive ridley turtles. On the eastern and southern seaboards deserted beaches – broad tan, chocolate, and black stretches of sand – welcome top-notch surfing waves, while world-class sport fishing takes place off the legendary 'Tuna Coast,' with many enthusiasts using understated Pedasí as a base.

The Western Azuero, on the other hand, is an oft-forgotten sliver of the Provincia de Veraguas that trickles down the seaboard, ending in one of Panama's least explored wilderness areas, Parque Nacional Cerro Hoya. Veraguas also stretches northward across the continental divide and down to the Caribbean – the only province to enjoy both Pacific and Caribbean coasts. In the mountains of the Cordillera Central, the delightful village of Santa Fé stands out as a base for exploring the nearby national park

Main attractions
Azuero's festivals
Isla Cañas
Cerro Hoya
The Western Azuero
Santa Fé
Santa Catalina

Maps on pages 182 and 187

Brightly painted ceramics for sale.

⊙ Tip

Choose your time to visit the Azuero carefully; when fed by the rains (May–mid-Dec), the verdant pastures create a picturesque landscape, though off-the-beaten track places such as Cerro Hoya and the wetlands of La Ciénega de las Macanas become inaccessible. When the clouds dry up, the Azuero becomes parched and dusty as temperatures soar.

of the same name. Back down on the coast, the smaller Peninsula de Soná also pokes its nose into the Pacific. At its tip, the country's top surf spot, an erstwhile fishing village, Santa Catalina, serves as the launchpad for expeditions to the enigmatic island of Coiba, and the spectacular surrounding national marine park.

Panama's Spanish colonial heritage is also at its most visible and vibrant in the Azuero, from the cattle ranching, bullfighting, and Baroque churches to the elaborate costumes – the best examples of which are crafted on the peninsula – and distinctive music that enliven the numerous religious and folk festivals. This has led to the region being fondly dubbed the *cuña*

(cradle) of national culture and traditions by many Panamanians – a statement that takes little account of the cultural affinities or contributions of the country's non-*mestizo* populations, and conveniently ignores the existence of much earlier cultures. Vestiges of pre-Columbian communities, the most ancient of which was an 11,000-year-old fishing village at Sarigua – currently the oldest known settlement on the isthmus – provide evidence both of an earlier history and of the conquistadors' brutal efficiency in wiping it out. Still today you'll notice the region's lack of indigenous communities.

For all that is said about the Azuero's yesteryear feel, the pace of development is increasing: trucks rattle

along tarred rather than dirt roads; unprepossessing cement-block mini-supers and houses with zinc roofs and satellite dishes dot the townscapes; and vast tracts of land are being gobbled up by a mushrooming number of property developers and the occasional mining company, looking to force rapid and irrevocable social change. For the moment, though, cattle farming and agriculture still prevail in the interior while coastal communities continue to derive their livelihood from fishing.

BIRDWATCHING IN THE NORTHERN AZUERO

Peeling off the Interamericana at Divisa, the Carretera Nacional takes you down the eastern flank of the Azuero, part of the Arco Seco (Dry Arc) and some of the country's driest and hottest terrain. In quick succession are three areas mainly appealing to birdwatchers, and most easily accessed in a private vehicle, though there are taxis from nearby Parita, or even from Chitré. The first, and most impressive area, several kilometers east of the main highway, is **La Ciénaga de las Macanas ❶** (daily 8am–4pm), the region's largest freshwater wetland area. Approached via the village of El Rincón, it extends across Río Santa María's floodplains, attracting a fabulous abundance of resident and migratory birdlife. On the other hand, in excessively arid seasons it can dry up almost entirely. Since the collapse of the observation tower (due to be rebuilt), birdwatching is limited to a couple of shady picnic tables and the rickety jetty near the water's edge. In addition to waders and ducks, at certain times of year you might see Brahman cattle chomping through the greenery; they help regulate the invasive water hyacinth, though conservationists are keen to reduce the number of grazing livestock. The dirt road here is only accessible via 4WD in the rainy season, and amenities at the time of writing were virtually non-existent – though funds have reportedly been earmarked to improve the situation.

Another 15 minutes down the road, signposted off the highway and 4km

⊘ AZUERO'S FESTIVALS

The riotous, costume-rich festivals of the Azuero pull in crowds from all over the country, particularly for the major celebrations of Carnaval, in Las Tablas and Chitré, Corpus Christi in La Villa de los Santos, and the Festival de la Mejorana in Guararé. The festivities are hybrid affairs: solemn religious ceremonies combine with pagan rituals and hedonistic excess; traditional folk groups are followed by DJs blasting out reggaeton, bachata, and salsa; and stylized Andalusian-inspired dances such as the *tamborito* (Panama's national dance) and punto are imbued with African and pre-Columbian rhythms using drums, gourds, and seed pods. More than 500 festivals are held here annually.

MAIN EVENTS

Jan 6 *Fiesta de los Reyes Magos (Three Wise Men) and Encuentro del Canajagua* Traditional folk festival culminating in a re-enactment of the Adoration of the Magi, Macaracas.

Jan (second Sat) *Desfile de las Mil Polleras* Tourist-focused parade of various types of Panamanian *polleras*, Las Tablas.

Late Jan (date varies) *Feria de San Sebastián* Five-day agricultural fair, Ocú.

Feb (date varies) *Carnaval* The country's most lavish celebration occurs in Las Tablas.

Mar/Apr (date varies) *Semana Santa (Holy Week)* Celebrated most colorfully in La Villa de Los Santos, Pesé, and Guararé.

Late Apr *Feria Internacional de Azuero* Ten-day international agricultural extravaganza with plenty of entertainment too, La Villa de Los Santos.

May/June (date varies) *Festival de Corpus Christi*, La Villa de Los Santos.

June 24 *Patronales de San Juan* Five days of costumed fun with *diablicos sucios*, folk dancing, fireworks, and the patron saint paraded from the beach, Chitré.

July (third week) *Festival de La Santa Librada* and *Festival de la Pollera* Religious processions and partying in for the town's patron saint, followed by a parade of *polleras*, Las Tablas.

Aug (second week) *Festival del Manito* – the usual parades and festivities with a mock wedding and sword fights, Ocú.

Late Sept *Festival de la Mejorana*, Guararé.

Nov 10 *El Primer Grito (First Cry) para la Independencia* – parades of marching bands, speeches, and fireworks, La Villa de Los Santos.

(2.5 miles) along a tarred road, lies **Parque Nacional Sarigua** ❷ (daily 8am–4pm), 25km (15.5 miles) north of the provincial capital, Chitré. Its 80 sq km (31 sq miles) are squeezed between ríos Santa María and Parita on land, and stretch out into the Bahía de Parita. Birdlife is restricted to a coastal sliver of threatened mangrove; farther inland are vast salt flats and tracts of dry forest, and bleak saline-streaked gullies dotted with cactus, acacia, and snowy blobs of wild cotton. Less a tourist attraction (as it is often heralded) than a cautionary tale, this desert-like wasteland is testament to the devastating consequences of a century of slash-and-burn agriculture and overgrazing, though gradually patches are beginning to recover. Covered with a layer of surreal bronze-colored dust and home to a vast solar farm, it is the country's hottest and most arid area. The silver lining in this sad story of environmental degradation is that the resulting erosion helped uncover important archeological remains, including evidence of an 11,000-year-old fishing village, the oldest known settlement on the isthmus, and more recent traces (between 1,500 and 5,000 years ago) of an ancient farming community. When walking around the park it's easy to stumble on shards of ancient ceramics or discarded shells, just as the sparse vegetation makes it easier to spot boas curled around parched branches, armadillos digging in the undergrowth, or lizards and iguanas sunning themselves. The landscape is best appreciated from the top of the *mirador* by the ranger station, from where you can also make out distant shrimp farms. Rangers offer guided walks for a tip, since the park's several trails are poorly marked.

Farther down the coast stretches **Playa Agallito** ❸, which at high tide rarely disappoints. Despite the continued clearing of mangroves to make way for shrimp farms, these silty mud and salt flats still provide sustenance for thousands of shore birds and waders, many migratory, who return to the same spot to feed each year. It's one of the country's top spots for sighting the rare roseate spoonbill as well as American oystercatchers. You can easily catch a local bus here from Chitré bus station, where they depart every 30 minutes.

CHITRÉ AND AROUND

Chitré ❹, the capital of the Provincia de Herrera, lies about a 40-minute drive south of the Interamericana, and is the main urban center in the Azuero Peninsula. Offering a spread of accommodations – though nowhere outstanding – it makes an ideal base for exploring the surrounding area and for attending the region's numerous festivals. A laidback commercial town with an attractive central park, Chitré was founded in 1848, though indications are that conquistadors had been there since the mid-1500s.

CHITRÉ HIGHLIGHTS

The compact center of Chitré can easily be explored in around an hour and the

Ceramics workshop in Chitré.

formal gardens of the **Parque Unión** are the obvious place to start. Neatly clipped flowerbeds and swaying palm trees around a stately bandstand provide the backdrop for a melding of modernity and tradition: young suited executives hold forth on their cell phones while elderly campesinos in *montunos* and *sombreros de junco* – the traditional embroidered shirts and workday straw hats – discuss the local news. Along the park's eastern flank stands the imposing **Catedral de San Juan Bautista** (daily 6am–8pm; free). Built between 1896 and 1910, it underwent a major restoration in the late 1980s, which took the unusual step of exposing some of the exterior stone walls to provide a pleasing contrast with the snow-white facade and bell towers. The restrained, polished wooden interior also makes a refreshing change from the ornate decor in many Catholic churches, especially the gilded mahogany altar, which is complemented by bright stained-glass windows. A one-block stroll east brings you to **Parque Centenario**, a more low-key affair, where the most striking feature in the park is the majestic ancient *guachapalí* tree. Leaving the square past the vegetable stands on the corner, you'll hit Calle Manuel María Correra, the main commercial street, bulging with stores selling cheap clothing and household goods.

Follow the street northwest for several blocks; on the corner of tiny Parque Bandera stands the faded colonial mansion – and former post office – that houses the **Museo de Herrera** (Mon–Sat 8am–4pm). Sadly, as with most of Panama's museums, little has been done to maintain the modest collection since it was first put together in 1984. That said, it is still probably the best museum outside Panama City. The exhibition on the ground floor focuses on the pre-Columbian era: a couple of fine ceremonial metates stand out, as well as some impressive ceramics. A reproduction burial chamber shows a life-size model cacique decked out in his gold arm- and leg bands, while copies of gold *huacas* from the anthropological museum in Panama City line the walls. Upstairs, fast-forward several hundred years to the colonial and post-colonial periods, with displays of traditional musical instruments and costumes, including elaborate *polleras* and devil outfits, and various tools from rural life. Don't miss the pouch made from a bull's scrotum used to carry staples for mending fences. The museum also offers Spanish-language cultural tours of the area.

PARITA

A short bus ride north from Chitré's bus terminal takes you to pretty **Parita** ❺. Founded in 1556, it is one of the oldest, best-preserved, and most picturesque villages on the peninsula, named after the Guaymí *cacique* who ruled over the Azuero. Particularly attractive is the sparkling white 18th-century Iglesia Santo Domingo de Guzmán, with its attractive clay-tiled

⌾ MASK-MAKERS

Ghoulish devil masks, which form the centerpiece of Corpus Christi celebrations across the country and feature in other festivals throughout the year, make great souvenirs, though they don't exactly fit neatly into your luggage. Made predominantly from papier-mâché coated onto a greased clay or earthen mold, their horns, wooden teeth, and eyes – usually ping-pong balls or marbles – are added later. They're available in various craft centers and agricultural fairs, and you can also visit some of the mask-makers in their workshops. Expect to pay less than $10 for a small mask and up to $150 for a larger and more elaborate one. The most renowned artist, with over 50 years' experience, who makes both *diablicos sucios* and *limpios* (see page 189), is Darío López (tel: 974 2933 or tel: 6534 1958); his hard-to-miss home-based workshop is on the Carretera Nacional, just north of Parita, on the eastern side of the road. Honored in 2017 with the Medallo de Belisario Porras – one of Panama's highest accolades – Sr López is now passing on his skills to his children and grandchildren. Another well-known artisan is José González (tel: 996 2314); taxi drivers should be able to find his workshop in Llano Bonito, on the outskirts of Chitré, or ask at the Museo de Hererra for directions.

roof; peek inside and you'll see some ornately carved wooden altarpieces and an elaborate pulpit. Surrounding the plaza, terraces of pastel-colored traditional adobe (*quincha*) cottages with tiled roofs take you back in time, though a line of telegraph poles reminds you that the village was not totally bypassed by the 20th century. The days leading up to August 8, the anniversary of the village's foundation, mark a big fiesta in Parita.

THE CENTRAL PENINSULA

The best way to get a feel for rural life in the Azuero is to head west of the Carretera Nacional into the agricultural heartland of the peninsula. Here you pass rolling hills of pastureland sprinkled with giant hardwoods, fields of sugar cane, and flower-filled towns and villages where the unhurried pace of life is infectious. There are precious few accommodations in these places, but the main population centers, such as Ocú and Pesé, are well connected by public transportation on decent roads and two or three can easily be combined into a day-trip, though you might prefer to rent a car in Chitré, or join a tour.

PESÉ AND OCÚ

One of the prettiest towns within reach of Chitré, lying 24km (15 miles) southeast and surrounded by a carpet of sugar cane, is **Pesé** ⑥, known for its liquor and its Good Friday re-enactment of the Passion of Christ. The ironic juxtaposition of faith and booze is evident the moment you set eyes on the church, which looks disapprovingly across the road at the **Varela Hermanos distillery**. Founded in 1908 by Spanish émigré José Varela – ancestor of Panama's last president – as a sugar mill and refinery, Varela Hermanos became a distillery in 1936 and has never looked back. Today it supplies 90 percent of Panama's spirits, including the country's top rum, Ron Abuelo, and the national knockout tipple, *seco* (35 percent). A million cases of spirit a year are produced here, much of which ends up down the throats of revelers at the Azuero's many celebrations, including the Festival de la Caña de Azúcar held in Pesé at the end of March to mark the end of the harvest. Tours, which include rum tastings and lunch, are run in English or Spanish at the distillery's **Hacienda San Isidro** (tel: 974 9401; email: reservaciones@varelahermanos.com).

Twenty kilometers (12 miles) west of Pesé, the larger village of **Ocú** ⑦ makes up for its lack of quaint charm with its festivals and its hat-making – above all the distinctive white sombrero Ocueño, with a thin black trim, which is still produced in home-based workshops. Try Artesanías Ocueña (daily 9am–4pm; tel: 6458 4529), a women's cooperative in the center of town on Plaza Sebastian Ocú, which also produces fine *polleras*, *montunos* and other embroidered items. The **Festival del Manito** (second week of August) is Ocú's premier event. Aside

Pedasí musician playing a güiro.

from the usual parades, there are two stand-out elements: the tamarind duel (*duelo del tamarindo*) and the peasant wedding (*matrimonio campesino*). The latter is a wonderful sight: following a mock church wedding, the bride, decked out in an all-white *pollera*, is paraded on horseback through the streets while the groom holds an umbrella above her head to protect her from the sun (or rain). In contrast, the tamarind duel harks back to the bygone days of testosterone-fueled fights to the death over women, family honor, or simply from overdoing the liquor, re-enacted with swords and sabres in the middle of the plaza. The town's other five-day extravaganza, La Feria de San Sebastián (late January), is an agricultural fair honoring the patron saint.

Though Pesé and Ocú are the more common day-trip destinations in the central peninsula, it is a pleasant drive, by car, to cover the further 30km (19 miles) through **Las Minas** and **Los Pozos** before returning to Chitré or continuing southeast to Macaracas – by bus you'd probably need to return to Chitré and take another bus back out into the countryside. There's nothing particular to see or do in any of these places, except chill out and watch rural life unfold. The party most likely to attract outsiders occurs in Macaracas; celebrated in the church plaza every 6 January for almost 200 years, the Fiesta de los Reyes Magos (Three Wise Men) features a two-hour dramatization of the Adoration of the Magi.

RESERVA FORESTAL EL MONTUOSO

Up the valley from Las Minas, the seriously denuded peaks of the optimistically named **Reserva Forestal El Montuoso** ❽ pale in comparison with the richly forested mountain ranges in Chiriquí, Bocas, or the Darién, so if you're heading for one of those

locations, El Montuoso can easily be skipped. But if you're lingering in the Azuero and aching to get into the hills, this is the best place to come, until the rugged wilderness of Parque Nacional Cerro Hoya (see page 195) becomes more accessible. The 120-sq-km (46-sq-mile) reserve, dubbed the 'pulmón ('lung') de Herrera,' was created in 1977 to safeguard the five rivers that rise in the mountainous region and to protect the rapidly vanishing tracts of forest being eaten away by illegal farming and lumber extraction. In response, several reforestation projects have been initiated. Though only 20 percent of the reserve is now forested, what remains is concentrated around the reserve's highest point, Cerro Alto Higo (953 meters/3,127ft). Steep-sided mountains cleaved by river-eroded ravines harbor plenty of wildlife to interest the visitor, such as red brocket and white-tailed deer, howler monkeys, white-faced capuchins, and collared peccaries. This is also one of the easiest places to spot the endemic brown-backed dove, while

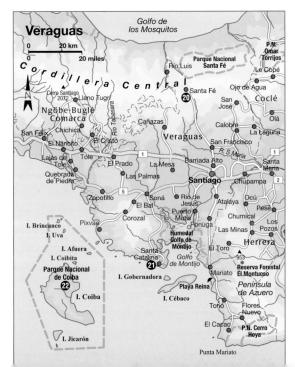

⊙ Tip

If you haven't time to hang around for several days to experience all the Corpus Christi celebrations, catch the 'highlights show' performed on a stage in the main plaza the following Saturday as part of the Día del Turismo. Sunday's Día de la Mujer offers Santeñas a chance to dust off their *polleras* and join in the fun.

Sarigua National Park.

other specialties include violet sabrewings and blue-throated goldentails – both hummingbirds – and the ever-acrobatic orange-collared manakin. To camp or bed down in the bunkhouse in the reserve you should enquire first at the Áreas Protegidas section of the MiAmbiente office in Las Tablas, along the road to Pedasí (tel: 500 0921; Mon–Fri 8am–4pm).

The reserve park office is set in a lovely orchard, where a short, pretty route crisscrosses the nascent Río La Villa up to a cascading pool. The main trail, Sendero Alto Higo, leads up the mountain of the same name, heading off to the left after Chepo, at a place known as the Caras Pintadas (Painted Faces), an imaginative reference to the petroglyph near the start of the path, where rare sundews are in evidence in winter. A moderately strenuous hike of just over an hour brings you out at a peak by a radio mast, which offers a tantalizing restricted view – thanks to some unfortunately located trees – toward the Golfo de Montijo.

THE ROAD TO LAS TABLAS

Just south of Chitré, the Carretera Nacional crosses the Río La Villa, the peninsula's longest river, which marks the provincial boundary between Herrera and Los Santos provinces, and continues southeast, running parallel to the coast. It bypasses the important yet tiny town of **La Villa de los Santos** ⑨, famous for the vibrant costume-clad celebrations of Corpus Christi, a historic rebellion against Spanish colonial rule, and the Feria Internacional de Azuero, the peninsula's annual 10-day agricultural jamboree in April.

LA VILLA SIGHTS

If you arrive outside party time, though, it's easy to be disappointed with 'Los Santos,' or 'La Villa,' as the town is usually called; it is much smaller and quieter than neighboring Chitré, and not as spruced up or as vibrant as Las Tablas. You'll need little more than an hour to check out La Villa's two main attractions, the church and museum, both on the central plaza. The square is named after the great Latin American liberator Simón Bolívar, to whom the town's influential citizens addressed a letter on 10 November 1821 asking to join his revolutionary movement against Spain. This unilateral declaration, called the Primer Grito de la Independencia (First Cry for Independence), started the domino effect that led to national independence from Spain 18 days later; it is celebrated annually with the customary flag-waving parades of marching bands, traditional folk costumes, speeches, and fireworks. On the north side of the square, the beautifully restored **Museo de la Nacionalidad** (tel: 966 8192; Tue–Sun 8am–4pm) marks the occasion, showcasing the room in which the townspeople's famous letter to Simón Bolívar was penned, complete with original furniture.

The museum, which was formerly a school and then a prison, overflows with details (in Spanish) of leading figures in the independence movement, and is therefore likely only to be of moderate interest to the casual visitor. The central attraction in the main plaza, and the focal point of the Corpus Christi celebrations – which are head and shoulders above those held elsewhere in the country – is the gleaming white **Iglesia San Atanasio**. The church contains a series of magnificent carved altars, a profusion of spiraling columns adorned with vine leaves, winged cherubs and flowers, all dripping with gold. Most splendid of all is the main altar, framed by an even more opulent archway that predates the completion of the church. Though the first stones were laid sometime between 1556 and 1559, the edifice was not completed until 1782. Note also the painted wooden tracery above the nave and the life-size entombed Christ figure in the glass sepulcher, which is paraded around the streets on Good Friday in a candlelit procession.

Three blocks southeast of Parque Simón Bolívar, at the southeastern end of town, the small **Parque Rufina Alfaro** celebrates the possibly apocryphal local heroine of the independence movement, Rufina Alfaro. A monument to the plucky Santeña has her seemingly emerging from a swamp. The story has it that Alfaro exploited the local Spanish commander's affections and secured crucial intelligence about when to attack the army barracks, and that she then headed the march there that cemented the bloodless coup.

GUARARÉ

Heading farther south along the Carretera Nacional, you'll pass roadside stands selling fruit and vegetables, occasionally with dangling strings of pork sausages or *chorizos*, a local specialty. Six kilometers (4 miles) before Las Tablas, the road skirts the tiny somnolent town of **Guararé** ⑩, which springs to life once a year when enthusiastic crowds arrive in droves to enjoy the famous Festival de la Mejorana (www.festivalnacionaldelamejorana.com; see page 191). Panama's largest and most vibrant folk festival, it is named

⊘ LA VILLA'S FESTIVAL DE CORPUS CHRISTI

By far the most fascinating and famous of La Villa's celebrations is the Festival de Corpus Christi, a heady mix of Christian and pagan imagery in an exciting narrative of dance, drama, and dialogue. It features a cast of larger-than-life characters and dancers decked out in extravagant costumes, interwoven with a series of religious ceremonies. Corpus Christi became an important tool in Spanish colonization across Latin America, as the invaders attempted to woo the indigenous population to the Christian faith by incorporating elements of their traditions and rituals into the ecclesiastical ceremonies. Though there is plenty of local variation, the basic good-versus-evil plot is the same.

In La Villa, the action starts on the Saturday before Corpus Christi when church bells at noon bring hordes of *diablicos sucios* (dirty devils) rampaging onto the streets. Clad in crimson-and-black-striped jumpsuits, wearing ferocious devil masks with flame-colored headdresses and letting off firecrackers at will, they terrify all to the beat of drums and whistles. Fast-forward to Wednesday, several Masses later, when at 11.30am on the Eve of Corpus Christi, the Diabla or Diablesa (though as

with all roles, performed by a male) also races around the town announcing the arrival of her husband, the Diablo Mayor, who convenes with three other devils in the central plaza. Joking and knocking back the booze, they carve up the globe in a bid for world domination. Before dawn on Corpus Christi, Santeños roam around town, on foot and on horseback, in search of the Torito Santeño – a man in a bull's costume – who is causing havoc, but is eventually rounded up in the Danza del Torito as the party proceeds through the streets to a large communal breakfast. The centerpiece of the drama unfolds mid-morning before the church, on a magnificent carpet of petals, as the Archangel Michael and the *diablicos limpios* (clean devils), distinguishable from the bad guys by their white sleeves and a rainbow of silk handkerchiefs attached to the waist, vanquish the villains in the Danza del Gran Diablo, or Danza de los Diablicos Limpios, before allowing them in to the service. All the dance troupes – including an assortment of dwarves, roosters, vultures, Mexican conquistadors, and escaped African slaves – attend the Mass, which then relocates outside as Holy Communion is offered to the townsfolk before the serious partying begins.

after the country's five-stringed guitar, the *mejoranera*. The five-day jamboree, which coincides with the *patronales* for the Virgen de la Mercedes in late September, is for lovers of Hispanic traditions; there's rarely a techno-beat in earshot and although, just as at most Panamanian festivals, the booze flows, it's a less hedonistic affair than many. The plaza resounds with folk music day and night, with dancers and musicians from around the country converging to entertain and compete. Adults and children vie for medals in playing violin, accordion, or *mejoranera*, and drumming, singing, or dancing, while the festival's *reina* (queen) looks on from her throne, decked out in all her *pollera* finery. There are even competitions for traditional work clothes – a kind of rural beauty pageant for both men and women. Bullfights are also on the agenda, usually dominated by seco-sodden guys staggering around a muddy field waving a filthy rag at a tired bull, cheered on by supporters – a far cry from the celebrity matadors of Spain. The festival highlight on Sunday

morning is the Gran Desfile de Carretas, when superbly decorated ox-carts parade through the town, accompanied by *tunas* (African-inspired bands of call-and-response singers and drummers).

The man whose brainwave it was to start up the festival in 1949, a local teacher, is heralded with a small museum in his name, **Casa Museo Manuel Fernando Zárate** (Mon–Sat 8am–4pm, Sun 9am–noon; free), five blocks north of the main square. Zarate's nostalgia for Panama while studying abroad made him realize the need to promote and preserve the country's cultural traditions. The museum chronicles Zárate's life and the festival's history. Walls are plastered with photos, including portraits of previous *reinas*, some antique *polleras*, and menacing devil costumes.

LAS TABLAS

Famed for hosting Panama's wildest Carnaval (see page 162), the provincial capital of **Las Tablas** ⓫ moves at a much more sedate pace for the rest

Las Tablas sign.

of the year. In comparison with neighbouring Chitré, Las Tablas is a modest town, but it possesses a sprinkling of tourist amenities as well as an attractive church and a small museum dedicated to Belisario Porras, three-time president and Las Tablas' most famous citizen.

Spanish nobles apparently founded the town in 1671; after fleeing Panamá Viejo – following its sacking by pirate Henry Morgan – they were swept by fierce winds onto the shores of the Azuero. The name Las Tablas is thought to have derived from the planks (*tablas*) salvaged from the ships and used to construct the initial houses. Once on dry land – so the story goes – an image of the Virgen de Santa Librada appeared before them as a statue, which they interpreted as a sign that their new settlement should be established on that very spot. Santa Librada, unsurprisingly, was adopted as the patron saint and is commemorated annually in the third week of July in the **Festival de Santa Librada**. Though it is less frenetic and a shade less hedonistic than Carnaval, there is no shortage of boozing and carousing, plus all the usual attractions of traditional costumes, dancing and music, street food, bullfighting, fireworks and, of course, religious devotions. For tourists the most interesting aspect is the **Festival de la Pollera**, which offers a chance to see streams of women in Panama's glorious national dress sashaying through the streets. A more recently established dusting off of the *polleras* occurs at the end of the second week of January in the **Festival de las Mil Polleras**. Thousands of women from all over the country converge on Las Tablas to show off regional variations of the national dress, accompanied by tuna bands.

TOWN HIGHLIGHTS

Most business in Las Tablas is conducted along the two main streets, Avenida Belisario Porras and Avenida 8 de Noviembre (also Av Carlos López), which is lined with stands, some selling local artesanía. The streets converge in the leafy main plaza, Parque

Local cowboy.

⊘ FESTIVAL QUEEN

Becoming a festival queen – La Reina del Festival de la Mejorana – is a national honor that lasts beyond the queen's year-long reign, such that wealthy families are prepared to shell out thousands of dollars for the privilege – and that's just for starters. Should there be more than one candidate at the pre-fiesta deadline, a run-off is held over three rounds (*escrutinios*) lasting several months, during which the candidates' families have to compete in fundraising. The belle with the most financial backing at the end gets to wear the crown; her rivals have to settle for being princesses. Some of the vast sums raised goes toward the queen's regalia – the elaborately embroidered *polleras de gala* and accessories cost several thousand dollars – and on other necessities such as dancing lessons and float decoration.

Belisario Porras. The vortex of the maelstrom that is Carnaval, at any other time the plaza is a tranquil shady spot to enjoy a snow-cone or ice cream. **Iglesia Santa Librada**, which overlooks the western side of the park, features a figurine of the patron saint set at the facade's apex. The magnificent golden altar, which suffers from an overdose of pale-faced cherubs, illuminates the otherwise pedestrian interior – look out for the reliquary said to contain a segment of the saint's leg. Although originally built in 1789, a lot of the church structure visible today dates from the late 1950s. Diagonally across the square from the church the neat, red-tiled **Museo Belisario Porras** (tel: 994 6326; Tue–Sun 8am–4pm) celebrates the life of Panama's most illustrious president in the house of his birth. Ironically its most striking exhibit is the Napoleonic-size tomb intended to house Porras's remains, which lies empty as family members wrangle over whether the bones should be moved from the prestigious Cementerio Amador in Panama City, where they

are currently interred. Walls in the single display room are plastered with faded photos, certificates, and memorabilia, which only partly succeed in conveying (in Spanish) the extent of his many achievements (see page 49).

Besides the church and the museum, the only other building of note is the **Escuela Presidente Porras**, with a smart maroon-and-cream exterior, and a distinctive clock tower and majestic portal. Built in 1924, this immaculately kept state school possesses high ceilings, large windows, and beautiful louvered shutters.

Midweek evenings are quiet unless there's a baseball game on at the Estadio Olmedo Solé (www.fedebeis.com; Jan–May) – a highly entertaining party atmosphere to be savored even if you don't know a home plate from a dinner plate. On weekends, many Tableños head for the nearest beach at **Playa El Uverito**, a broad belt of chocolate-colored sand 10km (6 miles) east of town, served by a regular bus service; here families tuck into platefuls of fresh fish at the beachside restaurants or picnic on the sand. There's also a sprinkling of smart foreign-owned accommodations dotted along the ordinary, occasionally garbage-strewn beach.

PEDASÍ AND ISLA IGUANA

Near the southeastern corner of the peninsula, 40km (25 miles) south of Las Tablas, is the small sleepy town of **Pedasí** ⓬ – though it springs to life for Carnaval and the Festival de Santa Catalina (November 25 & 26), which involves a parade of decorated floats and letting a bull loose to rampage round the square. A former small fishing village, it was catapulted into the national consciousness in 1999 as the birthplace of Panama's first female president, Mireya Moscoso, whose giant portrait greets you on arrival. There's nothing much to do here once you've glanced around the main square, but it is a tranquil place

Desfile de las Mil Polleras, Las Tablas.

to hang out, and provides a base for trips to Isla Iguana and Isla de Cañas, as well as being within easy reach of a string of great surfing beaches.

Other activities that can be organized, depending on the season, include kayaking, horseback riding, whale and turtle watching – the latter on Isla de la Cañas (see page 195). The growing expat community means there are some comfortable accommodations and decent restaurants, though places tend to come and go.

Undoubtedly the best day-trip from Pedasí is to the Isla Iguana, 4km (2.5 miles) offshore. This tiny lump of basalt, covered in dry scrub and grass, forms the centerpiece of the **Refugio de Vida Silvestre Isla Iguana** ⑬, created in 1981 to protect one of the largest and oldest coral reefs in the Golfo de Panamá. Home to more than 200 species of colorful fish, the coral itself is not in the best condition since a large chunk of the reef was blown off in the 1990s when two large bombs – relics of US training during World War II – had to be detonated. The best time

to visit is between May and December, when the calmer conditions mean crossings are smoother and snorkeling more rewarding; the sea can be so rough between January and March that it's sometimes too dangerous to set out. In the migratory season (June–Dec, especially Sept & Oct) humpback whales are visible, sometimes in the company of dolphins. The area's rich marine life also makes it popular with scuba divers. Tour operators and many lodgings can easily organize a visit.

NEARBY BEACHES

The rugged coastline of guano- and cactus-covered basalt is interrupted by two coral-sand beaches: the larger **Playa El Cirial**, where all boats pull up, accommodates the park office and a modest visitor's center. Playa El Cirial's small crescent of silky sand backs a sheltered cove of translucent water barely covering coral formations inhabited by a rainbow of reef fish, making it a superb spot for swimming and snorkeling. A short path across iguana-favored scrub takes you to **Playita del Faro**. Strong offshore

Banana tree flower.

⊙ LOS CARNAVALES DE LAS TABLAS

Las Tablas is synonymous with Carnaval, the nation's wildest party, a five-day bacchanal attended by an estimated 80,000 people. The festival is a crush, so it's not for the claustrophobic or faint-hearted. The festivities revolve around a Montagues-versus-Capulets-style feud between loyal supporters of either Calle Arriba (www.carnavalescallearriba.com) or Calle Abajo (www.calleabajolastablas.com), during which water pistols are substituted for swords. The calles shell out at least $500,000 each year to compete for the best music, supporters, fireworks, costumes, floats, and queen. Friday night sees the coronation of the new queen in a blaze of fireworks, followed by dancing until dawn in a swirl of *seco* and sweat. Mornings kick-start around 10am with *culecos* or *mojaderos* – being doused by hosepipes from large water tankers as you dance in the street. The queen and princesses parade around the square enthroned on gigantic themed floats, followed by percussion and brass murga bands, who work themselves up into a frenzy to inspire the tunas – the all-singing all-dancing support groups – to pump up the volume and outdo the opponents with insulting lyrics. The glam factor is ratcheted up a few notches at night, both on the streets and on the even more extravagant and glitzy floats, and general hedonism takes off. The good times are formally ended when a sardine is symbolically buried in the sand at dawn on Ash Wednesday.

currents mean swimming and snorkeling are sometimes prohibited here, but at low tide rock pools offer plenty to explore. The basalt outcrop to the left as you reach the beach provides a vantage point for one of the island's main attractions: Panama's largest colony of magnificent frigatebirds, estimated to be around 5,000. January to April offers the best chance of seeing males puffing out their extraordinary inflatable scarlet pouches, yet nesting goes on all year.

The southeastern tip of the Azuero Peninsula offers desolate beauty: kilometers of smooth dark sands punctuated by rocky outcrops and pounded by surf. Though the best surfing conditions are encountered between March and November, the coastline is surfable year round. Playa El Toro and Playa La Garita, both wide belts of sand, are a walkable 3km (2 miles) or short taxi ride east of Pedasí. But for surfers and non-surfers alike, the chocolate sand and rocks as well as fabulous ocean views at **Playa Los Destiladeros** ⓮ and nearby **Playa Escondido**, 10km (6 miles) south of Pedasí, are the most rewarding.

THE AZUERO'S SOUTHERN COAST

The imposing 3km (2-mile) swathe of charcoal-colored sand that is **Playa Venao** ⓯ (or Venado), 30km (19 miles) southwest of Pedasí, is the region's best-known surfing spot, providing waves suitable for beginners and more experienced surfers alike. A glorious arc, Playa Venao's beauty has been somewhat diminished in recent years by controversial developments at the eastern end of the beach. Thankfully, there are still a couple of mellow places to stay on the western end of the bay, which are fine spots to unwind, whether or not you are into surfing. In particular, Eco Venao (www. ecovenao.com) offers horseback riding, a waterfall trail – also open to non-residents – and a tour of its reforestation project. A few kilometers out from the bay, the guano-flecked rocky stacks of Islas Frailes are at times covered in thousands of nesting sooty terns and other passing seabirds; you'll need a good pair of binoculars to get a decent view from the boat, since landing is impossible.

In the bay to the west of Playa Venao, nestled among the mangroves and a stone's throw from the swampy shoreline, lies the long sliver of land that is **Refugio de Vida Silvestre Isla de Cañas** ⓰. The island is known for its turtles, which arrive annually in their thousands, availing themselves of a glorious 14km (8.5-mile) band of sand to lay their eggs. Turtles are not the only attraction, however. The reserve extends into a muddy tangle of mangroves both on the island's shore-side and along the mainland, providing roosting and nesting sites for waterbirds, which can be seen close up on a round-the-island boat tour, which also takes in a pre-Columbian archeological site (though with little to see) and a strangely formed cave dubbed the 'casa de piedra.' You can also enjoy a couple of hours' gentle fishing or a ride in a horse and cart around the island's

Beach on the Azuero Peninsula.

beaches and cultivations – rice, maize, banana, and cocoa are all grown alongside vast quantities of juicy watermelons, which demand to be sampled. Such excursions can be organized directly with the local community association Isla Cañas Tours (tel or What's App: 6718 0032; www.facebook.com/islacanastours), or through a tour operator in Pedasí.

For most people Playa Venao is remote enough, but if you're a die-hard surfer or an adventurous traveler with your own vehicle, you might want to swing by the even more out-of-the-way picturesque spots along the rugged coastline around **Cambutal**, a small fishing village 60km (37 miles) west. The journey takes you through undulating cattle country – spectacularly lush in the rainy season, desperately barren once the moisture has been sucked out of it.

THE WESTERN AZUERO: THE SUNSET COAST

The little-explored coastline of the Western Azuero has a very different feel to the dry, flat stretches of sand that line the eastern seaboard. Receiving much more rain, the countryside is greener and lusher, despite the cattle ranching and occasional rice cultivation, and so far, blissfully free of billboards advertising real estate. As the sole access road threads its way more than 90km (56 miles) south from the Interamericana through an increasingly undulating landscape, it offers tantalizing glimpses of rocky coastline, hidden coves, and foaming surf. Best of all, since the beaches face west, they witness glorious sunsets. Sprinkled along the coast, some delightful new lodgings make ideal spots for kicking back for a few days. Key areas for exploring include the pebble-and-sand **Playa Reina** ⑰, which stretches south to the mouth of the Río Negro – a haven for birdlife; the hilltop hamlet of Torio; and farther south, the headland of Punta Duarte. The increasingly roller-coaster road comes to a halt before one of the country's most inaccessible national protected areas.

Tucked away in the southwest corner of the Azuero Peninsula, **Parque**

An olive ridley turtle laying her eggs.

⊘ TURTLE WATCHING

Five species of turtle nest on Isla de Cañas, the most numerous being the world's tiniest sea turtle, the olive ridley. Their extraordinary mass nesting, or *arribada* (arrival), when thousands storm the beach over several nights, is a sight to behold. Pacific green turtles also nest in large quantities alongside significantly fewer loggerhead, leatherback, and hawksbill. Nesting occurs mainly between May and November, though timing your visit to coincide with an *arribada* – generally several days either side of a full moon – is tricky. The island was designated a protected area in 1994 and a number of the 800-strong population are involved in protecting the turtles – for which they are permitted to harvest a percentage of the eggs for consumption and sale.

Nacional Cerro Hoya  covers 325 sq km (125 sq miles) of the most ancient volcanic rocks of the isthmus, and contains more than 30 species of endemic plant. This is one of the country's most inaccessible parks; transportation is tricky, and formal trails and accommodations are lacking. But the rewards are plenty: giant mahogany, cedar, cuipo, and ceiba trees soar above the forest canopy, and carpets of moist forest rise up from the sea to lofty Cerros Hoya (1,559 meters/5,115ft), Moya (1,478 meters/4,849ft), and Soya (1,326 meters/4,350ft). A few scarlet and great green macaws maintain a fragile foothold in the forest, as does the endemic Azuero parakeet; other critically endangered species include the Azuero spider and howler monkeys, while substantial populations of white-tailed deer pick their way through the forest floor, shared with agoutis, collared peccaries, and coatis. As the park's name suggests – *hoya* means riverbed – the massif nourishes more than 10 major rivers, home to caimans and otters, and hundreds of streams that tumble down to the coast, leaving natural swimming pools and waterfalls in their wake.

The protected area also extends out into the sea, including precious mangroves and secluded coves enclosed by sheer cliffs, providing sheltered sands for hawksbill, olive ridley, and even some leatherback turtles to lay their eggs. Created in 1985, in a desperate attempt to stop the Azuero's hemorrhaging of forest through destructive agricultural practices, the national park and its protecting agencies are helping the population of about 20,000 – scattered around 25 communities – to make a livelihood from sustainable agroforestry, ecotourism, animal husbandry, and fishing projects. The best time to visit is early in the dry season when the views are more spectacular, the mud less overwhelming, and the hiking more pleasurable, yet the waterfalls and rivers – two of the major attractions – still hold sufficient water to impress. The handful of comfortable foreign-owned guesthouses and B&Bs sprinkled along the coast can usually organize a guide here, and trips to Isla

Santiago market stall.

Cébaco as well as to local community turtle-conservation projects in the season (July–November).

SANTIAGO AND AROUND

The administrative, economic, and cultural capital of Veraguas province, **Santiago ⑲** is a bustling center of around 40,000 inhabitants. Founded in its present location in 1637, and previously of great agricultural importance, it is now a thriving commercial hub – evidenced by the proliferation of banks and a state-of-the-art baseball stadium. Located almost halfway between Panama City and David, Santiago is a major transit point as well as a marketing center for the livestock, rice, maize, and sugar from the surrounding farmlands. If you're traveling round Panama by public transportation, it's highly likely that at some stage you will, at the very least, spend time in the bus terminal, though there's little incentive to venture farther into town unless you happen to coincide with the patronales, around July 25, which draw in the crowds for some serious partying.

Most of the businesses are strung along the Interamericana and Avenida Central, which branches west off the highway heading into the town center, coming to an abrupt halt in front of the impressive exterior of the **Catedral Santiago Apóstol**, stunningly illuminated at night. Adjacent is Parque Juan Demóstenes Arosemena, the city's main plaza; it takes its name from the former president, revered here for choosing the town as the site for Panama's first teacher-training institution. The college, **Escuela Normal Juan Demóstenes Arosemena**, lies several blocks northeast of the plaza on Calle 8A Norte and is the architectural jewel of Santiago, with a majestic Baroque frontispiece.

Across the main plaza from the cathedral stands the rather uninspiring – save for a few pre-Columbian ceramics – **Museo Regional de Veraguas**

(Tue–Sat 8am–4pm; free), housed in the former prison where three-time president Belisario Porras was incarcerated during the civil war.

Within easy reach by bus from Santiago's bus terminal lie two moderately interesting contrasting churches. **Iglesia Atalaya**, 8km (5 miles) southeast of the city, resembles an inauspicious two-tier wedding cake from the outside; inside, its lofty vaulted ceilings covered in splendid frescoes and its lovely stained-glass windows more than compensate. Tucked away in a side altar, the Cristo de Atalaya, said to date back to before 1730, is one of Panama's most venerated icons, a magnet for thousands of pilgrims every first Sunday in Lent. In the opposite direction, and in total contrast, the diminutive **Iglesia San Francisco de la Montaña** flanks the road to Santa Fé, north of Santiago, in a village of the same name. The simplicity of the small stone church, believed to have been built around 1727, belies the wonderfully elaborate wooden interior, with nine intricately carved Baroque altarpieces betraying both Spanish and

Museo Regional de Veraguas.

indigenous influences. You are likely to have to ask around to get someone to open up.

SANTA FÉ DE VERAGUAS

A hilltop village about 60km (37 miles) north of Santiago, **Santa Fé** ⓴ (not to be confused with its much larger namesake in the Darién) is a jewel of a mountain retreat that has been a well-kept secret for years. Surrounded by a stunning necklace of verdant mountains sprinkled with sparkling cascades and serene stretches of river, with easy access to a forested swathe of national park, it is a hikers' and bird-watchers' dream.

Thanks to its 500-meter (1,640ft) altitude, Santa Fé de Veraguas – to give it its full name – enjoys a pleasant, fresh climate, though the new highway over the Cordillera to the Caribbean coast is likely to have a major impact. For the moment, though, its absence of traffic and low population density, with houses strung across the tree-dotted hillside, gives it a peaceful village feel. Santa Fé is famous for its

flowers, boasting more than 300 species of orchid; the annual three-day orchid festival in August, when most are in bloom, attracts aficionados from around the country – contact the tourist office in Santiago for dates. The annual agricultural fair (late Jan–early Feb) also pulls in the crowds. Daily activity centers on the small covered market area, where fresh local produce is on display alongside a smattering of predominantly Ngäbe craft stands. Across the road stands a monument to Santa Fé's most famous resident, Padre Héctor Gallego (see page 16); a non-profit foundation that bears his name continues his community development work, offering support and skills training to local farmers and artisans. More visibly, the priest's legacy resides in the continued success of the cooperative he helped create. Today, it includes a couple of supermarkets, several grocery stores, a restaurant, bus and taxi services, and – the jewel in the crown – the local organic coffee mill, **Café El Tute**. Tours (in Spanish) of the processing plant, where you can buy some of

Avenida Central, Santiago.

⊘ PADRE HÉCTOR GALLEGO

On arrival in Santa Fé in 1967, the community's first parish priest, Héctor Gallego, was appalled at the exploitation of the local farmers by the wealthy merchant elite. So he set about helping the peasant population to establish a cooperative so their products could be sold directly to the market, bypassing the merchants. Perceived as a threat to the authorities – which included the first cousin of Omar Torrijos – Gallego was subjected to a campaign of intimidation, which escalated into arson and culminated in his final 'disappearance' at the hands of Manuel Noriega's National Guard in 1971. His tortured remains were uncovered years later, but were only unequivocally identified in 2018. Before his abduction, he had announced, in Spanish: 'If I disappear, don't look for me. Continue the struggle.' His prophetic words now figure on the monument dedicated to him in the village.

the delicious product, and to a nearby organic coffee farm, can be organized via the Fundación Héctor Gallego (up the road from the bus terminal).

The area's natural beauty makes it perfect for hiking, birdwatching, and bathing in clear streams and rivers – provided the weather holds – though the mountainous topography means there'll be steep inclines wherever you wander. River tubing is also popular here. A good start is to head down to the river, near the entrance to the village, below the Hotel de Santa Fé, or follow the road up toward Alto de Piedra and the Parque Nacional Santa Fé, which like many national parks does not yet have any noticeable trails. If you intend to tackle the area's loftiest peaks, Cerro Tute (930 meters/3,051ft) and Cerro Mariposa (1200 meters/3,937ft), cloaked in montane forest, or want to penetrate the wilderness areas of the park, then hiring a guide is a must. More accessible hiking destinations include the impressive Salto Alto de Piedra and Salto El Bermejo, as well as the 30-meter (98ft) cascade of El Salto, slightly farther afield. Your accommodations should be able to provide directions and/or a sketch map. For the hardcore, it's possible to organize a multiday hike over the cordillera to the Caribbean coast.

SANTA CATALINA

Though dwarfed by the Azuero Península to the west, the hilly Península de Soná attracts its own share of tourists. Small cattle farms cover the interior of the peninsula and fishing communities dot the rocky coastline, which protrudes into the Golfo de Chiriquí. Meanwhile, at the southern end of the peninsula, Panama's surfing capital, **Santa Catalina** ㉑ – the destination for most visitors – is expanding as a launch pad for excursions to the rainforests and coral reefs of Isla Coiba, which offers some of the world's finest

scuba diving, snorkeling, and sport fishing. As a result, this fishing village has developed into a pleasantly bohemian tourist hub, with mostly foreign-owned small-scale operations scattered along the main road in, or spilling off the paved road that leads to, **Playa El Estero**, the main beach and a scenic broad flat belt of soft sand. Though initially just a hangout for surfers and divers, Santa Catalina's tourist menu has expanded to include birdwatching, hiking, kayaking, snorkeling, and fishing, or just generally chilling out.

For specialized trips you're best off going with one of the tour operators whose offices are spread along the 200 meters/yds of main road from the junction to Playa Santa Catalina. For general snorkeling, surfing, fishing, or jaunts to Isla Cébaco or Coiba you may pay less by organizing things through your accommodations or by negotiating directly with the fishermen hanging out on the beach by their *pangas* (small flat-bottomed metal boats) or advertising outside their houses.

> **⊘ Tip**
> Note that park fees are often not included in tour prices to Coiba and that there is no ATM in Santa Catalina; the nearest ATM is in Soná, though Santiago bus terminal also has some.

Monument to Cacique Urracá, Santiago.

⊘ THE PENAL COLONY ON COIBA

For almost 80 years, Coiba was synonymous with fear and brutality, as horror stories of forced labor and torture, political assassinations, and gang warfare leaked from the island. Designated as a penal colony in 1919, it was intended to be an open prison, staffed by civilians and aimed at reforming serious offenders – hence the inclusion at the main camp of a school, rehabilitation center, and church. But with up to 3,000 prisoners on the island at one stage, scattered around various camps, most offenders were unable to access these resources. Prisoners worked 12-hour shifts on farmland and forest on only one meal a day, suffering violence from gangs and guards, malnutrition, poor sanitation, and scant medical care. A peek inside the decaying high-security block is sobering; prisoners shared a humid, windowless cell no more than 3 meters (10ft) across, with nine bare concrete 'beds' and a hole for a toilet, with no exercise, no visitors, and little chance of release. Unsurprisingly, escape attempts from the island were frequent but usually failed, as those who managed to get through the island's dense undergrowth, avoiding the crocodiles and snakes, generally came to grief in the shark-infested waters and strong sea currents. During Panama's military dictatorships, Coiba was a prime location for 'losing' political opponents. The penitentiary finally closed in 2004; the only former convict still remaining on the island is 'Mali-Mali,' now the park's most famous ranger and much-sought-after tourist guide.

PARQUE NACIONAL DE COIBA

'Abundance of fish' is one possible meaning of the name 'Panama,' in the indigenous Cueva language, and nowhere is this more apparent than in the crystalline waters of **Parque Nacional de Coiba** ㉒. The 2,700 sq km (1,042 sq miles) of reserve encompass Panama's largest island, Isla Coiba, plus eight smaller islands and 40 islets, but the vast majority consists of ocean brimming with spectacular sea life, including the second largest coral reef along the eastern Pacific. As part of the nutrient-rich Central Pacific Marine Corridor, the park is on the migration route of humpbacks (June–Sept), orcas, pilot, and sperm whales. Diving conditions are good year-round, but for land-based activities it's better to visit the island in the dry season since the trails are less boggy and there's a better chance of spotting mammals.

For years, the island's gruesome history as a penal colony helped protect its forests and waters, but the colony's animals (cattle, buffalo, and dogs) still roam free – though there was an attempt to capture and remove many of the cattle – threatening the ecological balance. Incursions by large fishing vessels (limited artisanal fishing is permitted), illegal timber extraction, and resort development could also damage the reserve, and ongoing negotiations between the government, environmental pressure groups, and interested businesses will have a critical impact on Coiba's future.

The island possesses large tracts of virgin forest, most of it still unexplored, home to numerous mammal and bird species. Of the estimated 2,000 different types of plant, under half have so far been formally classified. The surrounding oceans contain countless varieties of fish, ranging from delicate sea horses to vast manta rays, with 33 species of shark – including tiger, hammerhead, and whale sharks, though most are harmless reef varieties.

That said, the points of access within the park are limited. At the main camp, where rudimentary cabins constitute the only accommodations on the island, you can spend a pleasant day just hanging out. There's an interpretive center, moderate snorkeling in the sandy cove, and a couple of easy short walks affording pleasant views and tranquil birdwatching. Iguanas and agoutis are frequent dawn visitors to the lawn-cum-part-time-soccer-field fronting the main beach, and spider monkeys are often sighted swinging through the surrounding vegetation. The most rewarding hike is the **Sendero de Santa Cruz**, which leads from the ranger station through primeval rainforest, crossing crocodile-infested rivers to the island's west coast at Santa Cruz. You'll need to engage one of the park wardens as a guide; if you hire a boat and its captain, you can hike the trail one way (2–3hr) and arrange a pickup time to be ferried back to the MIA station. The more commonly tramped trail, and

Playa Banco, Veraguas.

usually the first stop on the basic tour, is just a short ride from the ranger station: the 1km (0.6-mile) **Sendero de los Monos**. You'll need to be here early to encounter the elusive white-faced capuchins or the island's unique variety of howler monkey. Just across the water from the trail is one of the most popular snorkeling spots, **Granito de Oro** ('the little grain of gold'), a speck of soft sand surrounded by translucent water, plentiful coral, and prolific fish, including the occasional nurse shark and turtle.

Just south of Punta Damas, almost halfway down the island, is the main camp of the former **penal colony** (see page 199), whose crumbling, eerie buildings are slowly being reclaimed by nature – though some parts have recently been 'cleaned up' for the tourists. Farther south, across Bahía Damas, the aquamarine reef-filled shallows of the eastern coast provide many of the prime diving and snorkeling sites. Panama's last remaining nesting site of the spectacular scarlet macaw is at the south of the island, near **Barco Quebrado**, though these magnificent birds are more easily heard than seen in the forest canopy. Some tours take a plunge in the invigorating thermal springs at Punta Felipe or venture into tangled mangroves at Boca Brava, or at Punta Hermosa, on the less-explored west coast. These more distant sites from the ranger station cost much more to visit because of the extra fuel required.

Most visitors to the island go on a day-trip from Santa Catalina, but this can be both costly and a little disappointing since the lengthy journey plus the unavoidable form-filling at the ranger station mean that you miss the best time for wildlife spotting. As there are no limits on day visitors to the national park, vacation periods and summer weekends should be avoided at all costs. Overnight stays are more rewarding, but you'll need to be prepared to forego creature comforts as the only accommodations are in the extremely basic MIA cabins, with shared kitchen amenities.

> ⊙ **Tip**
>
> In high season, book ahead if you want to stay overnight on Coiba, either through a Santa Catalina tour operator or your accommodations. If you are traveling independently, book via the MIA office in Santiago (national park desk; tel: 998 4271). Remember to bring plenty of repellent, and a flashlight, as power cuts are frequent.

A spot to relax in Santiago's main plaza.

Río Chiriquí Viejo.

CHIRIQUÍ AND WESTERN PANAMA

Cloudforests and coffee clad Panama's highest peaks, providing spectacular scenery and adventure activities galore. Down in the Pacific, tropical islands promise idyllic relaxation.

Most visitors to western Panama head for the forested Highlands, or Tierras Altas, of Chiriquí, at the eastern limits of the Cordillera de Talamanca, which rise out of the hot coastal plains round David, Panama's second largest city. Much of this stunning mountain scenery lies within the contiguous national parks of Amistad and Volcán Barú. These pristine forests are home to abundant wildlife including jaguars, pumas, tapirs, and gorgeous resplendent quetzals, with trails offering some of the best hiking in Panama. The region is also known as the country's 'canasta de pan' (bread basket), with the Highlands outside the reserves supplying most of the country's horticultural produce, while farther down the slopes, dairy and sheep farming are important, and in the lowlands, maize, rice, beans, and sugar cane are cultivated, alongside cattle farming.

Two roads wind up into the highlands on either side of Volcán Barú (3,475 meters/11,400ft), Panama's highest peak. The first climbs due north to Boquete, the country's main mountain resort, set in a picturesque flower-filled valley, surrounded by coffee estates and verdant mountains, laced with trails and waterfalls. The scenery, which is magnificent in its own right, also provides the perfect setting for a range of exhilarating outdoor

adventures: from zip lining to whitewater rafting, rock-climbing to horseback riding and hiking.

West of the volcano, the second road runs north from the Interamericana, through countless dairy farms to the smaller less touristy settlement of Volcán, which also provides access to its namesake. The road then threads its way through a steep-sided valley to lofty Cerro Punta, the highest village in Panama, which provides access to the cloudforests of Parque Internacional La Amistad. In contrast, down on the

⊙ Main attractions

Boquete adventure activities
Coffee tour
Sendero de los Quetzales
Highlands birdwatching
Volcán Barú
Parque Internacional La Amistad
Parque Nacional Marino Golfo de Chiriquí

⊙ **Map on page 205**

Parque Nacional Marino Golfo de Chiriquí.

coast, the Golfo de Chiriquí is dotted with unspoiled islands, some hosting dreamy exclusive resorts, where you can kayak through mangroves, snorkel the protected reefs, or simply loll in a hammock by the beach.

REGIONAL HISTORY

The earliest evidence of human habitation in the Gran Chiriquí region relates to the Barriles culture – so named after the barrel-shaped stones they carved – though little is known about them. For a long time, it was thought that a major eruption from Volcán Barú brought an end to this society around AD 600, but some geologists now suggest that the eruption happened much later, just before the Spanish Conquest. When the conquistadors did show up, they encountered various different groups, collectively referred to as Guaymí – ancestors of the present-day Ngäbe and Buglé, who were gradually pushed farther into remote mountain areas. From there, they repeatedly attacked Spanish settlements in the lowlands, though some eventually succumbed to

Coffee-bean production.

the colonizers' evangelizing efforts in mission centers such as San Félix, San Lorenzo, and Tolé – communities that lie along the southern fringes of the present-day Comarca Ngäbe-Buglé. Of the three main colonial outposts in the region, only David survived, eventually to become the thriving commercial provincial capital it is today. Under Spanish colonial rule, Chiriquí formed part of Veraguas, and was only established as an independent province in 1849. Following the separation from Colombia, the province gained its own railroad in 1916, which was expanded to reach Puerto Armuelles once the United Fruit Company (see page 216) began banana production. Though the railroad has long since ceased to function, there is talk of a Panama-China collaboration to build a new high-speed train link between the capital and David.

BOQUETE

Set in a scenic valley on the banks of the Río Caldera, 37km (23 miles) north of David and 1,000 meters

⊘ CHOOSING YOUR COFFEE TOUR

Going on a coffee tour, even if you don't like coffee, is de rigueur in the Chiriquí Highlands – either round Boquete or over near Volcán – and there are an increasing number to choose from. Most tours offer English-speaking guides and range from a 45-minute nuts-and-bolts introduction to three-hour interactive marathons involving roasting and a lesson on how to hone your cupping skills (see page 219). All provide an opportunity to sample and purchase the product at the end. Some even offer accommodations and other related activities on the farm, such as birdwatching or hiking. Other factors to consider include: the kind of coffee you want to taste (and probably buy afterward); whether the beans are specialty, gourmet, organic, or a combination of the above; whether the tour takes place in the coffee processing plant, or takes you out into the plantation; and does it offer value for money? Increasingly, some visitors are considering ethical and sustainability issues related to the estate's measures to conserve water, or reduce wastewater contamination, or their treatment of the Ngäbe workforces, such as providing schooling and meals for the children. Pay rates for pickers vary considerably among *fincas*.

(3,280ft) above sea level, **Boquete ❶** is the largest town in the Chiriquí Highlands, with a population of around 25,000. It is to specialty coffee what Bordeaux is to fine wine, with an array of informative *finca* tours to choose from that can tell you all about it. Boquete is also a popular weekend resort for Panamanians, and offers some of the country's best hiking, birdwatching, and adventure sports in the surrounding cloudforested mountains, in a delightfully refreshing climate. There's plenty to occupy you for several days – longer if you take a Spanish course at one of the town's acclaimed language schools (www.hablayapanama.com; www.spanishatlocations.com).

Technically, Boquete, spread out along the west bank of the Río Caldera and set against a mountainous backdrop, is separated into Alto Boquete – on the lip of the escarpment leading into the valley – and Bajo Boquete, which is considered to be Boquete proper. The slopes surrounding the latter are dotted with shady coffee plantations, lush gardens, and orange groves, rising to rugged peaks. Brooding Volcán Barú is frequently hidden behind cloud; only when the sky clears can you see its imperious peak dominating the town to the northwest.

Though the Guaymí were the first inhabitants of this remote valley, seeking refuge from the conquistadors, formal settlement only started in 1911, when European and North American migrants joined the existing population. Drawn to Panama during the canal construction eras, these pioneering settlers started up the various coffee estates and hotels as Boquete continued to develop – especially when, in 1916, the (now defunct) national railroad improved connections with David and other lowland centers – an old railcar from those times now rests outside the post office. Today, many Guaymí, known these days as Ngäbe, are only resident for the duration of the coffee harvest (Oct–Mar, depending on the estate), when families migrate from across the province for the tiring work of picking the 'cherries,' the

Gray-tailed (white-throated) mountaingem.

earnings from which have to support many for the rest of the year.

Since the 1990s the influx of foreign retirees and the associated real-estate boom, driven by the government's attempts to increase foreign investment, has forced major changes on the tranquil mountain community, and resulted in increasing deforestation. Lower down the slopes toward David, new middle-class residential developments have sprung up to accommodate city commuters.

BOQUETE SIGHTS

Laidback Boquete itself is rather unremarkable, with life revolving around the small **Parque Central** and the main street, Avenida Central, which are both dotted with souvenir shops, tour operators, and real-estate agents. The one low-key attraction is the quirky garden known as **Jardín El Explorador** (tel: 720 1989; Mon–Fri 9.30am–5pm, Sat & Sun 10am–7pm, closed Mon and reduced hours in low season) in the neighboring hamlet of Jaramillo Arriba. Cross the bridge in

town and turn left, following the road north alongside the river. Turn right at the fork, from where it's a stiff uphill walk to Jaramillo Arriba. The gardens are steep and decorated with tin men and scarecrows, with plants protruding from rubber boots and old TVs, plus scattered homilies in Spanish. On a clear day, the views of the valley below and Volcán Barú from the rose garden are fabulous.

While sights may be in short supply, there's plenty to enjoy in Boquete; specialty and more general tour operators offer a range of activities, from leisurely coffee tours and birdwatching to adrenaline-fueled, action-packed entertainment, including Panama's longest and most exhilarating zip lining and whitewater rafting. A couple of operators even organize water sports down in the Golfo de Chiriquí. Once the sun sets and the mountain chill sets in, most visitors retreat to one of the many fire-warmed restaurants, and midweek the town goes to bed early. On summer weekends or during festivals, however, you'll find several spots

where you can listen to live music and party until late.

Popular with foreign retirees, and Panamanians on a weekend break, Boquete also assures tourists a comfortable stay, with accommodations and restaurants to suit all tastes and budgets, and tour operators that can help you make the most of the area.

CLOUDFOREST HIKES

Hiking and **birdwatching** are the most established activities round Boquete, with trails ranging from a gentle undulating stroll round Finca Lérida to an eight-hour slog up and down Volcán Barú, with several scenic options in between. The shorter routes can easily be tackled independently, by taking a local minibus or taxi from outside Supercentro Bruña, close to Boquete's Parque Central, which will drop you off at, or close to the trailhead. Alternatively, local tour operators organize excursions to most places. For the longer hikes it's essential to go with a suitably qualified guide as routes are often poorly marked, and every year, ill-clad or poorly prepared tourists have to be rescued from the mountains, while every couple of years someone fails to make it home at all.

The **Finca Lérida ecolodge** (tel: 720 111; daily 7am–4.30pm) offers good-value birdwatching through the 10km (6 miles) of trails on its estate; birds to look out for include quetzals (Jan–Apr/May), highland hummingbirds such as the white-throated mountain gem, sulphur-winged parakeets, silver-throated tanagers, and the impressive black guan. Much of the trail network actually lies within the Parque Internacional Amistad (see page 213). Even as a non-resident, you can join a guided hike for a fee, which includes lunch, or pay for a sketch map and head off up through the coffee fields and cloudforest on your own. An Alto Quiel/Bajo Mono minibus from Boquete can drop you off at the entrance (taking 25 minutes). A more demanding proposition is the **Sendero Il Pianista**, which is a whole day's outing, and should be undertaken with a guide. Starting from the Il Pianista restaurant at the hamlet of Los Naranjos, 6km (4 miles) north of Boquete on the Palo Alto bus route, it leads you across farmland and up into the cloudforest, ascending as far as the continental divide, where, if you're lucky, you'll be treated to some superb valley views.

Many of the area's mist-swathed, jade-colored cloudforests above Boquete lie within the boundaries of **Parque Nacional Volcán Barú ②**, which stretches west toward the town of Volcán. This is prime birdwatching territory, and the favored habitat of the metallic green resplendent quetzal, the Holy Grail of Boquete birding. Quetzals are at their most visible from January to April, just after first light, when breeding pairs can sometimes be seen on the path. Since they are elusive birds, your best chance of sighting one is with a knowledgeable local

⚙ Tip

You are strongly advised to engage an experienced guide (armed with a first-aid kit) to go up Volcán Barú, or for hiking the Sendero de los Quetzales, or Il Pianista trail. While the routes are largely navigable on a clear day, if the weather turns bad, it is easy to get lost. In all cases, do not hike alone, be prepared for bad weather, and inform your accommodations where you are going before you set out.

⚙ SHORT TRAILS AROUND BOQUETE

Several short trails provide enjoyable alternatives to some of the more strenuous hiking in the mountains round Boquete. An easy introductory walk is the **Sendero Pipa de Agua** (daily 8am–3pm), northwest of Boquete – take a Bajo Mono bus and get off at the entrance by the T-junction. This easy 4km (2.5-mile) trail, also known as the Cascada Escondida (Hidden Waterfall), is a bird-watchers' favorite, following a water pipeline up a relatively gentle incline in a dead-end valley to an impressive waterfall. Also along the Bajo Mono route, on private land just over a kilometer (half a mile) after the T-junction on the way to the Sendero de los Quetzales, is the current tourist favorite, **Sendero de las Tres Cascadas** (tel: 6691 9144; www.thelostwaterfalls.com; daily 7am–3pm). Also known as the 'Lost Waterfalls,' this delightfully scenic cloud-forest trail takes in three waterfalls, each of which tumbles into a (cold) natural swimming pool. The first two are the most accessible, though still involve some moderately strenuous patches, especially when muddy. The last cascade involves more boulder clambering. Inevitably, the route is at its wettest when the falls are at their most impressive, but even in the dry season, be prepared for some mud.

guide, who will know their preferred courtship, nesting, and feeding spots.

The tedious haul up **Volcán Barú** (3,474 meters/11,397ft), Panama's highest point, is rewarded at the summit, which on a good day boasts a truly breathtaking and unique panorama of the Pacific and the Caribbean, both dotted with a myriad of islands. The dry season (roughly mid-December to April) is the best time to attempt the ascent but even then clouds and rain can close in quickly. To maximize your chance of a clear view, you should attempt some, or all, of the climb at night – for which you'll need a guide and a headlamp or flashlight – in order to arrive at dawn. The 13.5km (8.3-mile) ascent takes four to six hours (depending on your fitness); if you set off from the small park office, which marks the trailhead, between 11pm and 1am, you'll arrive at the peak in time to enjoy the unique spectacle of seeing the sun rise over both Atlantic and Pacific oceans. No rock-climbing skills are necessary, just the grit to plod up a boulder-strewn track and

endure a little rock-scrambling. You'll need warm, waterproof clothing – it's cold on the summit – plenty of water, and the usual hiking essentials.

Climbing Volcán Barú from the western side, from Volcán or Cerro Punta, is more physically demanding, and is usually spread over two days. However, the route is more rewarding as you are taken up a path, albeit very indistinct in places, rather than a road, and across more varied terrain. This trail, which you're likely to have to yourself, should definitely not be undertaken without a guide.

A far more beautiful, rugged hike than tramping the brooding volcano it skirts, the 8km (5-mile) **Sendero de los Quetzales ❸** offers the additional thrill of a possible glimpse of a male quetzal in full regalia, though quetzals may be more easily spotted in other locations, such as Finca Lérida. Though formerly easily doable on your own, severe floods and landslides have made the trail difficult to navigate in places, and hiring a guide will substantially enhance your chances of spotting a

Bienmesabe from Chiriquí.

⊘ THE QUETZAL

It may be the national bird of Guatemala, but the splendid resplendent quetzal is also the most highly prized avian sighting in the Highlands of western Panama. Solitary creatures for most of the year, feeding on insects and fruit, the male and female only come together during the mating and nesting period (Jan–Apr). Then the male complements his shimmering ruby breastplate by displaying his trailing iridescent tail. His acrobatic courtship display is a sight to behold, becoming a synchronized duet with a female if he manages to arouse her interest. The eggs are laid in a hollowed out tree, and both parents takes turns incubating them and feeding their offspring.

quetzal as well as allowing you to learn more about other fauna and flora. If you go on an organized tour, which is strongly advised, transportation to/from Boquete will be provided; if you decide to walk the trail on your own toward Cerro Punta, you can get your luggage transferred for you so that you don't need to return to Boquete.

The trail can be hiked in both directions, though conventional wisdom has it that it's easier to start from the Cerro Punta side (over 2,400 meters/7,874ft) because of the drop in altitude between there and the eastern trailhead at Alto Chiquero (over 1,800 meters/5,905ft). A moderately fit person soaking up the scenery and making occasional stops to spot the odd shy bird in the undergrowth should count on five to six hours to complete the trail, including the extra few kilometers to get to/from the official trailhead on the Cerro Punta side.

VOLCÁN AND AROUND

To reach the western side of Volcán Barú necessitates a return trip down to the baking heat of the Panamericana, before heading back up into the highlands; if you're traveling by bus, you'll need to head to David to take one bound for Cerro Punta. That may change, as work has started on a new link road connecting the two sections of the Tierras Altas. Turning off the Panamericana at Concepción, the road starts to rise through increasingly green countryside – the heartland of Panama's dairy farming.

Some 20km (12 miles) north of Concepción, at the mini-super in the hamlet of Cuesta de Piedra, a worthwhile short detour turns right to the **Cañón Macho de Monte** ❹. After just over 2km (1.2 miles), the parking lot by the hydroelectric project announces that you're in the right place. Follow the adjacent path that leads to the precipice above a dramatic (less so in the dry season) waterfall that tumbles into a gorge. It's also a good birdwatching area, where orange-collared manakins and fiery-billed aracaris are the stars of the show.

⊙ Eat

The perfect spot to break for a coffee and an *empanada* is Mirador Alan-Her (daily 6.30am–7.30pm), just south of Cuesta de Piedra. It serves a cornucopia of regional sweet and savory snacks, such as 'sopa borracha' (literally 'drunken soup'), sponge cake soaked in milk and panela, and the view is great.

Feria de las Flores y del Café.

Back on the main road, a further 13km (8-mile) climb takes you to the uninspiring small town of **Volcán** ❺ (formally known as El Hato de Volcán), spreadeagled on the lower western slopes of Volcán Barú at an altitude of 1,700 meters (5,577ft). It is little more than a glorified road intersection en route to the more appealing fertile valleys of Cerro Punta and the cloud-forests of the Parque International La Amistad, or the little-used Costa Rica border crossing at Río Sereno. That said, on a clear day it offers the most impressive views of the volcano. As the retirement and real-estate boom gradually seeps west of Boquete, tourism is beginning to take root. There are a few diverting excursions, not least to scale Volcán Barú (see page 208), though most visitors push on to Cerro Punta and Guadalupe. Even if you don't overnight here, a couple of good restaurants and relaxed ambience make Volcán a convenient pit stop and anyone set on independent travel up in the mountains should stock up on supplies (leaving the fruit and vegetables to Cerro Punta) and visit a bank.

Close to Volcán lie a few modest attractions that will appeal to enthusiasts or may be worth swinging by if you've a free couple of hours and your own transportation. Three kilometers to the northwest, the **Lagunas de Volcán**, at 1,300 meters (4,265ft), are Panama's highest wetlands and an important sojourn for migrating birds. The lack of infrastructure means that they will really only appeal to birders keen to spot northern jacanas, masked ducks, and, in the forested fringes, the rare rose-throated becard. Consider some early morning birdwatching with Laguna Adventures (www.lagunaadventures.com), the tour company branch of the **Janson Coffee Farm** (www.jansoncoffeefarm.com) on whose estate the lakes are located. They also offer guided hikes, horseback riding, and, of course, coffee tours.

Five kilometers (3 miles) northwest of Volcán, meanwhile, on the road to Caisán, the private finca of the Landau family harbors one of Panama's

Horseriding in Bajo Boquete.

⊘ AGRICULTURE BOOM

In the century since the Cerro Punta valley was formally settled, partly by Europeans, agriculture has expanded so rapidly that the area now supplies more than 60 percent of all the vegetables consumed in Panama, with fields forming a tapestry of produce from lettuce, onions, and carrots to commercial flowers and strawberries. This agricultural boom has come at the expense of the surrounding forests. What's more, once cleared, the bare cultivated soils on steep slopes, prone to heavy rain, have suffered heavy erosion. That said, the villages here, frequently swathed in cloud, and the surrounding fields are still undeniably beautiful, filled with abundant flowers and buzzing with hummingbirds.

most important archeological sites, **Sitio Barriles** (tel: 771 4281 or 6575 1828; daily 7am–5pm). It is named after the barrel-shaped stones unearthed in 1947 that provided the first modern-day evidence of what is presumed to be the country's oldest pre-Columbian culture, which was prominent around AD 500. The most interesting artifacts have been carted away to Panama City's anthropology museum (see page 132), but the farm possesses a couple of petroglyphs – the pièce de résistance is a silky smooth slab of basalt, which, when doused with water, reveals yet more squiggles. There's also an unconvincing re-creation of an archeological dig chamber and a small, rather chaotic display of ceramics.

From Volcán, a well-paved road snakes its way westward to the small town of Río Sereno, which shares an infrequently used border crossing with Costa Rica (tel: 722 8054; daily 8am–5pm), and is served by infrequent buses from David. A spectacular drive, the road swoops round tight bends, across cascading rivers, and through coffee and banana plantations. The two main attractions off this route are delightful mountain hideaways, known to avid bird watchers, but blissfully tranquil places for casual nature-lovers to unwind too. The first, 18km (11 miles) northwest of Volcán, is **Mount Totumas** (tel: 6963 5069; www.mounttotumas.com). It's a special place in a fabulous setting, surrounded by cloudforest and brimming with birdlife – over 200 species including quetzals (Jan–Apr) and the extraordinary three-wattled bellbird (Mar–Aug). Thoughtfully designed lodgings, including a delightfully rustic treehouse, are made predominantly of wood and suit a range of budgets, offering a mix of rooms, vacation rentals, and fine-dining. All have plenty of deck and hammock space from which to admire the breathtaking views and the iridescent hummingbirds, while a vast network of trails to waterfalls, thermal springs, and mountains await the more active. If you are without a high-clearance 4WD vehicle, a pick-up can be arranged in

Birdwatching in the cloudforest in Parque Internacional La Amistad.

Volcán, though whatever the transportation, the bone-shaking journey there will provide a memorable kick-start to your stay.

Farther along the Río Sereno road at Santa Clara, the welcoming family-run, eco-friendly coffee estate, **Finca Hartmann** (tel: 6450 1853, www. fincahartmann.com) lies one kilometer (half a mile) north of the main road. A birding paradise, with over 280 species recorded, it's the best place in Panama to see the dazzling turquoise cotinga and fiery-billed aracari, as well as more than 60 different mammals. Birds are most easily spotted around the main farm at Palo Verde, where the coffee roasting and other operations take place. Taking a coffee tour in English or Spanish (best during harvesting season) also allows you to stroll the five trails on the estate, one of which leads up to Amistad park. Returning eastward along the main road to Volcán, on a clear day, you are rewarded with impressive dorsal views of Panama's dormant volcano, Barú.

CERRO PUNTA AND PARQUE INTERNACIONAL LA AMISTAD

Heading north out of Volcán, the road twists and turns endlessly, threading its way up a mist-filled ravine, through which the Río Chiriquí Viejo gushes. It's flanked by almost vertical pine-clad slopes dotted with alpine chalets, some established by early European settlers. Roadside stands overflow with local produce; it's worth stopping off to indulge in a bowl of strawberries and *natilla* – a local creamy custard – or to pick up a jar of home-made jam. The road snakes through the hamlets of Bambito, known for its trout farm, and Nuevo Suizo, with a handful of weekend and vacation retreats dotted along the way. The landscape then opens out to expose a patchwork of agricultural holdings and pastureland before arriving at **Cerro Punta** ❻. Set almost 2,000 meters (6,560ft) above sea level in a fertile basin-shaped valley – the scarcely recognizable crater of an extinct volcano – and surrounded by densely forested, rugged mountains, it is the highest village in Panama.

Farmland surrounding Volcán Barú.

Horse lovers can arrange a visit to a nearby stud farm. Haras Cerro Punta (tel: 227 3371, www.harascerropunta.com), which offers tours in Spanish, breeds racing stallions that have greater lung capacity than average due to the altitude. The foaling season (Jan–May) is probably the most rewarding time to drop by.

Three kilometers (2 miles) beyond Cerro Punta you arrive at **Guadalupe**, an enchanting flower-filled hamlet of around 400 inhabitants, dominated by the rustic Los Quetzales Lodge and Spa, which is the hub of activity. While in Guadalupe, orchid fanatics may fancy booking a guided tour of nearby **Finca Dracula** (www.fincadracula.com; Jan–Apr 9am–4pm, hourly) – a 15-minute walk from the lodge. Latin America's premier orchid farm, it boasts more than 2,000 varieties, as well as some lovely gardens. The area's spectacular scenery, together with the cool, crisp mountain air (temperatures drop to well below 50°F/10°C at night), make Cerro Punta and Guadalupe superlative bases for

hiking, and the pristine cloudforests of La Amistad (see page 213) and Volcán Barú (see page 208) national parks are both within easy reach.

From Guadalupe, the road (and bus) sweeps round to the left in a wide loop, before climbing back to rejoin the main road at Cerro Punta. Just 6km (4 miles) from Cerro Punta or Guadalupe, off the bus loop, the hamlet of Las Nubes provides access to **Parque Internacional La Amistad ❼** (International Friendship Park), often abbreviated to PILA or Amistad. Covering 4,000 sq km (1,544 sq miles) of precipitous forested mountains straddling Panama and Costa Rica, the park forms a crucial link in the biological corridor of protected areas running the length of Central America. Given its varied topography, Amistad is the most ecologically diverse park in the region, including more than 400 different bird species, making it the most important protected area in Panama after the Darién. Although almost all of the Panamanian section lies in Bocas del Toro, it is far more accessible from

Red and white double-bloomed amaryllis.

⊘ LOS QUETZALES LODGE AND SPA

The remarkable Los Quetzales Lodge & Spa (tel: 771 2182; www.los-quetzales.com) is the hub of life in tiny Guadalupe, and an unpretentious example of real sustainable development. Involved in environmental activism, it engages in sound environmental practices, such as recycling, use of renewable energy, composting, and reforestation. What's more, it is also deeply embedded in the community, employing and providing training for over 40 local people. An incredibly versatile place, Los Quetzales accommodates campers, backpackers, honeymooners, Panamanian families, and expats with consummate ease. While the standard hotel rooms are pleasant enough, overlooking flower-filled grounds brimming with hummingbirds, the glorious vacation rental cabins set deep in the cloudforest are truly special. Back in the lodge, all guests have access to the comfy bar-lounge and games room, full of books and couches, warmed by a log fire, and with table tennis. Activities include spa treatments, cycling, horseback riding, and guided cloud-forest walks. Even if you're only passing by, a meal in the restaurant (daily 6.30am–8pm) is a must. Drawing on produce from their organic gardens, dishes often include more vegetables than you are likely to see in a month elsewhere in Panama!

the Pacific side of the country. There are three short trails with *miradores* (viewing platforms) offering excellent vistas of some of the highest mountains in Panama (at least before the cloud descends) and a 50-meter (164ft) waterfall. A longer, steeper, and less distinct trail (8km/5-miles round trip) leads through virgin cloudforest to the summit of Cerro Picacho (2,986 meters/9,796ft), but you'll need to get one of the park wardens to guide you. A basic campsite and bunkhouse, shared with the park wardens, are the only accommodations. Since there is no phone coverage here, you either turn up or make enquiries in advance at the MiAmbiente office in David (on the road to the airport; tel: 775 3164; Mon–Fri 8am–4pm).

DAVID AND THE CHIRIQUÍ LOWLANDS

In contrast to the Highlands – the destination for the vast majority of visitors to the province – the oppressive heat of the Chiriquí Lowlands does little to attract tourists. Nor do endless fields

of maize, rice, bananas, sugar cane, and cattle. In the midst of this agricultural land sits **David** ❽, Panama's second largest city, with a population of over 140,000, and served by an airport with daily flights to Panama City and international connections.

Founded in 1602, David was the only one of three Spanish settlements in the area to survive repeated attacks from indigenous groups. Developing slowly as a remote colonial outpost, it only began to thrive when Chiriquí's population swelled in the 19th century. Today, despite being a busy commercial city and the focus of Chiriquí's strong regional identity, it retains a sedate provincial atmosphere. Devilishly hot and either humid or dusty, its unexceptional modern architecture is spread out on a grid that derives from colonial days. Although David has few attractions per se, its very ordinariness holds a certain appeal for a couple of days. It's also a good place to stock up before a trip to the highlands or break a journey between Panama City and Costa Rica or Bocas del Toro. For independent travelers it's hard to avoid the city, or at least its vast bus terminal, since virtually all the province's public transportation passes through here. Being located on the Interamericana, it's an important staging post between Panama City (only six hours away by bus) and Costa Rica, a mere 40-minutes away.

David's heart is the vibrant **Parque Cervantes**, where snow-cone vendors, shoe-shiners, and hawkers peddling sugar cane and fresh fruit juice all vie for business, overlooked by the nondescript Iglesia de la Sagrada Familia. With plenty of shady seating, it's a prime spot for watching urban life unfold.

A stroll three blocks southeast of Parque Cervantes down Calle 'A' Norte takes you back to the last vestiges of the city's colonial past in **Barrio Bolívar**. The decaying historic colonial

View from the summit of Volcán Barú.

mansion on the corner with Avenida 8 Este was occupied by successive generations of the distinguished Obaldía family – José Vicente was the president of New Granada (combined Colombia and Panama) and his son José Domingo became the second president of Panama. Though slated for restoration, time is running out for the dilapidated structure. Just east of here, the ancient colonial bell tower stands over the messily restored 19th-century Catedral San José de David, which contains some gaudy modern murals.

EXCURSIONS FROM DAVID

The few low-key attractions around David are within a short bus ride of the city. Beyond the airport, the road fizzles out at **Pedregal**, David's small port and marina, which provides entry by boat into the morass of mangroves and islands in the Golfo de Chiriquí. On weekends, *La Cocaleca* (tel: 730 5583, www.lacocalecapty.com), a popular booze-cruise boat, leaves the jetty at set times to tour the mangroves or venture farther out into the gulf. Heading 25km (15.5 miles) southwest out of the city takes you to unremarkable, grainy **Playa Barqueta**, the nearest spot to dip in the sea, which has a couple of informal places to eat and enjoy a beer. A large portion of the beach lies within the boundaries of the little-known **Refugio de Vida Silvestre de Playa Barqueta Agricola** (park warden tel: 6602 5770; daily 6am–3pm), whose 14km (8.5-mile) stretch of sand, scrub, and mangrove protects nesting sites for hawksbill, olive ridley, leatherback, loggerhead, and green sea turtles. Visits to check out the night-time nesting (late May–Oct is best) can be arranged with the park warden or at the MiAmbiente office in David (the road to the airport; tel: 775 3163). The reserve entrance lies east of Las Olas Resort, where the infrequent bus stops; alternatively the warden will come and pick you up. Visitors in their own vehicle will need a 4WD.

West of David, the Interamericana speeds along 47km (29 miles) of flattish terrain to the frontier with Costa Rica. En route it passes a more appealing

Golfo de Chiriquí beach.

place to cool off from the sweltering heat than David's local beach: **Balneario Barranca** (daily 11am–6pm) is a natural swimming pool with a rancho bar-restaurant and hammocks on a meander of Río Chirigagua, just north of the Interamericana. While a festive family atmosphere prevails on weekends, you can have the Tarzan swing all to yourself midweek. Any bus from David bound for Boquerón can drop you off at the entrance to walk 100 meters/yds up the track to the river.

Just before Panama's main border with Costa Rica at Paso Canoas (open 24 hours), the road veers off left down the narrow **Península de Burica**, weaving its way through banana and palm oil plantations. Aside from a handful of die-hard surfers and fishing enthusiasts, few tourists venture down to the distant tip of the peninsula, which resembles an upside-down bowling pin straddling the Costa Rican border. Here, 50km (31 miles) southwest of David, the remoteness is tangible and the sunsets spectacular. The gateway to the peninsula is Puerto Armuelles,

for more than 70 years Panama's thriving Pacific hub of the infamous United Fruit Company (now Chiquita Brands) until it pulled the plug in 2003. The rotting pier and abandoned wooden houses serve as poignant reminders of the town's former importance.

Ten to 15 minutes east of David, a road peels north off the Interamericana, heading up into the mountains. Traversing the continental divide to the Caribbean coast this serpentine road is Panama's most spectacular drive. On a clear day you get breathtaking views; conversely, if you find yourself peering through thick fog to see the edge of the asphalt, it can be one of the scariest journeys you ever make. During the October and November rains, landslides are frequent, sometimes blocking the route for days. Midway across the cordillera, before descending into Bocas del Toro province, you cross the dam wall of Lago Fortuna, Panama's main source of hydroelectric power.

Only 17km (10.5 miles) up the road from the Panamericana/Interamericana, just north of the village of

Isla Coiba in the Golfo de Chiriquí.

Gualaca, the sparkling waters of Río Este squeeze through a narrow, shallow canyon, known as **Los Cangilones de Gualaca 9** (Dec–Apr daily 7am–6pm), creating a refreshing natural swimming pool – an ideal place to cool off in the summer, though it's packed on weekends. The flat slabs of volcanic rock either side of the canyon are thought to have come from lava slides from Volcán Barú, through which the river has eroded its path over time. There are no amenities beyond washrooms and changing rooms, but it makes a delightfully tranquil picnic spot provided you avoid the weekend crowds. Buses run here regularly from David and the cangilones feature on the tour menus of several Boquete tour companies.

GOLFO DE CHIRIQUÍ

There's not much to the laidback fishing village of **Boca Chica 10**, 30km (19 miles) southeast of David as the vulture flies, beyond a small supermarket, a couple of fishing lodges and a couple of inexpensive *fondas*. It does,

however, provide the gateway to one of the province's most prized natural treasures: **Parque Nacional Marino Golfo de Chiriquí 11**, a nirvana for scuba-diving, snorkeling, and sportfishing enthusiasts. Created in 1994 to protect almost 150 sq km (58 sq miles) of terrestrial and marine wildlife, the park comprises 25 islands and 19 coral reefs, teeming with hundreds of fish in a rainbow of colors. The coastline to the west of Boca Chica, meanwhile, is thick with mangroves – which means you'll have to venture to the more distant islands to find white sand or crystalline waters. Note that when the wind drops in the rainy season, sandflies can be a nuisance, so bring repellent. Just outside the village are a couple of classy guesthouses, while the islands themselves host some great accommodations, ranging from exclusive resorts to Robinson-Crusoe-style rustic *cabañas*.

Within the reserve, **Isla Parita** is by far the largest land mass, and along with the much smaller **Isla Paridita** it is the only inhabited island, on

Fisherman repairing his net at Boca Chica.

account of its fresh water sources. The rest are generally small, low-lying, sedimentary outcrops that enjoy a tropical savannah climate, with beaches backed by coconut palms and manchineel trees, where the only visitors to disturb the hermit crabs and iguanas are nesting hawksbill and leatherback turtles.

Across the narrow water channel in front of Boca Chica's jetty is **Boca Brava**, an island hosting two contrasting lodgings, while on the mainland a couple of upscale fishing lodges and boutique guesthouses do little to disturb the tranquility of the place. Snorkeling trips head out into the national park, to the gorgeous white-sand coves of **islas Bolaños** and **Gámez**, but there is even better snorkeling and diving to be had around the more remote (and pricier) **Islas Secas**, **Islas Ladrones** and **Isla Montuoso**. The marine life is breathtaking, from sea horses and starfish to giant manta and eagle rays, pods of dolphins, turtles, sharks, and vast schools of fish swirling round volcanic

Ngäbe woman on horseback.

pinnacles, with humpback whales arriving to calve from June. Islas Secas hosts Panama's most exclusive island resort, and includes its own private airstrip.

The impressive broad belt of flat tan-colored sand of **Playa Las Lajas** ⑫ is by far the most popular weekend destination for urbanites from David, some 80km (50 miles) away, and even from Santiago, over 120km (75 miles) away, in need of sand, sea, and surf. However, since the beach – backed by wafting palms – stretches for a long way in both directions, there's plenty of space to escape the crowds, except over the weekends leading up to Carnaval, when you can expect all-night partying on the sands. The benign waves are more suited to body surfing and playing around than serious surfing. There is an assortment of small accommodations clustered round the entrance to the beach, and a couple of options in the village of Las Lajas, some 7km (4.5 miles) back from the sea, and around 12km (7.5 miles) south of the Interamericana.

⊘ VISITING THE NGÄBE

Though the Ngäbe are Panama's most numerous indigenous citizens by far, they see considerably fewer tourists than the Guna or Emberá, and are understandably wary of outsiders given the recent history of conflict with both the Panamanian authorities and international mining corporations. Undertaking a homestay in the mountain community of Soloy, in the southwest corner of the Comarca Ngäbe-Buglé, provides a unique opportunity to begin to learn about the Ngäbe, their traditions, and their present-day challenges, though you'll need some Spanish to make the most of it, and be prepared for very rudimentary lodgings and simple food. The village itself has no nucleus, but rather is strung out several kilometers along the main road and the Río Soloy. The river is crucial to community life and provides the basis for tourist activities; visitors can also learn the processes of extracting plant fibers and mixing natural dyes to make a traditional *kri* (string bag). Homestays are currently only arranged by a handful of families as many remain suspicious of tourism. Contact tourist coordinator and white-water rafting guide, Juan Carlos Bejerano (tel: 6638 0944; email: carlito559@hotmail.com).

In eastern Chiriquí, the community of San Félix has a major Ngäbe population; lying just north of the Interamericana, it is more accessible.

⌕ COFFEE

As with fine wine, the world of specialty coffee tasting is full of hype, jargon, inflated prices, and an exuberant use of epithets.

One of Panama's lesser-known distinctions is as one of the world's finest producers of specialty coffee. The rich, volcanic soils of the mountainous slopes above Boquete, at the ideal elevation of 1,500–2000 meters (4,920–6,560ft), provide perfect conditions for growing high-quality coffee. Round Boquete coffee is 'shade-grown' – planted under a canopy of mixed trees – which provides a plethora of benefits: slower maturing beans that increase the natural sugars, which in turn enhance the flavor; tree cover that helps retain moisture in the soil; improved biodiversity, including more birds, which in turn help control insect pests and aid pollination. In short, a virtuous circle par excellence. After that, however, it's down to a labor-intensive and skilled production process to produce the highly prized beans.

Specialty coffee (www.sca.org) is basically single-origin coffee, where the farm manages the whole process 'from the seed to the cup,' according to strict protocols. All Boquete's coffee is Arabica, with Catuai, Pacamara, and Typica among the quality varietals grown, though Geisha is the star plant that has made waves across the coffee world. Once seedlings are planted, it takes around four years for the tree to produce the fruit, in which the precious coffee beans reside. The careful nurturing and back-breaking work of harvesting the 'cherries' by hand falls to the poorly paid Ngäbe workers, who migrate en masse from the comarca and live on the farm for the duration.

In Chiriquí, most of the estates harvest from October to March. Once picked, the beans are either wet (or washed) or dry-processed, or some hybrid combination of the two. In wet processing, the cherry is passed through a pulping machine first to remove the skin and pulp, before the beans are dunked in water to separate out the fully ripe beans – heavier ones that sink – from the unripe and defective, which float. The chosen beans are then fermented in water for up to two days, rinsed, and dried. In the ancient dry-processing method, the cherries are spread out to dry and ferment in their flesh in the sun (or whizzed round in a tumble-dryer like machine), raked, and turned periodically to ensure they don't get too moist and prone to bacteria, or too dry and brittle. The bean is then extracted. Milling follows next, where the remaining unwanted bits of husk or parchment are removed through hulling.

Beans are even polished in some cases – to improve their appearance – before grading and sorting, by size, shape, and color, with the aid of a host of machines and by hand.

COFFEE CUPPING

Tasting, or 'cupping' of small samples of beans occurs at various stages, to determine quality and taste. For specialty coffee the strict SCA regulations specify everything from dimensions of the room and table in the laboratory, to the size and shape of the cup, the temperature of the water, and the metal of the spoon. As with wine, cupping involves plenty of sniffing and smelling before slurping and tasting, and then spitting the coffee out so as not to ruin the palette for the next sample. The final tasting occurs at the all-important annual evaluation in May. Here, blind-tasting by certified cuppers leads to marks out of 100 being awarded; beans that score over 80 have the right to be labeled 'specialty.' A guided tour with one of the estates in Boquete should help you to untangle the mysteries of coffee-making.

Coffee berries.

BIRDWATCHING

The magnificently powerful harpy eagle, the resplendent quetzal, and the brilliant blue cotinga are just three residents that make Panama a top birding destination.

If you're one of many who regard birdwatching as a dull pastime, involving hours trying to identify one indistinguishable LBJ (little brown job) from another, a trip to Panama is likely to make you think again. Boasting around 1,000 species, including over 100 regional endemics, in a country slightly smaller than South Carolina (or Ireland), Panama acts as a magnet for serious twitchers laden with tripods, checklists, and hefty avian tomes. But even the casual nature lover cannot fail to be impressed by some of Panama's most colorful encounters: shimmering tanagers and hummingbirds, flashes of squawking macaws in flight, or the giant painted bills of toucans as they swoop across the treetops. What's more, many birds can be spotted around Panama City and in the nearby national parks around the canal, with the cloudforested highlands of Chiriquí and the rainforests of Darién the country's other birding hotspots.

Montezuma oropendolas live in groups, usually at the edge of lowland forests. They have spectacular bicolored bills.

Cinnamon woodpeckers feed on ants and termites, as well as fruit. They can be spotted foraging singly or in pairs.

Since many of these glamorous avian creatures spend much of their time tantalizingly high up in the treetops or flying overhead, it is worth acquiring a pair of binoculars, which will significantly enhance your birdwatching experience. So too will engaging a guide. Operators in the capital can arrange high-quality bi- or multi-lingual tours across Panama, while small companies and individual local guides dotted around the country can offer a morning or full day's outing. Alternatively, book into one of the many stunning birding lodges, such as the canopy collection (www.canopytower.com), which also have observation towers and decks and their own experts on hand.

A good introduction are the monthly morning birdwatching-for-beginners walks in the Parque Natural Metropolitano in Panama City; organized by the Panama Audubon Society (tel: 232 5977; www.facebook.com/audubonpanama), they are open to all and highly rewarding.

Pale-billed woodpecker.

Hummingbirds

Found only in the Americas, these diminutive, iridescent nectar-feeders are as fascinating as they are visually stunning in sunlight. Worldwide, well over 300 species make up the hummingbird family (*trochilidae*), with around 60 recorded in Panama. The 'humming' derives from the buzz you hear from the extraordinarily rapid wingbeat; some can manage up to 80 beats per second and can whizz past at speeds of up to 55kph (34mph). They can also fly sideways and backward – the only bird that can. To sustain all this activity, hummingbirds have to feed every 10–15 minutes, visiting well over 1,000 flowers a day, and are fiercely territorial as they defend their food source from rivals. At night, these hyperactive birds need to recover, so go into 'torpor,' a kind of temporary energy-saving hibernation which slows down their metabolism. Prevalent across Panama, your best chance of seeing a wide variety of hummers is in the accessible cloudforests of Chiriquí; star sightings include the glittering violet sabrewing, the sparkling blue crown and gorget of the magenta-throated woodstar, and the tiny scintillant hummingbird – only 3cm (1.2in) long and weighing no more than dime, it's one of the world's smallest.

Rufous-winged woodpecker has a dazzling red head
ch, which extends to become a crest on the male.

-winged flycatcher-shrikes often join mixed flocks to
age for insects.

The Talamanca or admirable hummingbird is found in the highlands of Western Panama and Costa Rica.

Bocas del Toro souvenirs.

BOCAS DEL TORO

The Caribbean islands of Bocas del Toro reel in water-sport enthusiasts, nature-lovers, and party-goers in equal measure, but there are treats on the mainland too, including some magical wetlands and an enticing, remote national park.

The Caribbean archipelago of Bocas del Toro ('Mouths of the Bull'), by the Costa Rican border, is one of the most beautiful areas in Panama. It's also one of the most isolated – the mainland portion of the province is connected to the rest of Panama by a single spectacular road that carves its way over the continental divide, often blocked by landslides during the heaviest rains, while the island chain requires a boat ride to reach.

For most people, Bocas means the tropical islands – Isla Colón and Bastimentos, in particular – which attract more visitors than anywhere else outside Panama City and the Canal. They offer opportunities for surfing or relaxing on pristine beaches, and snorkeling and diving among coral reefs in a maze of tangled mangroves and undisturbed rainforest. Some of this natural paradise lies inside Parque Nacional Marino Isla Bastimentos. Some visitors, however, come for the nightlife: cocktails, waterside dining, and places to dance until dawn. Yet the archipelago only constitutes a small percentage of the province, which lost a large chunk of land to the Comarca Ngäbe-Buglé in the east when it was formed in 1997. The lowlands of the mainland, often dismissed as an endless stream of banana plantations, also offer a couple of notable attractions. Panama's

banana capital and the province's main commercial center, Changuinola, provides access to the marvelous Humedales de San San Pond Sak, the country's main refuge for the manatee and an important beach for nesting marine turtles. Inland, on the banks of the picturesque Río Teribe, a stay with the Naso, one of the less-well-known indigenous peoples, provides an opportunity for intercultural exchange in a stunning natural setting, with the potential to head farther upriver into the inaccessible but spectacular

⊙ Main attractions
Bocas Town
Playa Bluff
Bastimentos beaches
Parque Nacional Marino
  Isla Bastimentos
Río Oeste Arriba
Humedales de San San
  Pond Sak
Hiking with the Naso in
  Amistad

**Map on pages
224 and 226**

Playa Estrella.

Talamanca mountain range; its lofty peaks form the backbone of the vast Parque Internacional La Amistad, which boasts an awe-inspiring array of wildlife.

Archeological evidence suggests that indigenous peoples inhabited the islands and mainland of present-day Bocas del Toro 2,000 years ago, long before an ailing Christopher Columbus limped into the bay on his final voyage in 1502 in search of a route to Asia. Later, during the colonial era, the calm waters of the archipelago provided shelter for European pirates and by the early 19th century the islands were becoming the multicultural melting pot that they are today. British and US trading merchants came with their West African slave workforce, founding the town of Bocas del Toro in 1826. Following construction of the Panama Railroad and the French canal effort, West Indian migrants continued to drift into the area. Despite the arrival of other nationalities, it is still the languid pace of the dominant Afro-Caribbean culture and its distinctive vernacular

wooden architecture that most clearly defines the islands.

The archipelago's unique history has made it the most ethnically diverse region in Panama outside the capital; its Afro-Caribbean, Panamanian-Chinese, *mestizo*, and indigenous Ngäbe residents have been joined in recent years by North American retirees and US and European hotel owners. Though the rise in tourism and real-estate speculation has generated employment, it has increased the cost of living and put pressure on the area's scarce resources and fragile ecosystems.

Most tourists make a beeline for the **Archipiélago de Bocas del Toro**, barely setting foot on the mainland except to catch a bus or a boat. Despite the existence of several hundred atolls, islets, and cays scattered across the bite-shaped gulf that shelters much of the archipelago, most tourist activity is centered on the handful of larger islands. Covered in rainforest and fringed with mangroves, they are populated by small Ngäbe communities or,

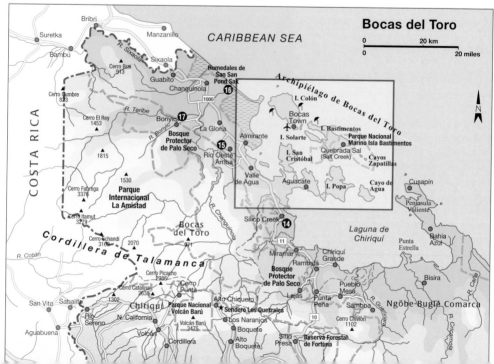

Bocas del Toro

in the cases of Islas Colón and Bastimentos, largely Afro-Antillean settlements. The majority of visitors stay in the laidback provincial capital Bocas del Toro, which spills off a peninsula at the southeast tip of **Isla Colón**, the archipelago's largest and most developed island.

ISLA COLÓN

BOCAS TOWN

The first port of call in the archipelago for almost all visitors – whether arriving by plane or boat – is **Isla Colón**, or, to be more precise, **Bocas Town ❶**, the provincial capital of Bocas del Toro. On a small headland off the southern tip of the island, and connected by a slender isthmus, Bocas explodes with tourists in high season (mid-Dec–Apr), and is the easiest base from which to explore the islands, beaches, and reefs of the archipelago. It is home to a small airport, with daily flights to Panama City, and to San José in Costa Rica, as well as the archipelago's only banking facilities and a host of accommodations, bars, restaurants, tour operators, and an increasing number of supermarkets.

Arriving in Bocas Town, you are welcomed to the island's casual melee by a spread of rickety, wooden, pastel-painted buildings, and a laidback population, many of whom speak English. After falling into decline with the collapse of the banana trade, the town was catapulted into another era by a steady trickle of backpackers and American retirees in the 1990s, followed by a country-wide real-estate boom. In the 1990s there were only three hotels here; now there are over 100. There's no sightseeing as such – experiencing Bocas is more about hanging out in the waterfront bars and restaurants, soaking up the relaxed vibe, chatting to the local populace, getting out on the water during the day, and partying at night.

Bocas is laid out on a simple grid system, with most activity centered on Calle 3, the broad main street that runs north–south, spilling into Calle 1, which bulges out into the bay.

⊙ THE NGÄBE AND BUGLÉ

The province's highest-profile indigenous peoples are the Ngäbe (pronounced 'NO-bay') and the less numerous Buglé. Collectively they are the oldest surviving ethnic groups on the isthmus, descended from the great Guaymí warrior tribes, whose best-known chief, Urracá (see page 34), features on the 1¢ coin. Forced into remote and mountainous lands by the Spanish, where many have remained, the majority live within the Comarca Ngäbe-Buglé, a semi-autonomous area established in 1997, covering almost 7,000 sq km (2,700 sq miles) in the eastern half of the province and pockets of Veraguas and Chiriquí. With poor access to potable water, health care and education, the comarca suffers Panama's highest levels of poverty – a situation not helped by the constant threats to land, lifestyles, and livelihoods by hydro-electric dams and mining, which the Ngäbe and Buglé continue to oppose.

Most Ngäbe and Buglé practice subsistence agriculture, supplemented by hunting, fishing, and limited cash crop cultivation. Struggling to survive in an increasingly cash-based economy, some make seasonal migrations to the banana, coffee, or sugar plantations, where they do the harshest jobs for the worst wages. A few of the women produce traditional handicrafts (see page 74) to sell; others have abandoned the rural areas altogether. Some of the Ngäbe communities in Bocas province, such as Silico Creek and Río Oeste Arriba, successfully manage seasonal community-based tourism.

Traditionally, both the Ngäbe and Buglé have lived in small kinship groupings – half a dozen thatched huts with dirt or wooden floors, though coastal communities prefer rectangular lodgings built on stilts – which control access to land and work in cooperation. These, and other cultural practices, such as the Ngäbe custom of polygamy (the Buglé have always espoused monogamy), have been eroded by missionary and other outside influences. One of the traditions that clings on in some places for special occasions – despite attempts to outlaw it – is the *krün* (*balsería* in Spanish), a violent 'sport' in which men of two teams take turns to try and knock their opponent off-balance by hurling a wooden pole at their calves. The contest is a core part of the four-day *chichería*, which involves plenty of its namesake, the potent maize-based *chicha fuerte* brew, alongside dancing and music.

Here the decks of attractive wooden hotels, bars, and restaurants stretch over the water on stilts. Halfway up the main drag, lined with supermarkets, souvenir shops and stands, hotels and hostels, sits **Parque Bolívar**, the social heart of the town, shaded by coconut palms and fig trees, with a bust of El Libertador, the town's sole monument.

During the day, launches brimming with tourists scatter outward, heading for the reefs, beaches, mangroves, and forests of the neighboring islands of Bastimentos, Solarte and Carenero, or the distant cays of Zapatillas. Other popular destinations include the Laguna de Bocatorito, often dubbed Dolphin Bay for the frequent sightings of dolphins, and the seabird colonies of Swan Cay off the north coast of Isla Colón. In late afternoon, the sandy streets of Bocas fill as the waterfront bars come to life. Dining options are plentiful and varied, reflecting the cosmopolitan population, and on weekends energetic visitors can usually find somewhere to dance till dawn.

ACTIVITIES FROM BOCAS TOWN

Bocas offers an ever expanding choice of tours and activities, from the traditional pursuits of surfing, diving, and snorkeling to options such as forest walks, kayaking, wildlife viewing, and visits to indigenous communities, as well as yoga and massage. The town is also the launchpad for excursions to other islands, though Isla Bastimentos also has a couple of tour operators, and the more upscale island retreats have their own boat and guide and so organize their own activities. Inevitably, in such a touristy area, there are plenty of sharks operating, so choose your operator wisely.

Diving and snorkeling – followed closely by surfing – are the most established diversions around Bocas Town. The area offers the healthiest coral on the Caribbean coast, covered in sponges and anemones, fed on by colorful reef fish and frequented by turtles and nurse sharks, while moray eels, lobsters, and crabs hide in the crevices. The main problem with snorkeling and diving in Bocas is

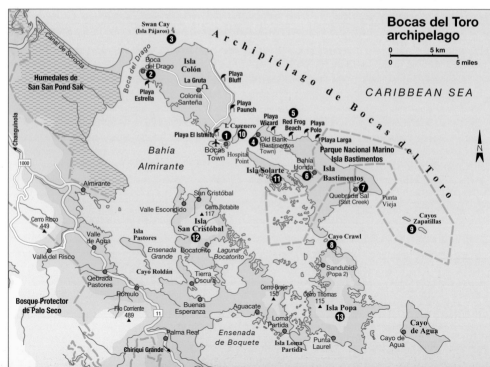

drastically reduced visibility caused by run-off from the mainland following heavy rains, which are frequent, even in the dry season. Strong winds and rough seas limit accessibility to more remote dive sites too. Snorkeling highlights include the distant Cayos Zapatillas in the national marine park, though currents are strong, and, off the southern tip of Bastimentos, the magical soft coral gardens of Cayo Crawl. Closer to base, the shallows by Hospital Point off Isla Solarte are favored by both snorkelers and divers, who can explore the impressive wall and rocky outcrop sheltering an abundance of fish. The best diving is undeniably Tiger Rock, a group of beautiful pinnacles visited by schools of large fish, which lies 40km (25 miles) offshore and requires a full day-trip and calm seas. The little-visited Escudo de Veraguas, an island at the far east of the archipelago, offers a variety of dive sites and can be visited on multi-day dive trips for experienced divers with La Buga Dive & Surf (www.labuga-panam.com).

Bocas also has a growing reputation for **surfing**, and while it can't match Santa Catalina (see page 199) for consistency of waves, it offers some excellent rides when conditions are right, generally between December and March. Most surf spots are for experienced or intermediate surfers, though everyone will need reef booties for the sharp reef breaks and to protect against sea urchins. On the east coast of Isla Colón, top billing goes to Playa Bluff, which can produce huge tubes when the swell is in and is only for experienced practitioners. Dumpers – nearer Bocas Town – provides a tricky reef-bottom left break, whereas the reef break at nearby Paunch is usually the place to take beginners. Over on Isla Bastimentos the left and right beach breaks of Playa Wizard and Red Frog Beach are also usually accessible to novice and intermediate surfers. Other hot spots for experts include the reef break that lies off Isla Carenero and along the northern coast of Bastimentos; and, between the two islands, the giant waves of Silverbacks.

Playing football in the street in Bocas Town.

Numerous places rent out boards in various states of repair and several places offer lessons, transfers to surf spots, and even guided surf tours.

The standard **day-trip** excursions combine snorkeling with other activities, and cater predominantly to budget travelers, depending on the destination and boat quality. Most leave at around 9.30am, returning about 4–4.30pm and stopping off for a seafood meal (not included in price) at a local restaurant along the way, though some trips include a picnic lunch. Bad weather can result in a change of itinerary or cancellation and the seas farther out can get very rough. Generally, you get what you pay for in a tour, in that the pricier operators tend to use better and safer boats, take fewer people, and show greater customer service and respect for the environment and the indigenous communities. Make sure you establish the itinerary and what's included in the price.

There are three popular itineraries offered by most operators. The first takes you to Laguna Bocatorito (Dolphin Bay), where you have a chance of seeing the rather shy bottle-nosed dolphins that live there year-round. This should be boycotted in high season when the place is overrun with boats, many engaging in potentially harmful practices. The next stop is the gorgeous, rainbow-colored soft coral of Cayo Crawl, where lunch is at one of the three over-the-water restaurants, before returning to lounge on Red Frog Beach – for which you have to pay a substantial landing fee – sometimes with an additional spot of snorkeling nearer home. Another similar but pricier option takes you on from Cayo Crawl to the national marine park and Cayos Zapatillas, for further snorkeling and beach lounging, stopping off at another snorkeling spot, such as Hospital Point, on the way back. The third option usually entails heading round Isla Colón to the easy shallows of Boca del Drago, with lunch at a restaurant on the beach, a visit to Playa Estrella, and a trip out to see the seabirds at Swan Cay before snorkel masks are donned once more at Punta

A leaping dolphin at – you guessed it – Dolphin Bay.

⊘ CULTURAL ECOTOURISM IN BOCAS

Several Ngäbe communities in the province have initiated cultural ecotourism projects to supplement their subsistence livelihood: Bahía Honda and Quebrada Sal (Salt Creek) on Bastimentos, Sandubidi on Isla Popa, and Silico Creek and Río Oeste Arriba on the mainland are all vying to attract visitors. The less well-known and less numerous Naso, too, are also active in community-based tourism (see page 240). While several day-tours from Bocas Town include communities in some of their itineraries, you learn and experience much more by staying overnight, and inevitably more of the money goes directly to the community if you organize it through them (usually in Spanish) – something your accommodations should be able to help you with if your Spanish is not up to the task. In addition to the obvious interest of being able to interact with the Ngäbe (or Naso) and learn about their traditional and changing cultures, the communities often offer traditional dishes, crafts for sale, and guided walks into the rainforest, with good wildlife-spotting opportunities and the chance to learn about medicinal plants. With some of the mainland communities, you can undertake more strenuous hiking. Details of how to contact the communities directly, and therefore ensure that all your money goes directly to them, are to be found in English and Spanish on the Red de Turismo Comunitario Bocas del Toro website, www.redtucombo.bocasdeltoro.org.

Manglar on the way back. In an attempt to avoid the crowds or offer some variation, some operators are now offering a visit to a Ngäbe village, such as Bocatorito or Bahía Honda. A more leisurely alternative to racing round the archipelago in a boat with an outdoor motor is to indulge in a **catamaran cruise**, which similarly rounds some of the islands, offering a spot of snorkeling, swimming, and sunbathing on deck while feeling the breeze in your hair. **Horseback riding** – more a 'walk' on horseback to appreciate the scenery than galloping across the countryside – takes place on Playa Bluff or on Isla San Cristóbal.

Excursions can be made to the mainland – to visit the wetlands of San San Pond Sak (see page 238) or embark on a chocolate tour of Río Oeste Arriba (see page 237) – though obviously prices will be cheaper if organized directly.

ISLA COLÓN BEACHES

Despite the lush primary and secondary rainforest on Isla Colón, most tourist activity happens on the wild and relatively deserted beaches of the east coast or the more sheltered shallows of **Boca del Drago** ❷, on the western point close to the mainland. These can be reached via boat or along one of the island's two roads.

The nearest stretch of sand to Bocas Town is tatty **Playa El Istmito**, on the eastern side of the causeway that links Bocas with the rest of Isla Colón. It is a decent place for a beer, especially during September's Feria del Mar festivities. The road follows the bay round, and after 3km (2 miles) divides at 'La Ye'; left takes you along a tarred road over the hilly terrain to Boca del Drago, 12km (7.5 miles) away, while the road to the right, which eventually becomes sand and gravel (4WD needed in the rainy season), hugs the coastline for another 5km (3 miles). Passing surfing hotspots Playa Paunch (or Punch) and Dumpers, it eventually reaches the glorious 4km (2.5-mile) swathe of sand that is **Playa Bluff**. As well as being another surfing paradise, it is an important nesting site for leatherback and green turtles.

Casa Acuario, Isla Carenero.

None of these beaches is suitable for swimming, with powerful waves and strong currents, but the thundering breakers on Bluff beach are a sight to behold and the golden sands provide a lengthy, scenic promenade. A clutch of secluded, tranquil retreats surrounded by lush vegetation and a stone's throw from the beach pepper the coastline. As well as attracting surfers, Playa Bluff is a popular day-trip destination, with the sun loungers and bean bags of the mellow beachside bar of La Punta providing the perfect pitstop while you watch the waves.

Taking the left-hand fork to Boca del Drago, the bumpy undulating tarred road reaches the small *mestizo* settlement of Colonia Santeña, at about the halfway point. As the name suggests, the population originally hails from Los Santos province in the Azuero, but moved to Bocas, like many farmers from there, in search of new pastures for cattle. The only point of interest is **La Gruta** (the grotto; no fixed hours), a rather murky though sacred bat-infested cave signposted to the right-hand side of the road, from where it is a short walk. It's a place of pilgrimage on July 16 for the Festival de la Virgen del Carmen. Push the fronds of greenery aside and, depending on the time of year and the amount of rain, you'll be wading in a delightful freshwater creek or a stream of guano. The shrine to the Virgin is near the entrance; shine a flashlight around and you'll see the bats clinging to the rock.

At the far northern end of the island, the road reaches a T-junction, just before the beach. To the left, the road soon comes to a halt at the Ngäbe community of Boca del Drago. Supposedly the first place in Panama that Christopher Columbus set foot on, Boca del Drago can be a pleasant place to spend a relaxing day, outside holiday weekends. The beach, though slight, consists of lovely white palm-fringed sand, but the real appeal is the sheltered translucent water, perfect for safe bathing and snorkeling while you wait for your seafood order at the most popular beachfront restaurant, Yarisnori. A regular bus

Pristine Bocas del Toro beach.

⊘ TURTLE WATCHING

A community tourism organization on Playa Bluff, ANABOCA (tel: 6843 7244; www.anaboca.bocasdeltoro.org) leads two turtle watches per evening (8.30pm & 10.30pm) in the breeding season (May–Sept). Transportation from Bocas is not included, so it means getting a taxi. The Sea Turtle Conservancy Office (see page 237) will help to get groups together to reduce transportation costs.

While turtle watching can be a captivating experience, bear in mind that female turtles can easily be spooked into not depositing their eggs. Avoid bright clothes and try to go when there is a good moon, so as not to be tempted to use a flashlight (unless it's infrared). Leave your camera behind and maintain a respectful distance from the turtle.

service from Bocas Town runs here though it's also a popular destination for more energetic tourists who rent bicycles for the day.

A 15-minute walk along the shoreline from Boca del Drago takes you to **Playa Estrella**, whose shallows were once dotted with an amazing number of orange cushioned starfish. Sadly, thanks to a combination of increasing numbers of water-taxis and thoughtless actions by some tourists, touching or picking up the starfish for photos, numbers have dwindled. Here the beach is backed by a string of informal seafood restaurants and bars, which are packed on weekends and during the vacation season, with music blasting out across the sand. However, if you visit midweek, or out of season, you'll encounter a more tranquil scene (though fewer options for eating) and by snorkeling a little farther out from the beach, you might spot a few more starfish.

A 15-minute boat ride off the north coast (accessible only in good weather conditions), is one of the area's main attractions, **Swan Cay** ❸. Known locally as Isla Pájaros (Bird Island), this impressive 50-meter (164ft) stack, topped with cascading vegetation, is an avian sanctuary. Seabirds wheel above, with star billing going to the elegant white red-billed tropicbird, which shares this nesting spot with a colony of brown boobies.

ISLA BASTIMENTOS

The sprawling and beautiful 52 sq km (20 sq miles) of **Isla Bastimentos** boasts the mellow, Afro-Antillean fishing community of Old Bank, marble-sand surfing beaches, and lush inland forest inhabited by strawberry poison-dart frogs. Most visitors are day-trippers: some come independently to tuck into tasty Creole seafood in Old Bank or to hike across the island to the beaches; others visit with organized tours, which generally cut across the narrowest part of the island to the much vaunted Red Frog Beach. If you want to escape the tourist scene in Bocas, Bastimentos is a good place to hang out and the place where you're

Snorkeling off Isla Bastimentos.

Tip

You'll get a cheaper ride from Bocas Town to Bastimentos if you go to Boteros Bastimentos, down at the lower end of Calle 3, rather than with any of the other water-taxi operators. Note also that if you take the water-taxi to Red Frog Beach you will have to pay a substantial landing fee, as the path to the beach from the jetty crosses the property of the Red Frog Beach resort.

Red mangrove tree.

most likely to hear the local Jamaican English patois, embellished with Spanish and Ngäbere. The island's two Ngäbe communities of Bahía Honda and Quebrada Sal both welcome tour groups and independent visitors (see page 228).

A quick jaunt by water-taxi from Bocas Town will drop you at the main jetty in **Old Bank**, or **Bastimentos Town**  – affectionately referred to as Basti – the island's main settlement. With a population of around 900, it sits on the westernmost point. An undulating, cracked concrete path acts as its main thoroughfare, snaking its way between tightly packed houses built out over the water on stilts, passing reggaeton beats, discarded bikes, and old men slamming down dominoes, and winding up to a steep, green hillside dotted with precariously built wooden homes. A jungle path, occasionally impassable after heavy rains, leads to several glorious beaches 20 minutes away on the other side of the island. Periodically, there have been muggings along this path – though

police security is better these days – so enquire beforehand and make sure you don't take valuables or go alone.

Renowned for riptides that claim lives every year, the sea that pounds the northern surfing beaches of Bastimentos is often too dangerous to swim in, but there is lots of good walking to be had along these curved broad belts of creamy sand backed by palms and thick vegetation. Heading along the overland path from Old Bank, you reach **Playa Wizard** (Playa Primera) after 15 to 20 minutes, and, farther east, Playa Segunda, before coming to **Red Frog Beach** – though you won't find its namesake waving to you from a beach towel. A short hike farther east brings you to **Playa Polo**, a smaller, sheltered cove protected by a reef, though it's been rather taken over by the plush new Red Frog Beach resort beach club. Even so, it's good for snorkeling, and the eponymous Polo, who lives on the beach (or thereabouts), happily cooks up the catch of the day with coconut rice for visitors when he's around. An alternative route to Playa Polo takes

you on an adventurous 2- to 3-hour hike through the rainforest, which you need to organize in advance with local tour operator Bastimentos Alive (tel: 6514 7961; www.bastimentosalive.com), which has an office on the main drag. Even farther east along Bastimentos' northern shore lies another surfing stretch of sand, Playa Larga. If you're planning a whole day at the beach, take enough water with you.

Six kilometers (4 miles) southeast of Bastimentos, the 25 or so thatched homes of the dispersed Ngäbe community of **Bahía Honda** ❻ (tel: 6726 0968, ask for Rutilio Milton (in Spanish); www.timorogo.org) are hidden among a dense tangle of mangroves at the eastern end of the bay of the same name, with a few across the water on Isla Solarte. In addition to a chapel and primary school, they have a restaurant, the heart of the community tourism project – whose star attraction is a guided excursion up the Sendero del Peresoso (Trail of the Sloth) to the Cueva Nivida. You'll be paddled up a nearby creek, where you can often see the trail's namesake furled round a branch and crabs and caimans in the shallows, before heading off on foot through forest that was once a cocoa plantation, to wade through a series of caves thick with stalagmites and coated with several species of Bastimentos bats. If you ring a day in advance, you can stop off at the community restaurant on the way back and sample traditional dishes such as *morongodo*, a green plantain pancake. They can arrange to pick you up at the dock by the *mercado municipal* in Bocas.

The other Ngäbe community on the island is **Quebrada Sal** ❼ (Salt Creek; tel: 6142 1476; www.aliatur.bocasdeltoro.org), on the southeast coast, but over toward the eastern end by Punta Vieja. It is often visited by guests at the upscale lodges at that end of the island. The surrounding wetlands and nearby Playa Larga – part of the marine park that occupies a swathe of the island – can be explored via several trails, which also provides a chance to learn about medicinal plants and other aspects of Ngäbe culture.

Carnaval celebration on Isla Colón.

ⓒ BOCAS FESTIVALS

While arguably every night is party night in Bocas, the town's main festival is the Feria del Mar, held on Playa El Istmito in late September; endless rows of exhibition stands, craft vendors, mountainous fry-ups, and late-night partying on the sands draw visitors in their thousands. Other dates for the diary include 16 November, when Bocas' main street becomes the focus of multiday celebrations for the foundation of Bocas del Toro province, marked by daytime parades with marching bands and *pollera*-garbed women, and night-time drinking and dancing to DJs and live music. Carnavales, though less wild than in the Azuero, involve a fair amount of partying nonetheless – the strong Afro-Panamanian influence ensures regular street outings of Congo bands and *diablitos* brandishing whips.

At the southern tip of Bastimentos amid a myriad of mangrove islets lies tiny **Cayo Crawl** N, where three thatched restaurants do a roaring trade in seafood lunches. After rounding the point, you come to the gorgeous soft coral fields of the same name, which feature on many day-trips. In order to protect the coral, fins are not allowed when snorkeling.

One of the archipelago's major attractions is the **Parque Nacional Marino Isla Bastimentos**. This 130 sq km (50 sq miles) of boomerang-shaped reserve sweeps across a central swathe of Isla Bastimentos; it includes a chunk of the northern coastline, dominated by the 6km (4-mile) **Playa Larga**, which is an important nesting site for hawksbill, leatherback, and green turtles (Mar–Sept; see box). Southeast of Isla Bastimentos, but still within the park boundary, are the **Cayos Zapatillas** N (Little Shoes), so named because they resemble a pair of footprints in the sea. The two dreamy, coral-fringed islands, encircled by powdery white sand, offer snorkeling

off the beach, where you'll find more and larger fish than in Cayo Crawl. The main reef is exposed to the ocean, often with strong currents and choppy water. With permission from the MIA office in Bocas Town (Calle 1 between avenidas Central and 'E'; tel: 757 9244; Mon–Fri 8am–4pm), camping is possible on the prettier northern island, where there is a short trail, allowing you to watch the stars and share the sand with nesting turtles.

OTHER ISLANDS

The closest island to Isla Colón and a short water-taxi ride from Bocas Town, **Isla Carenero** N presents a 2km (1.2-mile) sliver of low-lying land. It is surrounded by shallow waters and a thin necklace of beach that periodically dissolves into mud, tangled roots, and – around the northeastern end – jagged rocks, where one of the archipelago's best surf breaks pounds the reef. Most of the 400 occupants are squeezed onto the southwestern tip, in makeshift wooden housing on littered and extremely boggy ground. Though

Strawberry poison-dart frog.

⊘ POISON-DART FROGS

Probably Bastimentos' most famous residents, the dazzling strawberry poison-dart frogs, no larger than a thumbnail, are actually widespread along the Caribbean lowlands from Nicaragua to western Panama. But nowhere is their coloration and size – 'morphs' as they are termed – as varied as in the archipelago, where they can vary from island to island. Ironically, the place you're least likely to spot these amphibians is on Red Frog Beach, where local kids have captured many of them to impress tourists and charge for photos – or the frogs have simply scarpered. The most commonly sighted poison-dart frog in the area is the smart 'blue-jeans' morph, whose scarlet torso fades into cobalt blue or purple legs; on Bastimentos these seductive amphibians span red, orange, gold, green and white, and are often speckled with black.

the settlement is quieter than Bocas Town, which could be a plus, the island has a reputation for vicious sandflies; moreover, there's not much to do or see. Most visitors hop across for a drink or a bite to eat – there are a couple of pleasant over-the water bar-restaurants – or just a change of scene.

Sheltered in the leeward crook of Isla Bastimentos, thin, hilly **Isla Solarte** ⑪ – also known as Cayo Nancy, a corruption of 'nance,' the cherry-sized yellow fruit much in evidence on the island – is surrounded by tranquil waters. Its most famous feature, Hospital Point, at its northwestern tip, was the location of a hospital built by the United Fruit Company in 1900 during the banana boom to quarantine malaria and yellow-fever sufferers. The point is now one of the most popular dive and snorkel spots, at the end of many day-trip itineraries, with a healthy reef of cauliflower and brain coral and an impressive wall full of tropical fish, shelving off a pencil-thin strip of beach. Solarte is home to a Ngäbe village of around 250, which has a school and even a soccer field. Most of the villagers live from fishing and subsistence agriculture. More recently, new tourist lodgings have taken root on the southern side of the island.

A large mangrove-fringed island, nestled in the Bahía de Almirante facing the mainland peninsula of Cerro Brujo, **Isla San Cristóbal** ⑫ is home to three Ngäbe communities: Bocatorito, in the south, which overlooks a bite-shaped lagoon populated by dolphins, much visited on day-trips from Bocas Town; and Valle Escondido and San Cristóbal to the north. While cacao, yucca, and rice cultivation provides much of their diet, fishing is still the mainstay of these villages. Look out for the navigation lights on the north side of the island, used to guide the banana cargo boats into Almirante.

Just off the southern tip of Isla Bastimentos lies the archipelago's second largest land mass, **Isla Popa** ⑬, home to five Ngäbe fishing communities and the only island where you can spot toucans. The northern village of

Relaxing on Isla Colón.

Sandubidi (Popa 2) has a community-based tourism project that offers walks along a trail with a local guide, and a community homestay (www.meringobe.bocasdeltoro.org). Nearby, on the island's northeastern tip, you'll find several thin, sandy beaches leading off into coral-filled shallows and acres of rainforest.

MAINLAND BOCAS

Mainland Bocas covers the vast majority of the province, yet its imperious jagged peaks clad in virgin forest, its boggy wetlands, and its powerful rivers are ignored by most visitors. That said, while the three mainland towns of Chiriquí Grande, Almirante, and Changuinola have little for tourists, the Humedales de San San Pond Sak, home to countless aquatic birds and the endangered manatee, and the spectacular wilderness Parque Internacional La Amistad are definitely worth the effort to reach. The two main obstacles to exploring the region – poor accessibility and lack of infrastructure – have helped preserve the province's natural heritage; today, however, the indigenous Bri-Bri, Naso, and Bokota populations' livelihoods are under threat from hydroelectric projects.

The only main road into the province leaves the Interamericana at the village of Chiriquí, 14km (8.5 miles) east of David. Affording splendid views on a clear day, it winds over the Fortuna hydroelectric dam, cresting the continental divide that marks the entry into Bocas del Toro, before descending to the small town of Chiriquí Grande, the Atlantic terminus of the Trans-Panama Oil Pipeline. The road then hugs the crinkled coastline for 60km (37 miles) to the port of Almirante, before continuing to Changuinola. Few visitors venture east of Chiriquí Grande into the increasingly deforested Comarca Ngäbe-Buglé, where rivers cut through the Caribbean slopes of the Cordillera Central, flowing into the Golfo de los Mosquitos. The 29km (18-mile) Playa Chiriquí here is home to a major turtle conservation program (see page 237).

Bocas Marine & Tours hut.

ALONG THE COAST ROAD

At Km 25 of the coast road to Changuinola, at Punta Peña, between Chiriquí Grande and Almirante, lies the Ngäbe community of **Silico Creek** ⑭. It's a dynamic village that has successfully retained some traditional values while adapting to the modern economy though community tourism (tel: 6558 6913; www.uraribocasdeltoro. org). Though day-visits are common, you can also stay in the community's thatched *cabañas* or even arrange a homestay, giving you more time to learn about the organic permaculture projects in coffee, plantains, banana, yucca, and, most successfully, cocoa. In addition to cocoa tours, you can hike through the rainforest to a waterfall, or undertake a whole-day trek to visit an indigenous organic farm. Some English is spoken on tours, and the community is easier to reach than many as the David–Changuinola buses pass through the community.

Another 40km (25 miles) along the road takes you to the ramshackle port of **Almirante**, its rusting tin-roofed wooden houses propped up on stilts over the Caribbean, which functions as the departure point for water-taxis to the Bocas del Toro archipelago. Like Bocas, the port is a product of the banana boom, and suffered a similar decline afterward. Unlike Bocas, there is no tourism-fueled renaissance on the horizon. Basic services are lacking, unemployment and its associated ills are a major concern, and most visitors pass through as quickly as possible. Buses stop at the interregional bus terminal on the main road at 'La Ye' – the turn-off into town – where everyone piles into shared taxis for the short transfer to the water-taxi jetties.

A short local bus-ride into the forested hills from Almirante takes you to **Río Oeste Arriba** ⑮, a small Ngäbe settlement that runs an excellent community tourism venture based around their artisanal chocolate making. Like Silico Creek and other communities in the area, they harvest organic cacao to sell the beans to the cooperative in Almirante, which in turn exports the cacao to Switzerland

⊙ Tip

If you happen to miss the last water-taxi to Bocas at 6pm, the Hotel Alhambra (tel: 758 3001) on the road to the port is about the only option in this deprived port. It's very basic, but clean and safe.

Looking out for wildlife on a boat trip.

⊙ MARINE TURTLES IN BOCAS

Of the five species of turtle found in the country, four are known to nest along the beaches of Bocas del Toro. Historically the hawksbill (*eretmochelys imbricata*) and green turtle (*chelonia mydas*) reproduced prolifically on the province's sands but over the last 60 years, as eggs were overharvested and adults killed for their meat and shells, the populations were decimated – though significant numbers of hawksbill still nest on Islas Zapatillas (May–Sept). The 29km (18-mile) expanse of Playa Chiriquí, which lines the Golfo de los Mosquitos, east of the Península Valiente, is the most important rookery in all Central America for gigantic leatherbacks (*dermochelys coriacea*). Measuring around 1.5 meters (5ft) on average and weighing half a tonne, these leviathans dig 7,000 nests annually (Mar–June). In contrast, there are scarcely any records of loggerheads (*caretta caretta*) nesting in Bocas, though they can occasionally be spotted swimming in the archipelago's shallows.

If you're interested in volunteering (minimum one week; Mar–July), monitoring and tagging turtles and patrolling beaches – most likely on Playa Soropta in the Humedales de San San Pond Sak (see page 238) – contact the Sea Turtle Conservancy in Bocas Town on Calle 2, just south of the park (tel: 757 9186 or 6661 2533; www.facebook.com/SeaTurtleConservancyBocas; Mon–Fri 9am–6pm).

and the US. You can take a tour and participate in all the processes, plus sample some of the chocolate paste in a drink at the end. The community has an English-speaking guide. Some very basic rustic accommodations are also available if you want to stay overnight.

The undulating road continues to twist and turn the remaining 29km (18 miles) from Almirante to the hot, dusty town of **Changuinola**. It is Panama's most important banana center, and lies just 17km (10.5 miles) from the Costa Rica border. Surrounded by flat, drained wetlands, a patchwork of plantations and pastureland, this bustling, unattractive town of around 50,000 possesses little of interest for visitors but does provide a launch pad for trips to the Humedales de San San Pond Sak, Naso communities, or the Parque Internacional La Amistad. It is also the best place to stay if you are too late to make it to the Costa Rican border. Most of the action occurs along the congested Avenida 17 de Abril, where the crowded central pavements overflow with cheap goods. There are a few very basic hotels and a couple of restaurants. From Changuinola, the road runs 17km (10.5 miles) to the border with Costa Rica at Guabito–Sixaola (daily 8am–5.45pm), where, on the Panamanian side, there is little more than a handful of stores. It's a short walk from immigration across the old railroad bridge to Costa Rica (an hour behind Panama time), where you can change currency in the town of Sixaola.

NATURAL ATTRACTIONS

One of the premier natural attractions of mainland Bocas is the **Humedales de San San Pond Sak 16** (with numerous variant spellings), which encompasses more than 160 sq km (62 sq miles) of coastal wetlands stretching from the Costa Rican border, past Changuinola, to the Bahía de Almirante. Only a small section of the reserve is accessible to visitors but its mix of seasonally flooded swampy forests, dense mangroves, and peat bogs makes for a magical boat trip, especially at first light when the prolific birdlife – 160 species at the current tally – is at its most active. As you glide along the river, keep an eye out for caimans and river otters lurking in the waters. A dawn visit will also heighten your chances of spotting the wetlands' most celebrated inhabitant, the shy, endangered manatee. Though there are now an estimated 150–200 in the area, they remain fairly elusive except when banana leaves are provided at the viewing platforms when tour boats enter the reserve. The river eventually fills out into a coastal lagoon before emptying into the sea, its progress blocked by a sandbank on which there is a poorly maintained refuge. Behind the hut lies Playa Soropta, a long stretch of beach where hawksbill, leatherback, and green turtles nest. A boat trip has to be organized at least a day in

⊘ THE WEST INDIAN MANATEE

Occasionally called a 'sea cow,' the West Indian manatee (*trichechus manatus*) resembles a cross between a sea lion, a hippo, and an elephant. Its barrel-like greyish-brown body is propelled by two flippers and a spatula tail, and its large snout is equipped with a prehensile upper lip that helps it feed. Adults average 3 meters (10ft) in length, though can reach 4.5 meters (15ft), including tail, and weigh in at 200–600kg (440–1,300lbs); to sustain such a size, they have to spend six to eight hours a day munching floating or submerged greenery. When not feeding, they often rest, floating like large logs on or below the surface, frequently surfacing to breathe. Moving easily between freshwater and marine environments, the shy yet playful mammals are surprisingly agile, and can exceed 25km/h (15mph) for short bursts. In Panama, the vast majority of these aquatic behemoths inhabit the wetlands of Bocas del Toro, though in 1964 a small number were relocated to Lago Gatún by the Americans in a failed attempt to tackle the rampant spread of water hyacinth in the Canal. Though lacking natural predators, manatees are threatened by human activity, experiencing collisions with motorboats and getting tangled up in fishing nets or canal locks, while suffering from loss or pollution of habitat. What's more, since they only give birth to a single calf every three to five years, it takes a long time to replenish numbers.

advance through AAMVECONA (tel: 6679 7283; www.aamvecona.com), an environmental NGO that has an office right by the bridge over Río San San, about 15 minutes along the road to the border with Costa Rica. This is also the departure point for the boat trip. The staff does not speak English so, if necessary, ask your lodgings to make the reservation for you; alternatively, book with a tour operator in Bocas, though it will obviously be more expensive.

Divided equally between Panama and Costa Rica, the remote **Parque Internacional La Amistad** (International Friendship Park), often abbreviated to PILA or Amistad, covers a vast 4,000 sq km (1,544 sq miles) of the rugged Talamanca massif, with a topography and biodiversity unmatched in Central America. Precipitous volcanic tors clad in prolific cloudforest, containing the greatest density of quetzals in the world, plunge into deep ravines in Panama's most dramatic mountain scenery. Although it's easier to visit from the Pacific side, in Chiriquí (see page 236), most of the park lies on the Caribbean side of the cordillera, in Bocas del Toro.

From the treeless *páramo* of Cerro Fábrega (3,336 meters/10,945ft), the park's highest peak, to the Caribbean rainforests only 40 meters (130ft) above sea level, the park encompasses an incredible range of flora and fauna, including many endemics and endangered species. All five of Panama's resident cat species prowl the forests while the soaring canopy is pierced by impressive specimens of ceiba, *almendro*, and cedar, home to endangered harpy and crested eagles and great green macaws. A crucial link in the biological corridor of protected areas running the length of Central America, it is now under threat from agricultural incursions, illicit timber extraction, and poaching, but most of all from the ill-considered hydroelectric projects under way. As well as imperiling the area's unique biodiversity, the projects are threatening numerous indigenous communities. Given the park's remoteness

The West Indian manatee is a gentle giant.

and the ruggedness of the terrain, any visit to Amistad proper from the Caribbean side is a major undertaking, to be made with a good guide, suitable hiking and camping gear, a readiness for rain (more than 5 meters/200in tips down annually in places) and mud, plus a spirit of adventure. Most visitors content themselves with a trip organized through one of the Naso communities dotted along the banks of the Río Teribe, in the buffer zone of the Reserva Forestal de Palo Seco, a haven for colorful butterflies, dazzling birdlife, and a host of other wildlife.

NASO COMMUNITIES

Upriver from Changuinola live the **Naso**, one of the country's least numerous indigenous groups, and Central America's last remaining monarchy. They number about 3,500, around a third of whom have been assimilated into Latin culture and are living and working in Changuinola. The remaining Naso live in 11 settlements up the **Río Teribe**, generally inhabiting wooden houses built on stilts covered in thatch

The Naso king, Reynaldo Alexis Santana.

or occasionally zinc, practising animal husbandry and subsistence agriculture supplemented by fishing and hunting. For decades the Naso have been campaigning for their own *comarca*, which has finally been passed by the national assembly, and is on the verge of being signed off, which would cover their spiritual heart in their ancestral lands high up the Río Teribe's headlands. Teribe is thought to be a corruption of *Tjër Di*, meaning water of Tjër, their grandmotherly guardian spirit – one of the more tangible traces of a sorely eroded culture. For the moment, their modern-day capital, and home to the modest royal palace, is the largest community, **Seiyik**.

Since the completion of a controversial dam up Río Bonyic – which sorely divided the community and resulted in the previous king being deposed and exiled – there is now road transportation as far as the community of **Bonyic** ⑰, where residents farther upriver have to get into their motorized dugouts. Within Bonyic, two organizations are involved in ecotourism projects: a women's group, OMUB (www.acicafoc.org/proyecto/ecoturismo-etnico-naso-omub) and the more established OCEN (www.ocen.bocas.com). Both give visitors the chance to participate in a variety of activities: learning about Naso history and culture, including plants used for traditional medicine, making traditional bread or artisanal chocolate, hiking in the rainforest, making and traveling on a traditional bamboo raft (*balsa*), and visiting Seiyik. Slightly downriver, in Soposo, a community tourism venture set up by a US Naso couple is better patronized and English is spoken (www.soposo.com). The Naso are warm and welcoming and the spectacular river trips set against the brooding backdrop of the Talamanca range alone make a visit worthwhile, though to do the place and the people justice you should plan at least a two-night stay.

BOCAS AND THE BANANA BOOM

Long before Bocas del Toro became a vacation playground it was the center of the burgeoning global banana trade.

Though the humble banana has its origins in Asia, it was in Panama that cultivation of the world's most harvested fruit began on an industrial scale destined for export. Small plantations started up on the Bocas mainland in the 1880s, but were soon swallowed up into the US trans-national behemoth, the United Fruit Company. By 1895, bananas from Bocas accounted for more than half of Panama's export earnings, and Bocas Town, where the company's headquarters were first established in 1899, was booming. At one time, the place boasted five foreign consulates, three English-language newspapers, and the country's first lottery.

Workers predominantly from Jamaica – with experience of banana cultivation – were soon pouring into the region to work on the plantations, at the same time as they were migrating farther east to dig the canal. The wealth sloshing around from the banana economy attracted merchants from as far away as Canada, Europe, the Lebanon, and China, though the average plantation worker saw very little of the money, toiling long hours under the scorching sun, or in torrential rain and mud, prey to the usual array of tropical diseases.

In its heyday, the United Fruit Company employed around 6,500 people and was responsible for building the telegraph network and the now-defunct mainland railroad system that operated between Almirante – the banana port it established – and Changuinola, the center of banana production. To accommodate its workers, the company constructed, staffed, and managed entire towns, complete with hospitals, schools, entertainment, and sporting amenities. Some of the basic infrastructure established then is still in use today.

Cut off from the majority of Panama – the single tarred road over the cordillera that connects Bocas to the rest of the country was only completed in 1984 – the Bocas del Toro region therefore developed as a classic banana republic, operating in isolation from government, according to the needs and regulations of the United Fruit Company.

But the banana boom was short-lived. Blighted repeatedly by Panama Disease – so named as it was first identified in Bocas del Toro – in the early 20th century, the harvests constantly failed, causing the trade in 'oro verde' (green gold) to languish. Thanks to the initially disease-resistant Cavendish banana, trade revived in the 1950s and 1960s, accompanied by the use of noxious pesticides, such as DDT, with severe health consequences for the workers. Even today, the daily drone of the crop-spraying plane is ubiquitous on the mainland round Changuinola, and laborers – predominantly Ngäbe – struggle with poor health and a below-average life expectancy.

Currently, Panama's banana trade is confined to the plantations around Changuinola – the headquarters of Bocas Fruit Company, part of Chiquita Brands International, the current incarnation of 'the company.' Around 17 million boxes of bananas are exported each year, and with a workforce of about 5,000, Chiquita is still by far the most important employer in the province, though wages are still pitifully low. A beacon of light on this otherwise gloomy horizon is Coobana, an independent Fair Trade banana workers' cooperative that started in 2010 and is flourishing, selling predominantly to European and New Zealand markets. Around 40 percent of its 550-strong workforce are members, but all stand to gain from the cooperative's investment in healthier plantations and its program to build better housing for workers.

Banana tree.

Guna woman in traditional dress.

COMARCA GUNA YALA

Guna Yala is like nowhere else in Panama: a mixture of idyllic palm-topped islets, congested island-villages, and a fiercely independent indigenous nation fighting to preserve its traditions while simultaneously adapting to change.

The Guna (pronounced 'Guna' or 'Kuna', depending upon the dialect) – or the Dule (pronounced 'Dule' or 'Tule'), as they call themselves – are Panama's highest-profile indigenous people. They inhabit a vast semiautonomous region (or *comarca*) along the eastern Caribbean coast, which stretches some 375km (233 miles) from the Golfo de San Blas to Puerto Obaldía and comprises almost 400 islands and a swathe of land whose limits extend to the peaks of the Serranías de San Blas and the Darién. Around 33,000 Guna live within the Comarca de Guna Yala, with a further 47,000 predominantly spread among two smaller inland *comarcas* in eastern Panama (see page 265) and Panama City, though populations are fairly fluid given the constant toing and froing between the capital and the *comarcas*. For the most part, people are packed onto a chain of 36 low-lying coral outcrops close to the shore, with 11 communities established on the coast and two farther inland. In recent years, frequent flooding caused by rising sea levels has encouraged some island-based families to relocate to the mainland. Plans are afoot for entire communities to join them over the coming years, as it becomes increasingly likely that their homes will become permanently submerged.

There are basically two types of islands of interest to tourists. First,

are near-deserted islands, topped with coconut palms and surrounded by white-sand beaches that shelve into turquoise waters, where coral reefs provide great opportunities for snorkeling (diving is prohibited across the *comarca*). The waters of the western archipelago, in particular, are dotted with these pristine islets, which are predominantly distinguished by their accommodations, ranging from simple cane *cabañas* with a simple home-made bed, to slightly more comfortable lodges, all owned by families

Main attractions

Cayos Limones
Cayos Holandeses & Coco Bandero
Feria de Isla Tigre
Armila

Map on page 244

Guna Yala beach.

or communities from the more densely populated village-islands.

The villages, in contrast, are overcrowded coral outcrops chock-full of cane-and-thatch build-ings interspersed with cement structures, schools, medical cent-ers, and the occasional store. Very rarely do they have a beach. Women are often dressed in their striking traditional attire (see page 73) and cannot help but attract your atten-tion. To the casual visitor, the village-islands are very much alike: jetties hold tethered dugouts and traditional over-the-water toilets, with garbage often floating among the pilings, while sandy streets gravitate toward the center, where meeting and *chicha* houses and basketball courts stand out. Only by spending at least a couple of nights in different places will you begin to appreciate the subtle varia-tions among communities. Trips to the luxuriantly rainforested mainland are magical, whether gliding upriver in a dugout, hiking to a waterfall, or seek-ing out the spectacular birdlife.

These attributes make Guna Yala a potentially idyllic and fascinating location for a vacation, yet the Guna's relationship with tourism remains ambivalent, and their suspicion of outsiders (*uagmala*) and determina-tion to ensure that tourism is con-ducted on their terms has been born of bitter experience. This can make a trip to Guna Yala fairly challeng-ing, though the benefits far outweigh any frustrations or inconveniences, but to appreciate its unique nature, engaging with Guna culture in all its variations, complexities, and contra-dictions is essential.

GUNA HISTORY

Guna oral history traces their origins to the Sierra Nevada de Santa Marta of present-day Colombia. Fleeing from peoples such as the Emberá, in the 15th or 16th century, they took ref-uge in the mountainous areas of the Darién, including Mount Tacarcuna – the highest peak in eastern Panama (1,874 meters/6,148ft), lying just out-side the *comarca* – which became a

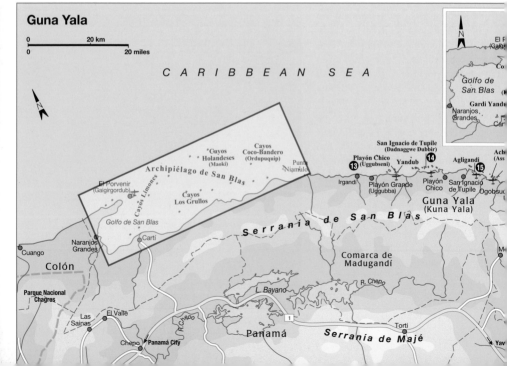

sacred place in folklore. Violent conflict ensued against the Spanish, with the Guna often forming unlikely alliances with English and French pirates, and gradually being forced toward the Caribbean. Colonization of the islands they inhabit today did not start until the mid-19th century as they sought greater access to passing traders and escape from disease-carrying insects on the mainland. Geographical isolation ensured the Guna were pretty much left alone until Panamanian independence in 1903, when the new state refused to recognize the Comarca Dulenega, which had been established by Colombia in 1870. It covered Guna territories straddling the two countries and had guaranteed a certain measure of independence. Tension between the Guna Congress and Panamanian authorities soon escalated as the latter granted concessions to outsiders to plunder resources in Guna territory and persistently attempted to suppress Guna culture – banning women's traditional attire and forcing missionaries and colonial schooling onto the communities. Matters came to a head in 1925, when a gathering of Guna leaders on Ailigandi – today's Agligandi – resolved to declare independence and rose up in what is proudly commemorated as the Revolución Dule (Guna Revolution). Around 40 people lost their lives, and only the intervention of the US, which was concerned for the safety of the Canal, prevented further government reprisals. A settlement was finally reached in 1938, when the Guna agreed to recognize Panamanian sovereignty in exchange for a clearly defined *comarca* and a high degree of political autonomy.

WHERE AND WHEN TO GO

There are more than 400 islands to choose from, most with two names (one in Dulegaya, one in Spanish). However, the fact that only 36 of them support villages, and that many are conveniently arranged in identifiable clusters, simplifies planning. During one visit most travelers are satisfied to explore just one cluster, and indeed, if you go on a package tour, as most

Tropical grilled fish.

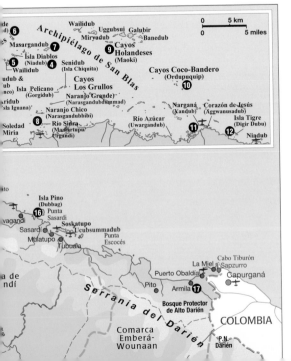

⊙ Tip

As tap water is not drinkable in Guna Yala, some lodgings provide purified water for guests at meals; most charge. Bottled water is on sale in most islands, but it is expensive and its disposal an environmental headache; it's far better to use a water filter or purifying tablets if you can.

people do, where you go and what you do will be arranged for you.

Choosing where to go is the first consideration. The islands in the western area of the archipelago, such as those in the Cayos Limones or Holandeses, or north of Río Sidra, are the most visited, possessing the greatest sprinkling of tiny Robinson Crusoe-style beaches, the best snorkeling, and plenty of accommodations. Moreover, they – together with a handful of islands in the central region – are generally the most geared up for tourism. These attributes, along with improvements in the access road (Guna Yala is now just a three-hour drive from Panama City), have led to a great increase in visitor numbers in recent years, including day-trippers. This in turn has put great strain on the islands' natural resources, and sometimes on Guna-tourist relations, and has undoubtedly diminished the appeal of this particular group in high season. Visiting the more isolated eastern islands, such as Aligandi or Mamitupu, you'll experience greater cultural engagement with the

Guna – provided you can speak Spanish – since you may well be the only outsider there.

Choosing when to go is also important. Peak tourist season in Guna Yala, as elsewhere in Panama, is the dry season (roughly mid-Dec–Apr) though for some of the period, the archipelago is buffeted by the trade winds (Dec–Feb), which whip up the waters into large waves, making travel to the islands uncomfortable – and scary at times – impairing snorkeling and leaving the outer islands inaccessible. Late March and April are more appealing times to visit, although water levels can be low on the mainland, restricting river trips. If possible, avoid the popular palm-topped islets of western Guna Yala – Isla Perro Chico above all – on weekends or during vacation periods in the dry season. At this time hundreds of weekenders and day-trippers flock here from Panama City, saturating the beaches with deckchairs, vast cooler boxes, and sound systems, making it almost impossible to see the sand, never mind sit on it.

Buying fish fresh off the boat.

PACKAGE STAYS IN GUNA YALA

Given the complexities of traveling independently around the archipelago, the easiest way to visit the region is on a package tour. In fact, most hotels only offer package deals – the Guna prefer this as it affords them greater control over tourist activities. The majority of lodgings are aimed at budget travelers; there are few mid-range accommodations and no luxury lodgings – the nearest lies 25km (15.5 miles) west of El Porvenir (www.corallodge.com). Panama City hostels and hotels can help organize a multiday trip, or you can make arrangements yourself for the same price – a minimum stay of three days and two nights is recommended. Itineraries may change depending on sea conditions.

Most packages in the western region include: return transportation by boat from the Cartí docks, though some charge for the transfer; three basic meals; rustic accommodations; and a daily excursion. This might entail a trip to a near-deserted palm-fringed island (there's usually someone living there to look after the place), or a cultural visit to an inhabited island or to the mainland to visit a cemetery or a waterfall. The *comarca* taxes – payable by all non-Guna – and the 4WD transportation fees are usually additional. There is usually a fuel supplement to visit the Cayos Holandeses, which offer the best snorkeling in the *comarca* but are sometimes inaccessible due to rough seas for much of the peak season (Dec–Feb/early Mar). You also have to pay a small fee for the dock at Cartí or Barsukum and for any island you visit during your stay, even if you're only there for a short time.

On the sandy atolls, all of which are privately owned, accommodations are usually in simple white-cane *cabañas*, with makeshift beds and thin mattresses, and perhaps somewhere to keep your belongings out of the sand. Increasingly, some islands are offering camping, though you usually have to bring your own tent. Whichever option you choose, the often-basic toilets (which may have to be flushed with sea water from a bucket) are usually

Beautiful Caribbean beach in Guna Yala.

⊙ GUNA NAMES

All island communities have a Guna name, which often has several variant spellings, and a Spanish name. Matters have been further complicated by the standardization of the Guna alphabet in 2011 in which the letters 'p,' 't,' and 'k' were removed and replaced by 'b,' 'd,' and 'g,' which are sometimes doubled to give 'bb,' 'dd,' and 'gg'; the letters 'l,' 'm,' and 'n' are also doubled in some contexts. However, this standardization has not yet permeated all of Guna society. When introducing a place, we have tried to use the more commonly used name first (be it in Spanish or in Dulegaya) and given the alternative – and sometimes a variant spelling – in parentheses.

Nusagandi Forest Reserve was created by the Guna.

shared, and electricity is not a given; you may have to wash under overhead cold showers, or use a barrel of water and a jug or calabash (gourd). On weekends in peak season, fresh water for washing may run out on islands that have to transport it from the mainland.

For more comfort, several lodges in the central islands, such as Akwadup, fit the bill, offering cabins with private bathrooms (flush toilets, hand basins, and cold-water showers), often with private balconies, fancier cuisine, and English-speaking guides.

Costs depend heavily on fuel prices, and may be negotiable in low season. Accommodations and package rates in Guna Yala – be they for private or shared/dorm *cabañas*, tents, or hammocks – are almost always quoted per person, sharing.

Day-trips and overnight camping trips from Panama City are also offered in high season, though the day-trips are rarely worth the time and expense, given the six hours needed to get to and from the dock, plus the boat travel time.

In theory only Guna-owned companies are entitled to operate within the *comarca*, though several others do. The overnight stays organized by the tour companies tend to be more expensive than tours arranged directly with the accommodations concerned, though in some cases you're paying the extra for an English-speaking guide to accompany you.

You have to take all the cash you might need with you, in small denominations – the *comarca*'s only bank, in Narganá, does not give credit-card withdrawals. Some of the more expensive lodges accept online credit-card payments for a basic package, but extras – drinks, community taxes, extra tours, snorkel rental, and so on – will usually need to be paid for in cash.

EL PORVENIR AND AROUND

The diminutive, scarcely inhabited island of **El Porvenir ❶** (Gaigirgordub) belies its status as administrative capital of Guna Yala. A sliver of bare land, it barely manages to squeeze on an airstrip (no longer in use) alongside a handful of buildings, including a police post, hotel, museum, and craft shop, plus a clump of palm trees. Though this is not one of the more popular destinations, the water off El Porvenir's thin bar of sand is cleaner than at the more heavily populated neighboring islands. It's worth dropping in at the **Museo de la Nación Guna** (tel: 316-1232; Mon–Sat 8am–4pm), though you may have to ask around to get someone to open up. The exhibition hall displays photos of festivals and numerous ceremonial artifacts such as a necklace of pelican bones worn by the absoguedi's (chanter's) assistant and a headdress decorated with macaw feathers. There's also a model Guna kitchen and a notable collection of basketry and bamboo flutes. Limited information is given in English, Spanish, and Dulegaya.

A short hop across the water takes you to **Wichub-Wala**, a bustling yet relaxed island that's often visited by cruise ships, hence the proliferation of arts and crafts on sale. In addition to the usual sandy pathways and cane-and-thatch huts there are some decaying cement structures, including a former swimming pool now full of large tropical fish. To the west, the tiny semi-submerged private coral outcrop of **Ukuptupu** was formerly home to a Smithsonian marine research station until the institute was ejected from the *comarca* in 1998. The islet, on which the accommodations are the only building, provides a mellow hideaway – there's nowhere to stretch your legs, but Wichub-Wala and Nalunega are a stone's throw away.

Just south of Ukuptupu lies **Nalunega**, 'the house of the macaw' in Dulegaya; these brightly colored birds were resident on the island when it was first colonized. A more appealing village than Wichub-Wala, with a population of around 500, it has broader streets dotted with shady trees populated with parrots, while traditional cane-and-thatch buildings rub shoulders with occasional aluminum-topped

cement structures. At the center is a primary school, the meeting hall, and the basketball court. Nalunega's tiny **museum** (daily 7am–6pm) houses an unusual collection that is particularly worthwhile if you have some Spanish. The curator, Teodoro Torres, offers a fascinating narrative of Guna culture illustrated through his woodcarvings and paintings from recycled materials, such as boat sails that have washed up on the beach.

THE GARDI ISLANDS AND AROUND

The road connecting to Panama City funnels backpackers and day-trippers into the Cartí docks. Just a coconut's throw away, the **Gardi (Cartí) Islands**, together with the tiny uninhabited palm-covered retreats of Icodub (Isla Aguja), Achuerdub (Isla Ansuelo), and Aridub (Isla Iguana) nearby, experience the greatest number of tourists in the archipelago, and day-trippers in particular. The best recommendation is to stay on one of the smaller islands – Gardi Yandub if you want to sample

Indigenous Guna fisherman.

Guna village life, or Icodub for the desert-island experience – and drop by Gardi Sugdub during the day to visit the excellent museum, or in the evening if there's a community event.

Close to the mainland, densely populated **Gardi Sugdub** ❷ forms the stadium-sized hub of this island group and, with around 2,000 inhabitants, is one of the *comarca*'s busiest communities, with motorized dugouts constantly coming and going, but it's not a desirable place to spend the night. The center comprises a few large, functional cement buildings, including a secondary school, medical center, library, and post office, standing amid a maze of cane and thatch. There are a couple of restaurants, and numerous stands selling soft drinks and snacks. The large number of people passing through and the increasing proliferation of consumer goods has resulted in garbage piling up in the streets and at the water's edge, and the place should be avoided at all costs when a cruise ship has dropped anchor, as Guna women selling *molas* appear from every

doorway and the population almost doubles. The main feature of interest is the **Museo de Cultura y Arte Guna** (tel: 669 1390; daily 8am–4pm). Stuffed full of artifacts, with pictures from floor to ceiling, it covers many aspects of Guna culture – *mola* making, funerary rites, traditional medicine, religious beliefs – with some bilingual signage in Spanish and English. The place really comes alive through the informative explanations of the curator, José Davies, who is happiest conducting tours in Spanish but can manage some English.

Southeast of Gardi Sugdub, very close to the coast, four families occupy the tiny outcrop of **Nurdub**, welcoming visitors to their simple *cabañas*. Provided your Spanish is up to the task, this intimate environment is ideal for deepening your understanding of Guna culture. Although there's no beach, daily trips are arranged to beaches.

CAYOS LIMONES

The gorgeous islands that comprise **Cayos Limones** ❸ are clustered east and northeast of El Porvenir. Once

Cayos Limones.

dedicated to harvesting coconuts, they now function mainly as prime day-trip destinations, and with no limits on visitor numbers, they are completely overrun during vacation periods and summer weekends, when water for showers and toilet-flushing often runs out. At other times, it's worth staying overnight, allowing you to soak up the tranquility by a campfire and admire the sparkling night sky.

Isla Perro Chico (Assudubbibi) – also known as Perro Uno and not to be confused with nearby Isla Perro Grande (Assudubdummad), or its more populated namesake with the airstrip much farther east – is the most visited of the Cayos Limones, so it is usually overwhelmed with day-trippers on summer weekends and vacation periods. It offers the best snorkeling in the area, around an accessible reef and a sunken cargo boat in the narrow channel separating it from adjacent Isla Diablos. A further draw is the beachside restaurant that offers an à-la-carte menu, though the two-story cement structure that houses it is less appealing. A short

hop (or strong swim – beware of currents) from the island's midsummer mayhem is **Isla Diablos** ❹ (Niadub). It lays claim to a modest, thin stretch of beach with a sheltered swimming area, a volleyball court, and two pleasant backpacker accommodations with good restaurants, neither of which attracts too many day-trippers during the season.

Wailidub ❺, tucked away behind a mangrove-fringed islet just southwest of Diablos and Isla Perro Chico, is arguably the nicest place to stay in the area, offering slightly more upscale cabins on stilts, and generally better service. Favored by passing sailboats, which stop off at the well-known bar-restaurant at Cabañas Wailidup, it comprises a windward stretch of alabaster sand, shelving into crystalline shallows sprinkled with starfish, and an open grassy patch surrounded by willowy palms. It also has the rare luxury of a fresh water supply. But beware of the bugs when the wind drops.

Heading north, toward the outer perimeter of the archipelago, the large

Kuna Yala sign (an alternative spelling of Guna Yala).

⊙ GUNA GLOSSARY

The most essential word to grasp in Dulegaya (Guna language) is the versatile 'nuedi,' meaning 'hello,' 'yes,' and 'it's good/OK' or 'welcome.' 'Nuegambi,' meaning 'thank you' is also useful. Other key cultural terms include:

Bab Dummad and *Nan Dummad* Great Father and Mother, the creators
Baba Nega heavenly spirit world
boni evil spirits
dule masi traditional Guna fish and plantain stew
Iberogun Guna prophet and religion
Innamudigi initial puberty ritual held at a girl's first menstruation
inna nega chicha house
innasuid second puberty ritual for girls when they are officially named
nainumar cultivated lands on the mainland
neg uan burial ground
nele traditional healer or shaman
nuchu carved wooden totem to ward off evil spirits
onmagged nega meeting house
saila chief
uaga (uagmala) outsider(s)
ulu dugout canoe

Eat

The seafood can't get any fresher at the breezy, over-the-water deck of Restaurante Banedub (tel: 6119 4743; daily 8am–7pm), which is popular with the yachting fraternity. They serve high-quality seafood – fish, conch, octopus – alongside rice and a smidgen of salad, as well as various sizes of lobster.

Classroom on Isla Corbisky, which educates its pupils in both Spanish and Dulegaya (the Guna language).

palm-covered **Chicheme Grande** ⑥ (www.ichubdubdummad), home to a handful of families, attracts both day and weekend visitors. In addition, sailing vessels on the Puerto Lindo or Portobelo to Cartagena route often stop here for the night. Waves thunder over the protective outlying reef, which prevents garbage from washing up on the gorgeous beach, and the island's relative size coupled with its isolation engender an away-from-it-all feel – outside peak periods – though it's not really a place for snorkeling.

Just off the eastern end of the Cayos Limones, and about an hour's boat ride from Cartí en route to the Cayos Holandeses, lies **Masargandub** ⑦ (Isla Bambú). A gem of an island and one of the largest in the *comarca*, it takes a full hour to circumnavigate on foot. Starfish, stingrays, and dolphins inhabit its translucent waters, iguanas peek out through the undergrowth, and hawksbill turtles dig their nests in the soft sand (late Apr–July). Two family associations from the central isles run camping-only operations here.

RÍO SIDRA AND AROUND

Some 15km (9 miles) east of Cartí, just off the mainland, lies **Río Sidra** ⑧; formerly a key portal into the archipelago until its airport was closed a few years ago, it is still an important settlement within the *comarca*. Originally two separate islands, Urgandi and Mamartupu combined to make Río Sidra – a community of almost 2,000 – by reclaiming the land in between. Each retains its own identity, maintaining separate *sailas*, meeting houses, and churches – and each charges a community visitors' tax – though they share a school and basketball court. As you face the town from the main jetty, Urgandi lies to the right, Mamartupu to the left; the main drag, a broad sandy boulevard with a number of grocery stores, bisects both, running the length of the island.

The island is convenient for visiting Nusadub (Isla Ratón) and Isla Maquina (Mormagedub). Famous for its *molas*, the latter is a popular village excursion for the backpacker islands of Senidub, Naranjo Chico, and Isla Pelicano. Other

scenic diversions in the area include the lovely sandy island of Bigirdub and starfish haven of Isla Salar, while the mainland attractions include a boat trip up the Río Masargandi, calling in at the cemetery at its mouth, and a trek through luxuriant rainforest to the once-sacred waterfall of Saiba, where you can cool off in the delightful fresh-water pool at its base.

North of Río Sidra lie some of the archipelago's most renowned back-packer retreats, in particular the postage-stamp-sized islands of **Isla Pelicano** (Gorgidub) and **Senidub** (Isla Chiquita). Crowned with coconut palms and fringed with strips of soft sand, they offer the cheapest pack-ages in the *comarca* and stays are easily organized through Panama City hostels. As a result there can often be something of a budget-resort atmos-phere on them. Of the two, Senidub is the slightly larger and better tended, though it's rather cluttered with *cabañas*. Possible excursions from both take in the village of Soledad Mirya (Mirya Ubgigandub), which is noted for fine *molas*, or the glorious white-sand beaches of Piderdub.

Belying its diminutive tag, **Naranjo Chico** (Narasgandubbibi) is the second largest island in the area after Naranjo Grande (Narasgandubdummad). It is particularly lovely for its distinctive hourglass shape, its gorgeous swathe of white-powder sand – from which you can snorkel – and its vegetation of coconut palms, shrubs, and delightful hibiscus flowers. Several families run lodgings here but with most *cabañas* set back off the sand, nestled in the undergrowth, the nicest stretch of beach remains unspoilt.

As you approach the wafting coco-nut palms of **Guanidub**, 10km (6 miles) north of Río Sidra, a serried rank of 12 smart cane-and-thatch *cabañas* at the edge of the sparkling white sand seem-ingly stand to attention. Though idylli-cally located, within striking distance

of the Cayos Holandeses, the teardrop-shaped island offers relatively little shade and the beach is small.

CAYOS HOLANDESES AND OTHER CAYS

Three groups of predominantly unin-habited cays provide the archipelago's most spectacular underwater scenery. Marking the outer limit of the comarca, 30km (19 miles) from shore, **Cayos Holandeses** ❾ (Maoki) are the most remote, yet the most visited, of the three as they are often offered as day-excursions from the island-hotels of western Guna Yala, though a fuel sup-plement is often charged. Effectively out of bounds during the fierce winds and high waves of December to the end of February, at other times this chain of around 20 densely forested islands acts as a magnet for yachts drawn to the sheltered anchorage and shal-low, translucent waters. Protection is afforded by the outlying Wreck Reef, which has ensnared Spanish galleons and the odd drug-smuggling vessel, parts of which still protrude through

Sunken ship in the crystalline waters off Isla Perro Chico (Assadubbibi).

the pounding surf. The resulting bays form clear natural swimming pools displaying a stunning array of sponges and soft and hard corals – fire, elkhorn, brain, fan – that attract rays, reef sharks, moray eels, starfish, and a plethora of polychromatic fish.

Much nearer to the mainland and strung out along the 30km (19-mile) expanse of sea between Río Sidra and Narganá and Corazón de Jesús are **Cayos Los Grullos** and **Cayos Coco-Bandero** ⑩ (Ordupuquip). These two clusters of around a dozen or so cays comprise thin powdery beaches peppered with driftwood encircling densely forested isles and coral-filled shallows. Their isolation and lack of landing space means they avoid the hordes of backpackers or day-trippers. Popular with cruising yachts, they attract Guna dugouts selling *molas* and fresh produce to the visitors.

NARGANÁ AND CORAZÓN DE JESÚS

A quick glance round either **Narganá** ⑪ (Yandub) or Corazón de Jesús

(Aggwanusadub), two islands at the heart of central Guna Yala, and it's easy to forget you're in Guna Yala. The paved squares are dotted with benches, lampposts flank wide sandy streets, evening sound systems blast out reggaeton and bachata, and traditionally clad women are conspicuously absent. Some Guna see the twin islands as a warning of the fate of the *comarca* if the spread of uaga burba – the spirit of outsiders – proceeds unchecked. On the plus side, the location of the two islands is enchanting, nestled in a bay and fringed with mangroves fronting forest-clad hills. Moreover, if you've been traveling around the *comarca*, you might find Narganá's Hostal Parks – with proper mattresses, cable TV, and a/c – a welcome relief.

Corazón de Jesús, in keeping with its name, has a statue of Christ in its central plaza, which is illuminated at night. Other than that, the island's main features are its currently disused airstrip, a handful of government buildings, and a church; there's a small cemetery at the northern tip.

Guna woman with a parrot.

⊘ GUNA BURIAL RITUALS

A traditional Guna burial ground (*neg uan*) is usually a mass of thatched rooftops that protect the graves from rain. Underneath, an elongated mound of earth represents the pregnant belly of *Nabguana* (Mother Nature) as she gives birth to the deceased in the heavenly spirit world (*Baba Nega*). Everyday utensils, clothing, and food are also left to accompany the deceased on their journey. The body is laid to rest in a deep grave in a hammock, oriented toward the rising sun in the east. This is symbolic of new life, which is also sometimes alluded to by laying cotton threads – representing the umbilical cord – across the corpse. A dugout tethered nearby is left to carry the deceased to their ancestors.

Most of the action occurs down at the wharf and at its opposite number across the dividing channel of water in Narganá: boats load up with supplies and drop off passengers, and yachts bob at anchor.

Across the bridge in Narganá, the gleaming golden statue of Carlos Inaediguine Robinson, educator and major player in the 1925 Guna Revolution, stands as if in defiance at the center of the main plaza. Spacious sandy streets lead off the square in grid formation, in stark contrast to most Guna communities' cramped, labyrinthine layouts. Cement houses, occasionally surrounded by a hedge or garden, alternate with traditional cane-and-thatch dwellings, sometimes sprouting satellite dishes. Given that the first missionaries to the *comarca* settled in Narganá, it's no wonder the place has four churches.

If you have the means to get there, consider a trip up Río Azúcar (Uwargandub) on the mainland, a few kilometers west of Narganá. It is one of the most beautiful rivers in the *comarca*, brimming with birdlife, with the occasional crocodile idling on the bank.

ISLA TIGRE

Of greater appeal, east of Narganá is the populous yet spacious, elongated **Isla Tigre** ⑫ (Digir Dubu), which has the rare luxury of a couple of slender beaches. This island is managing better than most to sustain Guna mores while opening up to tourism, partly due to partitioning off the village from the grassy community-run tourist areas. In the latter you can loll in a hammock, enjoy a beer at the community restaurant, or sit on the sliver of beach in your swimwear – provided you cover up to go into the village. Possible inexpensive excursions include a visit to the mainland cemetery, a three-hour hike to waterfalls, or a snorkeling trip around one of the nearby islands, where coconuts are harvested.

Some aspects of traditional living are still practiced: families rotate to harvest coconuts, and workers take it in turn to staff the community restaurant. The island also has its own NGO and

Fresh lobster.

is actively involved in lobster protection and recycling practices. The Guna dance – involving men playing panpipes and women shaking maracas – originated here, and during the mid-October Feria de Isla Tigre dance troupes from across the *comarca* compete for prizes. You can catch them rehearsing on some evenings and weekends.

PLAYÓN CHICO AND SAN IGNACIO DE TUPILE

Two cemeteries atop hills on the mainland announce your arrival at the sprawling administrative hub of **Playón Chico ⑬** (Uggubseni), home to around 3,000 people. A large, flat, coral-filled pancake packed with cane-and-thatch dwellings, interspersed with functional concrete buildings, the island is wrestling to balance traditional customs with modern developments, but is a vibrant and welcoming place for all that. The wharf opens out onto the main-square-cum-basketball-court, and a painted stage. A concrete footbridge leads to the mainland, where a soccer field, airstrip, and several

Gorgeous fish mola.

government buildings, including a high school, are located. Westernizing influence is evident in the numerous churches scattered round the island, and in the presence of electricity, which allows for a weekend movie night at the community hall by the basketball court, and results in the sound of competing TVs penetrating paper-thin walls as you try to sleep. Attractive excursions include hikes into pristine rainforest taking in the cascading waterfall of Saibar Maid; birdwatching up the Río Grande; and lazy sun-lounging, moderate snorkeling, and fishing off nearby coconut isles.

Ten kilometers (6 miles) southeast of Playón Chico, midway along the *comarca*, lies the well-organized widely-evangelized community of **San Ignacio de Tupile ⑭** (Dadnaggwe Dubbir). As you step out of a boat at the community pier, you are greeted by a statue of the Virgin Mary. Though tourists rarely visit, the vibe among the 1,500 inhabitants is relaxed and welcoming, particularly if your visit coincides with the patron saint festivities (July 28–31), when you can join in the celebrations marked by rowing races and various competitions.

Beyond the statue stands the elementary school, where a wide main boulevard peels off left. The streets are kept spick-and-span, as community regulations mean families are held responsible for disposing of garbage on the mainland. Rules are equally strict about getting a permit to leave the island, aimed at curbing what elders see to be the moral decline among some of the younger members of the community. Squeezed between two old public phone booths, the strangely whitened face of General Inatikuña, the community's first *saila* following relocation from the mainland to the island in 1903, stares out across the street.

Excursions are available to the unremarkable nearby beach on Ilestup ('Isle of the Englishman'), named after a gent who lived there in the 1700s, and to the Río Yuandub Gandi, where alligators laze on sandbanks and a rainbow of birds flit in and out of the foliage.

THE EASTERN ISLES

What might loosely be described as the eastern isles stretch over the whole of the eastern half of the *comarca*, which, outside the sprinkling of lodges near Achutupu (Assudub) and Mamitupu (Mammidub), sees precious few outsiders beyond the odd yacht and Colombian trading vessel. Here, lacking the protection of an offshore reef, the seas are rough and transportation between communities sparse. After storms, garbage jettisoned from boats will wash up on the shore in places. Westernmost of these islands, overlooking coastal mangroves, is **Agligandi** ⑮ (previously Ailigandi). As the first place of organized resistance in the Guna Revolution of 1925, the community has cemented its place in Guna history – hence the many revolutionary flags fluttering proudly above the rooftops – and is a good place to experience the annual revolutionary celebrations in February.

A pivotal figure in the rebellion was Chief Olokindibipilelel (Simral Colman), whose statue – incongruously clad in suit and bowler hat – claims a central position on the densely populated island of around 1200, next to the obligatory basketball court. A warren of pathways weaves through tightly packed thatched dwellings, in the midst of which is squeezed the tiny **Museo Olonigli** (no fixed hours). As with other museums in the *comarca*, it comprises a single room stuffed with artifacts whose significance only becomes clear through the explanations (in Spanish) of the owner-curator. He elaborates on traditional culture drawing on his own woodcarvings, which depict Guna symbols and rituals.

Five kilometers east of Agligandi, the unusual crescent-shaped island of **Achutupu** (Assudub), dotted with banana trees and coconut palms, has a deceptively spacious feel. The village has an elementary school, health center, and restaurant by the pier,

Church in Playón Chico (Uggubseni).

alongside a basketball court. It's inadvisable to swim off the strip of sand that might optimistically be called a beach, due to pollution. There's nowhere to stay on the island itself, but a couple of lodges can be found on nearby islets.

Just a few hundred meters/yds east of Achutupu, **Mamitupu** (Mammidub) has ten *sailas* governing a traditional village of about 1,200. Photography is forbidden here, though it is permitted on excursions to the mainland.

Beyond Mamitupu, completing the remaining 75km (46.5 miles) to the eastern limit of the *comarca*, you pass the densely matted, thatched rooftops of the *comarca*'s most populous communities: the 4,000-strong twin settlements of **Ogobsucum** and **Usdub**, renowned for their gold craftwork. The next notable community is the pine-clad **Isla Pino** ⑯ (Dubbag), which unlike any other island in the *comarca* has a large hill; though only a little more than a square kilometer (0.4 square miles) in size, it boasts a couple of forest trails and a picturesque waterside thatched village.

Travelers rarely venture this far east to these more traditional communities, where you will need to check in with the police and ask permission of the *saila* to visit or stay on an island – make sure you are appropriately clad. It is usually possible to negotiate with a family for a hammock or bed, pay for meals, and engage the services of someone to explore the rivers and rainforest on the mainland. The seas along this stretch of coastline are particularly rough and should only be navigated in a sturdy boat, with life jackets – not the shallow leaking dugout favored by many boatmen.

ARMILA AND PUERTO OBALDÍA

Tucked away in the remotest corner of mainland Guna Yala, close to the Colombian border, is the unusual and welcoming Guna community of **Armila** ⑰. It is idyllically located at the base of a forest-cloaked hill, where two rivers empty into the sea. Atypically spacious, and run by five *sailas*, the village boasts an intriguing mix of traditional cane cabañas and

The Armila Guna community performing a welcome dance.

more substantial Afro-Antillean-style wood-and-thatch houses, sometimes painted or on stilts. Beyond, more than 4km (2.5 miles) of cream-colored windswept beach extends along the coast, one of the world's most important nesting sites for leatherback turtles. The visitor community fee goes toward the settlement's conservation and monitoring project (www.facebook.com/yauggalu). Indeed, turtle watching is a major tourist activity during the nesting season (Feb–Aug). During the annual turtle festival in the third week in May, involving traditional music and dancing, a three-night package deal is usually offered to visitors, and camping is permitted. Other activities include jungle walks, river trips by dugout, and swimming in the local freshwater lagoon. Provided the sea is calm, beach and snorkeling trips can be organized to the lovely Playa Blanca at La Miel, by the Colombian border. A calm sea also means visitors can be transferred to the community by boat from the border town of Puerto Obaldía – the entry point for most, who fly in from Panama City. When the sea is choppy, however, reaching Armila entails a 90-minute hike over a forested hill, though villagers can carry your luggage if necessary.

Puerto Obaldía is the last major settlement before the Colombian border. Despite a tidy park, a fine playing field, clean streets, and a scenic seaside location, it is still an unendearing encampment, where the frontier police in combat gear guard against drug runners, Colombian guerrillas, and smugglers. Though technically within the *comarca*, the community has a mixed population of Guna, Colombian refugees, and non-Guna Panamanians, plus fluctuating numbers of migrants and refugees attempting to reach North America. The town is served by daily flights to and from Panama City, which are heavily oversubscribed, and the occasional speedboat to/from Cartí, in western Guna Yala. Not only does the boat cost more than the air fare (if you include the Guna taxes and onward transportation to the capital), but it's often an extremely uncomfortable, hair-raising six- to eight-hour ride.

The twin islands of Narganá (Yandub) and Corazón de Jesús (Aggwanusadub).

📷 TRADITIONAL DRESS

While distinctive traditional attire is still everyday wear for many indigenous women, most Panamanians only don their vibrant and varied costumes for celebrations and festivals.

What counts as traditional dress depends very much on who you are. Even then, these markers of identity are hybrid and constantly evolving, with tangled cultural roots in indigenous, Spanish, and African heritage, shaped by a history of missionaries, colonialism, and resistance.

Panama's traditional clothing is as diverse as its multicultural population: from the world-renowned *molas* (colorful, embroidered cloth panels) and beaded forearms and calves (*wini*) of Guna women, to the bright wraparound skirts (*uhua*) and body painting of the Emberá, or the pants and shirts made from bark of the *cucuá* tree by a little-known community in Coclé. Geometric designs and patterns in such attire are full of symbolism, often related to groups' belief-systems – the perfectly aligned, interlocking triangles adorning the flowing Ngäbe dress (*nawa* or *nagua*), for example, reflect their harmony with the world around, such as mountains, valleys, and rivers. Other aspects of traditional clothing signify the gender or life-stage of the wearer, such as the Guna gold nose-ring (*olasu*), which is only worn by women after puberty.

Panamanian men tend to wear subdued variations of more modern Western-style clothing, whatever their affiliation. Arguably, the most distinctive look – emblematic of the Azuero Peninsula – is the classic *montuno*: a buttoned, loose white shirt, worn over long pants, accompanied by a straw hat.

Young Emberá women in traditional dress: their brightly colored skirts called uhua were once made using plant fibers; today, they are generally imported from China.

Guna women have their septum pierced in puberty and thereafter wear a gold nose-ring (olasu).

Guna calf bracelet (wini).

A flamboyant headdress usually accompanies the pollera.

The pollera

With plenty of regional variation, the multi-layered *pollera* is Panama's undisputed national dress, consisting of a blouse (*camisa*) and a full skirt (*pollerón*). With probable origins in Afro-colonial slave dresses, the colorful patchwork *pollera Congo*, unsurprisingly, features heavily in the pre-Lenten Congo celebrations along Colón's Caribbean coast (see page 158). In contrast, a plain *pollera montuna*, comprising full skirt and simple white blouse, was later adopted and adapted by the Panamanian social elite, culminating in the *pollera de gala*, a wedding-cake-like confection embellished with intricate stitching, appliqué, and embroidery. Taking up to two years for even the most skilled seamstresses to make, working out of their homes around Las Tablas, these ornate items of clothing are either passed down as family heirlooms or made to order at costs of up to several thousand dollars. Attend any of the Azuero's numerous folk festivals, and you'll see a wealth of *polleras* sashaying through the streets. Best of all, catch the annual Desfile de la Mil Polleras in Las Tablas (see page 190), which showcases this spectacular dress in all its forms in an endless joyous parade of music and dance.

...mbrero pintao.

...ite is usually the base color of the pollera de gala, ...corated with floral designs. Most have a large pompom ...the top of the blouse.

Panamanian woman donning a traditional pollera de gala as part of the Desfile de la Mil Polleras festival in Las Tablas.

Emberá woman in traditional attire, her body painted in jagua dye.

DARIÉN AND THE EAST

No region of Panama captures the imagination quite like the Darién. One of the last true tropical wildernesses, it encompasses swathes of mountainous forest, teeming with wildlife and promising adventure.

Map on page 264

Mention of the Darién – Panama's largest province, abutting Colombia – conjures up a host of images, some alluring, others less so; some true, others vastly exaggerated. The biggest attraction in this sparsely populated, rugged region is Parque Nacional Darién. Panama's largest national park, it boasts towering ancient forests that harbor a staggering array of flora and fauna, and provide opportunities for serious hiking and superb birdwatching. Yet travelers are increasingly drawn to the Darién by its people as much as its compelling scenery; remote communities of the closely related Emberá and Wounaan – the region's main indigenous peoples – have opened up to tourists, offering insights into their daily lives and ancient yet changing traditions. The region's other main draw, 100km (62 miles) east of Panama City, is Lago Bayano, a vast reservoir that enjoys a picturesque setting in an increasingly deforested landscape, and has an impressive network of caves.

Darién's history, both old and more recent, is peppered with violence. In colonial times, the region bore witness to some of the bloodiest confrontations between the invading conquistadors, greedy for gold and power, and the indigenous groups desperate to defend their territories. This occurred most notably at Santa María La Antigua del Darién, the first successful Spanish settlement on the mainland since the time of Columbus (across the border in present-day Colombia). Balboa took Santa María in 1510, and later intercepted an attempt to reclaim the city, led by Cacique Cémaco, a pivotal figure in the indigenous resistance. The Spaniard captured all the alliance's chiefs, bar Cémaco, and had them hanged as an example. It is therefore perhaps only fitting that Balboa, who first espied the Pacific from the Darién, also met his

Main attractions

Lago Bayano
Parque Nacional Darién
Río Sambú
Visiting an Emberá/
    Wounaan community
The Pacific Coast

Taking a break in Darién National Park.

end here – beheaded on the orders of Pedrerías Dávila, governor of Castillo de Oro, in the coastal town of Acla (in present-day Guna Yala). Shortly afterward, Santa María was abandoned by the Spanish in favor of Panama City, and was later razed to the ground by indigenous forces in 1524.

PEOPLE OF THE DARIÉN

The indigenous peoples most in evidence today in the Darién are the Emberá and Wounaan. Both groups may have migrated from the Chocó regions of Colombia (which is why they are often referred to collectively as Chocós). Guna presence is still recalled in some of the place names, notably the snaking Río Tuira, and though most

Guna moved to the Caribbean coast, pockets remain in the more recently formed *comarcas* of Madugandi and Wargandi, and in isolated communities in Panamá and Darién provinces. The other substantial population, dominant in the regional capital of La Palma and in settlements lining the Golfo de San Miguel, are the Afro-Darienites (also Afro-Coloniales). These are descendants on the whole of the *cimarrones* – escaped slaves brought over from Africa by the Spanish, who fled and waged warfare from their own strongholds (*palenques*) in the rainforest, forming strategic alliances with pirates and indigenous communities. Some of their communities are now mixed with Emberá and Wounaan, and, in some

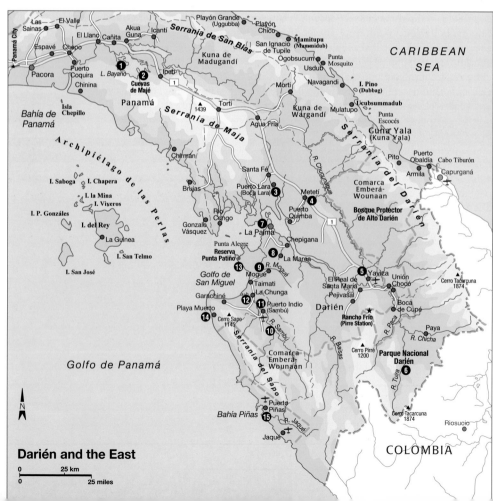

Darién and the East

0   25 km
0   25 miles

parts, with Afro-Colombian refugees, who fled the more recent civil conflict across the border.

The completion of the Interamericana to Yaviza in 1979 opened the floodgates to *'colonos,'* the name often given to migrating *mestizo* cattle ranchers and farmers predominantly from the Azuero Peninsula. Pursuing their traditional way of life, these farmers have now cleared vast tracts of land along the highway for pasture, and constitute around 50 percent of the total population of Darién province. The settlers' thirst for new land for grazing has resulted in increasingly violent clashes with indigenous communities defending their land that was demarcated in the joint Comarca Emberá-Wounaan in 1983, which covers around a quarter of Darién province. At the same time, indigenous authorities have been wrangling with successive governments for decades over the collective land rights of communities that lie outside the *comarca* but within declared protected areas.

LAGO BAYANO

Heading east out of Panama City toward the Darién, the first tourist destination of note is **Lago Bayano ❶**, some 90km (56 miles) to the east and still within the confines of the Provincia de Panamá. Named after Bayano, a charismatic leader of a major settlement of *cimarrones* (see page 264), the picturesque 350-sq-km (135 sq mile) reservoir is a popular day-trip destination from the capital. On weekends, families spill out of vehicles at the impressive **Puente Bayano**, which fords the lake's narrowest point, and pile into motor launches bound for island picnics, fishing trips, or tours of the lake, on the lookout for caimans, crocodiles, and otters slithering around the muddy banks.

The reservoir's charm and tranquility, however, belie the anger of indigenous communities that were displaced when the reservoir was formed in 1976 and are still awaiting full compensation from the government. The tips of dead tree trunks that protrude eerily from the water act as poignant reminders of the acres of forest that were submerged when the Río Chepo (or Río Bayano) was dammed to supply Panama City with more hydropower. Comprising much of Lago Bayano's northern shores is the hilly Guna **Comarca de Madugandi** (see page 243); elsewhere, scattered around the reservoir, are various Emberá, Wounaan, and Ladino settlements, many of which make a living from the commercial fishing of tilapia.

Lago Bayano's biggest draw is the **Cuevas de Majé ❷**, a kilometer (half-mile) -long series of limestone caverns at the southwestern end of the lake, with atmospheric calcitic formations that are home to thousands of bats. Toward the end of the dry season, it's possible to wade your way (up to your chest) through the entire system, marveling at the sparkling stalactites, before emerging in a steep-sided

⊘ Tip

Several tour operators run day-trips from Panama City to Lago Bayano and the caves, but it's easy to get here by bus, though you need to arrange boat transportation in advance – avoiding summer weekend crowds if possible.

⊘ SAFETY IN DARIÉN

For many years the rule of thumb for safety in the Darién has been to draw an imaginary line from the Caribbean Colombian border, through Yaviza, to Bahía Piñas and Jaqué on the Pacific coast, beyond which you should not travel. Rancho Frío excepted, this still holds; however, due to the occasional flare-up in violence and drug-trafficking-related incidents, other places may be temporarily off limits too. You should always check with your consulate before traveling, and continue to seek local advice on your travels, especially from the frontier police (SENAFRONT) and village authorities. For a few years, independent foreign travelers were required to obtain a (free) permit from SENAFRONT, and although this restriction was lifted in 2016, security is tightened up again after any major incident. Any independent traveler would be well advised to pass by the SENAFRONT office in Corozal (opposite the Panama Railroad station; tel: 527 1000; Mon–Fri 8.30am–3.30pm) and make enquiries. Given the ever-changing regulations and security situation, it's no wonder that most people prefer to go on an organized tour. That said, the challenging environment still poses the greatest threat out here – trails are poorly demarcated and medical assistance is virtually inaccessible in the event of an emergency.

verdant gully, dripping with mosses and ferns. At other times, the raised water level means you'll need to go partway in a boat, or kayak, before stepping into the water, and may not be able to make it through on foot. Whatever the season, you'll need a headlamp – though guides sometimes provide flashlights – footwear with a good grip and a minimum amount of clothing that you're happy to get soaked (as well as something dry to change into). Most boat tours also take in the impressive rock walls that enclose the entrance to the nearby Río Tigre.

The indigenous community of Agua Yala at the western end of the Puente Bayano marks the entry to the Guna Comarca de Madugandi, established in 1996, which includes 80 percent of the reservoir's surface area and extends from the forested northern shores of the lake up the mountainous backdrop of the Serranía de San Blas. Well over 3,000 Guna inhabit the *comarca*, dispersed among 14 communities; some, such as Icanti, Pintupu, and Tabardi are beginning

to open up to tourists, but you would need to ask permission and find some transportation at the community dormitory in Agua Yala, by the bridge. Once in the village, it would be a case of slinging up a hammock in someone's home as there are no organized accommodations as yet.

THE INTERAMERICANA TO YAVIZA

Once past the first security checkpoint at the bridge, the road heads eastward. Some 50km (31 miles) or so farther on, just south of the Interamericana, at **Ipetí**, two adjoining Emberá communities provide the other main reason to stop en route to the Darién proper. Popular with day-trippers and budget tours from Panama City, the relatively barren location of Ipeti-Embera and Bahu Pono lacks the rainforest charm of other villages in Darién province. However, if you're keen to drop in, any bus bound for Yaviza, Metetí, or Agua Fría will let you off by the roadside, from where it's a 20-minute walk along a gravel road to the communities.

Geoffroy's tamarin.

⊘ EL 'REY NEGRO BAYANO'

El 'Rey Negro Bayano' was the most successful leader of the cimarrones and the undisputed king, referred to as such even by the Spanish. Commanding the loyalty of between 400 and 1,200 followers, he constructed an impenetrable hilltop fortress from where he repeatedly attacked Spanish forces and plundered mule trains on the Camino Real. After the governor of Panama had failed to quell Bayano's resistance, the Viceroy of Peru sent Captain Pedro de Ursúa to crush the rebellion. Aware he couldn't take the fortress by force, the conquistador resorted to deceit, pretending to offer Bayano a peaceful settlement and half the land. At the supposed celebratory feast – so the story goes – de Ursúa drugged the wine, resulting in the easy capture of Bayano and his men, and an end to six successful years of revolt against the Spanish Crown.

Agua Fría No. 1, a place easily missed were it not for the police checkpoint, marks the entry into the Provincia de Darién. From here, the road veers southeast, speeding through pastureland, past the turn-off to the province's first major settlement, the agricultural center of Santa Fé, which sees few visitors. In contrast, five kilometers downriver from Santa Fé, along the eastern bank of the Río Sabana – and accessible by road from the Interamericana – lies **Puerto Lara ❸**. One of the few communities to receive plenty of technical support and funding, this Wounaan village of around 600 people has a functioning fishing association and a computer center, and produces high-quality crafts (see www.puertolara.com). Though both Emberá and Wounaan are renowned for their basketry and tagua carving, it is the Wounaan who historically have been artists and have the greater reputation; many pieces from Puerto Lara are sent straight to Panama City for sale, but some can still be perused in the village, where workshops in *artesanía* are also held.

Simple cane *cabañas* accommodate overnight visitors. Beyond the village, boat trips, guided hikes (within a small patch of forest of modest appeal), fishing, and traditional dances can all be arranged by contacting the president of the tourism committee.

Arrival at the regionally important commercial and administrative center of **Metetí ❹**, a few kilometers farther along the highway, is heralded by another security checkpoint. Unendearing as Metetí is, you're likely to pass through the place more than once if you spend time in the area, as it offers good road transportation both to Yaviza – from where it's a shortish hop by boat downriver to El Real, the main gateway to the Parque Nacional Darién – and Puerto Quimba, which provides a water-taxi link to La Palma, capital of the Darién and access point for many of the Emberá and Wounaan communities. What's more, the handful of warehouse-like stores by the main intersection stock a greater range of supplies than you'll find in either Yaviza or La Palma, and better lodgings and

Boating on Lago Bayano.

⊙ Tip

Bordering the Reserva Serranía Hidrológica Filo de Tallo, the upscale, all-inclusive Canopy Camp Darién (www.canopytower.com/canopy-camp) is one of the very few comfortable places to stay in the region. Run by the owners of established birding lodges (the Canopy Tower and Canopy Lodge), this safari-style tented camp provides opportunities to seek out a harpy eagle and other rare birds, as well as visit a local community.

restaurants, though all at the budget end of the scale. The MiAmbiente office (tel: Mon–Fri 8am–4pm) by the bridge is an essential stop if you're en route to the national park. Most buses from Panama City turn in at the bus station in Metetí, where travelers change onto one of the frequent local minibuses that shuttle between here and Yaviza, or make the short ride to Puerto Quimba.

Around Metetí lies the protected area of the **Reserva Serranía Hidrológica Filo de Tallo**, though it has no amenities or recognized trails. Though lacking the wilderness appeal of the Darién national park, it constitutes a refreshing oasis of woodland in an increasingly denuded landscape. Along with the contiguous Reserva Forestal Canglón, it aims to protect the water source for 26 communities.

Back on the Interamericana, beyond Metetí, the undulating road passes the odd settlement and occasional teak plantation until it comes to a halt at the end of the road – literally – by the banks of the Río Chucunaque at

⊙ THE DARIÉN GAP

The fabled Darién Gap – roughly 12,000 sq km (4,633 sq miles) of dense tropical rainforest, swamp, and mountains straddling the Panama–Colombia border – constitutes the only break in the 30,000km (18,640-mile) -long Panamerican Highway that stretches from Alaska to the tip of South America. Teeming with danger, this untamed jungle has fascinated explorers, outlaws, scientists, and adventurers for hundreds of years. Over the last century, numerous attempts were made – only a handful successful – to cross in jeeps, motorbikes, and even by bicycle. In the 1980s a British travel company organized regular treks across El Tapón (the plug), as it is known in Spanish. By the 1990s, however, the Gap was off limits for all but the most foolhardy, as the impenetrable terrain provided hideouts for Colombia's FARC guerrillas, right-wing paramilitaries, bandits and drug traffickers. Since then, the area has been plagued with disappearances, kidnappings, and murders – some well publicized, others not even recorded. More recently, human traffickers have added their name to the list of Darién's undesirables, exploiting thousands of weak, vulnerable, ill-prepared migrants or refugees, all desperate to reach the US or Canada. While some survive the trauma and hardship of crossing the Darién Gap, only to be apprehended by the authorities, others fail to make it through the jungle at all.

Yaviza ❺. Here, hidden behind a high chainlink fence and reams of barbed wire, the river port buzzes with activity in the morning. Marking the official start of the infamous Darién Gap (Tapón del Darién – literally, Darién cork or plug), the 100km (62-mile) highway hiatus between Central and South America, Yaviza simultaneously exudes a lethargic end-of-the-road torpor and an edgy frontier-town feel. The mixed population of around 3,000 (Afro-Dariénite, Emberá, Wounaan, and *mestizo*) eyes outsiders warily, while gun-toting frontier police officers routinely patrol the town togged up in full camouflage combat gear.

Yaviza's only interest to visitors is as an unavoidable stepping stone to El Real, the gateway to Parque Nacional Darién, or to the Distrito Cémaco, the northern segment of the Comarca Emberá-Wounaan, which has been out of bounds to visitors for years on account of the security situation. During the day, most of the action occurs at the wharf, where buses pull in: supplies are loaded onto a flotilla of motorized piraguas headed for communities upriver, while mounds of plantain and yuca bound for the city are heaved onto trucks, and the surrounding makeshift *fondas* and restaurants do a thriving trade. There's essentially only one very basic lodging in town, and a nearby restaurant, both of which are often taken up with government or NGO workers.

PARQUE NACIONAL DARIÉN

At 5,790 sq km (2,235 sq miles), **Parque Nacional Darién ❻** is the most expansive protected area in Central America. Created in 1972, it outranks all of Panama's national parks in both size and reputation. Yet it's one of the least-visited protected areas in the country since reaching the park requires considerable organization. That said, the awe-inspiring greenery, laced with rivers and waterfalls and rich in wildlife, makes the effort well worth the time and money, providing a truly magical experience. Now that hiking across the Darién Gap has been consigned to history – though various specialty operators market their multi-day jungle adventures as such – visiting the national park these days means hiring a guide (who will help sort out the paperwork) and staying at the only permanent camp: MiAmbiente's bunkhouse at Rancho Frío, reached via El Real.

The park hugs the Colombian border, a forested carpet rising from the mangroves, coastal lagoons, and deserted beaches of the Pacific. It then ripples over the volcanic ranges of the Serranía del Sapo and Cordillera de Jungurudó northeast to the park's highest point of Cerro Tacarcuna (1,875 meters/6,150ft), on the continental divide of the Serranía del Darién, stopping just short of the Caribbean coast. Numerous important rivers scythe their way through the emerald mantle, including the Tuira, Sambú, and Balsas.

Reaching the park requires a boat trip on the deceptively fast-flowing waters of the Río Chucunaque as they snake down 6km (4 miles) from Yaviza through variegated walls of water chestnuts, banana plantations, expansive trees, and pastureland to the low-key grassy bank 'jetty' of **El Real** on the Río Tuira. A one-time fortified colonial settlement, El Real is now a pleasant if somnolent collection of houses constructed from various combinations of wood, zinc, and concrete, and a couple of churches, interwoven with a network of cement pathways. This is the jumping-off point for the rustic and rudimentary MiAmbiente refuge at **Rancho Frío**, a further couple of hours away, usually reached by a combination of vehicular and fluvial transportation and hiking, depending on the season and the tour package.

Scenically located on the shady banks of the Río Perescenico, Rancho Frío offers several trails leading off from the camp. These include the serious day or overnight trek to the cloudforest of **Cerro Pirre** (1,200 meters/3,937ft) – which requires hauling tent, sleeping bag, and provisions up the mountain;

Catching the sunrise from Cerro Pirre.

Tip

There are only two banks (with ATMs) in the whole of the Darién: one in Metetí and one in La Palma, so plan accordingly.

it can be chilly at night, so pack something warm. Alternatively, the Sendero de las Antennas provides a stiff day-hike that culminates in a hilltop police post, affording sweeping views of La Palma and the Golfo de San Miguel, with the Pacific as backdrop. Less strenuous walks can be had closer to camp, but still require a guide; the most popular is the two-hour circular Sendero Rancho Frío, which takes in a waterfall and natural *piscina* (swimming pool). During the wet months, the rivers and waterfalls are truly spectacular, though the refuge and mountain trails are often swathed in mist and the quantity of mud to wade through can scarcely be imagined, making even the shortest hike a major physical achievement. In the dry season, paths are easier to hike, views more frequently glimpsed, and your chances of spotting mammal life – driven to the river to drink – is greatly enhanced.

LA PALMA AND AROUND

Market stalls in La Palma.

Stacked up on a hilly peninsula, a ramshackle collection of wooden buildings

constitutes the unlikely provincial capital of **La Palma** ❼. The town juts out into the widening expanse of the Río Tuira as it empties into the **Golfo de San Miguel**, a large bite-shaped body of water penetrating into Panama's southeastern Pacific coastline. Resembling no other place in Panama, La Palma, a predominantly Afro-Diénite settlement of around 7,000, is the regional administrative and commercial hub. Here, motorized dugouts from the coastal and riverine communities jostle for position at the narrow and non-too-salubrious main jetty. The town's one sultry street is chock-full of hole-in-the-wall restaurants, bars, and hotels, and stores selling welcome piles of fresh produce and other goods that are regularly shipped in from Panama City.

Just across the water from La Palma, Isla El Encanto (or Boca Chica) hosts the scarcely visible, crumbling remains of the overgrown Fuerte de San Carlos de Boca Chica; though little more than a watchtower, it was a crucial link in a chain of defenses that safeguarded the Spanish gold mines at Cana. Sprinkled along the coastline amid the mangroves are several predominantly Afro-Diénite communities, whereas up the rivers that flow into the Golfo de San Miguel lie numerous Emberá and Wounaan villages. Indeed, most visitors only pass through La Palma to connect with transportation to these outlying communities. It's worth stocking up with supplies while here – the (pricier) village stores are unlikely to provide much beyond tinned fish, rice, and cookies. If you don't have the means to purify water, make sure you pick up a flagon or two of the bottled variety, to bring back out with you.

VISITING AN EMBERÁ OR WOUNAAN VILLAGE

Staying overnight in an Emberá or Wounaan village is a great way to interact with villagers and learn about their day-to-day activities, as well as giving you access to the rainforest. Accommodations will either be in a traditional communal house (raised, thatched, and open-sided) or in a family home. Communities that are used to greeting tour parties tend to offer slightly better amenities (showers, flush toilets, and maybe even mattresses and mosquito nets), whereas others may provide little more than a wooden floor or a hammock for you to sleep on, and possibly a fire to cook your own food and a bucket of water for washing.

As many settlements are located on tidal rivers only accessible at high tide, you may well have to hang around by jetties waiting for the water level to rise, or leave in the middle of the night. Generally, you need to be flexible and organized, taking food with you where possible, since many communities expect you to provide the food to cook and village stores are thinly stocked. Bottled water – or, better still, the means of purifying water – is necessary, as water can be scarce in villages. Beer is more widely available, though check on the village etiquette before indulging; discretion should be practiced when drinking, except when the whole village is having a party.

Most visitors head for communities around the Golfo de San Miguel or in the Distrito Sambú section of the Comarca Emberá-Wounaan, where you first need to report to the *comarca* office in Puerto Indio (see page 273) and pay the entry fee. Cell phone signals are fickle, and some communities have no coverage at all; given the difficulties in communication in the Darién, most independent travelers just turn up. The tourist coordinator (or president) is the person to ask for on arrival. They can tell you the prices and whether money needs to be paid to them (to be disbursed later to the relevant people) or directly to anyone who provides a service. They may also allocate you a personal tourist coordinator, who will organize all aspects of your stay. Since arrangements vary among communities, it is essential to sort out what's to be paid to whom from the outset to

⊙ WILDLIFE IN PARQUE NACIONAL DARIÉN

The wildlife in Parque Nacional Darién is staggering, even as its boundaries are threatened. More than 450 bird species have been recorded, including an array of vibrantly colored macaws and parrots and strange-named rarities such as the beautiful treerunner, scale-crested pygmy tyrant, and Chuck-will's-widow. Mammal species top 169, with numerous endemics and endangered animals lurking in the lush vegetation; the park offers the best chance, albeit slender, of glimpsing one of the big-five cats, or a Baird's tapir – though spotting their footprints in the early morning mud is more likely – and even the occasional spectacled bear has been sighted.

The plantlife in the Darién demands just as much attention, with over 40 endemic orchids, tracts of primary and secondary growth, and a towering canopy of *barrigón*, spiny cedar, and graceful platypodium. If you visit in March or April you will be treated to the golden crowns of flowering *guayacán*, heralding the start of the rains, and the russet bloom of the silvery *cuipo* trees, looking down on the already lofty forest canopy. The latter is the favorite nesting site for

the world's largest concentration of harpy eagles (see page 274). On the forest floor, the scene is very different: dark and dank, and dominated by gnarled tree trunks entwined with vines or studded with vicious spines, vast buttress roots, dangling lianas, ferns, and rotting leaf litter.

The park was declared a Unesco World Heritage Site in 1981 and a Biosphere Reserve in 1983, but such designations offer little protection in practice, as illegal hunting, logging, extraction of rare plants and animals, and slash-and-burn agriculture continue unchecked. In the buffer zone, the story is the same, compounded by expanding plantations of palm oil. Ironically, the long list of undesirables that have taken refuge in the rainforest in recent decades – guerrillas, paramilitaries, drug and human traffickers, smugglers, and bandits – have acted as unwitting conservationists by frightening off most settlers and major developments. That said, the constant stream of refugees from the long-running civil conflict over the border in Colombia – until the 2016 peace accord – has also contributed to deforestation, as the newcomers clear land for cultivations.

prevent misunderstandings. Costs are charged per person and often itemized separately, from a community fee, to accommodations, meals, the services of a cook – usually per group – and recreational activities. When it comes to organized activities, they generally include guided hikes – sometimes to a harpy eagle nest – fishing trips, boat trips, and body painting with jagua dye (made from the juice of a tropical berry mixed with charcoal). Of course, there are plenty of informal activities – helping to prepare food, tending the fire, or joining in a soccer or basketball game.

Sales of handicrafts are also an important aspect of village visits, displayed in a small shop or by the artisans themselves, and at set prices that are inevitably lower than in Panama City. If you don't intend to buy anything, alert the tourist coordinator to avoid embarrassment since otherwise the artisans will come and spread their wares out in front of you. If you are interested, try to spread your purchases round several artisans.

⊙ RIVER TRANSPORT IN THE DARIÉN

Once in the Darién proper, transportation is predominantly by boat, which can be a motorized dugout (*piragua*), or – if you're lucky, a more comfortable fiber-glass *lancha*. Traveling this way, while brilliantly atmospheric, often entails a lot of waiting around as many communities are on tidal rivers, only accessible at high tide, especially in the dry season. If you're an independent traveler, it's infinitely cheaper, though far less comfortable, to travel in a community boat or *colectivo* (*como pasajero* – as a passenger) already heading to your destination than to hire a boat privately (*viaje especial*). For the latter, you will have to cover the cost of the fuel (often for the return trip, even if you're only traveling one way), the captain, and probably a poleman. Find out fuel costs and the amount required for your journey from another source before negotiating a price, and note that if hiring someone's services to transport you for an overnight stay in a village, you may need to pay for their lodging and food too. The best place to enquire about transportation to villages around the Golfo de San Miguel, and deeper into the Darién, is at the jetty in La Palma, the region's main transit hub, though you may sometimes be lucky to catch a ride to a community directly from Puerto Quimba.

POPULAR COMMUNITIES TO VISIT

The popularity or readiness of communities to receive tourists often comes and goes, depending upon the dynamism of the community member or committee in charge of tourism, but the following places tend to be fairly reliable options.

Forty minutes' boat ride southeast from La Palma up the sinuous tree-lined Río La Marea, the small, welcoming community of **La Marea** ⑧ provides a perfect introduction to the Emberá way of life. The '*marea*' (tide) is crucial to village logistics since the place is only reachable at high tide, and even then, at the backend of the dry season the piragua scrapes along the riverbed. Traditional open-sided wood-and-thatch dwellings are dotted across a sloping expanse of neatly trimmed grass ending at the riverbank, where a small rancho is used for dance performances and craft displays; opposite this, a tiny store sells beer and a few tinned essentials.

An infectious tranquility pervades the settlement – aside from the two hours in the evening when the generator is on – and for most of the night it is illuminated by starlight and kerosene lamps. Unlike in some communities, many of the 160 villagers choose to go about their business clad in traditional attire, except when heading into town. The surrounding forest abounds in wildlife, worth exploring with a guide following a trail leading to a waterfall or a lake, or embarking on a substantial hike or a shorter horseride. Otherwise, the days can happily slip by interacting with villagers, getting your body painted in *jagua* dye, and cooling off in the river.

Heading southwest of La Palma takes you to the popular village of **Mogué** ⑨. There's a *Heart of Darkness* feel about entering the Río Mogué, enclosed by forbidding walls of mangroves, flecked with perching white ibis, which eventually clear at a scenic mooring, 10 minutes' walk from the village itself. The name derives from Mogadé, a mythical Emberá creature that lived in the mountains and ate people – though Panama City would seem to have devoured more of the dwindling village population as they leave in search of employment. Besides a little tourism, agriculture – plantain, yucca, and a variety of other fruits and vegetables – constitutes the economic mainstay of the community, though a minority still fish or hunt iguanas, agoutis, and other small animals with traditional arrows or a gun. Another important source of income is basketry – especially masks – for which Mogué is justifiably renowned. Mogué is also the most likely community to have an active harpy eagle nest (see page 274), where a willingness to stake the place out for several hours can often be rewarded by a truly special sighting: a parent returning with a monkey in its talons, which is ripped apart, before tiny morsels are fed to the chick with incredible delicacy. The focus of community life is the zinc-roofed *casa comunal*, where on Saturdays or Sundays the leaders preside over the weekly village gathering. The tri-weekly evangelical services are also a draw for a large number of the community, while in the late afternoon the soccer field provides an important social focus for both the men's and women's teams, and visitors are welcome to join in.

Other popular destinations lie farther afield. The portal to the 12 communities of the Distrito Sambú of the Comarca Emberá-Wounaan, 12km (7.5 miles) up the serpentine **Río Sambú** ⑩, is the twin settlement of **Sambú** and **Puerto Indio** ⑪. They are reached by river at high tide and the boat trip, sweeping round the river's tortuous bends, causing flocks of white ibis to fly off in unison, is highly atmospheric.

While Sambú and its counterpart Puerto Indio, connected by a footbridge, are pleasant enough places, they serve more as a gateway to swathes of primeval forest and a serpentine waterway leading to Emberá and Wounaan

Traditional Emberá woven baskets.

communities farther upriver. The contrast in mood and architecture between the two villages is striking. In bustling Sambú – where all accommodations and eating options are located – cement pathways wind between tightly packed houses of various architectural styles, sheltering a mixed population of Emberá, Wounaan, *mestizos*, and Afro-Dariénites. Across the river, quieter Puerto Indio, at the western limit of the Distrito Sambú, of which it is the capital, comprises an indigenous population living in traditional wooden housing raised on stilts, where afternoon social activity centers round the basketball court or soccer field.

Closer to the mouth of the Río Sambú, a small tributary navigable only at high tide leads to the hamlet of **La Chunga** ⑫, named after the ubiquitous palm used for basketry. At other times, you land at a pontoon on the main river, from where it's a 20-minute walk along a boardwalk through mosquito-infested swamp to the village. An avenue of cedar trees marks the entrance, opening out onto an overgrown basketball court surrounded by a handful of traditional homes. Basketry is still widely practiced by the women. Make sure you check out the village stocks (*sepo*); miscreants who commit an offence and are unable to pay the fine are placed there for a couple of hours, an experience made particularly painful by being made to sit on a pile of cooked rice, which attracts vicious ants that tuck in to the penitent's buttocks. La Chunga currently has a well-functioning tourism operation (www.traveldarien-panama.com), which can arrange an English-speaking guide to accompany you from Panama City (at extra cost) if the thought of negotiating public transportation as far as Puerto Quimba is too daunting.

The Wounaan community of Semaco, known for its exquisite basketry, music and dance, is just a two-hour hike away. A village guide can take you birdwatching upriver, or perhaps to a harpy eagle nest.

As the Río Sambú's waters swell during the rainy season, *piraguas* can penetrate as far upstream as the tiny village of **Pavarandó**.

RESERVA PUNTA PATIÑO

Established in the early 1990s, **Reserva Punta Patiño** ⑬ is Panama's first and, at 300 sq km (116 sq miles), largest private reserve, occupying the entire headland at the tip of the choppy Golfo de San Miguel, just beyond the lively Afro-Dariénite fishing village of Punta Alegre. While the landscape is nowhere near as dramatic as the jungle-carpeted peaks of the interior, the regenerating hinterland forest – once devastated by cattle ranching, timber extraction, and coconut plantations – is filling up with native hardwoods, though it's an hour's hike to primary forest. The area also covers a stretch of charcoal beach, an important expanse of mangroves, and mud and salt flats that attract an abundance of resident and migratory seabirds.

⊘ THE HARPY EAGLE

Instantly recognizable for its splendid slate-grey back, brilliant white chest, and distinctive crest, the harpy eagle (*águila harpía*) is the largest eagle in the Neotropics, and one of the most powerful worldwide, with talons the size of a grizzly bear's claws. The larger female can weigh up to twice as much as the male, and despite its vast wingspan of more than 2 meters (6ft), it can reach speeds of up to 80km/h (50mph) while accelerating through trees to stab its prey. After declining in numbers for many years due to loss of habitat and hunting, the raptor is making a comeback: an increasingly successful breed-and-release program (www.peregrinefund.org) has resulted in Panama now having the greatest concentration of harpy eagles in Mesoamerica, with an estimated 800 pairs or more. It will be a long recovery process, though, as harpy eagles are lethargic breeders, though devoted parents, nurturing the chick in the nest for around six months, and taking care of it for a further two years. Working with local communities and conducting educational campaigns in schools, the conservation project has succeeded in heightening public awareness and interest in the harpy eagle. Fittingly, the raptor is now Panama's national bird, and even has its own national day. Indigenous communities in the Darién can often guide you to the location of an active nest, which is the easiest way to catch sight of this magnificent bird.

Managed by the environmental organization ANCON, the reserve is not without its critics, not least the Emberá, who feel the land should be theirs. Moreover, the area can only be visited by splashing out on an all-inclusive four-day tour through ANCON Expeditions, which includes a day or overnight excursion to Mogué. Still, there's no denying that this is a magical spot to soak up glorious sunsets, aerial displays by diving pelicans, and occasional sightings of bottle-nosed dolphins and humpback whales. On land, mammals to look out for include the weasel-like tayra, grey foxes, and the extraordinary-looking capybara, the world's largest rodent, which resembles a giant guinea pig and weighs in at 55kg (120lbs). Needless to say, the location necessitates lashings of insect repellent to ward off the prolific uninvited guests.

Set against the imposing backdrop of Cerro Sapo (Toad Hill), the small, neglected fishing community of **Garachiné** is only of interest to visitors who intend to hike the overland route to Playa Muerto (see page 275), or are trying to reach Sambú via a bumpy road (which often costs more than the transfer by boat), which then loops back to the coastal Wounaan community of Taimatí. Unless you arrive at high tide, you'll be wading knee-deep across alluvial mud flats to the shore.

THE SOUTHEASTERN PACIFIC COAST

The Darién's Pacific coast is as remote and unexplored as the jungle-filled interior: to the northwest of the Golfo de San Miguel, the coastline is dominated by mangroves, but to the southeast it comprises kilometers of deserted beaches interspersed with rocky outcrops, cliffs, and expanses of pristine forest, with the brooding serranías del Sapo and Jungurudó a dramatic backdrop.

Attractively located amid serried ranks of coconut palms backing a chocolate swathe of sand, **Playa Muerto** ⑭ is the only Emberá community on the Pacific coast. Its gruesome name ('Beach of the Dead') derives from the

Chestnut-mandibled toucan in Darién National Park.

⊘ Tip

You cannot visit the Darién National Park without a guide; if you don't travel with a tour operator, you will need to engage an independent guide (see companion App for listings). Indigenous communities usually have their own local guides, who can accompany you on hikes, and who will have varying levels of knowledge about the rainforest and its wildlife, but are unlikely to speak English.

corpses that used to wash ashore following sea-battles between bullion-laden Spanish galleons and pirate ships in colonial times. Isolated, and inaccessible by boat in winter, when the waves are huge, the village is well worth a visit. When the Pacific is calm boats between La Palma and Jaqué will drop off and pick up passengers. Otherwise, the only access is a one- to two-day mountainous jungle trek across from Sambú or Garachiné, via other small communities. You could arrange for a local community guide (and mule if you don't want to carry a pack) by contacting the authorities in Puerto Indio or Playa Muerto (satellite phone: 386028), which doesn't have cell-phone coverage. Beyond use of the village stocks – which are still used to punish wrongdoers – Playa Muerto has lost most of its traditions, but the setting is attractive, and the pace relaxed. You can have your body painted in *jagua* dye, hike through the rainforest, or take a short stroll to a nearby waterfall and natural pool.

The only real tourist enterprise on this section of coast is the Tropic Star Lodge (www.tropicstar.com), an internationally renowned sport fishing lodge tucked away in a sheltered cove, staffed primarily from the adjacent village of **Puerto Piñas** ⓯. Less edgy and much smaller than the neighboring frontier community of Jaqué, Puerto Piñas has a more impressive setting, encircled by forested mountains, in a protected bay – the safest anchorage along this part of the coast – and boasts a substantial beach and riverside location, though accommodations, as elsewhere, are rudimentary. From here you can organize a day-hike over the mountains to the cream-colored sands of Playa Blanca, which offers sheltered snorkeling, or to the Wounaan village of Biroquera. From here, it's a half-hour boat trip down to **Jaqué**, Panama's heavily-garrisoned Pacific border town, which actually lies around 40km (25 miles) from the Colombian border. A short hop by boat from Jaqué back round the headland will return you to Puerto Piñas. Puerto Piñas and Jaqué are the only destinations in the Darién that are served by plane from Panama City.

A competitor wields his bow and arrow during the Ancient Games, held at a community in the Darién.

SCOTLAND'S DOOMED DARIÉN ADVENTURE

In one of Panama's lesser-known historical footnotes, in the late 1600s the Scots gambled their country's future on a trading colony in the Darién, in the hopes of transforming Scotland into an imperial power to rival England.

The undertaking was the brainchild of William Patterson, one of the founders of the Bank of England, who, having failed to convince the English government of the plan's viability, succeeded in arousing the nationalist pride of the Scots. He persuaded rich and poor alike to pour their savings into forming the Company of Scotland. Yet, in the excitement that accompanied preparations, the fact that Patterson had never set foot in Panama and was wholly ignorant of the conditions there passed unnoticed. Soon, a sizeable proportion of the country's wealth belonged to the company.

In July 1698, 1,200 Scots, including Patterson and his family, set sail across the Atlantic in five ships laden with the most unlikely collection of personal possessions and trading goods. These included: 4,000 wigs, 25,000 pairs of shoes, and 1,500 bibles. Within days, many of the ships' supplies – including meat, butter, and cheese – had spoiled, rations were cut, and the crews became demoralized. After four months at sea, the fleet finally anchored in a bay off the Caribbean coast of the Darién. There, they labored a further five months to build a settlement they named New Edinburgh (in modern-day mainland Guna Yala). This was some feat given their constant battles with disease, low rations, and drunken in-fighting – 5,000 gallons of brandy had been transported there alongside copious amounts of rum and claret – not to mention the harshness of the tropical environment. To make matters worse, the English king had forbidden any of the Caribbean colonies to assist the Scots, in order not to upset the Spanish.

Only the Guna were prepared to help – the Scots seeming preferable to the Spanish – though they were as uninterested as everyone else in the Scots' bizarre trading wares. After ten months of struggle, and news that a Spanish fleet was on its way, the colony's council decided to abandon the settlement and weigh anchor. Only one ship made it back to Scotland, carrying a quarter of the original population, including Patterson, whose family lay buried in Panama.

When rumor of the colony's abandonment reached the ears of the company's directors, it was roundly dismissed. They refused to believe that the men they had sent forth 'could be guilty of so much groundless cowardice, folly and treachery,' so sanctioned a second fleet of four ships and 1,300 would-be settlers, no better equipped than the first. Arriving in the Darién to find a deserted colony, this second expedition soon encountered much the same problems as the first, compounded by the fact that their presence riled the Spanish along the coast in Portobelo. Small battles soon broke out between the Scots, aided by the Guna, and the Spanish, though in April 1700, only six months after their arrival, the Scots were forced to surrender. Thanks to the respect they were accorded by the Spanish governor, they were allowed to leave – although none of the ships made it home to Scotland and only a handful of folk survived.

This failed Darién venture crippled Scotland financially, leaving the country at the mercy of England. In 1707, England agreed to compensate all investors as part of a deal that saw Scotland reluctantly agree to the creation of the United Kingdom of Great Britain.

Depiction of the departure of the Darién expedition in 1698 from Leith.

Cruise ship at port in Colón.

PANAMA

TRANSPORTATION

Getting there 280
   By air 280
   By sea 280
   By bus 280
Getting around 281
   To/from the airport 281
   By air 281
   By bus 281
   By car 281
   By rail 282
   By taxi 282
   By boat 282
   By bicycle 282

A – Z

Accommodations 283
Addresses 283
Admission charges 284
Budgeting for your trip 284
Children 284
Climate 284
Crime and safety 285
Customs regulations 285
Disabled travelers 285
Eating out 286
Electricity 286
Embassies and consulates 286
Etiquette 286

Festivals and events 286
Health and medical care 287
Internet 287
Left luggage 288
LGBTQ travelers 288
Maps 288
Media 288
Money 288
National parks and
   protected areas 289
Opening hours 289
Photography 289
Postal services 289
Public holidays 290
Religious services 290
Restrooms 290
Shopping 290
Tax 290
Telephones 290
Time zone 291
Tourist information 291
Tour operators and
   travel agents 291
Visas and passports 291
Websites and apps 291
Weights and measures 291

LANGUAGE

Pronunciation tips 292
Greetings 292

At the hotel 292
Shopping 292
Traveling 293
Sightseeing 293
Eating out 293
Menu decoder 293
   Essentials 293
   Vegetables 293
   Meat and poultry 293
   Cooking terms 293
   Seafood 293
   Fruit 293
   Snacks 294
   Drinks 294
Health 294
On the road 294
Emergencies 294
Useful words/phrases 294
Days of the week 294
Months of the year/seasons 294
Numbers 295

FURTHER READING

The Canal 296
Pirates and politics 296
Guna culture 296
Fiction 297
Biography 297
Birdlife 297

TRANSPORTATION

GETTING THERE

By air

The vast majority of visitors to Panama arrive by air, landing at Tocumen International Airport in Panama City. Bear in mind the crucial distinction between Panama City in Central America (airport code PTY) and Panama City in Florida (airport code PFN).

Panama's reliable no-frills national carrier, Copa Airlines (www.copaair.com), often offers good rates and has an efficient online booking service. It flies to and from several US cities and numerous destinations in Latin America and the Caribbean, with three connecting flights a day from Tocumen to the airport at David, capital of Chiriquí province, in the far west of the country. The new Panamá Pacífico International Airport, formerly the US Howard Air Force base in the Canal Zone, 9km (6 miles) southwest of Balboa, accommodates a couple of Latin American low-cost airlines and charter flights. Río Hato, farther west, serves the Pacific coast resorts with charter flights. The other (small) international airport is on Isla Colón, in the Bocas del Toro archipelago, though its only international routes are from Costa Rica.

From the US and Canada

There are numerous daily flights direct to Panama City from various US hubs. Operators include Delta (www.delta.com), United (www.united.com) and American Airlines (www.aa.com), alongside Copa (www.copaair.com), Avianca (www.avianca.com) and Spirit (www.spirit.com). The main portal is Miami, offering several daily connections, but there are also direct flights from New York, Washington, Los Angeles, and Orlando. There are no direct flights from Canada;

connections have to be made in the US or Mexico, making it at least a nine-hour journey. Slightly cheaper charter flights can sometimes be bought in high season (Dec–Apr) through Transat (www.transat.com) from Calgary, Montréal, and Toronto, or through Sunwing (www.flysunwing.ca) from Montréal and Toronto, to Río Hato airport at Playa Blanca.

From UK, Ireland & the Rest of Europe

Although there are currently no direct flights from the UK or Ireland, several airlines operate daily flights from mainland Europe: Lufthansa (www.lufthansa.com) from Frankfurt; KLM (www.klm.com) from Amsterdam; and Air France (www.airfrance.com) from Paris. Iberia (www.iberia.com) has frequent, more expensive departures from several Spanish cities. The cheapest route from the UK or Ireland is sometimes via the US with a US carrier, though the lengthier flying time and the extra hassle of clearing US immigration generally makes this less appealing than flying via Europe.

From Australia & New Zealand

It is a long, expensive haul to Panama from Australia or New Zealand, with no direct flights. Most routes travel via the US. Your best bet is with United Airlines (www.united.com) via Houston, though flights via Santiago or Buenos Aires are also possible with the journey time (26hr-plus) staying much the same.

From Africa

From Johannesburg, South Africa, or Nairobi, Kenya, you can travel to Panama via Frankfurt with Lufthansa or Amsterdam with KLM, which both take around 24hrs in travel time.

From Central & South America

Various countries in Latin America have direct connections with

Panama through Avianca or, more usually, through Copa, which connects with more than 40 destinations across Latin America and the Caribbean. In Costa Rica, award-winning Nature Air (www.natureair.com) operates daily flights from San José, Costa Rica, to Bocas del Toro, while Panama's domestic carrier, Air Panama (www.airpanama.com), has daily departures from San José to Albrook Airport in Panama City. Copa's low-cost airline, Wingo (www.wingo.com), offers cheap deals from several Colombian destinations, as well as San José in Costa Rica, landing at the new Panamá Pacífico airport. Note that because of the Darién Gap – the 87km (54-mile) swamp-and-jungle hiatus in the Panamerican Highway between Colombian and Panama – flying is by far the safest way to travel between the two countries.

By sea

Cruise ship visitors dock at the terminals in either Colón, at the Caribbean end of the Panama Canal, or on the Calzada de Amador in Panama City, on the Pacific side. Sailing boats carrying backpackers from Cartagena in Colombia usually unload passengers in Puerto Lindo or Portobelo, along the coast in Colón province. Other yacht arrivals usually call in at the Balboa Yacht Club on the Calzada de Amador or at the Shelter Bay Marina west of Colón.

By bus

It is possible to travel overland along the Pan-American Highway from Tapachula in Mexico to Panama City (with drop-offs at David and Santiago in Panama), with Ticabus (www.ticabus.com). Buses are comfortable and air-conditioned, offering the obligatory diet of Hollywood movies; they pick up (and drop off) passengers at the major Central American cities on the way, though you will have to spend a couple of nights in hotels, which increases the cost. Since there is no road between Colombia and Panama, on account of the Darién Gap, terrestrial transportation between the two countries is non-existent.

GETTING AROUND

Panama City is the country's transportation hub for both international and national traffic, with two international airports, one domestic airport, a port, a cruise ship terminal, and a gigantic bus terminal. When it comes to moving on, most people use the country's efficient and extensive bus system, though internal flights are plentiful, reasonably priced, and simple to arrange – and particularly useful for reaching the islands of Guna Yala and Bocas del Toro.

To/from the airport

There are several ways to get to/from Tocumen International Airport (tel: 238 2703), which lies 24km (15 miles) northeast of Panama City. The easiest way is by taxi, which takes about 30–40 minutes to reach the city center, depending on traffic. Alternatively, you can go by *colectivo* (shared taxi), provided there are sufficient passengers. The official taxi desk, with the published rates, is in the arrivals hall. If you're feeling more adventurous, buy a Metrobus card, which can be used on the Metro and the Metrobus. The Metrobus stop is outside the terminal, at the other side of the road, and the bus will take you to the main bus terminal at Albrook via the city center. This is not safe at night, however. Getting to the airport by bus is easier: Metrobuses displaying 'Tocumen Corredor' leave from the front of Albrook Bus Terminal (6am–midnight; every 20–40 mins), picking up passengers at the new Cinco de Mayo–Marañon metro station and at stops along the Cinta Costera. Passengers alight at a bus stop 200 meters/yds from the terminal entrance. A Metro link between the airport and Metro Line 2, with connections to the city center, is under construction. If you arrive at Panamá Pacifico International Airport a taxi is the only option.

☉ Panama City's Metro and Metrobus

Panama City's Metro currently has one line, with 12 stations, though a second is nearing completion, with a link to Tocumen International Airport planned. It's a very quick, safe way to get around. The line runs from Albrook, via Plaza Cinco de Mayo – the de facto city center – toward the hotel and business district of El Cangrejo and beyond. Metrobuses, which leave outside the main bus terminal, can take you to the Miraflores Locks, the Amador Causeway, Cinta Costera, and Panamá Viejo, among other places, and have designated bus stops. There is no public transportation to the historic center; you will have to take the Metro to Cinco de Mayo and then walk, or get a taxi. To use either the Metro or the Metrobus, you need a rechargeable swipe card, which you can buy at the airport, in the main bus terminal, at supermarkets, or in Metro stations. ID needs to be shown at purchase; the card can then be recharged in the machines. The card also allows access to the provincial and inter-regional transportation departure area of the main bus terminal. Old *diabo rojo* chicken buses still operate in some parts of the city, for cash, which is paid to the driver on exit.

By air

Flying within Panama is convenient, safe, and relatively inexpensive. Internal flights depart from or arrive at Marcos A. Gelabert Airport (tel: 238 2700), more commonly known as Albrook Airport (after the former US Air Force base it occupies), 3km (2 miles) northwest of Panama City center, and a short hop by taxi from the main bus terminal. Air Panama (www.airpanama.com), the country's one domestic airline, serves around 20 destinations: the major urban areas, several locations along the largely inaccessible Comarca Guna Yala, and currently two destinations in the Darién, which are impossible to reach by road. Tickets theoretically can be bought online but the website often doesn't work. Note that luggage allowances are 12kg (26lbs) plus 2.3kg (5lbs) carry-on, but full-size surfboards incur an extra charge. Flights to David, Bocas, and Guna Yala fill up quickly in advance of a holiday weekend.

By bus

The Gran Terminal de Transportes de Panamá, in Albrook, more commonly referred to as 'El Terminal,' is the center of both the city's and the country's bus networks, as well as the end stop on Metro Line 1. Comfortable long-distance regional buses run between the main cities, whereas smaller, less comfortable Coaster buses do shorter journeys, though all are air-conditioned. The main centers, such as Santiago,

Chitré, and David, also have large efficient bus terminals on the outskirts of town complete with washrooms, left-luggage desks, ATMs, and cafeterias. In provincial towns, buses fan out to the surrounding area. Most local bus services run from dawn to dusk. In the more rural areas, transportation may include more battered minibuses or even chivas (converted pick-up trucks), which may only leave when full. In Panama City, you need to purchase a ticket at the relevant ticket office. In most other parts of the country, you buy the ticket on the bus.

There are many good paved roads in central and western Panama, even to small villages up in the mountains, and dirt roads are also generally well graded, though in the rainy season (roughly May to mid-Dec) they can soon become boggy. East of Panama City there are few roads of any description. The main road east, the final stretch of the Interamericana is paved as far as Yaviza, in the Darién, but every year after heavy rain a section or two gets damaged, resulting in a quagmire. However, expect several police checkpoints along this stretch of road, as well as along the western section of the Interamericana, as you near the Costa Rican border.

By car

Though driving around Panama City is a nightmare, driving elsewhere in central and western Panama is fairly straightforward, with very good, well-signposted roads connecting the main urban centers. Car rental too is easy in Panama City and David. It's advisable to use public transportation while in Panama City and then rent a vehicle when you want to leave the capital. The Interamericana, Panama's main thoroughfare, and part of the Pan-American Highway, runs 486km (302 miles) from the Costa Rican border at Paso Canoas in the west, skirting several major cities, crossing the canal and bludgeoning its way through the capital before continuing another 282km (175 miles) and grinding to an abrupt halt in Yaviza in the Darién. Traffic for the Azuero Peninsula peels off onto the Carretera Nacional at Divisa, 34km (21 miles) east of Santiago (just under a 3hr drive from Panama City), and branches off north across the Cordillera Central at Chiriquí for the sinuous journey across the continental divide down to the islands of Bocas del Toro in western Panama's only transisthmian route. Though an excellent paved road, it is sometimes blocked by landslides during the wettest months of the rainy season (roughly May to mid-Dec). Two roads connect the capital with the country's second city of Colón: the frequently log-jammed Transístmica, and the Autopista Panamá–Colón, a faster parallel toll road. The only other route across the isthmus lies an hour east of the canal, beyond Chepo; heading north from the Interamericana at El Llano, 40km (25 miles) over the mountains to Cartí, this is the only terrestrial link with the Comarca Guna Yala. It's accessible most of the year, and although it's paved, only 4WD vehicles are granted access. It is not advisable to drive yourself to the Darién.

Car rental

Car rental is easy, but not particularly cheap. The usual international agencies (eg Avis, Budget, Hertz) have online booking and desks at Tocumen and Albrook airports and along Vía España in Panama City. In David, they have desks at the airport and/or in town, whereas in Colón, there are a couple of offices at the cruise ship terminal. The usual minimum age for car rental is 25, but companies usually accept younger drivers on payment of a supplement.

Road regulations

Despite Panama's decent road network, driving at night is best avoided because there's little illumination outside the urban centers, and drink driving, one of the main causes of accidents nationally, is common. Though there is a legal limit of 86mg, it is rarely adhered to or enforced. If you are involved in a car accident, Panamanian law requires that you should not move the vehicles but should wait near them until the traffic police (Transito) arrive; a statement from them is required in order to file any insurance claim. Unless otherwise indicated, the speed limits are 40km/h (25mph) in urban areas, 60km/h (37mph) on secondary roads, and 100km/h (62mph) on primary roads – but these limits are neither widely advertised nor followed. Two of the most dangerous roads are the Interamericana, along which copious buses and heavy trucks thunder, and the route across the Cordillera Central to Bocas del Toro, when bad weather can make the hairpin bends even scarier.

By rail

The only functioning line is the weekday commuter and tourist service on the Panama Railroad (tel: 317 6070; www.panarail.com), which is not cheap, though it only takes 50 minutes and offers splendid views of the Canal.

By taxi

Taxis are a reliable, relatively inexpensive way to get around and can be flagged down on the street. Only get in an official yellow taxi. White tourist taxis with SET number plates are in better condition, with guaranteed a/c, and are more expensive. Theoretically there are set fares, but in practice, prices are down to supply and demand and your negotiating skills in Spanish. Agree a fare before you get in. Hiring the services of a taxi for the day to go sightseeing (to visit both sides of the Canal, for example) is often cheaper than going on a tour, especially for more than one person. Prices are higher for multiple people, and at night.

By boat

With two coasts and well over 1,000 islands, you will almost inevitably need to take a boat at some stage of your trip to Panama. Before you commit to a boat ride it pays to check the seaworthiness of the vessel and availability of life-jackets. Robust ferries leave the Amador Causeway to go to Isla Taboga and Contadora in the Pearl Islands according to regular timetables. To reach the archipelago of Bocas del Toro, you need to take a water-taxi from Almirate on the mainland – they usually leave every 30 minutes (6am–6pm) – to Bocas Town on Isla Colón. Once there, you can continue your journey by taking another water-taxi to one of the other islands. In Guna Yala, most boats these days used to transport tourists are fiber-glass lanchas, though in the less touristed, more remote islands you may find yourself in a motorized (and sometimes leaking) dugout (cayuco). If you buy a package tour, as most people do, your boat transportation will be organized for you, but note that between December and February the sea can be very rough.

In Darién, river transportation is the only way to get about: from Yaviza down to El Real, to access the national park, or from Puerto Quimba (by Meteti) for La Palma and the Golfo de San Miguel, if you're visiting one of the indigenous or Afro-Darienite communities. Depending on the community, transportation can be in a fiberglass lancha or motorized dugout (piragua). Note that as most communities are on tidal rivers, timetables are dependent on the tides, which may entail traveling at night and not all boats have lights (though they should). If a boat is already heading your way, you can travel in a colectivo 'como pasajero.' Otherwise, private boat rental ('viaje especial') is very expensive.

By bicycle

Away from the Interamericana and Panama City, cycling is pleasant – with wonderful views and quiet roads – and growing in popularity both as recreation and a means of transportation (though you won't find cycle lanes or cycle routes outside the Cinta Costera in Panama City). Mountain bike rental is on the increase in tourist areas such as El Valle, Boquete, Bocas, and Santa Fé, though the quality of the bicycle on offer varies. In Panama City you'll find rental places on the Amador Causeway and the Cinta Costera, where on Sunday mornings the road is closed to traffic so that you can cycle all the way to the Panama Viejá ruins. Exodus (www.exodus.co.uk) and Explore (www.explore.co.uk) offer cycling holidays in Panama.

A

Accommodations

From secluded mountain ecolodges to thatched cane *cabañas* on deserted islands or smart boutique hotels, Panama offers a wide range of accommodations, some of it very comfortable, and set in glorious surroundings. Panama City has the greatest variety, though prices are generally a lot higher than elsewhere. In touristy areas such as Bocas and Boquete prices are creeping up and more lodgings now exist at the higher end of the market, with an increasing number of mid-range lodges (often foreign-owned) and B&Bs – but there is still little outside Panama City that could truly be described as luxury. Lodges in remote areas offer all-inclusive packages since, obviously, there is nowhere else to eat. In Guna Yala or the Darién you might be snoozing on a thin mattress in a traditional dwelling – although you are more likely to be visiting on a package tour organized from Panama City, which will also be all-inclusive.

Most mid-range and high-end accommodations operate a dual pricing system. High-season rates (mid-Dec to Apr) generally coincide with the dry season, whereas the rest of the year counts as low season, when it's possible to find significant discounts, especially for online bookings. On top of high-season rates, some establishments in Panama City and the major vacation destinations hike their prices even further for Carnaval, Easter (Semana Santa), Christmas, and New Year, or for a popular local festival. In places that are primarily weekend retreats, such as Isla Grande and El Valle, lodgings charge more from Friday to Sunday, occasionally demanding

a two- or three-night minimum stay over the weekend.

Note too that in mid-range hotels a double room often means a room with two double beds, and you might have to specify one double bed (una cama doble, or una cama matrimonial) if you want to keep costs down. Room costs are usually based on two people sharing, but many rooms have an extra single bed, which a third person can have for an extra $10–15. Children under 12 are often allowed to stay for free.

Various mid- to high-end establishments, especially if foreign-owned, have online booking systems that take credit card or Paypal reservations. Many use Booking.com. Less expensive establishments usually take a reservation by phone (in Spanish), and payment in cash.

Types of hotel

Posadas and lodges usually offer a fair degree of comfort in pleasant natural surroundings, whereas places prefaced with *hospedaje*, *pensión*, or *residencial* are generally very basic small family-owned lodgings. The word *cabaña* may conjure up an image of a simple thatched hut in an idyllic natural setting, but can just as easily mean a dark, windowless cement cell in an unremarkable location. *Hostal* may signify a place with dorms for backpackers but is also a synonym for a family-run hotel. The term hotel, too, can cover a mixed bag from a plush international five-star high-rise to a dilapidated shack. As for the much-abused prefix 'eco,' it may simply denote pleasant natural surroundings, and is no guarantee of sustainable environmental practices or social responsibility.

Amenities

Neither name nor price is much of an indication of what you'll get for

your money, though a private bathroom is often squeezed into even fairly rudimentary and minuscule lodgings. In the lowlands, even the cheapest establishments usually have a/c, though not necessarily hot water; in the highlands a/c and fans are unnecessary and usually absent, though hot water is almost always available. Wi-fi is widely available, and almost always free. Guna Yala and the Darién are the two exceptions: in the former there is virtually no wi-fi, and in the latter coverage is limited and unreliable. Cell-phone coverage too can be patchy in these areas. As in most other Latin American countries, toilet paper should not be put down the toilet, but into the adjacent wastebasket because it can clog the system in all but the most modern top-end hotels. If in doubt, enquire at reception. Water shortages can occur in Bocas, Darién, and Guna Yala. Power can also be an issue in these isolated areas, where there may not even be electricity.

Breakfast is usually provided in accommodations though it may not be included in the rates.

Addresses

Finding your way round Panama City and David – the only two sizeable cities you are likely to be walking around – is not easy. Street maps don't really exist and street signs are not common in Panama, so when asking directions you are more likely to be directed to a landmark. Broadly, *avenidas* are the main roads, and *calles* are the streets, which are usually numbered, followed by a suffix 'norte' (north) 'sur' (south), 'este' (east), and 'oeste' (west). These broadly relate to how they are oriented in relation to a main street or road. Thus, in Casco Viejo, for example, on one side of Avenida Central lies Calle 7 Este, and on the other, Calle 7 Oeste. This is quite logical in David, which is laid out in a classic grid system, but is rather random in parts of Panama City, compounded by the fact that in some areas, such as Bella Vista, there are two number systems. In the capital buildings may have a number, though it may not be visible. In smaller towns, buildings may not be numbered, nor streets necessarily named.

Admission charges

Many natural attractions are on private or communal land, so fees are varied, though are usually half-price for children under 12. A new ruling regarding national park fees was brought out in 2018, stating that fees should only be charged for Coiba ($20), and that other parks should waive fees, given the poor infrastructure. However, the various park offices are either unaware, or are ignoring the ruling, so you are likely to be charged (usually $5 or $10) provided there is someone at the office when you arrive to relieve you of your fee.

Most of Panama's museums are either under renovation, in disrepair, or are very small (consisting of a room or two), so rightly only charge a token entrance fee. The BioMuseo is the country's only decent functioning museum at the moment, and is very expensive, although there is a discount for children.

B

Budgeting for your trip

Costs are much higher in Panama than in Central American countries such as Guatemala and Nicaragua, but are generally lower than Costa Rica. Panama City and Bocas prices are higher than the rest of the country. Since the national currency is the US dollar (often called a Balboa, locally), prices are all quoted in dollars. Staying in hostel dorms, eating in inexpensive local restaurants, and using public transportation, you can easily survive on $50 a day, less if camping, with anything from $35–150 on top for a full day's guided excursion – snorkeling, surfing, fishing, horseriding, or kayaking, for instance. Staying in more

comfortable accommodations and eating in more touristy restaurants can mean a daily food and lodgings budget of $150 with excursions and car rental on top, though a lot depends on where you spend most of your time. High-end accommodations are only really available in Panama City and at a handful of resorts across the rest of the country; expect to be charged from $175 for a double room in high season.

Sample costs

A local beer: In a bar in the interior $2; in a bar in Panama City $6
A glass of house wine: $4–5
A meal: menu del día $5: Main dish at a moderately priced restaurant $12; main dish at a fine-dining establishment from $20–25
A taxi journey: around Panama City $4–8; from the city center to Tocumen International Airport $30; around Panama's other towns and cities $2–3
A bus ticket: Panama City–David $15 for a 6hr journey; budget for around $2.50–3 per hour of travel
A Metro journey: 35 centavos

C

Children

Latin cultures are very family-oriented and Panama is no exception. While there is no pre-packaged entertainment for children such as theme parks, there's plenty to enjoy, including boat trips, snorkeling, horseback riding, exploring the Canal, and walking in the rainforest. Many hotels have extra beds or pull-outs in rooms for children and under-12s are often accommodated free, with older kids admitted at discount rates. Activity prices and entry fees are also usually half-price for children.

The large resort hotels – the Decameron at Farallón on the Pacific coast (www.decameron.com), the Hotel Meliá on Lago Gatún (www.melia.com), and the Gamboa Rainforest Resort (www.gamboaresort.com) – have special activities laid on and child-minding services. Children are sometimes not permitted in small B&Bs and ecolodges, while a number have a minimum age of 12 or 14.

Habla Ya Language Centre (www. hablayapanama.com) in Boquete

offers family and children's Spanish courses, while various tour operators in the UK and North America (check out www.wildland.com in the US, www.familiesworldwide.co.uk in the UK, and www.audleytravel.com for both the US and UK) include family-oriented itineraries. Traveling to Guna Yala and to the Darién, which can be challenging enough for adults, is very hard work with kids in tow. Sticking to Panama City and the Canal area, the Pacific beach resorts, El Valle, Bocas, and Boquete is much easier and more enjoyable all round.

Climate

Being in the tropics, Panama is hot year-round (at least 85°F/29°C), even at night in the lowlands. In the highlands, daytime temperatures in the sun can be high too, though they can descend to around 60°F (16°C) at night.

The Pacific coast

Dry season
The dry season is also referred to as *verano* (summer) and broadly runs from mid-December through April. In terms of activities, the firmer going underfoot makes it easier to travel on unpaved roads and explore the rainforests, and the reduced rainwater run-off ensures clearer waters to swim in. Also, many tourist places, especially in out-of-the-way spots in any part of Panama only really function during the season ('la temporada').

Rainy season
The rainy season, or *invierno* ('winter') stretches roughly from May to

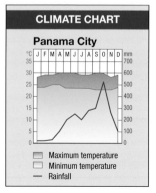

CLIMATE CHART

Panama City

■ Maximum temperature
□ Minimum temperature
— Rainfall

mid-December, Although the mountainous and rainforested regions in Panama are best avoided during the wettest months, since peaks are constantly swathed in cloud and tracks are boggy, if you stick to the lowland areas on the Pacific coast, the downpours, while frequent and intense, rarely last more than a few hours. This leaves plenty of sunny, dry periods to enjoy. In particular, the otherwise parched Azuero Peninsula offers much more picturesque scenery during its understated rains.

The Caribbean coast

On the Caribbean side, the seasons are not as marked, and a great deal more rain falls – and more often – though there can still be rain-free days. In Bocas del Toro, September to October and March are two windows when there's usually slightly less rainfall. Possibly of greater significance is the fact that the Trade Winds are at their strongest between December and February, which can make seas rough and outer islands harder to reach.

Needless to say, climate change, including the greater frequency of the El Niño effect, is making weather patterns less predictable.

What to wear

Loose, light clothing is ideal for everyday wear, given the heat. Shorts are fine for the beach, but not for urban areas, visiting churches, or indigenous communities. Similarly, open-toed sandals and flip-flops are ideal when by the sea, but you would be turned away from a club in Panama City for wearing such informal footwear. By the same token, packing a light 'smart casual' outfit is recommended if you intend to sample some of Panama City's gourmet restaurants. Also useful, even on a beach vacation, are a long-sleeved shirt and loose long pants, to protect from biting insects; for the rainforest, they're essential. So too are some robust shoes, long socks and breathable waterproofs. Since it's cool in the mountains in the evening – and some of the a/c on buses is ferocious – a thin fleece or jumper is a good idea. It can also get quite cold if you're traveling by boat for a while and there's a wind blowing. If you intend to climb Volcán Barú, a thicker fleece, gloves, and hat would be wise.

Crime and safety

The presence of FARC (now disbanded) guerrillas, drug-smugglers, people traffickers, and other criminals in the Darién has helped promote the popular misconception that Panama is a highly dangerous country to visit. In fact, even though crime seems to be on the increase, especially in urban areas, Panama is still a lot safer than most other Central American states, with only a few areas to avoid or in which to take special care – as in any country. Check the latest government advice before you go (e.g. www.fco.gov.uk in the UK; or travel.state.gov/travel in the US) and, more importantly, make enquiries with your tour operator and on the ground once you reach Panama.

The eastern strip of the Darién and Guna Yala that borders Colombia tops the danger list as a no-go area. However, there are still ways of visiting some areas of the Darién safely both in an organized group with a local tour operator, and – if you're a seasoned adventurer with a decent command of Spanish – as an independent traveler. It is also possible to cross to Colombia on the Caribbean side by boat.

The second major trouble spot is Colón, where extreme caution needs to be taken even during the day, as it's an exceedingly impoverished city and drug crime is rife. Panama City also has several areas to avoid, generally poor neighborhoods with inadequate housing and high unemployment. Violent crime is on the increase, but 90 percent of this is estimated to be drug-related, often among rival gangs; petty crime too is on the rise in some areas, especially where there are significant economic disparities between the general population and those who are making decent money from tourism, such as in Bocas. That said, the vast majority of visitors enjoy their time in Panama without incident, with the main issues being theft of money and/or passport and the odd traffic accident. The usual common-sense guidelines apply.

The police

If you are a victim of crime, report to the Policía de Turismo (Tourist Police) in Panama City or the main police station in other towns. Even though your possessions are

Beside the seaside.

unlikely to be recovered, a police report (*denuncia*) will be required to make an insurance claim. At the police station, you will probably need to present your ID, which by law you should always carry with you, though it is acceptable to carry a photocopy of your passport details provided it also includes a copy of the entry date stamp on the same page.

Customs regulations

Panama allows you to bring 3.8 liters of alcohol, 400 cigarettes or 500g of tobacco, and $10,000 into the country, but no fruit, animal, or vegetable products.

D

Disabled travelers

Organized tourism is in its infancy in Panama and awareness of the needs and rights of disabled travelers is a fairly recent phenomenon – they were only granted equal rights by law in 1999. As a result, Panama isn't really geared up to accommodate disabled travelers. That said, Tocumen International Airport and many mid-range and luxury hotels in Panama City have wheelchair access, as do most cruise ships that take in Panama, though none address the spectrum of special needs. Eco-Adventure International (www.eaiadventure.com) and Disabled Holidays.com (www.disabledholidays. com) both organize customized tours to Panama for disabled travelers.

E

Eating out

Eating out takes several forms, depending on where you are. By far the widest range of dining options is in Panama City, from Lebanese to Vietnamese food, an Argentinian streak house to a Japanese Sushi joint, and innovative Nueva Cocina Panameña (see page 96), as well as a plethora of Italian restaurants and places serving international staples. There are a few mid-range options, especially round El Cangrejo, and some seriously chic – and expensive – fine-dining establishments in Casco Viejo and in the Obarrio and San Francisco neighborhoods. But the dress code is never more than smart casual. For a Friday or Saturday evening you'd be advised to make a reservation. After the capital, Bocas del Toro offers the best variety of restaurants, though prices are quite high too because, as well as being a tourist destination, a lot of the food has to be transported over from the mainland. Boquete and David have a reasonable range of places to eat, too.

Inexpensive self-service cafeterías and fondas (informal restaurants) can be hard to spot in central Panama City, but are ubiquitous in other parts of the country. Fondas and local restaurants in the interior tend to open daily, from 6.30–7am to catch workers for breakfast, and may close around 7–8pm, or even earlier. Formal dining establishments tend to open for lunch (noon to 2.30–3pm) and then reopen for dinner around 6pm. Note that the latter will also add 7 percent service tax (ITBMS) to your bill, which is rarely included in the advertised menu prices.

Electricity

The voltage in Panama is 110 volts. Receptacles (sockets) take flat two- and occasionally three-pronged plugs. Power outages are common in remote areas, especially in the rainy season. In some islands of Guna Yala and in much of the Darién, in national parks or in isolated villages, there is limited or no electricity at night, so a flashlight is essential.

Embassies and consulates

Australia

Refer to the embassy in Mexico (www.mexico.embassy.gov.au)

Canada

Torres de las Américas, Tower A, 17th floor, C 53 Este, Punta Pacífica (tel: 294 2500; www.canadainternational.gc.ca/panama)

Colombia

Edif. Oceania, Torre 2000, 17th floor, Punta Pacífica (tel: 264 9513; www.panama.embajada.gov.co)

Costa Rica

Galerías Balboa, primer alto, Avenida Balboa (tel: 264 2980; ww.embajadacostaricaenpanama.com)

Ireland

Honorary Consul, Torre Delta, 14th floor, Vía España (tel: 264 6633; email: irishconsulatepma@gmail.com)

South Africa

Edif. Plaza Guadalupe, fourth floor, Oficina 404, C 50 at C 69, San Francisco (tel: 302 2750; email: jmantovani@westmar.com.pa)

UK

Humboldt Tower, fourth floor, C 53, Marbella (tel: 297 6550; www.gov.uk/world/panama)

US

Avenida Demetrio Basilio Lakas, Clayton (tel: 317 5000, www.pa.usembassy.gov)

Etiquette

Verbal courtesy is the norm in Panama. Saying 'Buenos días/Buenas tardes/Buenas noches,' or the abbreviated 'buenos' or 'buenas,' and waiting for the appropriate response is usual when asking for something at a store or ticket office, for example, as is adding 'señor' or 'señora' (in this instance similar to the US 'sir' or 'ma'am').

On meeting someone for the first time, it is customary to shake hands. On being introduced to someone, people are likely to say 'con mucho gusto,' meaning 'it's a pleasure,' and you should do the same. On departure you will more often than not be told ¡Que le vaya bien! – literally meaning 'May all go well with you;' it

☉ Emergency numbers

Medical emergency: 911
Directory enquiries: 102
Fire brigade: 103
International operator: 106
Tourist police: 511 9260

often translates better as 'Take care' or 'Travel safely.'

Before eating it is polite to wish someone 'buen provecho' (bon appétit). Toast others with salud – and you can also say this when someone sneezes.

F

Festivals and events

Panama is awash with festivals and public holidays. A festival calendar is available on the national tourism website: www.visitpanama.com/events-and-festivals.

January

Festival de las Mil Polleras Second Saturday in Jan. An unashamedly touristy event in Las Tablas. Groups from all over the country dance through the streets to the sound of music, showing off the different regional polleras.
Feria de las Flores y del Café Mid-Jan. Ten-day celebration in Boquete to mark the coffee harvest with carpets of flowers, food, and craft stands. Daytime family entertainment is followed by night-time discos.

February

Revolución Dule 25 Feb. Celebrates the Guna Revolution of 1925, their Independence Day, with colorful reenactments of battles against the Panamanian authorities held across the comarca.
Carnaval Five days, ending at dawn on Ash Wednesday (occasionally in March). Wild partying and processions – celebrated countrywide, but especially in Las Tablas and Panama City, with an aquatic parade on the Saturday in Penonomé.

March

Semana Santa or Holy Week Mar–Apr. Celebrated everywhere, but most colorfully on the Azuero Peninsula.

Festival de los Diablos y Congos
Usually the second or third weekend of Mar. Vibrant biennial weekend event (odd-numbered years) in Portobelo, showcasing Afro-Colonial culture and resistance to the Spanish conquest in a mass of devilish costumes and dances.

April

Feria de las Orquídeas Five days in early Apr. Boquete festival featuring copious orchids, craft stands, and cultural events.
Feria Internacional de Azuero Ten days in Apr. Major agricultural fair in La Villa de Los Santos with vendors, presentations, and competitions reflecting the area's colonial and cattle-farming traditions.

May/June

Festival de Corpus Christi Late May/early June. Celebrated across the country but most spectacularly in La Villa de Los Santos, with processions and dramatic devil dances.

July

Fiestas Patronales de la Virgen del Carmen 16 July. On Isla Taboga the Holy Virgin gets to circumnavigate the island in a procession of decorated boats.
Fiestas Patronales de la Santa Librada 20–22 July. A mix of religious and folkloric parades in Las Tablas, incorporating the Festival de la Pollera, which showcases Panama's gorgeous national dress.

August

Festival del Manito Ocueño Thu–Sun, dates vary. In Ocú, on the Azuero Peninsula, this lively folk festival features a mock duel and peasant wedding.

September

Feria del Mar Sept. Bocas' big bash, spread over five days, is filled with Caribbean traditional food, drink and dance, a midway, vendors, boat races, and fishing competitions.
Festival de la Mejorana Late Sept. Panama's premier folk festival, in Guararé, on the Azuero Peninsula, involving five days of traditional music, dancing, and parades.

October

Feria de Isla Tigre Mid-Oct. Multiday festivity of Guna culture, celebrated in Isla Tigre (Digir Dubu), Guna Yala.

Festival del Cristo Negro 21 Oct. The most revered pilgrimage in the country, attracting thousands decked in purple robes to Portobelo.

November

Primer Grito de la Independencia 10 Nov. The 'First Cry of Independence,' celebrated in La Villa de los Santos as part of 'El Mes de la Patria.' Patriotic flag-waving parades and marching bands, attended by the president.

H

Health and medical care

Most of Panama poses little threat to your health: yellow fever has been eradicated; malaria only persists in a few isolated areas; tap water is safe to drink in most of the country; and sophisticated medical care is widely available in the main population centers. Your most likely medical ailment will be travelers' diarrhea from a change of diet and climate, or sunburn from overdoing it on the beach. That said, you should ensure that your basic inoculations are up to date and consult a travel medical-center professional to help you decide what other precautions to take. If you intend only to explore the Canal area and chill on the beach, you'll probably need little more than sun block and insect repellent, but if you're bent on venturing into the Darién jungle, all kinds of insect- and water-borne hazards need to be considered. Medical insurance is essential.

Most inoculations that involve multiple injections need six to eight weeks to complete. There are no compulsory vaccinations to visit Panama but in addition to ensuring that your routine injections are current (tetanus, diphtheria and polio, and MMR), hepatitis A and typhoid are generally recommended, though you can also have a combined hepatitis A and B inoculation, advisable for long-term travelers. Yellow fever is nearly always flagged up as a hazard on health websites in relation to Panama, although the last documented case was in 1974. Nevertheless, there is still deemed to be a very slight risk of the disease in the Darién and remoter parts of Guna Yala. You may need to show proof of yellow fever inoculation if you travel to Panama from or via an infected area.

Rabies is another potential hazard, more from vampire bats in cattle-ranching areas than from feral dogs, and one that should only really be considered by travelers expecting to spend a lot of time in the remoter rural areas.

Good private options include Clínica Hospital San Fernando, Vía España, Las Sabanas, next to McDonald's (tel: 305 6300; www.hospital sanfernando.com), and Centro Médico Paitilla, Avenida Balboa at C 53 (tel: 265 8800; www.centromedico-paitilla.com). The Centro de Medicina Natural on C 42 Este at Avenida Mejico, Edif, Guadalupe (tel: 225 0867) offers natural and traditional treatments. For a dentist, try Clínica Dental Fábregas (tel: 399 4251) in Hospital Punta Pacífica or the Eisenmann Dental Clinic (tel: 269 2750), C 53 at Avenida Samuel Lewis. Staffers at both speak English.

I

Internet

Where Internet connectivity is available, almost all lodgings offer free

Primer Grito de la Independencia.

wi-fi. There are also numerous government wi-fi hotspots, called Internet Para Todos, though you have to register and the speed is very slow. However, Internet access – along with cellphone coverage – is very limited in the Darién and Guna Yala. In the former, wi-fi is restricted to a few places in the major settlements of Metetí, La Palma, Yaviza, and Garachiné; in the latter it is only available in Puerto Obaldía, unless you manage to catch a signal outside a government office on one of the larger village-islands. We indicate in the Guide where wi-fi is available in these regions, though even then you should bear in mind that the service is often unreliable, especially in the rainy season (May–mid-Dec).

In general, the exponential spread of smartphones has led to a decline in the number of Internet cafés across the country, though in most towns the local library, at the very least, usually has a couple of PCs. Rates are generally $1 an hour – note that the '@' sign is usually achieved by pressing ALT, '6,' and '4' keys simultaneously.

L

Left luggage

Reliable left-luggage facilities are available in Tocumen International Airport and in the major bus terminals.

LGBTQ travelers

Homosexuality was finally decriminalized in Panama in 2008, which illustrates not only the country's prevailing social conservatism but also the fact that things are changing. The Asociación de Hombres y Mujeres Nuevos de Panamá (AHMN) is active in campaigning for LGBTQ rights and low-key Gay Pride parades have been held since 2005. The LGBTQ scene is discreet; the clutch of nightclubs is not widely advertised (see www.ellgeebe.com). However, on the Panama pages of LGBTQ travel websites (for example www.purpleroofs.com/centralamerica /panama.html, www.gayjourney.com/hotels/panama.htm, and www.globalgayz.com) the number of openly 'gay-friendly' accommodations listings, though small, is gradually increasing.

M

Maps

Country maps of Panama tend not to be updated very often, so easily get out of date given that road construction is happening all the time in Panama. That said, the following two are of good quality: International Travel Maps (1:300,000; available online at www.itmb.com and www.amazon.com) – updated in 2014 – and National Geographic (www.nationalgeographic.com). Both companies produce good maps of Panama, though the latter updated only the text, not the map itself, in 2016. There are also some rudimentary trail maps for the parks in the former Canal Zone, usually available from the park offices.

Media

Aside from one government TV channel and one radio station, the media in Panama is privately owned. The five national daily Spanish-language newspapers – and three Chinese-language papers, catering to the country's 60,000-strong Chinese-Panamanian community – are widely available from street vendors in urban areas, and in supermarkets countrywide. It's hard to escape TV in Panama – screens adorn most eating and drinking establishments, even upscale restaurants, and are standard in most hotel rooms. The most respected, if conservative, paper is *La Prensa* (www.prensa.com), which also produces informative supplements with in-depth writing and interesting features on tourism, history, and culture. *La Estrella de Panamá* (www.laestrella.com.pa) and *Panamá América* (www.pa-digital.com.pa) also count as 'quality press,' with *El Siglo* (www.elsiglo.com) and La Crítica (www.critica.com.pa) the popular tabloid options.

Given the large US expat population, there is no shortage of English-language news, including the imported Miami Herald International Edition and USA Today.

On evenings in a bar or *cafetería* you're likely to catch an unremittingly awful soap opera (*telenovela*) on one of Panama's four terrestrial television channels. Even the cheapest accommodations tend to offer satellite TV. Check out www.

coolpanama.com for a list of radio stations, frequencies, and their musical preferences (in Spanish).

Money

Panama adopted US dollars (referred to as *dólares* or *balboas*) as its currency in 1904, shortly after separation from Colombia. Although the country uses US paper currency, it mints its own coinage: 1, 5, 10, 25, and 50 centavo pieces, and a dollar coin, which are used alongside US coins. Both $100 and $50 bills are often difficult to spend, so try to have $10 or $20 as the largest denominations you carry.

Most banks are open Mon–Fri 8am–3.30pm and on Sat 9am–noon, though busier branches in the capital have extended hours; almost all branches have ATMs, as do many large supermarkets.

It is difficult to change foreign currency in Panama – convert any cash into US dollars as soon as you can. There are two Travelex currency exchange counters in Tocumen International Airport, and several branches of Red Plus (www.gruporedplus.com) in the city, which are open every day: Multicentro houses the main office, but there are also branches in Albrook Mall, Multiplaza, and Metro Mall. Foreign banks will generally change their own currencies.

Money transfers can easily be carried out through Western Union (www.westernunion.com), which has more than 100 offices sprinkled around the isthmus, with a concentration in Panama City.

Tipping is not universally expected and should be reserved for good service. While 10 percent is customary in mid-range (or more expensive) restaurants, it should not be automatic. In local fondas you might round up a $3.80 lunch to $4. Bell hops are usually tipped $1 per bag, which is also the going rate at Tocumen International Airport. In hotels you might consider leaving a tip of $1–2 per day for housekeeping staff, but it's not de rigueur. It's not usual to tip taxi drivers or guides on organized tours. If, however, you hire the services of a park warden (guardaparque) to take you on a guided hike, you should ask what the going rate is; if there isn't one, $15–20 should be adequate for a full-day outing.

Overtipping is not helpful; it sets a precedent which other travelers may not be able to live up to, and can upset the micro-economy, particularly in small villages.

Cards and ATMs

With more than 1,000 ATMs across the country, the most convenient way to access your money is by drawing out cash on a credit card (you'll need your PIN). Debit cards such as Maestro and Cirrus are valid in many ATMs, though they sometimes do not actually work in practice. Most home banks charge a fee for credit and debit card withdrawal – check before departure – and almost all ATMs in Panama levy $5.25 per transaction. You can avoid paying the ATM fee by withdrawing cash against your credit/debit card over the counter at a bank. Make sure to inform your bank at home that you are traveling to Panama before you leave so that they don't block your credit or debit card when you try to use it, although note that your card may still be blocked when undertaking swipe rather than chip-and-pin transactions.

Visa and MasterCard are the most widely accepted credit cards across the country, both at ATMs (recognizable by the red Sistema Clave sign outside) and to pay for services such as plane tickets, tourist hotels, restaurants, goods in stores, and car rental. Most establishments in Bocas del Toro, Guna Yala, and the Darién only accept cash; denominations of $20 and below are preferred because of problems with counterfeit $50 and $100 notes. Note that there are no ATMs in Guna Yala (only one bank in Narganá), one in the archipelago of Bocas del Toro (in Bocas Town, Isla Colón), and just two in the Darién (in Metetí and La Palma).

Note also that heading into a major holiday weekend ATMs may run out of money, especially if there is only one in town.

National parks and protected areas

Visiting Panama's protected areas independently can be frustrating at times, as infrastructure is sorely lacking in many instances: there are no reliable maps and few well-signed or marked trails. Campgrounds or bunkhouses, where they exist, are often in poor repair, and missing basic utensils. In recognition of these shortcomings, perhaps, the government decided to abolish all park fees in 2018 – except the hefty entrance fee to visit Coiba. Despite this ruling, many parks still levy charges (see page 284). Fees for camping or staying in a park bunkhouse (refugio), where this is possible, remain in place.

The parks are managed by the Dirección de Áreas Protegidas y Biodiversidad, within the Ministry of the Environment (Ministerio de Ambiente, often shortened to MiAmbiente, or MIA). Dealing with tourists is theoretically the job of Panama's national tourist agency, the ATP, but MIA staff in the regional and local offices (Mon–Fri 8am–4pm), as well as the guardaparques (park wardens), are likely to be of more direct use, though they will probably only speak Spanish. In theory, there should be a full-time resident warden at each park entrance, although it is not always the case – if so any amenities are likely to be locked. If you decide to organize your visit by telephoning one of the MIA offices – listed in the Walking App – ask to talk to someone in Áreas Protegidas, and note that most MIA employees only speak Spanish.

If you have not organized a guide in advance through a tour company you can sometimes engage the services of one of the park wardens on the spot. They may not necessarily have an extensive knowledge of the flora and fauna – though some will – but they will at least ensure that you don't get lost.

Silver coin.

P

Photography

People are fascinating subjects, but be sensitive. How would you like to be photographed all the time? If you want to snap one or more human beings, rather than a market scene with people in it, you should ask their permission, and offer a tip or buy some artesanía from them. In indigenous villages in particular, ask the village chief or the head of the tourist committee what the protocol is – some villages do not permit photography at all. Tour groups on a village may be encouraged to snap away, but you should still always ask for permission from the individuals concerned.

Postal services

Mail is reliable, but if speed is of the essence the standard Panamanian postal service is probably not for you; a letter from Panama can take five to 10 days to reach North America (25¢ stamp) and a couple of weeks or longer to meander to Europe (35¢ stamp), Australasia or South Africa (60¢ stamp). In Panama City the main post office is opposite the Basílica Don Bosco on Avenida Central, between C Ecuador and C 34 Este. Other convenient branches are on Plaza Concordia (below the Hotel El Panamá), in El Cangrejo, and in Balboa at the end of the Prado on Avenida Arnulfo Arias Madrid. Opening hours vary but are generally Mon–Fri 8am–5pm, Sat 8am–noon. Alternatively, use one of the more

O

Opening hours

Opening hours vary but generally businesses are open Mon–Sat 8/9am–5/6pm. Government office hours are Mon–Fri 8am–4pm. Stores usually open their doors Mon–Sat 9am–6pm, though places selling souvenirs and crafts to tourists may open on Sundays too, and Chinese-Panamanian supermarkets often open early (6.30–7am) until late (10pm–midnight); some of the larger branches of the major supermarket chains, e.g. Super 99, Extra, and El Rey, are open 24 hours.

N

expensive private mailing or courier services that are widely available, such as Fedex (www.fedex.com/pa) or Mail Boxes Etc. (www.mbe.com).

Post offices also offer an entrega general (poste restante) service, keeping letters for up to a month. Passport ID needs to be shown when claiming mail and you can't collect on behalf of another person. The sender should address items as follows: receiver's name, Entrega General, name of town, name of province, República de Panamá. If you are receiving mail in Panama City then the postal zone also needs to be specified – enquire at the branch in question.

Public holidays

Most government offices, businesses, and stores close during national public holidays. Note that services shut down in Panama City on August 15 to celebrate the foundation of Panamá La Vieja, while other towns and cities have their own multiday festivities during which most places close. Check www.qppstudio.net/publicholidays.htm.
Jan 1 Año Nuevo. New Year's Day.
Jan 9 Día de los Mártires. Martyrs' Day, in remembrance of those killed by US troops in the 1964 flag riots.
Feb Carnaval. Five days up to and including Ash Wednesday.
Mar/Apr Viernes Santo. Good Friday.
May 1 Día del Trabajo. Labor Day.
Nov 3 Separación de Panamá de Colombia. Anniversary of the 1903 separation from Colombia and primary Independence Day.
Nov 4 Día de la Bandera. Flag Day.
Nov 5 Día de Colón. Celebrating Colón's separation from Colombia.
Nov 10 Primer Grito de la Independencia. 'First Cry for

Independence,' marking the unilateral declaration of independence from Spain in La Villa de Los Santos.
Nov 28 Independencia de Panamá de España. Celebrating independence from Spain in 1821.
Dec 8 Día de la Madre. Mother's Day.
Dec 25 Día de Navidad. Christmas Day.

Religious services

Panama is a Catholic country, with around 70 percent identifying themselves as Catholic. There are also a substantial number of Protestants and Evangelical Christians, especially among indigenous communities, who often practice traditional religion alongside Christianity. Panama is generally tolerant of other religions and there are strong Jewish, Muslim, Buddhist, and Hindu populations in Panama City. Panama also has one of the world's 10 Baha'i houses of worship.

Restrooms

Public restrooms are thin on the ground in Panama. You will generally find them in airports and bus terminals, which require payment of a few cents to an attendant, who in return will hand you an inadequate few sheets of paper – always travel with an emergency toilet roll. Other options are fast-food joints, cafeterias, and gas stations. Most places outside top-end or very modern hotels with their own septic system require you to throw used toilet paper into an adjacent basket. In Guna Yala a toilet cistern is no guarantee of a water treatment system;

everything may still flush straight out to sea.

Shopping

Despite all the hype about duty-free shopping in Panama City, there's very little around. Though the streets are bulging with malls and stores, you're unlikely to be impressed with either the selection or the prices. The Zona Libre in Colón, the second-largest duty-free shopping zone in the world after Hong Kong, is not designed for the casual shopper either; it's aimed mainly at Latin American and Caribbean customers who, on the whole, buy in bulk and resell in their home country. Local arts and crafts, however, are a different matter.

Bargaining for goods is not the norm in Panama. If you're buying several items from a single stand in a craft market you can usually negotiate a slight discount (descuento), but it's rarely the lengthy social ritual it can be in some countries. Bear in mind too that while $40 for an intricate mola or $80 for a Panama hat may seem like a lot, they are likely to have taken several weeks to make.

Tax

Places with more than nine rooms are subject to a ten-percent tourist tax (though even smaller lodgings sometimes charge), which is not always included in the advertised rate.

Telephones

Making a call

To make a call to Panama you need to dial the international prefix (generally 00), followed by 507 – the country code for Panama – followed by the number. Local calls to landlines anywhere in Panama cost a pittance and are usually free from a hotel room. International calls are also relatively cheap provided you do not use a hotel phone. Some Internet cafés (and Cable & Wireless offices) also have phone booths and offer decent rates for international

Church on Isla Taboga.

calls as well as a degree of comfort, quiet, and privacy. Off-peak time for international calls is between 6pm and 6am, and on weekends. Landline numbers have seven digits, cell phones have eight.

Cell phones

Cell phones, and smartphones in particular, have mushroomed in Panama, which now has more different numbers – 6 million – than it does people. There are four providers: Mas Móvil (from Cable & Wireless), Digicel, Movistar, and Clarocom. Crucially, though, coverage varies depending where you are in the country, as there are places where only one provider works. Digicell, for example, is the main provider for Guna Yala, where there is often no service at all. Ask locally which provider is best before you buy a SIM card. If you have an unlocked cell phone on an 850 GSM (the setting for much of the Americas), you can easily buy a SIM card on arrival for a few dollars, from numerous convenience stores in Panama City, or from Albrook Bus Terminal. Only expensive phone packages (around $40) are available at Tocumen International Airport. Once the initial credit has expired, you can buy prepaid airtime cards from stores around the country. Alternatively, you might consider renting a cell or satellite phone; the executive business hotels can usually procure one for you. Incoming calls are all free in Panama.

Time zone

Panama is four hours behind Greenwich Mean Time throughout the year, the same as Eastern Standard Time in the US, though note time changes for daylight-saving hours. Panama is one hour ahead of Costa Rica. If in doubt, consult www.timeanddate.com.

Tourist information

The official tourist agency, the Autoridad de Turismo Panamá (ATP; www.atp.gob.pa), has a slowly improving website (with some English too) at www.visitpanama.com, though the swanky air-conditioned tourist offices in the major towns and resort areas are still not geared up to assisting passing tourists. You may be lucky enough to get a pamphlet and, if you have a specific

question, the employee will probably do their best to help you, but do not expect lists of local accommodations or tourist attractions, nor assume the person will speak English. Accommodations reception staff are a far better bet for information.

Panama's national parks and other protected areas, which encompass many of the country's natural wonders, are administered by the Ministry for the Environment, or MiAmbiente. The Áreas Protegidas section in regional and local park offices can provide you with information (in Spanish).

Tour operators and travel agents

Although there are good specialty tour operators at home that can arrange a tour of Panama, you will reduce costs by buying an air ticket separately, either online or via a travel agent, and contracting one of the high quality bilingual tour operators in Panama City (listed in the App) for when you arrive. Independent travelers can easily organize their own accommodations and transportation as they travel, signing up for a tour with a local operator, in whichever part of the country, for a particular activity, such as scuba diving or hiking.

V

Visas and passports

Tourists from most European countries, plus the US, Canada, Australia, New Zealand, and South Africa, do not need a visa to enter Panama. They can get their passport stamped for 180 days on arrival provided they can produce a passport valid for at least six months after departure, an onward (or round-trip) bus or plane ticket, and proof of funds (usually $500 or a credit card).

That said, check for the latest regulations at a Panamanian consulate in advance and don't forget that if you are traveling from Europe via the US, you will need a transit visa, or a visa waiver (ESTA) application in advance of travel (see www.usimmigrationsupport.org), as well as a machine-readable passport. The Panamanian immigration authorities' website is also worth checking (www.migracion.gob.pa).

Airport information board.

If you are arriving from one of the WHO-listed yellow fever countries there is a very small chance you might be asked to produce your vaccination certificate.

W

Websites and apps

www.visitpanama.com. The official website of Panama's tourism authority is patchy, in terms of usefulness, though it has plenty of inspirational photos.
www.thevisitorpanama.com. This bilingual weekly paper offers a bland summary of Panamanian news and features plus a decent listings section of events in Panama City, Bocas, and Boquete.
www.degustapanama.com. A good restaurant review website (in Spanish) with a rating system for service, ambience, and food.
www.bocasbreeze.com. Bilingual paper run primarily by ex-pats but with some interesting articles and listings.
www.whatsapp.com. Very popular in Panama; most hotels, and tour operators use it to confirm bookings, times, etc.
www.livewalkpty.com. Informative app designed by Panamanians to give a comprehensive walking tour of Casco Viejo.

Weights and measures

The metric system is used for weights and measurements.

Spanish is the official language of Panama and the first language of more than 2 million of the population, though a recorded 13 other first languages are spoken across the country. The latter are mainly indigenous but include Panamanian Creole English, preferred by around 100,000 Afro-Antillean Panamanians, primarily resident in Bocas, Colón, and Panama City, and Cantonese or Hakka, spoken by around 60,000 or more Chinese-Panamanians. While many urban middle-class Panamanians speak English, some of whom are bilingual, the 'everybody-speaks-English' myth is easily dispelled. Official estimates reckon around 14 percent of the population can communicate in English, but in small towns and rural areas you'll find many speak virtually no English and in a number of the remote indigenous communities some villagers, especially older women, do not even speak much Spanish. Your travel experience in the country will be greatly enhanced by learning at least the basics of Spanish before you arrive.

PRONUNCIATION TIPS

In Spanish, each word is pronounced as written according to the following guide:
A somewhere between the 'A sound of 'back' and that of 'father'
E as in 'get'
I as in 'police'
O as in 'hot'
U as in 'rule'
C is soft before E and I, otherwise hard; *cerca* is pronounced 'SERka.'
G works the same way – a guttural 'H' sound (like the 'ch' in a Scottish 'loch') before E or I, a hard G elsewhere; *gigante* is pronounced 'HiGANte.'

H is always silent.
J is the same sound as a guttural 'G;' *jamón* is pronounced 'ham ON.'
LL sounds like an English Y; *tortilla* is pronounced 'torTIya.'
N is as in English, unless there is a '~' over it, when it becomes like the N in 'onion;' *mañana* is pronounced 'maNYAna.'
QU is pronounced like an English 'K' as in 'kick.'
R is rolled, RR doubly so.
V sounds like a cross between B and V, *vino* almost becoming 'beano.'
X is a soft 'SH,' so that *Xela* becomes 'SHEla;' between vowels it has an 'H' sound – *México* is pronounced 'ME-hi-ko.'
Z is the same as a soft C; *cerveza* is pronounced 'serVEsa.'

GREETINGS

Hello ¡Hola!
Good morning Buenos días
Good afternoon Buenas tardes
Welcome Bienvenido
How are you? (formal/informal) Cómo está?/ Qué tal?
Very well Muy bien
And you? (formal/informal) Y usted?/ Y tú?
What is your name? ¿Como se llama? **My name is...** Me llamo...
Pleased to meet you ¡Mucho gusto!
I am British/American/Canadian Soy británica(o)/norteamericana(o)/ canadiense
See you tomorrow Hasta mañana
See you later Hasta luego
Goodbye (formal/informal) ¡Adiós!/ ¡Ciao!
Good night Buenas noches

AT THE HOTEL

Do you have a room available? ¿Tiene una habitación disponible?

I have a reservation Tengo una reserva
I'd like... Quisiera...
a single room una habitación individual (sencilla)
a double (with one double bed) una habitación (con cama) matrimonial
a double (with two double beds) una habitación (con dos camas) doble
a room with twin beds una habitación con dos camas
for one night/two nights por una noche/dos noches
with a sea view con vista al mar
Does the room have a private or shared bathroom? ¿Tiene la habitación baño privado o baño compartido?
Does it have ... ¿Tiene... ?
hot water agua caliente
air-conditioning aire-acondicionado
a fan abanico
a fridge una nevera
a mosquito net mosquitero
Could you show me another room, please? ¿Puede mostrarme otra habitación, por favor?
I would like to change rooms Quisiera cambiar la habitación
How much is it? ¿Cuánto cuesta?/ ¿Cuánto sale?
Do you accept credit cards? ¿Se aceptan tarjetas de crédito?
What time is breakfast/ lunch/dinner? ¿A qué hora es el desayuno/el almuerzo/la cena?

SHOPPING

Where can I find...? ¿Dónde hay...?
Where is the nearest...? ø¿Dónde está el/la... más cerca?
ATM cajero automático
bank banco
I'm just looking Sólo estoy mirando, gracias
How much is this? ¿Cuanto cuesta/ sale?
Do you have it in another color? ¿Tiene en otro color?

Do you have it in another size? *¿Tiene en otro talle/número?*
smaller/larger *más pequeño/más grande*
I would like some of/half a kilo of... *Quisiera un poco de/un medio kilo de...*
A little more/less *Un poco más/menos*
Would you like anything else? *¿Quiere algo más?*
That's enough *Está bien*
expensive *caro*
cheap *barato*
clothes store *tienda de ropa*
bakery *panadería*
market *mercado*
supermarket *supermercado*
shopping center *centro comercial*

TRAVELING

luggage, bag(s) *equipaje, bolsas*
bus *bus/autobús*
bus stop *parada de bus/autobus*
bus terminal *terminal de autobuses*
one-way ticket *boleto de ida*
roundtrip, return ticket *boleto de ida y vuelta*
fare *pasaje*
What time does the bus/boat/ferry [leave/return?] *¿A qué hora [sale/regresa] el autobús/la lancha/el ferry?*
Is this seat taken? *¿Está ocupado este asiento?*
Could you please advise me when we reach/the stop for...*? ¿Por favor, puede avisarme cuando llegamos a/a la parada para...?*
Is this the stop for...? *¿Es ésta la parada para...?*
Next stop please *La próxima parada, por favor*
subway *metro*
taxi *taxi*
car *auto*
4WD/4x4 *doble tracción/cuatro por cuatro*
car rental *alquiler de autos*
fuel/gas *gasolina*
dock/jetty *muelle*
ferry *ferry*
sailboat *velero*
ship *barco*
dugout canoe *cayuco/piragua*
plane *avión*

SIGHTSEEING

Where is/are..? *¿Donde ésta(n) ...?*
the viewpoint *mirador*
the main square *la plaza principal*
the restrooms *los baños/servicios*

What time does/do ... open? *¿A que hora se abre(n) ...?*
What time does/do ... close? *¿A que hora se cierra(n) ...?*
the museum *el museo*
the cathedral/church *la catedral/la iglesia*
the ruins *las ruinas*
the tourist office *oficina de turismo*

EATING OUT

I'd like to reserve a table *Quisiera reservar una mesa, por favor*
Do you have a table for...? *¿Tiene una mesa para...?*
breakfast *desayuno*
lunch *almuerzo*
dinner *cena*
starter *entrada*
main course/dish *plato fuerte*
dessert *postre*
I'm a vegetarian *Soy vegetariana(o)*
May I/we have ....? *¿Puede traerme/traernos).....?*
the menu *la carta/el menu*
wine list *la carta de vinos*
the bill *la cuenta*
a bottle of... *una botella de...*
a glass of... *un vaso/una copa de...*
What would you recommend? *¿Qué recomienda?*
fixed-price menu/lunch *el menú del día/el almuerzo*
What would you like to drink? *¿Qué quiere tomar?*
Is service included? *¿Incluye el servicio?*

MENU DECODER

Essentials

aciete **oil**
ají **chili pepper**
ajo **garlic**
arroz **rice**
azúcar **sugar**
mantequilla **butter**
pan **bread**
pimiento negra **black pepper**
sal **salt**

Vegetables

aguacate **avocado**
cebolla **onion**
champiñon (hongo) **mushroom**
ensalada **salad**
espinaca **spinach**
frijoles **beans**

gallo pinto **mixed beans and rice**
lechuga **lettuce**
lentejas **lentils**
maíz **sweetcorn/maize**
menestra **bean/lentil stew**
papa **potato**
papas fritas **French fries**
tomate **tomato**
zanahoria **carrot**

Meat and poultry

bistec/lomo **carne steak**
cerdo **pork**
chuleta **pork chop**
jamón **ham**
mondongo **tripe and chorizo stew**
pollo **chicken**
pork **chop ham**
res **beef**
ropa vieja **shredded spicy beef and rice**
sancocho **thick red meat or chicken soup with root vegetables**

Cooking terms

a la parrilla **barbecued**
a la plancha **griddled**
apanado **breaded**
asado **roast**
encocado **in coconut sauce**
frito **fried**
guisado **stewed**
picante **spicy hot**
puré **mashed**
revuelto **scrambled**

Seafood

almejas **clams**
atún **tuna**
calamares **squid**
camarón **shrimp**
cangrejo **crab**
ceviche **raw seafood marinated in lime juice with onion and cilantro**
corvina **seabass**
langosta **lobster**
langostina **king prawn**
mejillónes **mussels**
mero **grouper**
pargo rojo **red snapper**
pulpo **octopus**
trucha **trout**

Fruit

aceitunas **olives**
chirimoya **custard apple**
coco **coconut**
fresa **strawberry**
guanábana **soursop**
guayaba **guava**
guineo **banana**

limón **lemon/lime**
manzana **apple**
maracuyá **passionfruit**
marañon **cashew**
mora (zarzamora) **blackberry**
naranja **orange**
piña **pineapple**
plátano **plantain**
sandía **watermelon**
uva **grapes**

Snacks

empanada **pasty**
emparedado **sandwich**
hojaldre **deep-fried doughy pancake**
patacones **fried green plantains**
platanitos **plantain chips**
salchichas **sausages**
tortilla **thick fried maize/corn patty**
tortilla **de huevos omelette**
tostada **toast**

Drinks

agua mineral **mineral water**
...con gas **sparkling**
...sin gas **still**
agua potable **drinking water**
aromática **herbal tea**
batido **milk shake**
café **coffee**
cerveza **beer**
jugo natural **pure fruit juice**
leche **milk**
licuado **fresh fruit shake**
refresco/soda **soft drink**
té **tea**

HEALTH

shift duty pharmacy *farmacia de turno*
hospital/clinic *hospital/clínica*
I need a doctor/dentist *Necesito un médico/dentista (odontólogo)*
I don't feel well *Me siento mal*
I am sick *Estoy enferma(o)*
It hurts here *Duele aquí*
I have a headache/stomachache *Tengo dolor de cabeza/de estómago*
I feel dizzy *Me siento mareada(o)*
Do you have (something for)...? *¿Tiene (algo para)...?*
a cold *un resfrío*
flu *gripe*
cough *tos*
a sore throat *dolor de garganta*
diarrhea *diarrea*
fever *fiebre*
heartburn *acidez*
aspirin *aspirina*
antiseptic/antihistamine cream *crema antiséptica/antihistamínica*

insect/mosquito bites *picaduras de insectos/mosquitos*
insect repellent *repelente contra insectos*
sun block *bloqueador solar*
toothpaste *pasta de dientes*
toilet paper *papel higiénico*
tampons *tampones*

ON THE ROAD

Where can I rent a car? *¿Dónde puedo alquilar un auto?*
Is mileage included? *¿Está incluido el kilometraje?*
comprehensive insurance *seguros comprensivos*
How do I get to...? *¿Cómo se llega a...?*
Turn right/left *Doble a la derecha/izquierda*
At the next corner/street *en la próxima esquina/calle*
Go straight ahead *Siga recto/derecho*
How long does it take to get there? *¿Cuánto tiempo lleva para llegar?*
driver's license *licencia de conducir/manejar*
gas station *gasolinera*
I would like to fill the tank *Quisiera llenar el tanque*
Where can I find a car repair shop? *¿Dónde hay un taller mecánico?*
Can you check the...? *¿Puede revisar/ chequear...?*
There's something wrong with the... *Hay un problema con...*
gasoline *gasolina*
diesel *diesel*
oil *aceite*
water *agua*
air *aire*

EMERGENCIES

Help! *¡Ayuda!*
Stop! *¡Pare!*
Watch out! *¡Cuidado! ¡*
I've had an accident *He tenido un accidente*
Call a doctor/the (transit) police *Llame a un médico/la policía (de transito)*
Call an ambulance *Llame una ambulancia*
Where is the nearest hospital? *¿Dónde queda el hospital más cercano?*
I want to report an assault/a robbery *Quisiera reportar un asalto/un robo*
Thank you very much for your help *Muchísimas gracias por su ayuda*

USEFUL WORDS/PHRASES

yes *sí*
no *no*
thank you *gracias*
you're welcome *de nada*
okay *está bien*
please *por favor*
Excuse me (to get attention) *¡Perdón! ¡Por favor!*
Excuse me (to get through a crowd) *¡Permiso!*
Excuse me (sorry) *Perdóneme*
Wait a minute! *¡Un momento!*
Can you help me? *¿Me puede ayudar?* **Do you speak English?** *¿Habla inglés?*
Please speak more slowly *Hable más despacio, por favor*
Could you repeat that please *¿Podría repetírmelo, por favor?*
I (don't) understand *(No) entiendo*
I'm sorry *Lo siento/Perdone*
I don't know *No lo sé*
No problem *No hay problema*
Where is...? *¿Dónde está...?*
I am looking for... *Estoy buscando*
That's it *Eso es*
Here it is *Aquí está*
There it is *Allí está*
Let's go *Vámonos*
At what time? *¿A qué hora?*
late *tarde*
early *temprano*
yesterday *ayer*
today *hoy*
tomorrow *mañana*

DAYS OF THE WEEK

Note that the Spanish form takes a lower-case initial letter.
Monday *lunes*
Tuesday *martes*
Wednesday *miércoles*
Thursday *jueves*
Friday *viernes*
Saturday *sábado*
Sunday *domingo*

MONTHS OF THE YEAR/SEASONS

Note that the Spanish form takes a lower-case initial letter.
January *enero*
February *febrero*
March *marzo*
April *abril*
May *mayo*
June *junio*
July *julio*
August *agosto*

September *septiembre*
October *octubre*
November *noviembre*
December *diciembre*
Summer *verano*
Winter *invierno*

NUMBERS

1 *uno*
2 *dos*
3 *tres*
4 *cuatro*
5 *cinco*
6 *seis*
7 *siete*
8 *ocho*

9 *nueve*
10 *diez*
11 *once*
12 *doce*
13 *trece*
14 *catorce*
15 *quince*
16 *dieciséis*
17 *diecisiete*
20 *veinte*
21 *veintiuno*
30 *treinta*
40 *cuarenta*
50 *cincuenta*
60 *sesenta*
70 *setenta*
80 *ochenta*
90 *noventa*

100 *cien*
101 *ciento uno*
200 *doscientos*
300 *trescientos*
400 *cuatrocientos*
500 *quinientos*
600 *seiscientos*
700 *setecientos*
800 *ochocientos*
900 *novecientos*
1,000 *mil*
2,000 *dos mil*
1,000,000 *un millón*
2,000,000 *dos millones*
first *primer(o)/a*
second *segund(o)/a*
third *tercer(o)/a*

FURTHER READING

Bookstores are far from plentiful in Panama. The main chain is Hombre de la Mancha (www.hombredelamancha.com), which has branches in many of the shopping malls across Panama City, as well as a small outlet in Santiago and another in David. The stores generally stock a small, pricey selection in English.

As regards Panamanian authors, though native novelists are scarce, there are a few short-story writers, but very little is available in English. Even the colossus of contemporary Panamanian literature, Enrique Jaramillo Levi – internationally acclaimed short-story writer, poet, essayist, editor, and critic – has had relatively few works translated into English, despite such accolades. New Afro-Panamanian author, Melanie Taylor Herrera, has English versions of her short stories and poetry scattered round various journals, some of which are accessible online.

THE CANAL

The Canal Builders: Making America's Empire at the Panama Canal Julie Greene. Long overdue focus on the men and women who, in dreadful conditions and facing all sorts of discrimination, worked to realize America's grandiose dream of empire. You also meet the big players whose ambition ignored the human cost.
The Building of the Canal in Historic Photographs Ulrich Keller. A clear case of pictures speaking louder than words, as 164 detailed black-and-white photos evoke the lives of both rich and poor engaged in the monumental struggle to build the Canal.
The Path Between the Seas: The Creation of the Panama Canal, 1870–1914 David McCullough. Though this is a detailed scholarly work of 700 pages, the plot-twisting narrative and larger-than-life characters

sweep the reader along, together with a focus on understanding the underlying causes of events.
Hell's Gorge: The Battle to Build the Panama Canal (also published as Panama Fever) Matthew Parker. A gripping account of the struggle with jungle, disease, engineering impossibilities, and disastrous ignorance, which is a meticulously researched yet wide-ranging narrative that focuses on the oft-neglected labor force that lived and died digging the Big Ditch.

PIRATES AND POLITICS

Panama Kevin Buckley. Written by a former *Newsweek* correspondent, this book provides what many consider to be the most reliable account of events leading up to the US invasion of Panama in 1989. Buckley vividly brings the complex web of corruption and political intrigue to life.
The Sack of Panama: Captain Morgan and the Battle for the Caribbean Peter Earle. Swashbuckling account of the real-life pirates of the Caribbean and the Spaniards' efforts to defeat them, focusing on the Welsh privateer Henry Morgan and his exploits, culminating in the sack of Panama in 1671.
The Pirates of Panama: True Account of the Famous Adventures and Daring Deeds of Sir Henry Morgan and Other Notorious Freebooters John Esquemeling. Based on a lively first-hand account originally written in Dutch, the first English edition was published in 1684. The author was barber surgeon to Henry Morgan and accompanied him on his notorious expedition against Panama City.
Path of Empire: Panama and the Californian Gold Rush Aims McGuinness. A look at the key role played by the isthmus during the Gold Rush in the mid-1800s as the fastest link between New York and San Francisco, the consequences of

building the Panama Railroad, and the first of many military interventions by the US.
The Panama Papers: Breaking the Story of How the Rich and Powerful Hide Their Money Bastian Obermayer and Frederik Obermaier. Both gripping and disheartening in equal measure. Insights into the exposé on how the global political, commercial, and celebrity elite use perfectly legal offshore accounts for tax avoidance, while their funds are used to launder drug money.
Emperors in the Jungle: The Hidden History of the US in Panama John Lindsay Poland. A human-rights campaigner and investigative journalist explores the role of the US military in Panama and the dubious uses to which it put the land it acquired.
The Darién Disaster John Prebble. Highly detailed and often turgid exploration of the doomed attempt by the Scots to colonize the Darién. The minutiae, such as the numbers of cases of rum loaded onto the ships, obscure the depth of the tragedy that bankrupted Scotland.
The Politics of Race in Panama Sonja Watson. This thoughtful, scholarly work, which examines the way that race and identity are inscribed differently by authors from the Afro-Caribbean and Afro-Hispanic communities, leads you to wish more of these authors' writings were available in English.
Panama: Made in the USA John Week and Phil Gunson. Written in 1991, this much-praised analysis of the 1989 American invasion of Panama and its historical background deals with the legal implications and political consequences, while shining a light on the part Noriega played leading up to the attack.

GUNA CULTURE

Chiefs, Scribes and Ethnographers: Kuna Culture from Inside and Out James Howe. Written by a professor of anthropology who has spent considerable time among the Guna over a 35-year period, this recent book deals with accounts that the Guna chiefs themselves have given of their life and culture. Like his previous books, it's a serious but rewarding read.
The Art of Being Kuna: Layers of Meaning among the Kuna of Panama. Salvador Mary Lyn (ed.) Glossy

coffee-table book full of fascinating photos and scholarly insights on the interweaving of Guna art, culture, and environment.

Magnificent Molas Michael Perrin. Lavishly illustrated, this book explores the *molas* or fabric 'paintings' of the Guna women, tracing the links between the patterns used and traditions and rituals in the lives of the women.

Stories, Myths, Chants and Songs of the Kuna Indians Joel Sherzer. The author, a linguistic anthropologist, lived among the Guna people photographing and recording their oral tradition of songs and ritual performances.

Plants and Animals in the Life of the Kuna Jorge Ventocilla, Heraclio Herrera, and Valerio Nuñez. Written by two Guna biologists and their non-Guna Panamanian colleague, this book is aimed at the Guna reader as well as outsiders, providing fascinating insights into the Guna perspective on ecology and cosmology as they relate to environmental issues.

FICTION

Two Serious Ladies Jane Bowles. An avant-garde classic of 1943, this story follows two women seeking freedom from the confines of social convention. On holiday in Panama, one falls in love with a young prostitute and leaves her husband to live in the brothel in Colón.

The World in Half Cristina Enríquez. Debut novel from US author Cristina Enríquez who draws on her Panamanian heritage to narrate a young woman's search for identity as she leaves her ailing mother to find the father she never knew in Panama. The same author's award-winning *Come Together Fall Apart* contains a novella and a handful of short stories, which provide deft close-ups of a range of Panamanian characters in the turbulent 1980s.

The Rising Sun Douglas Galbraith. A detailed, somewhat rambling historical novel about the Scottish expedition to the Darién, fueled by human greed but leading to unbelievable hardship and the eventual bankruptcy of Scotland. It is difficult to warm to the main character who tells the story, but the horror comes across.

The Tailor of Panama John Le Carré. With an explicit nod to Graham Greene's *Our Man in Havana*, this satirical spy thriller is a classic. Set just before the US handover of the Canal, a young unscrupulous British agent embarks on an elaborate fiction of intrigue, which spirals out of control. While both American and British intelligence services are lampooned as much as Panamanian high society, the novel, nevertheless, caused some upset in Panama upon publication.

The Shadow: Thirteen Stories in Opposition Enrique Jaramillo Levi. Short stories by Panama's pre-eminent (post) modern writer, though some tales are scarcely more than vignettes. You'll either be seduced by the originality of his imagination and fluid prose or left baffled and irritated as meaning slips through your grasp.

BIOGRAPHY

Is There a Hole in My Boat? Tales of Travel in Panama Without a Car Darrin Du Ford. The author sets out to explore Panama using public transportation or hitching a lift, by dugout or on foot, aiming to get closer to the life and culture of the people than the average tourist; he never seems to turn down a new experience.

⊙ Send us your thoughts

We do our best to ensure the information in our books is as accurate and up-to-date as possible. The books are updated on a regular basis using local contacts, who painstakingly add, amend and correct as required. However, some details (such as telephone numbers and opening times) are liable to change, and we are ultimately reliant on our readers to put us in the picture.

We welcome your feedback, especially your experience of using the book "on the road". Maybe you came across a great site or new attraction we missed. We will acknowledge all contributions, and we'll offer an Insight Guide to the best letters.

Please write to us at:
Insight Guides
PO Box 7910
London SE1 1WE

Or email us at:
hello@insightguides.com

Hands of Stone: The Life and Legend of Roberto Durán Christian Giudice. Meticulously researched biography of Panama's most famous boxer and one of the sport's all-time greats, drawing on plenty of fascinating original interview material. A warts-and-all rags-to-riches tale that tracks his rise to fame from the slums of Panama City.

Getting to Know the General: The Story of an Involvement Graham Greene. A personal slant on Omar Torrijos, the country's most charismatic leader, whom the author befriended during his time in troubled late 1970s and early 1980s Panama.

Fire Under My Feet: A Memoir of God's Power in Panama Leo Mahon. The moving story of a compassionate Roman Catholic priest sent in 1963 to a poverty-stricken town in Panama to found a church.

The Darién Gap: Travels in the Rainforest of Panama Martin Mitchinson. An entertaining account of 18 months spent in the trackless jungle trying to retrace the route to the Pacific made by the first European, Balboa, in 1513. It's a successful blend of personal experience, history, and local lore.

America's Prisoner: The Memoirs of Manuel Noriega Manuel Noriega and Peter Eisner. The other side of the story of a leader who was vilified, arrested, and put on trial by the US. A controversial book, it is worth reading for its revelations about the American attitude to Panama and Latin America.

BIRDLIFE

A Bird-finding Guide to Panama George Angehr, Dodge Engleman, and Lorna Engleman. You need to read the title carefully – this excellent, detailed guide tells you where to find the birds and how to get there by car, but is not a bird identification manual.

A Guide to the Birds of Panama Robert Ridgely and John Gwynne. This weighty tome is *the* birding bible for Panama, although it's in desperate need of updating.

A Guide to the Common Birds of Panama City Jorge Ventocilla and Dana Gardner. Excellent, beautifully illustrated pocket-size book aimed at the average nature-lover – perfect for anyone basing their stay in the capital and wanting to identify the city's surprisingly abundant birdlife.

298

CREDITS

PHOTO CREDITS

Alamy 7MR, 9TL, 9BR, 28, 30/31, 33, 37, 44/45T, 45BR, 45TR, 55, 58, 68, 77, 93, 136, 137, 156, 162/163T, 163BR, 167, 168, 170, 174, 176, 177, 178, 181, 184, 186, 190, 191, 196, 197, 199, 204, 209, 210, 211, 212, 213, 214, 215, 216, 217, 233, 240, 249, 250, 251, 253, 257, 258, 259, 263, 269, 270, 276, 277
Getty Images 4, 9TR, 10/11, 16, 18, 24/25, 26, 27, 29, 32, 34/35, 36, 38, 39, 40R, 40L, 41, 42/43, 44BR, 44BL, 45BL, 46, 47, 48, 49, 50, 51, 52, 53, 54, 60, 61, 63, 64, 65, 67, 71, 88, 89, 95, 98, 102,

149, 150, 153, 154, 155, 161, 162BR, 162BL, 163ML, 163BL, 163TR, 164, 175, 179, 192, 193, 194, 195, 198, 202, 206, 218, 228, 235, 236, 237, 245, 246, 248, 252, 254, 262, 266, 275, 291
Hemis/AWL Images 12/13, 128
iStock 1, 6MR, 6BL, 6MR, 6ML, 7ML, 7MR, 7ML, 7TL, 8T, 8B, 14/15, 17T, 19, 20, 21, 22, 23, 45ML, 56/57, 59, 62, 66, 69, 70, 72, 73, 74, 75, 76, 78, 79, 80, 81, 82, 83, 84/85T, 84BR, 84BL, 85ML, 85BL, 85TR, 86, 90, 92, 94, 96, 97, 99, 100, 101, 103, 104/105, 110, 111T,

111B, 116, 117, 121, 124, 125, 127, 130, 131, 132, 133, 135, 138, 139, 140, 141, 143, 145, 146, 152, 165, 203, 208, 219, 220/221T, 220B, 221ML, 221BR, 221BL, 221TR, 222, 223, 227, 229, 230, 231, 232, 234, 239, 241, 242, 243, 255, 256, 260/261T, 260BR, 260BL, 261ML, 261BR, 261BL, 261TR, 273, 278, 282/283, 285, 287, 289, 290, 292, 296
Shutterstock 7BR, 17B, 85BR, 87, 91, 106/107, 108/109, 118, 119, 123, 129, 147, 148, 157, 158, 159, 173, 180, 188, 200, 201, 247, 267, 280

COVER CREDITS

Front cover and Spine: Mola *Getty Images*
Front flap: (from top) Old Panama *Shutterstock*; Empanadas *iStock*; Typical Caribbean house *iStock*; hand-made souvenirs *iStock*
Back flap: Resplendent Quetzal *Shutterstock*

INSIGHT GUIDE CREDITS

Distribution
UK, Ireland and Europe
Apa Publications (UK) Ltd;
sales@insightguides.com
United States and Canada
Ingram Publisher Services;
ips@ingramcontent.com
Australia and New Zealand
Woodslane; info@woodslane.com.au
Southeast Asia
Apa Publications (SN) Pte;
singaporeoffice@insightguides.com
Worldwide
Apa Publications (UK) Ltd;
sales@insightguides.com
Special Sales, Content Licensing and CoPublishing
Insight Guides can be purchased in bulk quantities at discounted prices. We can create special editions, personalised jackets and corporate imprints tailored to your needs. sales@insightguides.com
www.insightguides.biz

Printed in China by CTPS

All Rights Reserved
© 2019 Apa Digital (CH) AG and
Apa Publications (UK) Ltd

First Edition 2019

Every effort has been made to provide accurate information in this publication, but changes are inevitable. The publisher cannot be responsible for any resulting loss, inconvenience or injury. We would appreciate it if readers would call our attention to any errors or outdated information. We also welcome your suggestions; please contact us at: hello@insightguides.com

www.insightguides.com

Editor: Helen Fanthorpe
Author: Sara Humphreys
Head of DTP and Pre-Press: Rebeka Davies
Managing Editor: Carine Tracanelli
Picture Editor: Aude Vauconsant
Cartography: Carte

Legend

City maps

	Freeway/Highway/Motorway
	Divided Highway
	Main Roads
	Minor Roads
	Pedestrian Roads
	Steps
	Footpath
	Railway
	Funicular Railway
	Cable Car
	Tunnel
	City Wall
	Important Building
	Built Up Area
	Other Land
	Transport Hub
	Park
	Pedestrian Area
	Bus Station
❶	Tourist Information
✉	Main Post Office
	Cathedral/Church
☾	Mosque
✡	Synagogue
⚑	Statue/Monument
	Beach
✈	Airport

Regional maps

	Freeway/Highway/Motorway (with junction)
	Freeway/Highway/Motorway (under construction)
	Divided Highway
	Main Road
	Secondary Road
	Minor Road
	Track
	Footpath
	International Boundary
	State/Province Boundary
	National Park/Reserve
	Marine Park
	Ferry Route
	Marshland/Swamp
	Glacier Salt Lake
✈	Airport/Airfield
∴	Ancient Site
⊖	Border Control
	Cable Car
	Castle/Castle Ruins
	Cave
	Chateau/Stately Home
✝	Church/Church Ruins
	Crater
	Lighthouse
▲	Mountain Peak
★	Place of Interest
�	Viewpoint

CONTRIBUTORS

This brand new guide to Panama was commissioned, managed, and copyedited by **Helen Fanthorpe**. It was written by **Sara Humphreys**, a freelance writer and researcher. Sara has lived and worked in various countries in Latin America and sub-Saharan Africa. In addition to this guide, she has worked on books to Ecuador, Peru, the Dominican Republic, and Namibia. When not island-hopping or tramping through the rainforests of Panama, she can be found on the beaches of Barbados. This title was proofread and indexed by **Penny Phenix**.

ABOUT INSIGHT GUIDES

Insight Guides have more than 45 years' experience of publishing high-quality, visual travel guides. We produce 400 full-colour titles, in both print and digital form, covering more than 200 destinations across the globe, in a variety of formats to meet your different needs.

Insight Guides are written by local authors, whose expertise is evident in the extensive historical and cultural background features. Each destination is carefully researched by regional experts to ensure our guides provide the very latest information. All the reviews in **Insight Guides** are independent; we strive to maintain an impartial view. Our reviews are carefully selected to guide you to the best places to eat, go out and shop, so you can be confident that when we say a place is special, we really mean it.

INDEX

MAIN REFERENCES ARE IN BOLD TYPE

A

accommodations 283
tax 290
Achiote 156
Centro El Tucán 156
Achutupu 257
activities 87
addresses 283
admission charges 284
adventure sports 17
Afro-Antillean people 225
Afro-Panamanian music 69
Afro-Panamanian people 61
Agligandi
Museo Olonigli 257
Agligandi 257
agriculture 210, 237
Aguadulce 178
Iglesia de San Juan Bautista 178
Ingenio Santa Rosa 179
Museo Regional Stella Sierra 178
Agua Fría No. 1 267
Agua Yala 266
air travel 280
Albrook Airport 281
Alfanno, Omar 67
Alfaro, Rufina 189
Almirante 237
Altos de Campana National Park 165, 166
Amador Guerrero, Manuel 49
Amistad International Park 17, 207, 213, 224, 239
Amphibian Ark project 85
amphibians 81
anteaters 81
Antón 172
ants 83
ants, leafcutter 83, 152
apps 291
Arboleda, Carlos 136
archeology 29, 31
Archipiélago de la Perlas 119
Arco Seco 19, 176
Ardito Barletta, Nicolás 52
Área Protegida San Lorenzo 155
Áreas Revertidas 53, 144
Arias de Ávila, Pedro 35
Árias de Calvo, Cuquita 96
Arias Madrid, Arnulfo 50
Armila 258
art and crafts 73
art galleries. See museums and galleries
Aspinwall, William 143
ATMs 289
Attenborough, David
Life in Cold Blood 169
Azuero Peninsula 21, 19, 111, 165

B

bags 75

Baha'i House of Worship (Panama City) 137
Bahía de Panamá 136
Bahía Honda 233
ballet 70
Balneario Barranca 216
bananas 223, **241**
Bancroft, H.H. 154
Barriles culture 30, 204
Barroso, Anita 67
basilisks 83
basketry 75
Bastimentos 111
Bastimentos Town 232
bats 80, 265
vampire bats 287
Bayano, 'El Rey Negro' 266
beaches
Azuero Peninsula and Veraguas 192, 193, 195
beach hazards and safety 90
Bocas del Toro 228, 229, 231, 232, 236
Caribbean Coast 157, 160, 161
Central Panama 165
Chiriquí and Western Panama 215, 218
Guna Yala 243, 246, 253, 255
Pacific Coast 165, 167
Pearl Islands 139
beer 97, 284
birdlife and birdwatching 17, 79, 156, 155. See also national parks
Azuero Peninsula and Veraguas 182, 184, 187, 193, 194
birding lodges 220
Bocas del Toro 238, 239
Central Panama 167, 168, 172, 179
Chiriquí and Western Panama 207, 210, 211, 212
Darién and The East 271
field guides 297
guided walks and packages 147
in national parks 147
in Panama City 130, **136**
migrations 79
Panama Audubon Society 220
Pearl Islands 139
raptors 79
Blades, Rubén 67, **71**
Blue Apple 55
boat travel 282
Boca Brava 218
Boca del Drago 229, 230
Bocas del Toro 19, 23, 33, 60, 89
eating out 286
water taxis 282
Bocas Fruit Company 241
Bocas Town 87, 224, 225, 241
activities 226
Parque Bolívar 226
Sea Turtle Conservancy 237
tours 226

water taxis 237
Bokota people 61
Bonyic 240
bookstores 296
Boquete 87, 111, 203, 205, 219
Jardín El Explorador 206
Parque Central 206
short trails 207
Boquete Tree Trek 91
Bri-Bri people 61
Bridge of the Americas 101
budgeting for your trip 284
Buglé people 60, 204, 225
Bunau-Varilla, Philippe 43, 47
Burica Peninsula 216
buses
fares 284
international 280
national network 281
Bush, President George H.W. 52
butterflies 83

C

caimans 83, 152, 265
Cambutal 195
Camino de Cruces 36, 147
Camino de Cruces National Park 145
Camino del Oleoducto 79, 148, 151
Camino Real 36
camping 88
Canal Zone 44, 47
Cañón Macho de Monte 209
Canopy Camp Darién 268
Canopy Tower Ecolodge 147, 148
capybaras 80
Caribbean coast 19, 155, 223, 226
climate 285
car rental 282
Carrera, Silvia 62
Carter, President Jimmy 51
Cascada Las Yayas 175
Cascada Tavida 175
Castrellón, Mario 96
cathedrals. See churches and cathedrals
Cayo Crawl 228, 234
Cayo Nancy 235
Cayos Coco-Bandero 254
Cayos Holandeses 253
Cayos Limones 250
Cayos Los Grullos 254
Cayos Zapatillas 227, 228, 234
cell phones 248, 291
Cémaco, Cacique 35
Central Panama 165
ceramics, ancient 30
Cerro Campana 167
Cerro Fábrega 239
Cerro Gaital 169, 172
Cerro Hoya National Park 195
Cerro Jefe 149
Cerro Marta 176
Cerro Peña Blanca 176

Cerro Pirre 269
Cerro Punta 210, 212
Cerro Punta agriculture 210
Cerro Santa Marta 176
Chagres National Park 149
Chagres, Río 48, 100
Changuinola 60, 223, 238
Chiari, Rodolfo 178
Chicheme Grande 252
Chiguirí Arriba 174
children 284
Chinese-Panamanian people 61
Chiriquí 203, 219
Chiriquí Highlands 87
Chitré
    Catedral de San Juan Bautista
        184
    Museo de Herrera 185
    Parque Centenario 185
    Parque Unión 184
chocolate 237
    cacao farm tours 237
Chorro El Macho 171
Chorro Las Mozas 171
churches and cathedrals
    Basílica de Don Bosco (Panama
        City) 134
    Basílica Menor Santiago
        Apóstol (Natá) 177
    Catedral de la Inmaculada
        Concepción de María (Colón)
        155
    Catedral de San Juan Bautista
        (Chitré) 184
    Catedral de San Juan Bautista
        (Penonomé) 173
    Catedral Metropolitana
        (Panama City) 121
    Catedral Santiago Apóstol
        (Santiago) 197
    Episcopalian Christ Church by
        the Sea (Colón) 155
    Iglesia Atalaya (Santiago) 197
    Iglesia de la Merced (Panama
        City) 121
    Iglesia del Carmen (Panama
        City) 134
    Iglesia de San Felipe (Portobelo)
        159, 160
    Iglesia de San José (Panama
        City) 125
    Iglesia de San Juan Bautista
        (Aguadulce) 178
    Iglesia San Atanasio (La Villa de
        los Santos) 188
    Iglesia San Felipe de Neri
        (Panama City) 124
    Iglesia San Francisco de la
        Montaña (Santiago) 197
    Iglesia San José (El Valle) 171
    Iglesia Santa Librada (Las
        Tablas) 191
    Iglesia Santo Domingo de
        Guzmán (Parita) 185
    Iglesia y Convento de San
        Francisco de Asís (Panama
        City) 123
    Iglesia y Convento de Santo
        Domingo (Panama City) 125
Churuquita Grande
    Festival de la Naranja 174

chytrid fungus 85
Ciénaga de las Macanas 182
Cienfue 68
cigars 175
Cinta Costera 55, 117
classical music 70
climate 19, 284
clothing 285
cloudforests 21, 79, 206, 207, 239
Club Unión 65
Coclé 165
Coclé, eastern 172
cocoa tours 237
coffee 198, 205, 219
    plantation tours 204, 210, 212
Coiba 20, 89, 90
Coiba National Park 200
Coiba penal colony 199
Collins, Charlie 96
Colman, Simral 49
Colombia, border with 259, 268,
    269, 285
Colombia, separation from 43
Colón 153
    Aspinwall monument 154
    Catedral de la Inmaculada
        Concepción de María 155
    Christ the Redeemer statue 155
    crime and safety 285
    Episcopalian Christ Church by
        the Sea 155
    New Washington Hotel 154
    Panama Railroad terminal 154
    Zona Libre 153
Columbus, Christopher 33, 224,
    230
Comarca de Madugandi 265
Comarca Guna Yala 60
Comarca Ngäbe-Buglé 218, 223,
    225
comarcas 59, 60, 64
Compagnie Universelle du Canal
    Interocéanique 40
Company of Scotland 277
Congos 158
conservation 22
consulates 286
Coobana 241
coral mining 23
coral reefs 83
    Azuero Peninsula and Veraguas
        193, 199, 200
    Bocas del Toro 223, 226, 228,
        234, 235
    Chiriquí and Western Panama
        217
    Guna Yala 243, 254
Corazón de Jesús 254
Cordillera Central 19
Corozal 265
Costa Arriba, eastern 161
Costa Rica, border with 211, 215,
    216, 223, 238
costs 284
crafts 73, 170, 267, 272
credit cards 289
crime and safety 153, 285
    drug-trafficking 265
    no-go areas 265, 285
crocodiles 83, 152, 265
cruise ships 280

Cucuá community 175
Cuevas de Majé 265
currency 284, 288
customs regulations 285
cycling 282
cycling holidays 282

D

Daddy Yankee 70
dance 67
Darién 263
    river transportation 282
    safety issues 265, 285
Darién Gap 268
Darién National Park 17, 111, 263,
    268
David 214
    addresses 283
    Barrio Bolívar 214
    Feria Internacional de San José
        de David 214
    Parque Cervantes 214
debit cards 289
deforestation 22
de Icaza, Amelia Denis 129
de Lesseps, Ferdinand 40, 99
Delgado, Roberto 67
de Nicuesa, Diego 33
dentists 287
de Ojeda, Alonso 33
devil dances 175
devil masks 185
devils 163, 172, 175, 189
disabled travelers 285
discos 68
diving 89, 139, 193
    Azuero Peninsula and Veraguas
        199, 200
    Bocas del Toro 226
    Chiriquí and Western Panama
        217
    Portobelo 160
Dolphin Bay 228
dolphins 81, 193, 228
Drake, Sir Francis 35, 36, 157, 161
dress code 286
driving 281
driving regulations 282
    speed limits 282
Dule (Guna) Revolution 49
Durán, Roberto 190
duty-free shopping 153

E

eastern isles 257
eating out 286
economy 53
ecotourism 156, 175, 228, 240
El Caño 30, 31, 165, 176
electricity 283, 286
El Nancito 31
El Porvenir 248
    Museo de la Nación Guna 248
El Real 269
El Valle 165, 169
    APROVACA Orchid Nursery 169
    Butterfly Haven 170
    Calle de los Millonarios 169
    El Nispero 170

El Nispero zoo 85
Iglesia San José 171
museum 171
pozos termales 171
embassies 286
Emberá communities
village stays 270
visiting 149, 151
Emberá people 17, 60, 263, 264
crafts 74, 75
emergency numbers 286
environmental issues 22
chytrid fungus 169
crop spraying 241
in the Bahía de Panamá 136
pollution 258
sustainable developments 213
Esclusas de Agua Clara 153
Esclusas de Gatún 152
Escudo de Veraguas 227
etiquette 286

F

Fair Trade initiatives 241
Farallón 169
ferries 282
festivals and events 65
Boquete Jazz & Blues Festival
68
Carnaval 162, 173, 193
chichería 225
Congos y Diablos (Portobelo)
157
Corpus Christi 163
Corpus Christi (La Villa de los
Santos) 162, 188, 189
Desfile de la Mil Polleras (Las
Tablas) 261
El Nazareño (Portobelo) 157
Feria de Isla Tigre (Isla Tigre)
253, 256
Feria de San Sebastián (Ocú)
187
Feria Internacional de Azuero
(La Villa de los Santos) 188
Feria Internacional de San José
de David (David) 214
Festival de la Caña de Azúcar
(Pesé) 186
Festival de la Mejorana
(Guararé) 189
Festival de la Naranja
(Churuquita Grande) 174
Festival de las Mil Polleras (Las
Tablas) 191
Festival del Manito (Ocú) 186
Festival del Nazareño
(Portobelo) 159, 160
Festival de los Cucuás (San
Miguel Centro) 175
Festival de los Diablos (Costa
Ariba) 158
Festival de los Diablos y Congos
(Costa Ariba) 158
Festival de Santa Librada (Las
Tablas) 191
Festival de Toro Guapo (Antón)
172
Festival Internacional de Música
de Alfredo de Sant Malo 70

festivals calendar 286
Fiesta de los Reyes Magos
(Macaracas) 187
Guna Revolution celebrations
(Agligandi) 253, 257
in Bocas del Mar 233
Mejorana festival 69
Ocean to Ocean cayuco race
(Panama Canal) 101
of the Azuero Peninsula 183
Panama Jazz Festival 67, 144
Finca Dracula 213
Finca Hartmann 212
Finca Lérida ecolodge 207
fine dining 96
fish 83, 152
fishing 91, 152
sport fishing 89, 91
flights 280
domestic 281
from Africa 280
from Australia and New Zealand
280
from Central and South
America 280
from the UK, Ireland and rest of
Europe 280
from the US and Canada 280
folk music 68
Fonsi, Luis 71
Fonteyn, Margot 124
food and drink 93
frigatebirds 193
frogs 81
golden frog 169
poison-dart 84, 234
Fuerte San Lorenzo 155
Fuerzas de Defensa de Panamá
52
Fundación Operá Panamá 70
fungus 85
further reading 296

G

Gaillard Cut 48
Galindo, Gabriel Lewis 138
Gallego, Héctor 198
Galván de Bastidas, Rodrigo 33
Gamboa 150
Garachiné 275
Gardi Islands 249
Gardi Sugdub
Museo de Cultura y Arte Guna
250
Gardi Sugdub 250
Gatún Dam 152
Gatún lake 100, 103
Gauguin, Paul 126
geography and geology 19, 29
Goethals, George 48, 99
golden frogs 169
golf 150
Golfo de Chiriquí 80, 89, 90
Golfo de Chiriquí National Park
217
Golfo de Panamá 21
Golfo de San Miguel 270
Gorgas, Colonel William 47
Gran Coclé 29
Guadalupe 213

Guanidub 253
Guararé 189
Casa Museo Manuel Fernando
Zárate 190
Guaymí people 205, 225
Guna (Dule) Revolution 49
Guna people 17, 49, 63, 64, 60, 244
books about 296
burial rituals 254
crafts 73
names and language 247
Guna Yala 20, 23, 89, 111
boat trips and ferries 282
safety issues 285

H

handicrafts 73, 170, 267, 272
harpy eagles 274
hats 76, 174
Hay, John 47
health 287
Herrera, Emiliano 42
highways 281. See
also Interamericana
hiking 87, 89, 147. See
also national parks
Central Panama 171
Chiriquí and Western Panama
207
equipment 89
safety guidelines 207
Hindu population 62
history 26, 29
homestays 218, 237
horseback riding 91, 161, 170, 229
horses 213
hostals 283
hotels 283
Humedales de San San Pond Sak
223, 238
hummingbirds 221
hydroelectric projects 23

I

iguanas 82
independence 39
India Dormida, La 171
indigenous peoples 17, 59, 60,
225. See also by individual group
names
insects 83
Interamericana 165, 167, 215, 265,
266, 268, **282**
hazards 282
Internet 287
Ipetí 266
Isla Barro Colorado 83, 152
tours 152
visits to 132
Isla Bastimentos 89, 223, 227, 231
water-taxi operators 232
Isla Bastimentos Marine National
Park 223, 234
Isla Bolaños 138, 218
Isla Carenero 227, 234
Isla Coiba 89, 200
Isla Colón 33, 223, 225, 227
beaches 229
Isla Contadora 138, 139

Isla de las Flores 126
Isla Diablos 251
Isla El Encanto 270
Isla Gámez 218
Isla Grande 161
Isla Iguana 192, 193
Isla Mamey 161
Isla Montuoso 218
Isla Paridita 217
Isla Parita 217
Isla Pelicano 253
Isla Perro Chico 251
Isla Pino 258
Isla Popa 235
Isla Saboga 138, 139
Isla San Cristóbal 235
Isla San José 138
Islas de las Perlas 138, 90, 137
   on TV 137
Islas Ladrones 218
Isla Solarte 235
Islas Secas 218
Isla Taboga 126
   ferries to 126, 128
Isla Tigre 255
Isla Viveros 138
Isthmian Canal Commission (ICC) 44

J

jaguars 80
jaguarundis 80
Janson Coffee Farm 210
jazz 67
jewelry 74

K

Kantule, Nele 49
kayaking 88, 149
kitesurfing 91, 168
krün 225

L

La Chunga 274
Lago Bayano 263, 265
Lago Gatún 89, 100, 103, 146, 150, 151
   boat trips 103
Lago Miraflores 100, 146
La Gruta 230
Laguna Bocatorito 228
Lagunas de Volcán 210
La Kshamba 67
La Marea 272
language 292
   Spanish courses 284
La Palma 270
La Pintada 174
   Artesanías Reinaldo Quirós 174
   Cigarros Joyas de Panamá 175
   Mercado de Artesanías La Pintada 174
La Rica 176
Las Minas 187
Las Rabanes 68
Las Tablas 190
   Carnaval 162
   Desfile de la Mil Polleras 261

Escuela Presidente Porras 192
Festival de las Mil Polleras 191
Festival de Santa Librada 191
Iglesia Santa Librada 191
Los Carnavales de los Tablas 193
Museo Belisario Porras 192
Las Tres Peñas 174
La Villa de los Santos 188
   Corpus Christi 188, 189
   Corpus Christi celebration 162
   Feria Internacional de Azuero 188
   Iglesia San Atanasio 188
   Museo de la Nacionalidad 188
   Parque Rufina Alfaro 189
La Villa de Los Santos 39
LBGTQ travelers 288
left luggage 288
Levi, Enrique Jaramillo 296
lobsters 256
Lolas 68
Lorenzo, Victoriano 42, 43, 125
Los Cangilones de Gualaca 217
Los Pozos 187
Los Quetzales Lodge & Spa 213

M

Mallarino-Bidlack Treaty 39
Mamitupu 258
manatees 81, 223, 238
mangroves 21
maps 288
Marcos A. Gelabert Airport 281
margays 80
marine life 80, 81, 193, 200, 218.
   See also coral reefs, dolphins, turtles, whales
marine parks 88
marine turtles. See turtles
Martinelli, Ricardo 54, 55
Masargandub 252
masks 73, 185
Maya, Julia 30
measurement system 291
media 288
medical care 287
Metetí 267
mining 23
Mirador Alan-Her 209
Miraflores lake 100
Mogué 272
molas 73
Monagrillo 29
money 288
monkeys 17, 82, 151
Monumento Natural Cerro Gaital 169
Morgan, Henry 35, 36, 117, 137, 155, 158
Moscoso, Mireya 53, 192
mosquitoes 48
Mossack Fonsecca 55
mountain bike rental 282
mountain-biking 91
mountain lions 80
Mount Tacarcuna 244
Mount Totumas 211
museums and galleries 284
   BioMuseo (Panama City) 128, 284

Casa Museo Manuel Fernando Zárate (Guararé) 190
El Valle museum 171
Museo Afro-Antillano (Panama City) 133
Museo Antropológico Reina Torres de Araúz (Panama City) 132
Museo Belisario Porras (Las Tablas) 192
Museo de Arte Contemporáneo (Panama City) 132
Museo de Arte Religioso Colonial (Panama City) 125
Museo de Cultura y Arte Guna (Gardi Sugdub) 250
Museo de Herrera (Chitré) 185
Museo de Historia de Panamá (Panama City) 121
Museo de Historia y Tradición Penonomeña (Penonomé) 173
Museo de la Nacionalidad (La Villa de los Santos) 188
Museo de la Nación Guna (El Porvenir) 248
Museo del Canal Interoceánico (Panama City) 122
Museo Olonigli (Agligandi) 257
Museo Regional de Veraguas (Santiago) 197
Museo Regional Stella Sierra (Aguadulce) 178
museum (Nalunega) 249
music 67
musical instruments 69
music and dance, indigenous 69
música típica 68

N

Nalunega 249
Naranjo Chico 253
Narganá 254
Naso people 60, 223, 240
   ecotourism 228
Natá 177
   Basílica Menor Santiago Apóstol 177
national parks 88, 145, 289. See also Parque Internacional Amistad
   Altos de Campana 165, 166
   Camino de Cruces 145
   Cerro Hoya 195
   Chagres 149
   Coiba 200
   Darién 17, 111, 263, 268
   fees 288, 289
   Golfo de Chiriquí 217
   Isla Bastimentos 223
   Omar Torrijos 165, 175
   Portobelo 160
   Santa Fé 199
   Sariqua 183
   Soberanía 147
   Volcán Barú 207
Ngäbe people 17, 204, 205, 60, 224, 232, 218, 225
   ecotourism 228
nightclubs 68

Nombre de Dios 35, 36, 161
Noriega, Manuel 51, 52
North Americans 62
Nuñez de Balboa, Vasco 35
Nurdub 250

O

Obaldía, José Domingo 215
Obaldía, José Vicente 215
ocelots 80
Ocú 186
  Feria de San Sebastián 187
  Festival del Manito 186
Odebrecht company 55
Odebrecht, Marcel 55
Ogobsucum 258
Old Bank 232
Olokindibipilele 49
Omar Torrijos National Park 165, 175
opening hours 289
orchids 21, 169, 172, 198, 213, 271
Orquesta Sinfónica Nacional de Panamá 70
Orquesta Yaré 67
outdoor activities 87

P

Pacific coast 203
  climate 284
Pacific Ocean 35
paddleboarding 91
Panama Canal 44, 17, 19, 111
  books about 296
  Centro de Capacitación Ascanio Arosemena (Panama City) 130
  Centro de Visitantes de Agua Clara 153
  Corte de Culebra 145
  Edificio de la Administración del Canal (Panama City) 129
  Esclusas de Agua Clara 153
  Esclusas de Cocolí 144
  Esclusas de Gatún 152
  Esclusas de Miraflores 144
  Esclusas de Pedro Miguel 145
  expansion project 54, 102
  ferries and bridges 101
  French Cemetery 145
  French project 40, 99
  Lago Gatún 146, 151
  Lago Miraflores 146
  locks 100
  Museo del Canal (Casco Viejo) 102
  Museo del Canal Interoceánico (Panama City) 122
  Ocean to Ocean cayuco race 101
  Puente Centenario 145
  Puente del Atlántico 152
  tours 146
  transit cruises 128, 146
  US project 44, 47, 99
  viewpoints 89, 102, 118, 144, 153
  visitor centers 102, 103
Panama Canal Railway Company 143

Panama City 36, 41, 111
  addresses 283
  airport 118
  airport transportation 281
  Altos de Ancón 127
  Asamblea Nacional de Panamá 131
  Avenida 'A' 125
  Baha'í House of Worship 137
  Balboa 118, 143
  Basílica de Don Bosco 134
  Bastión Mano de Tigre 126
  BioMuseo 128, 284
  Cabeza de Einstein 136
  Café Coca Cola 127
  Calzada de Amador 118, 127
  Casa de la Municipalidad 121
  Casco Viejo 117, **119**
  Catedral Metropolitana 121
  Causeway, El 127
  Central Hotel 121
  Centro de Capacitación Ascanio Arosemena 130
  Centro de Convenciones Atlapa 136
  Cerro Ancón 118, 127, 128
  Cinta Costera 134, 135
  Círculo Stevens 130
  Ciudad de Saber 143
  Corozal train station 143
  day trips from 137
  driving 281
  Earl S. Tupper Research and Conference Center 131
  eating out 286
  Edificio de la Administración del Canal 129
  Einstein's Head 136
  El Cangrejo 117
  El Chorrillo 52
  El Prado 130
  El Terminal 281
  El Tornillo 134
  Grandclément ice cream 119
  Hospital Santo Tomás 49, 135
  Iglesia de la Merced 121
  Iglesia del Carmen 134
  Iglesia de San José 125
  Iglesia San Felipe de Neri 124
  Iglesia y Convento de San Francisco de Asís 123
  Iglesia y Convento de Santo Domingo 125
  Instituto Nacional de Cultura 125
  Isla Taboga ferries 128
  Mahatma Ghandi statue 130
  Maito 96
  Marbella 117
  Mercado de Buhonería y Artesanías 132
  Mercado de Mariscos 132
  metro 118
  Metro 281, 284
  Metrobus 281
  Metrobus card 281
  Monumento a Goethals 129
  Monumento a Vasco Núñez de Balboa 135
  Museo Afro-Antillano 133
  Museo Antropológico Reina

  Torres de Araúz 132
  Museo de Arte Contemporáneo 132
  Museo de Arte Religioso Colonial 125
  Museo de Historia de Panamá 121
  Museo del Canal Interoceánico 122
  Obarrio 117
  Palacio Bolívar 123
  Palacio Municipal 122
  Palacio Presidencial 122
  Panamá Viejo 117, 136
  Parque Natural Metropolitano 130, 220
  Parque Recreativo Omar Torrijos 136
  Parque Santa Ana 126
  Parque Urracá 135
  Pearl Islands ferry 128
  Plaza Belisario Porras 133
  Plaza Bolívar 123
  Plaza Cinco de Mayo 131
  Plaza de Etnías y Culturas 127
  Plaza de Francia 125
  Plaza de la Catedral 121
  Plaza Herrera 126
  post office 289
  Puente de los Américas 142
  Punta Culebra Nature Center 128
  Punta Pacífica 117, 135
  Punta Paitilla 117, 135
  ramparts 124, 125
  San Felipe 119
  Scuba Panama 90
  Taboga Express 128
  taxis 281
  Teatro Balboa 130
  Teatro Nacional 124
  Tocumen International Airport 118
Panamá La Vieja 36
Panamá Pacífico International Airport 280
Panama Papers 55
Panama Railroad 39, 40, 103, 143
Pan-American Highway 282
Parita 185
  Iglesia Santo Domingo de Guzmán 185
Parque Arqueológico El Caño 176
Parque Internacional La Amistad 17, 207, **213**, 224, 239
Parque Nacional Altos de Campana 165, 166
Parque Nacional Camino de Cruces 145
Parque Nacional Cerro Hoya 195
Parque Nacional Chagres 149
Parque Nacional Darién 17, 111, 263, 268
Parque Nacional de Coiba 200
Parque Nacional Marino Golfo de Chiriquí 217
Parque Nacional Marino Isla Bastimentos 223, 234
Parque Nacional Omar Torrijos 165, 175
Parque Nacional Portobelo 160

Parque Nacional Santa Fé 199
Parque Nacional Sarigua 183
Parque Nacional Soberanía 147
Parque Nacional Volcán Barú 207
parrot fish 83
Partido Panamñista (PP) 50
Partido Revolucionario
    Democrático (PRD) 52
passports 291
Patterson, William 277
Pavarandó 274
Pearl Islands 138, 80
    ferries to 128, 139, 282
pearls 138
peccaries 81
Pedasí 192
Pedregal 215
Península de Azuero 165
Península de Burica 216
Penonomé 172
    Balneario Las Mendozas 173
    Catedral de San Juan Bautista
        173
    Museo de Historia y Tradición
        Penonomeña 173
    Plaza Bolívar 173
people 59
Pérez, Danilo 67, 68, 126
Perlas, Archipiélago de la 119
Pesé 186
    Festival de la Caña de Azúcar
        186
    Hacienda San Isidro 186
    Varela Hermanos distillery 186
petroglyphs 31, 171, 188, 211
phones 290
photography 151, 289
Piedra Pintada, La 31, 171, 172
pirates 36, 138, 35, 126, 224
plantlife 20
Playa Agallito 184
Playa Barqueta 215
Playa Bluff 227
Playa Coronado 168
Playa El Cirial 193
Playa El Estero 199
Playa El Istmito 229
Playa El Palmar 168
Playa El Salado 179
    Las Piscinas 179
Playa El Uverito 192
Playa Escondido 194
Playa Estrella 231
Playa Gorgona 168
Playa Las Lajas 218
Playa Los Destiladeros 194
Playa Muerto 275
Playa Polo 232
Playa Reina 195
Playa Río Mar 168
Playa Santa Clara 168
Playa Venao 194
Playa Wizard 232
Playita del Faro 193
Playón Chico 256
poison-dart frogs 84, 234
police 285
    SENAFRONT 265
pollera 261
Porras, Belisario 42, 49, 190
Portobelo 35, 36, 89, 157

activities 160
boat trips 160
Casa Real de la Aduana 159
Festival del Nazareño 159, 160
Fuerte San Fernando 159
Fuerte San Jerónimo 159
Fuerte Santiago 158
Iglesia de San Felipe 159, 160
Mirador El Perú 159
Portobelo National Park 160
postal services 289
Pozos Azules 174
Prestán, Pedro 41
privateers 35, 36, 126
protected areas 289
public holidays 290
Puente Bayano 265
Puente Centenario 102
Puente del Atlántico 102, 152
Puerto Indio 273
Puerto Lara 267
Puerto Piñas 276
pumas 80
Punta Chame 168
Punta Paitilla 65

Q

Quebrada Sal 233
quetzals 207, 208, 239
Quibián 33

R

rafting 88
rail travel 282
Rainforest Discovery Center 148
rainforests 20, 141, 147, 148, 152
Rancho Frío 269
rays 83
Red Frog Beach 228, 232
Refugio de Vida Silvestre de Playa
    Barqueta Agricola 215
Refugio de Vida Silvestre Isla de
    Cañas 194
Refugio de Vida Silvestre Isla
    Iguana 193
reggaeton 70
religious services 290
reptiles 81
Reserva Forestal de Palo Seco
    240
Reserva Forestal El Montuoso 187
Reserva Punta Patiño 274
Reserva Serranía Hidrológica Filo
    de Tallo 268
Reserva Serranía Hidrológica Filo
    de Tallo 268
restaurants 286. See also eating
    out, food and drink
    prices 284
    service tax 286
restrooms 290
Río Chagres 36, 89, 100, 147
Río Oeste Arriba 225, 237
Río Santa María 91
Río Sidra 252
roads 281
rock and pop music 68
Roosevelt, President Theodore
    43, 47

S

safety, personal
    beach hazards and safety 90
sailing 90, 139
salsa 67
salsa lessons 67
Sambú 273
San Carlos 168
Sandoval, Samy and Sandra 69
San Félix 218
San Ignacio de Tupile 256
San Ignacio de Tupile 256
San Miguel Centro 175
    Festival de los Cucuás 175
San Sebastián de Urabá 35
Santa Catalina 87, 89, 199
Santa Fé 87, 91
Santa Fé de Veraguas 198
Santa Fé National Park 199
Santiago 197
    Catedral Santiago Apóstol 197
    Escuela Normal Juan
        Demóstenes Arosemena 197
    Iglesia Atalaya 197
    Iglesia San Francisco de la
        Montaña 197
    Museo Regional de Veraguas
        197
Sarigua 29
Sarigua National Park 183
Scottish involvement 277
sea-kayaking 89
sea travel 280. See also boat
    travel, ferries
Sea Turtle Conservancy 237
    volunteer opportunities 237
sea turtles. See turtles
Seco Herrerano 95
Seiyik 240
Semaco 274
SENAFRONT (frontier police) 265
Sendero de la Plantación 147, 148
Sendero de las Tres Cascadas 207
Sendero de los Quetzales 208
Sendero Il Pianista 207
Sendero Pipa de Agua 207
Senidub 253
Señor Loop 68
sharks 83
Shelter Bay Marina 156
shopping 290
    bargaining 290
    duty-free 153
shrimp 179
Sierra, Stella 178
Silico Creek 225, 237
silver 36
Sinfonía Concertante de Panamá
    70
Sitio Barriles 211
Sitio Conté 30, 165
Sixaola, Río 61
slavery 34
sloths 81, 152
Smithsonian Tropical Research
    Institute field station 152
snakes 81, 152
snorkeling 89, 139, 193, 217
    Azuero Peninsula and Veraguas
        199

Bocas del Toro 226
Guna Yala 251
Portobelo 160
Soberanía National Park 147
soccer 54
social issues 63
Soloy 218
sombreros 75, 76, 174, 186
Ocueño 186
Spanish conquest 33, 225
sport fishing 181, 199, 217, 276
stand-up paddleboarding 91
Stevens, John 48, 99
stingrays 168
surfing 90, 168
Azuero Peninsula and Veraguas 192, 194, 199
Bocas del Toro 226, 227
tuition 168
Swan Cay 231

T

Taboga 119
Tacarcuna, Mount 244
Talamanca mountains 224
tamborito 69
tapirs 81
tax 290
taxis 282
fares 284
Taylor Herrera, Melanie 296
telephones 290
Teribe people 60
Teribe, Río 60
textiles 73
thermal baths 171
Tiger Rock 227
time zone 291
tipping 288
Tocumen International Airport 55, 118

ground transportation 281
Torres De Araúz, Reina 132
Torrijos, Colonel Omar 51
Torrijos, Martín 53, 55
Torrijos, Omar 176
tourism 23
tourist information 291
tour operators 291
travel agents 291
tubing 91, 161, 199
turtles 82. *See also* Sea Turtle Conservancy
Azuero Peninsula and Veraguas 181, 194, 195, 196
Bocas del Toro 223, 229, 230, 234, **237**, 238
Chiriquí and Western Panama 215, 218
Guna Yala 252, 259

U

Ukuptupu 249
United Fruit Company 216, 241
Urracá 178, 225
Urracal, Cacique 34
Usdub 258
US intervention 40

V

Van Ingen, William 129
Varela, Juan Carlos 54, 55
vegetation 20
Veraguas 165, 197
Vernon, Sir Edward 158
visas 291
Volcán 30, 210
Volcán Barú 17, 20, 30, 203, 204, 205, 207
hiking guidelines 207

W

Wailidub 251
War of Jenkins' Ear 156, 158
War of the Thousand Days 41, 47
water, drinking 246
Watermelon War 40
water shortages 283
websites 291
weights and measures 291
Western Azuero 195
western Panama 203
whales 80, 81, 193, 218
migration route 200
whale shark 83
whale-watching 89, 139
what to wear 285
whitewater rafting 88, 149, 206
Wichub-Wala 248
wi-fi 283, 288
wildlife 17. *See also* national parks
Azuero Peninsula and Veraguas 187
Darién National Park 271
in Panama City 118, 128, 130
Pearl Islands 139
windsurfing 91
wine 284
woodcarving 77
Wounaan people 60, 263, 264
crafts 74, 75
Wounaan village stays 270

Y

Yaviza 265, 268

Z

zip lining 91, 161, 171, 206
zoo
El Nispero (El Valle) 85

INSIGHT GUIDES

OFF THE SHELF

Since 1970, INSIGHT GUIDES has provided a unique perspective on the world's best travel destinations by using specially commissioned photography and illuminating text written by local authors.

Whether you're planning a city break, a walking tour or the journey of a lifetime, our superb range of guidebooks and phrasebooks will inspire you to discover more about your chosen destination.

INSIGHT GUIDES

offer a unique combination of stunning photos, absorbing narrative and detailed maps, providing all the inspiration and information you need.

PHRASEBOOKS & DICTIONARIES

help users to feel at home, when away. Pocket-sized with a free app to download, they go where you do.

CITY GUIDES

pack hundreds of great photos into a smaller format with detailed practical information, so you can navigate the world's top cities with confidence.

EXPLORE GUIDES

feature easy-to-follow walks and itineraries in the world's most exciting destinations, with our choice of the best places to eat and drink along the way.

POCKET GUIDES

combine concise information on where to go and what to do in a handy compact format, ideal on the ground. Includes a full-colour, fold-out map.

EXPERIENCE GUIDES

feature offbeat perspectives and secret gems for experienced travellers, with a collection of over 100 ideas for a memorable stay in a city.

www.insightguides.com

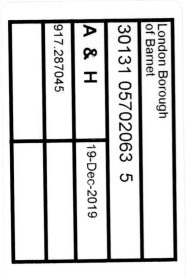

London Borough of Barnet

30131 05702063 5

A & H   19-Dec-2019

917.287045

Panama
6218300

Central Panama City

0   500 m
0   500 yds

Corredor Norte

Albrook

Av Dulcidio González

Avenid

Teatre Ascanio Arosemena

Av Omar Torrijos Herrera

Policía Nacional de Panamá

Avenida Ascanio Villalaz

Calle River

Río Curundú

Edificio de la Administración del Canal de Panamá

Goethals Monument

Calle Tomás Guardia

Calle Mindi

Calle Cascada

C. Gorgas

Lion Hill

C. J. R. McKay

Calle Bavano

C. Carlos Ortiz

Calle Tomás Guardia

Av Omar Torrijos Herrera

Tribunal Electoral

Calle Sta Cruz

Calle Juan Demóstenes Arosemena

Calle N

Calle O

Calle Q

Calle P

Calle María Reina

CURUNDÚ

C. Gorgas

Calle E. Méndez Icaza

Quarry Heights

Calle Juan Demóstenes Arosemena

Calle Evangelista G. Zamora

Calle Dr. José M. Vazquez

Calle Q

Craig

Corte Suprema de Justicia

Avenida Luis Clement

RESERVA CERRO ANCÓN

Calle Amelia Denis de Icaza

Cerro Ancón

Calle Gorgas

Calle N Navarro

Calle R López

Calle Arnoldo Walter

Av Simón Bolívar (Vía Transístmica)

Calle Evangelista G. Zamora

Basílica de Don Bosco

Avenida C

Bandera del Cerro Ancón

Cerro Ancón 199

Calle J. de Arco Galindo

Smithsonian Tropical Research Institute

Earl S. Tupper Research and Conference Centre

Calle Fr. J. Morales

Calle Mariano Arosemena

Archivos Nacionales

Avenida Perú

Avenida Central

Museo de Ciencias Naturales

Avenida C

Mi Pueblito

C. R. Alemán

Museo de Arte Contemporáneo

Asamblea Nacional de Panamá

Palacio Legislativo

Plaza J. Rremón Cantera

Calle 26 Este

Calle 31 Este

Calle 32 Este

Avenida Cuba

Catedral San Lucas

Plaza Cinco de Mayo

Museo Afro-Antillano

Av Cuba

Calle 27 Este

Loteria

Avenida de los Mártires

5 de Mayo

Avenida Justo Arosemena

Avenida Justo Arosemena

Calle 28 Este

Calle 29 Este

Calle 30 Este

Calle 32 Este

Calle Estudiante

Calle H

Calle 20 Este

Av México

Calle República de Nicaragua

Avenida México

Calle 25 Este

Calle 26 Este

Calle 27 Este

Avenida México

Avenida Balb

CEMENTERIO DE AMADOR

Calle 24 Oeste

Calle B Oeste

Calle J. de la Ossa

Calle Ancón

Calle 17 Oeste

Calle H

Calle 18 Este

Mercado de Buhonería y Artesanías

Calle República de Haití

Calle República de Belice

Avenida Balboa

Cinta C

Calle 23 Oeste

Calle 22 Oeste

Calle 21 Oeste

C. Pedro de Obarrio

Avenida A

Calle 8

Calle 16 Oeste

Calle 15 Oeste

Avenida Central (La Peatonal)

Avenida Balboa

Avenida B

EL CHORILLO

Calle 14 Oeste

Av Eloy Alfaro

Mercado de Mariscos

Muelle Fiscal

Calle B Oeste

Av de los Poetas

Calle 20 de Diciembre

C. M. Iturralde

Avenida A

Calle 18 Oeste

Calle 17 Oeste

Calle 16 Este

Calle 15 Este

Iglesia de Santa Ana

Avenida B

Calle 13 Este

Av Eloy Alfaro

Cinta Costera

Calle 14

PARQUE SANTA ANA

Avenida Central

SANTA ANA

Plaza V Centenario

Monumento de La Bandera de Panamá

Calle 13 Oeste

Calle 12 Oeste

Calle 11 Este

Iglesia de la Merced

Avenida A

Calle 8 Este

Av Eloy Alfaro

Cinta Costera

Cinta Costera

Iglesia de San José

Manglar del Casco Viejo

Avenida A

Catedral Metropolitana

Plaza de la Catedral

Plaza de Bolívar

Museo del Canal Interoceánico

Palacio Bolívar & Salón Bolívar

Iglesia y Convento San Francisco de Asís

CASCO VIEJO

Avenida A

Iglesia y Convento de Santo Domingo

Instituto Nacional de Cultura (INAC)

Plaza de Francia

B a h